SOCIAL POLICY REVIEW 22

Analysis and debate in social policy, 2010

Edited by Ian Greener, Chris Holden
and Majella Kilkey

First published in Great Britain in 2010 by

The Policy Press
University of Bristol
Fourth Floor
Beacon House
Queen's Road
Bristol BS8 1QU, UK

Tel +44 (0)117 331 4054
Fax +44 (0)117 331 4093
e-mail tpp-info@bristol.ac.uk
www.policypress.co.uk

North American office:
The Policy Press
c/o International Specialized Books Services (ISBS)
920 NE 58th Avenue, Suite 300 • Portland, OR 97213-3786, USA
Tel +1 503 287 3093 • Fax +1 503 280 8832
e-mail info@isbs.com

© The Policy Press/Social Policy Association 2010

British Library Cataloguing in Publication Data
A catalogue record for this book is available from the British Library.

Library of Congress Cataloging-in-Publication Data
A catalog record for this book has been requested.

ISBN 978 1 84742 712 0 paperback

The right of Ian Greener, Chris Holden and Majella Kilkey to be identified as editors of this work has been asserted by them in accordance with the 1988 Copyright, Designs and Patents Act.

Cover design by The Policy Press
Front cover: photograph kindly supplied by Nick Kane Architectural Photography
Printed and bound in Great Britain by Hobbs, Southampton
The Policy Press uses environmentally responsible print partners.

Contents

Part three: Service user involvement: Majella Kilkey

List of tables and figures

List of contributors

David Abbott is a Senior Research Fellow at the Norah Fry Research Centre, University of Bristol, UK.

Marian Barnes is Professor of Social Policy and Director of the Social Science Policy and Research Centre, University of Brighton, UK.

Peter Beresford is Professor of Social Policy, and Director of the Centre for Citizen Participation, Brunel University, UK, and Chair of Shaping our Lives, the national user-controlled organisation and network.

Paul Bridgen is a Senior Lecturer in Social Policy at the University of Southampton, UK.

Clyde Chitty is Emeritus Professor of Education at Goldsmiths College, University of London, and Visiting Professor of the Institute of Education, University of London, UK.

Charlie Cooper is a Lecturer in Social Policy in the Department of Social Sciences, University of Hull, UK.

Gary Craig is Visiting Professor at Durham University, UK, and Emeritus Professor of Social Justice and Associate Fellow at the Wilberforce Institute for the Study of Slavery and Emancipation, University of Hull, UK, where he led the team working on issues of modern slavery.

Chris Deeming is a Research Fellow at the University of New South Wales, Australia, and an Honorary Research Fellow at the London School of Hygiene and Tropical Medicine, UK.

Elena Gaia is currently a Policy Analysis Specialist in the Economic and Social Policy Unit at UNICEF Regional Office for CEE/CIS in Geneva. Previously she worked as a Research Analyst in the Social Policy and Development Programme at the United Nations Research Institute for Social Development (UNRISD).

Colin Gell is a founder member of the Nottingham Advocacy Group (NAG), and has more than 20 years' experience of activism in the UK.

Ian Greener is Reader in Social Policy at Durham University, UK.

Steffen Heinrich is a Research Associate at the Institute of East Asian Studies (IN-EAST), University of Duisburg-Essen, Germany.

Rachel Harding is Research Co-ordinator at Framework Housing Association, UK, where she focuses on many aspects of homelessness and associated issues.

Chris Holden is a Lecturer in Global Health in the Centre on Global Change and Health, London School of Hygiene and Tropical Medicine, UK.

Majella Kilkey is a Lecturer in Social Policy in the Department of Social Sciences, University of Hull, UK.

Mary Langan is a Senior Lecturer in Social Policy and Criminology at the Open University, UK.

Colin Lindsay is a Senior Research Fellow at the Employment Research Institute, Edinburgh Napier University, UK.

Sally Ruane is Deputy Director of the Health Policy Research Unit in the School of Applied Social Sciences, De Montfort University, UK.

Neil Stillwell is a former service user of Framework Housing Association's services. He has been a peer interviewer in a number of different research projects about homelessness in the UK.

Pat Thomas is Chair of Birmingham Carers Association, UK, and has more than 20 years' experience of activism.

Grahame Whitfield is Assistant Director of the Centre for Research in Social Policy (CRSP) at Loughborough University, UK.

Introduction

Ian Greener

Social policy faces difficult times ahead. The extraordinary debts that governments in developed nations have acquired since 2008 in order to try and deal with the financial crisis must be paid back, and the public spending deficits that they have created are becoming the source of considerable vexation. As I write this in January 2010 it seems that while the banking sector, where much of the crisis originated, is making substantial profits again, with the return of bonuses to bankers despite the anger expressed towards them by President Barack Obama and the British Chancellor Alistair Darling, welfare states across the world are facing a period of retrenchment and budget cuts.

The financial crisis appears frequently throughout this collection, which has three main sections. First there is a review of policy, structured around contributions from four leading writers in their areas who looked back over Labour policy in the UK since 1997; 2010 is an election year, so it is a good time to review Labour's approach to social policy in four key areas, as well as starting to look to the future to imagine what/who might come next. After these reviews comes the Social Policy Association's (SPA's) best postgraduate paper winner from 2009, before moving on to Part Two, current issues and debates. This section contains a mix of chapters, with two directly addressing the financial crisis, one that considers modern slavery and one that looks at reform in a developing country. Together they form an overview of the diversity of scholarship in social policy. Finally Part Three is a themed section on service user involvement which includes five contributions examining this issue, one that is central to thinking about social policy organisation in both present policy and in the future. Once again there is a premium on the diversity of scholarship, with outstanding work that examines the issues in getting users involved and engaged with policy from a range of perspectives.

Part One: Current developments – Ian Greener

The central theme of *Social Policy Review* (*SPR*) this year was to ask, in four key policy areas, what Labour have achieved since 1997, and then to look forward to what might happen next. The four areas chosen were those of *education*, because of former Prime Minister Tony Blair's claim before Labour came to power that his top three priorities would be 'education, education, education'; *children's social care*, because of the increased emphasis Labour have placed on the child, especially in respect of attempting to intervene early to equalise opportunity for children; *healthcare*, because of the continued importance of the National Health Service (NHS) in debates leading up to and beyond the next general election; and *pensions*, where there is now almost universally recognised to be a crisis of policy which Labour have periodically attempted to address, although arguably without noticeable success.

All four of these areas have seen considerable reform since 1997, with varying degrees of success and failure. All four areas affect all of our lives to a considerable extent, and were central to Labour's approach to social policy, so it is both appropriate and important to review what has been achieved over the past 13 years.

Clyde Chitty's chapter on education policy argues that policy since 1997 has been marked by confusion and contradiction, with Labour wanting to appear to be non-ideological in their approach to welfare reform in order to try and capture as much of the middle-class vote as possible, and so unwilling to tackle the question of the role of grammar schools in the education system, or that of how to deal with selection on entry to secondary schools. Labour's use of top-down initiatives such as the literacy hour and their extension of the National Curriculum left little room for teacher discretion in what syllabus ought to be covered, and Chitty links their use of academies to a fairly clear attempt to privatise education.

Chitty concludes by suggesting that there is now little to choose between the two main political parties in respect of education policy – in fact they appear 'interchangeable'. There is a new consensus based on the privatisation of education, the National Curriculum and the top-down regulation of teachers with little respect for their professionalism.

Mary Langan's chapter on social care suggests that Labour's approach to social care has been through a substantial discontinuity. Whereas between 1997 and 2005 the extension of the market and of managerialist principles was the central theme, after 2005 through Blair's last term in office and through to Gordon Brown's Prime Ministership, there has been a more fundamental move toward an individualistic, therapeutic ethos that is more concerned with the moral and spiritual welfare of the individual.

Langan's overview of policy in social care takes us through the events that shaped Labour policy, focusing on how we have come to regard young people as being in 'danger', and how we have come to fear sex offenders and to question parenting. Labour's approach, perhaps made most clear in *Every Child Matters*, was to try and intervene early in children's lives through policies such as Sure Start and Family Intervention Projects, which Langan describes and explores the role of in relation to Labour's larger policy goals. Langan then goes on to describe the role of 'positive psychology' in the greater therapeutic content of Labour's policy and how, despite negative evaluations, they have pressed on with their approach to trying to intervene in children's lives, transforming the relationship between the family and the state as a result.

Sally Ruane suggests that health policy under 'New Labour' is not entirely what it seems, exploring a number of contradictions in health policy and the role of 'spin' in government at the same time. She asks how it is that, despite Labour's health policy being more radical than even the previous Conservative Thatcher government, there is relatively little debate or discussion around the direction of policy, even despite the British people's emotional attachment to the NHS.

Ruane suggests that Labour's presentation of their health policy has been extremely important in understanding these tensions because they have managed to present their reforms as modernisation rather than privatisation, they have been able to claim significant increases in health expenditure, which again act as a distraction from their increased use of non-public providers of healthcare and which enable them to claim that the NHS is 'safe' with them, and finally, that ministers have claimed to have achieved far greater say in the NHS despite the absence of virtually any kind of accountability checks in Labour's reforms, the central theme of the chapter. Despite this lack of accountability, however, the NHS is now achieving the highest levels of satisfaction since the 1980s, but with the public not necessarily understanding much about the reforms that have been carried out over the past decade, or their consequences for healthcare in the future.

Last in the review section, Paul Bridgen considers Labour's difficulties in dealing with what has become an important but rather intractable problem – that of pensions. Bridgen takes us through the problems that Labour inherited in this area in 1997, with increased poverty rates resulting from low state provision of pensions, women disproportionately represented among the older poor, and much of the growth in inequality indexes coming from the growth in occupational pensions. Key factors in the considerations of the Pensions Commission and the 2007 and 2008 Pensions Acts were that Labour's attempts at 'stakeholder pensions' to address these problems did not appear to take off and the closure of defined benefit pension schemes in the private sector to new members.

Bridgen considers whether pensions reforms have made the subsequent system more social democratic. He considers entitlement, the public/private mix and benefit levels before coming to the conclusion that the 2007 and 2008 reforms represent a new direction for policy, but notes the lack of clarity as to whether these reforms will develop should there be a change of government in 2010. He particularly questions whether employer opposition to some of Labour's ideas might represent a significant test of the social policy credentials of David Cameron's Conservative Party.

Best postgraduate paper

This year's best postgraduate paper, decided by an SPA panel of reviewers, is Chris Deeming's 'Drawing semi-normative budget lines in household expenditure data'. This is a technical paper that deserves attention because of its unusualness in method in social policy terms, and because of the importance of its topic.

Deeming's paper is concerned with food poverty, especially with regard to poverty through insufficient household purchasing power. He uses a variety of statistical methods to attempt to determine the food poverty line, concentrating on a sample of older person households. He concludes that a budget line of around £110 per week for single people corresponds to the point where over 90% meet minimum dietary standards, with £170 per week corresponding to 80% of dietary standards for couples. This is not a measure of whether such income levels *can* secure a healthy standard of living, but rather whether they do so in practice, given actual spending choices made in households. Deeming's work therefore gives us, based on the data, an empirical measurement of the extent to which particular households are, or are not, likely to fall into food poverty, which is surely something that policy makers must pay close attention to.

Part Two: Current issues and debates – *Chris Holden*

The past two years have been ones in which the economic crisis has had
a profound impact on those aspects of social life and well-being central
to the study of social policy, and this is set to continue, with no area of
policy likely to escape. The first two chapters in Part Two engage directly
with the financial crisis, and are among the first serious attempts by social
policy scholars to get to grips with its consequences. One of the most
obvious ongoing results of the crisis is its impact on unemployment,
and Colin Lindsay's chapter provides an insightful appraisal of New
Labour's 'Work First' supply-side approach to unemployment policy in
these new circumstances. In doing so, he reconnects with earlier work by
Adrian Sinfield, from a previous period of mass unemployment, which
appealed to us to 'recognise more fully what unemployment means',
both for those who directly experience it and for society as a whole.
Lindsay reviews in some detail how the concept of 'employability' has
been interpreted and put into practice by New Labour, revealing in the
process the inadequacy of this approach, especially in a period when mass
unemployment requires that we analyse and take action on its demand-
side aspects. However, rather than rejecting the concept of employability
altogether, Lindsay instead offers an analytical framework that allows us
to recognise and make sense of the full range of factors that affect the
ability of individuals, particularly those who have been unemployed
long-term, to access meaningful employment. The concentration of
long-term unemployment in particular locations, especially following
processes of industrial restructuring, continued to be a problem even
during recent periods of economic growth, but in a period when mass
unemployment caused by failures in the macro-economy has given
rise to persistent lack of demand, the inadequacy of the 'Work First'
approach becomes impossible to ignore. Lindsay's chapter is of particular
importance at a time when the two major parties in the UK continue
to argue over the correct timing of the removal of fiscal stimulus and
the need for austerity to repair the government's balance sheet.

Steffen Heinrich's analysis of the nature of the two-tier labour markets
of Germany and Japan is also timely, following as it does changes of
government in both countries during the second half of 2009. He
shows that these two 'coordinated economies' have both been subject to
processes of deregulation of the second, non-regular, tier of the labour
market, even while workers in the first, regular, tier continue to enjoy
strong protection. The consequence of this in the present crisis has been
that non-regular workers have disproportionately borne the brunt of

recession. Heinrich examines the institutional and political dynamics of these labour market reforms in order to try to understand how the crisis might alter them and whether the possibility exists for a re-regulation of the non-regular tier. Reviewing the 'varieties of capitalism' and other literature, he evaluates the difficulties of German and Japanese policy makers in attempting to manage the conflicting policy goals of maintaining and supporting first-tier arrangements while also attempting to maintain or increase the labour market flexibility attained by the expansion of the second tier. He also evaluates the significance of political partisanship for the regulation of the second tier, and cautiously concludes that there is little evidence of a move towards the significant re-regulation of non-regular employment, although much will depend on how the crisis plays out.

The issue of labour market flexibility is also central to Gary Craig's chapter, which provides a comprehensive review of modern slavery in the UK, in the process dispelling the belief that such forms of extreme exploitation no longer exist in the country. Craig focuses on the two most common forms of modern slavery in the UK: forced labour and human trafficking for sexual purposes. He argues that the biggest driver of forced labour has been increasing deregulation of the labour market, with the UK the second least-protected developed country after the US and with large proportions of agency workers. In this environment, migrant workers are the group most at risk of becoming subject to working conditions that equate to forced labour. Poor conditions in sending countries are an important driver of trafficking for sexual purposes, and Craig shows that the globalisation of labour markets has had a substantial impact, in this case with labour moved to meet the demands of those willing to pay for sex. Craig's chapter thus provides an important illustration of the transnational nature of many contemporary social problems, and demonstrates that effective responses require international coordination as well as coherence between domestic agencies.

The final chapter in this section, by Elena Gaia, provides an appraisal of a significant policy innovation in a developing country, Guatemala. Conditional cash transfers (CCTs) were pioneered by Brazil and Mexico in the 1990s, widely promoted by The World Bank, and have since spread throughout Latin America and the world. CCTs link cash transfers to the behaviour of the target population, thereby combining short-term poverty alleviation with requirements aimed at improving long-term human development, such as school or health clinic attendance. Gaia provides a detailed analysis of the design and implementation of

Guatemala's CCT programme, *Mi Familia Progresa*. While the programme is the first that has been deliberately targeted at the poorest sectors of the population, thereby mitigating the regressive nature of previously existing social policy, Gaia concludes that there is more continuity with previous residual approaches than there is change. Gaia's chapter provides an important contribution to our understanding of the challenges of developing effective social policies in countries like Guatemala, where extreme poverty and inequality often exist alongside entrenched power differentials in a context of economic under-development.

Part Three: Service user involvement – *Majella Kilkey*

Part Three of this edition of *SPR*, traditionally a themed section, focuses on service user involvement. As many of the contributors to this part note, involving 'the public', 'citizens' and/or 'service users' in the governance, design, delivery and evaluation of publicly and other provided services has become a common feature in the UK and elsewhere. The ideological and political origins of this development, however, are multiple; as such the value base from which user involvement is advocated, and the outcomes that are sought, vary fundamentally. This has given rise to much contestation around the concept of service user involvement, which some of the chapters included here outline and reflect on. Still other chapters, while acknowledging the philosophical dilemmas, pay greater attention to the practice of service user involvement, particularly, but not only, in the field of social research. Collectively, the chapters cover a range of service user groups including: homeless people, disabled adults, disabled children and young people, carers, mental health service users and disadvantaged young people.

In the first chapter, Peter Beresford argues that the tensions inherent in the competing value systems around participation and involvement mean that there are risks for service users and their movements attached to participating in the state's and service system's user involvement agenda, an agenda which, through its origins in managerialist/consumerist approaches to social policy, he argues, is part of the pursuit of the marketisation of state welfare. Drawing on examples from the experiences of two UK service user movements – the disabled people's movement and the survivors movement – Beresford identifies two key risks. The first – co-option – is the danger that simply by getting involved, service users unintentionally and unwillingly become incorporated into policy makers' agendas, which are frequently at odds with their own. The second risk, and one which Beresford argues has received less attention, is that service users' ideas can be appropriated and transformed by policy makers to satisfy other, more regressive, policy priorities. Government plans for personalisation and self-directed support in social care, which Beresford demonstrates have their origins in the disabled people's movements' agenda around direct payments, is given as one example of this process, as are mainstream conceptualisations and projects around co-production, recovery, social capital and social inclusion. Given the observed challenges, Beresford concludes by arguing for increased reflexivity on the part of service users and their movements around participation and involvement, as well as greater recognition, ideally in partnership with service users and their organisations, within academic social policy of the importance of the issue.

Marian Barnes' chapter, written with Colin Gell and Pat Thomas, activists in the mental health service user movement and the carers' movement respectively, adopts a similarly evaluative approach, and offers some conceptual frameworks that could contribute to facilitating the increased reflexivity on the part of service users and their movements advocated by Beresford. Acknowledging the diverse origins of participation agendas, and partly in the light of this, the specific question posed by Barnes and her colleagues is whether initiatives around participation and user involvement can be considered as contributing to the creation of a more just society. In addressing that question, they first consider the principles that (should) inform participatory approaches to governance and service delivery, and specifically, the principles underpinning the issue of who precisely is to participate. In particular, the tensions between the principles of 'local representation' and 'local knowledge' – principles frequently and simultaneously in evidence in participatory processes of governance and service delivery – are explored in detail. In the second part of the chapter the question of the consequences of participation and user involvement for social justice is examined. Drawing on a conceptualisation of social justice as both recognition and redistribution, and a distinction between 'affirmative' and 'transformative' recognition and redistributive policy strategies, Barnes and her colleagues offer a framework for assessing the social justice outcomes of user involvement. In their concluding section, they then apply this framework to assessing whether and how the situation of people with mental health problems and carers has benefited from user involvement initiatives.

In the third chapter in this section, David Abbott continues the focus on a specific group of service users; in this case, disabled children and young people. His chapter is highly reflective, designed to take stock of 'where we are at' in terms of engaging disabled children and young people – a group with a long history of exclusion – in consultations about public services, as well as in the design and implementation of social research. Abbott begins the chapter by developing the case on *why* to involve disabled children and young people. Here, he reveals that one important reason is that research demonstrates that the views and concerns of children and young people often differ from those of their carers. The bulk of Abbott's chapter, however, represents a guide to best practice in the field, reviewing what we know from previous research about *how* to involve disabled children and young people in a 'meaningful' and 'non-tokenistic' way. Abbott reviews the evidence of what works best in terms of both how to consult with this group on the services they receive, as well as how to involve disabled children and young people in the research process. His consideration of the latter is notably reflexive, offering insights from his own experiences as a researcher working with disabled young people, and advocating greater awareness on the part of researchers about the motivations and values that inform their engagement with disabled children and young people.

Young people and the research process are also the focus of the fourth chapter, authored by Charlie Cooper. Here, Cooper examines how involving disadvantaged young people in research might contribute to improved understandings of their aspirations and the strategies that are required to achieve these. Specifically, Cooper outlines the rationale and approaches of a participatory action research agenda with young people (youth PAR). He situates the need for such an agenda within the context of, on the one hand, consistent evidence of a decline in the well-being of young people in the UK, and on the other hand, a dominant social policy response which locates the cause of this within the cultural and individual failings of young people themselves, without acknowledgement of the shifting structural contexts in which young people's expectations and experiences are constructed. A youth PAR approach, Cooper argues, would not only present policy makers with important lessons on how better to respond to the needs of young people, but by facilitating the meaningful involvement of young people in the research process it also has the potential to empower young people themselves to effect positive social change. While there is no fixed set of methods associated with PAR, Cooper, drawing on existing literature, outlines a toolbox for undertaking youth PAR, and offers several case studies of the approach in practice.

In the final chapter, Rachel Harding, Grahame Whitfield and Neil Stillwell continue with the theme of involving service users in research, focusing specifically on their involvement as *peer research interviewers*. This is an approach whereby those currently or recently receiving services interview their peers (that is, others receiving similar services) as part of a research project. The authors point out that this approach, while part of a wider methodological commitment to challenging the objectification of service users within research, represents just one method of doing so, and is notably distinct from 'user-led' research. Harding and her colleagues, one writing from the perspective of a peer research interviewer, draw on two studies undertaken within the social housing sector to outline the rationale, methods and ethics of peer interviewing, and to assess its strengths, as well as its risks. Reflecting on their own experiences, the authors argue that through this research approach, benefits can accrue to the peer interviewer (for example, increased confidence and self-esteem), the service user being interviewed (for example, increased comfort with the process) and the 'quality' of the research process and data gathered (for example, in accessing those often deemed 'hard to reach'). Crucially, however, they suggest that the benefits associated with peer interviewing are contingent on the effective management of the risks involved, which, while in the main relate to the fact, common to research in general, that people have to be trusted to behave ethically and professionally, are also specific to this research approach. In the final sections of their chapter, the authors provide useful guidance on how best to minimise risk and maximise the benefits of peer interviewing, while also advocating further evaluation of the research approach.

Part One
Current developments

Ian Greener

ONE

Education policy and policy making, 1997–2009

Clyde Chitty

Introduction

In the last hundred years – since, in fact, the end of the First World War – there have been two major pieces of legislation affecting the future of the education service in England and Wales: the Education Act of 1944 and the so-called Education Reform Act (ERA) of 1988. There have, of course, been an enormous number of other pieces of legislation, White Papers and Circulars relating to education promulgated over the same period, but the 1944 and 1988 Acts stand out as having special significance. They constitute the backdrop to the educational changes described in this chapter.

Administratively, the 1944 Education Act established what is often referred to as 'a national system, locally administered', with local education authorities exerting considerable control over the service provided in their area. More accurately, perhaps, it sanctioned the continued development of a partnership between central government, local education authorities and teachers that had grown up in the preceding 50 years. It was popularly believed in the 1940s and 1950s that most important policy decisions in education were taken over lunch at the National Liberal Club by a troika consisting of Sir William Alexander, Secretary of the Association of Education Committees, Sir Ronald Gould, the General Secretary of the National Union of Teachers and the Permanent Secretary at the Ministry of Education. At a time when the prevailing mood was one of cooperation and consensus, it was generally assumed that if these three individuals agreed on some major item of education policy, it would, more often than not, be implemented. Such, at any rate, was the general belief, and, as constitutional expert

Vernon Bogdanor has commented, 'even if it was a caricature, it is at least significant that it was widely held' (Bogdanor, 1979, p 161).

One of the main aims of the 1988 ERA was to begin the process of dismantling this post-war settlement, with the erection of a strictly hierarchical system of schooling, particularly at the secondary level, subject both to market forces and to greater control from the centre. The power of the local education authorities was to be steadily undermined, with the creation of a new tier of secondary schooling outside of local authority control and comprising city technology colleges (CTCs) and grant-maintained or 'opted-out' schools, schools financed directly by central government. The emphasis now was to be on choice and diversity, with local authorities required to distribute funds to their primary and secondary schools by means of a weighted, per capita formula and, theoretically at least, no school being allowed to continue to function as an institution independently of the choices which parents exercised.

It is interesting to note that the 1944 Education Act made no reference to the content of the school curriculum – the word 'curriculum' appearing only once in the entire Act – whereas the 1988 Act established a compulsory national curriculum consisting initially of three 'core' and seven 'foundation' subjects for all pupils in state schools aged five to sixteen. At first sight, this might appear to contradict what has already been said about the 1988 legislation to the effect that it was chiefly concerned with choice and diversity. In fact, the very idea of a national curriculum to be imposed on all state schools was bitterly opposed by many of Margaret Thatcher's advisers and could be shown to have validity only as the justification for a massive programme of national testing at 7, 11, 14 and 16, which would, in turn, result in differentiation, selection and streaming at both primary and secondary levels. At the same time, it has been argued (see, for example, Chitty, 1988, p 46) that the whole process of curriculum standardisation and testing was ideologically consistent with the rest of the 1988 Act if it could be seen as providing the raw data for a system of national league tables designed to provide parents with evidence as to the 'desirability' or otherwise of individual schools. In any case, whatever the motivation, not long after it passed into law, Conservative education ministers began the process of amending and indeed dismantling the National Curriculum's original archaic structure, and particularly with regard to the provision for 14- to 16-year-olds where little real thought had been given to the needs of older students in the last years of compulsory schooling.

In 1965, at a sort of midway point between the two Education Acts, Harold Wilson's Labour government issued Circular 10/65 to all

163 local education authorities in England and Wales, requesting them to prepare viable plans for comprehensive reorganisation in the areas for which they were responsible. It was possible to attempt to implement this major reform by means of a circular because, contrary to popular belief, the 1944 Act had laid down no specific blueprint for the way the secondary system would be organised in the post-war period. Then, in 1988, another of the principal aims of the ERA was to try to abolish the comprehensive system of secondary schools wherever it existed primarily by means of the creation of new types of school. In an interview with Stuart Maclure, editor of *The Times Educational Supplement*, published in April 1987, the then Education Secretary Kenneth Baker argued for a 'post-comprehensive system', where the new CTCs and grant-maintained schools would act as 'halfway houses' between state schools and the independent sector. 'I would,' he said, 'like to see many more of these "halfway houses", a greater choice, a greater variety' (Maclure, 1987).

In the period of John Major's 1992–97 Conservative administration, the new emphasis of education ministers was on the need to encourage the spread of specialist comprehensive schools, promoting the idea of 'selection by specialisation'. The then Education Secretary John Patten chose this as the theme of an article published in the *New Statesman and Society* in July 1992. 'Selection,' he said 'is not, and should not be, a great issue for the 1990s, as it was for the 1960s.... The new "s-word" for all socialists to come to terms with is "specialization"' (Patten, 1992, p 20).

By the time the Conservatives left office in 1997, there were still 164 grammar schools in England and Wales, concentrated in counties such as Buckinghamshire, Kent and Lincolnshire, and in many of the larger conurbations, together with 1,155 grant-maintained schools accounting for 19.6% of pupils in secondary schools and for 2.8% of primary pupils, 15 CTCs, 151 new colleges specialising in technology and 30 colleges specialising in modern languages. At the same time, it has to be conceded that many 'comprehensive' schools did not really deserve that appellation, and it was therefore a very divided and complex secondary system that Tony Blair's New Labour Party inherited from 18 years of Conservative government.

The meaning of Blairism

When New Labour came to power in May 1997 after a landslide general election victory, it faced an important choice in most areas of domestic policy: it could either repudiate the Thatcherite legacy, with its emphasis on the merits of privatisation and reliance on market forces and, having taken this radical step, move on to forge a new distinctive policy of its own based on a different set of values, or it could instead choose to continue with the Thatcherite agenda and attempt to present it in a new compassionate light. Broadly speaking, it chose to follow the latter path, particularly with regard to education policy.

In a short pamphlet with the ambitious title *Socialism*, written for the Fabian Society and published in July 1994 shortly after his election as Labour Party Leader, Tony Blair had actually argued that, if and when he became Prime Minister, he did not want to run 'a Tory economy with a bit of social compassion'. But the main purpose of his seven-page paper was to argue that the socialism of Marx – 'of centralised state control of industry and production' – was now dead. In Blair's view, this outdated form of socialism 'misunderstood the nature and development of a modern market economy; it failed to recognise that the state and public sector can become a vested interest capable of oppression as much as the vested interests of wealth and capital; and it was based on a false view of class that had become too rigid to explain or illuminate the real nature of class division today'. In its place, Blair put forward a set of values or beliefs – loosely defined as 'ethical socialism' – based around the notion of 'a strong and active society' committed to promoting the needs of the individual and the pursuit of enlightened self-interest. The basis of this new updated concept of 'socialism', or, to use Blair's preferred spelling 'social-ism', lay in the view that 'the collective power of all should be used for the individual good of each'. Individuals might well be 'socially interdependent human beings', but it was time to stop viewing 'socialism' or 'social-ism' in terms of the promotion of either 'a set of narrow timebound class or sectional interests' or 'a set of particular state-imposed economic prescriptions' (Blair, 1994, pp 3, 4, 6).

It all seemed very simple and straightforward to Tony Blair back in 1994, but, in the years that followed, he proved unable or unwilling to resolve the glaring contradictions involved in affirming a commitment to 'social-ism', however defined, while, at the same time, pursuing a set of competitive market policies in education, health and other important areas of the welfare state. Tony Blair's 'philosophy' – if you can give such a grand title to his motley collection of views – lacked intellectual rigour and consistency. Anxious to appeal to a number of different constituencies, in an attempt to make a success of what has been called 'big-tent politics', Blair often used words and phrases without appearing to grasp their actual meaning. For that reason, it is still remarkably difficult to be precise about what Blairism stood for on a wide range of issues.

It is often claimed that the new Prime Minister's thinking owed much to the concept of 'the third way', propounded by the leading sociologist Anthony Giddens (see Giddens, 1998, 2000), but that concept has itself been criticised for lacking precision and real content. Those close to the Prime Minister in the early days of his administration argued that it was this very 'lightness of ideological being' that had helped New Labour to come to power with such a huge and unexpected majority in May 1997, but, as awkward policy decisions had to be made, a perceived lack of commitment to traditional Labour Party values was widely blamed for deep-seated grass-roots disillusionment with the so-called Blair Project.

It has been argued by Professor David Marquand that Tony Blair's marked disdain for party boundaries and, on a deeper level, for the differences of ideology and interest that had sustained the concept of 'party' in Britain and other European democracies, was 'almost palpable'. According to Marquand, writing in 2000:

> Blair dreams of a united and homogeneous people, undifferentiated by class or locality, with whom he, as Leader, can communicate directly, without benefit of intermediaries. In his vision of it, at least, New Labour's vocation is to mobilize the suburbs as well as the inner cities; rich as well as poor; old as well as young; Christians as well as Unbelievers; hunters as well as animal-rights activists; believers in traditional family values as well as the opponents of Clause 28. Its warm embrace covers all men and women of goodwill, provided only that they are prepared to enlist in the relentless, never-ending crusade for modernization which he and his colleagues have set in motion. (Marquand, 2000, pp 73-4)

New Labour's education programme

In the field of education policy, that 'crusade for modernisation' meant a repudiation of the post-war settlement and a continuation, with very minor modifications, of the Thatcherite privatising agenda. Those who reviewed an edited book published in 1999 with the title *State schools: New Labour and the Conservative legacy* (Chitty and Dunford, 1999) made specific reference to the cartoon specially drawn for the cover by *The Guardian* and *Times Educational Supplement* cartoonist Martin Rowson which neatly summarised the essential message of all the book's contributors. In the picture, a gowned and mortar-boarded headteacher (unmistakably Margaret Thatcher) is shown handing a prize to a beaming, blazered pupil (unmistakably Tony Blair). The prize is a neat scroll of

Conservative education policies. By 1999, it was already clear that Tony Blair might talk in terms of a new commitment to the concepts of 'social justice', 'community' and 'educational opportunity for all', but, in reality, he was chiefly anxious to change the Labour Party's image and appeal to a wider section of the middle class by upholding the virtues of choice and competition and playing down the Labour Party's commitment to comprehensive schooling. Education would be allowed to continue as a market commodity driven by consumer demands, with parental choice of schools being facilitated by the continued publication of league tables of test and examination results.

It had been made clear, even before the 1997 General Election, that, in the event of a Labour victory, several key personnel would remain in their posts heading the major education quangos: Anthea Millett at the Teacher Training Agency (TTA), Nicholas Tate at the Qualifications and Curriculum Authority (QCA) and Chris Woodhead, a highly controversial figure with a thinly disguised contempt for many features of the state system, at the Office for Standards in Education (Ofsted), which had been set up by the 1992 Education (Schools) Act as a new 'independent' body responsible for contracting independent teams of inspectors to assess the progress of all primary and secondary schools. In his 2002 book *Class war*, Woodhead attacked the notion that, under his leadership, Ofsted inspections had invariably placed an intolerable strain on schools and teachers. 'If Ofsted has a fault,' he wrote, 'it is not that it has been too critical of schools and teachers; it is that too often, it has bent over backwards to be too kind' (Woodhead, 2002, p 20).

With regard to the vexed question of what should be done with the remaining 164 grammar schools, supporters of a *genuine* comprehensive system without selective enclaves had no reason to be optimistic. New Labour's strategy for dealing with selection had been outlined in the 1995 policy document *Diversity and excellence: A new partnership for schools* (Labour Party, 1995). It was made clear in this document that the Labour Party was 'implacably opposed to a return to selection by the eleven-plus', but it was also emphasised that a Labour government would not be prepared to deal with the grammar schools as 'an issue of national policy':

While we have never supported grammar schools in their exclusion of children by examination, change can come only through local agreement. Such a change in the character of a school could follow only a clear demonstration of support from the parents affected by such a decision. (Labour Party, 1995, p 11)

Delegates to the October 1995 Labour Party Conference were clearly unhappy with this clumsy formula, and in his reply to the rather tense education debate on 4 October, Shadow Education Secretary David Blunkett sought to placate his restless audience by affirming: 'Read my lips. No selection, either by examination or interview, under a Labour government'. That categorical assurance won the day for the Labour leadership, and a revolt, organised around demands for the remaining 164 grammar schools to be incorporated into the comprehensive system, collapsed, on the grounds that David Blunkett had clearly acceded to the rebels' demands.

It soon transpired, however, that the phrase 'no selection' actually meant 'no FURTHER selection', and when David Blunkett started using this new slogan in speeches and media interviews, he was accused by critics of reneging on the promise made in his conference speech. Responding to this charge on the BBC television 'Breakfast with Frost' programme on 30 November 1997, the new Education Secretary protested that when he had used the words 'no selection' in the 1995 debate, he had actually intended to say 'no further selection'. It had been a simple 'slip of the tongue'. He had not been under pressure from 10 Downing Street to change the formula and therefore the policy.

The White Paper *Excellence in schools*, published by the Department for Education and Employment in July 1997 just 67 days after the General Election, stipulated that under a Labour government, there would be *three* types of secondary school: community, aided and foundation. Community schools would be based on the existing county schools; aided schools would be based on the existing voluntary-aided schools; and foundation schools would have a degree of independence designed to make the category attractive to most, if not all, grant-maintained establishments. Where grammar schools still existed in England, their future would be decided, as laid down in the 1995 policy document, by ballots of eligible local parents and not by local education authorities (DfEE, 1997, pp 67, 72).

In an interview with *The Sunday Telegraph* in March 2000, David Blunkett left readers in no doubt that he had no intention of tackling the grammar school question. It was time, he said, to 'bury the dated arguments of previous decades' and reverse 'the outright opposition to grammar schools' that had been 'a touchstone of Labour politics for at least 35 years'. He went on:

> I'm just not interested in hunting the remaining grammar schools.... I'm desperately trying to avoid the whole debate in

education once again, as it was waged in the 1960s and 1970s, concentrating on the single issue of selection, when it should be concentrating on the raising of standards.... Arguments about selection are part of a past agenda. We have set up a system which says "if you don't like grammar schools, you can get rid of them"; but it simply isn't the key issue for the year 2000 and beyond. The real issue is what we are going to do about the whole of secondary education. (*The Sunday Telegraph*, 12 March 2000)

This remarkable interview was given just two days after the announcement of the voting figures in the first ballot on the future of grammar schools held as a result of the new government's policy of leaving the future of 11 Plus selection in the hands of local parents. The future of Ripon Grammar School in North Yorkshire, founded in 1556 and one of the oldest in England, was assured as parents decided by a majority of two to one to reject the proposition that the school be required in future to 'admit children of all abilities'. On a 75% turnout, 1,493 of the 3,000 or so parents who were 'entitled to vote' because their children went to one or other of 14 'feeder' state primary or independent preparatory schools voted to reject the proposition, with 748 voting in favour – a clear result that was immediately accepted by Education Minister Estelle Morris on behalf of the government:

> The Government respects the decision of parents to retain the current admissions arrangements at Ripon Grammar School.... At all stages of the Debate, the decision has been a matter for the parents, and they have all had the chance to express their views. (reported in *The Daily Telegraph*, 11 March 2000)

Whatever David Blunkett and Estelle Morris might say about the situation, those concerned about the future of 11 Plus selection felt that it was simply too important to be surrendered to the vagaries of local campaigns, affected as they might well be by a number of esoteric local factors. The Ripon experience had shown that the ballot regulations were very difficult to operate in practice and could be played out on an uneven pitch with, in this case, the 'pro-selectionists' having the resources to employ professional lobbyists.

At the same time, recent research had shown that 11 Plus selection could not be dismissed as part of a 'past' or 'out-of-date' agenda, since the continued existence of selective schools made a very real difference to the success or otherwise of neighbouring comprehensives. A survey of comprehensive schools in Britain carried out in 1994 had, in fact, clearly highlighted the educationally depressing effect that the 164 remaining grammar schools were having on other secondary schools in the vicinity. Where grammar schools were present in an area, the percentage of pupils in the neighbouring comprehensives falling in the 'top' 20% of the attainment range was 12%, compared with 24% for those comprehensives where there was *no* competition from selective schools. For those going on from 11–16 schools to some form of post-16 education and training, the figure was 57% as against 69%; for those staying on after the age of 16 in 11–18 schools, 49% as against 60%; and for those gaining five or more GCSE passes at grades A★-C, 29% as against 48%. The A-level point score averages were 10.6% and 13.4%, respectively. These figures led the authors of the 1994 survey to conclude that:

> Selection at secondary-school level did not actually render comprehensive education impossible, or deny it to parents and children; what it did do, however, wherever it was taking place, was decrease comprehensive education's effectiveness *for the majority* – and, in some cases, severely depress outcomes in the neighbouring schools. (Benn and Chitty, 1996, p 465, emphasis in original)

The other aspect of education policy that clearly pointed up New Labour's reluctance to abandon the concept of selection by 'ability' (or 'aptitude') related to the continuing emphasis on 'specialisation'. As we have already seen, the new government inherited 181 specialist schools and colleges: 151 specialising in technology and 30 specialising in modern languages. The 1997 White Paper *Excellence in schools* argued that 'there is value in encouraging diversity by allowing schools to develop a particular identity, character and expertise' (DfEE, 1997, p 66).

And it went on to give an assurance that schools with a specialism would continue to be able to give priority to children who 'demonstrated the relevant aptitude', as long as that was not 'misused' to 'select pupils on the basis of general academic ability' (p 71). This pledge was then given legislative backing in section 102 of the 1998 School Standards and Framework Act, which said that 'a maintained secondary school may make provision for the selection of pupils for admission to the school by reference to their aptitude for one or more prescribed subjects' where:

- the admission authority for the school is satisfied that the school has a specialism in the subject or subjects in question;

- the proportion of selective admissions in any relevant age group does not exceed 10% (p 80).

The Specialist Schools Project was given specific endorsement in the 2001 Green Paper on *Schools: Building on success: Raising standards, promoting diversity, achieving results*, where it was announced that there would be around 1,000 specialist secondary schools in operation by September 2003 and at least 1,500 by September 2006 (DfEE, 2001). In fact, there were already 1,955 specialist schools in existence in September 2004 covering a wide range of specialisms: technology, arts, sports, sciences, modern languages, maths and computing, business and enterprise, engineering, humanities, music and combined specialisms. The most popular and sought-after specialisms were technology (545 schools), arts (305) and sports (283). Those schools offering technology, arts, sports, languages and music were allowed to select up to 10% of their pupils on the basis of their 'aptitude' for the subject (DfES, 2004). It is, of course, very unclear what the term 'aptitude' actually means, and how it can be distinguished from 'general ability'. Professor Peter Mortimore, formerly Director of the Institute of Education in London, has argued that except in music and possibly art, 'it is simply not possible to diagnose specific aptitudes for most school curriculum subjects'. How, he asks, can headteachers know 'if the "aptitude" of a ten-year-old in German shows anything more than their parents' ability to pay for language lessons?' (quoted in Chitty, 2007, p 19).

Where the school curriculum was concerned, it was soon obvious that the new government was preparing to make major changes, particularly at the primary level. The 1997 White Paper announced that literacy and numeracy would now be a priority for all primary school pupils. Each primary school would be expected to devote a structured hour a day to literacy from September 1998 and introduce a daily numeracy hour in September 1999. This drive to improve children's literacy and numeracy skills would be assisted by rigorous assessment and testing at ages 7 and 11. There would also be new challenging national targets for the performance of 11-year-olds in English and maths. By 2002, 80% of 11-year-olds would be required to reach the standards expected for their age in English, and 75% would be expected to reach the required standard in maths. In the event, primary schools did not, in fact, reach their targets in 2002. It was announced by the government at the end of September 2002 that only 75% of 11-year-olds had reached Level 4 in English and only 73% in maths. And this failure to meet these well-publicised targets was to be cited in the media as one of the main reasons for Estelle Morris's unexpected resignation as Education Secretary on 23 October 2002.

In January 1998, the government announced that pupils under the age of 11 would no longer be required to follow the detailed national syllabuses in history, geography, design and technology, art, music and physical education. And this emphasis on literacy and numeracy, particularly for the morning sessions, has been seen by many commentators as having the undesirable effect of 'narrowing' and 'impoverishing' the curriculum for primary school pupils. Speaking on the BBC Radio 4 programme 'The World Tonight' on 16 May 2002, Mike Tomlinson, the former Chief Inspector of Schools, conceded that the broad and rich National Curriculum in primary schools was being steadily 'whittled away' to facilitate a harmful concentration on the issues of literacy and numeracy. In his view, there was a real danger that the emphasis on core skills amounted to 'a silent revolution', whereby little time was now available for such important subjects as history, geography, art and music. It was to be one of the main conclusions of the Cambridge Primary Review, published on 15 October 2009 (Alexander, 2009), that the New Labour government had introduced a primary school diet 'even narrower than that of the Victorian elementary schools' (reported in *The Guardian*, 16 October 2009).

In the case of the National Curriculum at Key Stage 4, very little was left of the original 1987 model by the time New Labour came to power in 1997. Maintained secondary schools in England were now required to teach the authorised programmes of study in: English, maths, science (as a 'single' or 'double' programme), design and technology (a short course being the 'minimum requirement'), information technology (as a separate subject or coordinated across other subjects), a modern foreign language and physical education. Secondary schools also had a statutory obligation to provide a programme of 'clearly identified' religious education, in accordance with a locally agreed syllabus, and a programme of 'carefully structured' sex education – although, in accordance with section 241 of the 1993 Education Act, parents now had the right to withdraw their children from all or part of the programme.

Careers education would become a statutory part of the curriculum from September 1998. And it had been decided that there would be 'greater scope' for vocational options by providing for courses leading to GNVQs (General National Vocational Qualifications). A Part One GNVQ course at either intermediate or foundation level would be expected to take about the same time at Key Stage 4 as two GCSEs and occupy a maximum of 20% of curriculum time. This was, of course, a very different curriculum framework from that envisaged by Education Secretary Kenneth Baker back in 1987. And further proposals for 'slimming down' the structure were contained in the 2002 Green Paper *14–19: Extending opportunities, raising standards* (DfES, 2002). The Key Stage 4 curriculum would now comprise: maths, English, science and information and communication technology (ICT), alongside citizenship, religious education, careers education, sex education, physical education and work-related learning. Modern foreign languages and design and technology would no longer be 'required study' for all students, but they would join the arts and the humanities as subjects where, in the words of the Green Paper, there would simply be 'a new statutory entitlement of access' (DfES, 2002, p 20). The decision to make French, German and other modern European languages 'optional' at Key Stage 4 would then be offset by the introduction of a foreign language into the primary school curriculum at Key Stage 2. This did little to placate the members of the Association of Language Learners (ALL), and it soon became clear that the majority of secondary schools planning to dispense with compulsory language lessons were those situated in deprived inner-city areas, raising legitimate fears that learning languages such as French and German to an advanced level would soon be seen as an 'elitist' activity confined to largely middle-class areas.

The privatisation of education

One important respect in which New Labour has been keen to follow the educational agenda of previous Conservative administrations concerns the continuing emphasis on the 'benefits' of privatisation, and here special attention must be paid to the origins and development of city academies.

The statutory basis for New Labour's academies project, launched in March 2000, was the collection of legislative powers taken from the 1988 ERA and originally designed to facilitate the establishment of a nationwide network of privately financed CTCs in the early 1990s. And this is a significant point because the academies initiative has been seen by many as a thinly disguised New Labour version of the Conservatives' ill-fated CTC programme.

When the project was launched, it was made clear by the then Education Secretary David Blunkett that it was to be seen as 'a radical approach' to 'breaking the cycle of underperformance and low expectations' in inner-city schools. Blunkett actually outlined his vision for the new academies in a speech delivered to the Social Market Foundation on 15 March 2000:

> These academies, to replace seriously failing schools, will be built and managed by partnerships involving the government, voluntary, church and business sponsors. They will offer a real challenge and improvements in pupil performance, for example through innovative approaches to management, governance, teaching and the Curriculum, including a specialist focus in at least one curriculum area. They will also be committed to working with and learning from other local schools.... The aim will be to raise standards in urban schools by breaking the cycle of underperformance and low expectations. To be eligible for government support, these academies will need to meet clear criteria. They will take over or replace schools which are either in special measures or are clearly underachieving. (www.dfes.gov.uk/speeches; see also Rogers and Migniulo, 2007, p 7)

The first of three academies opened in September 2002. Nine followed a year later, and five more opened in September 2004, making a total of 17 at the end of Tony Blair's second term in office. By this time, the word 'city' had been dropped, to allow for the creation of new schools in rural areas. The government's policy document *A five-year strategy for children and learners*, published in July 2004, indicated that the government intended to have 200 academies 'open or in the pipeline' by 2010, despite the fact that no evaluation had been made of their cost-effectiveness. Some would replace 'under-performing schools', while others would be entirely new, particularly in London, where there was a demand for new school places and where it was expected that there would be at least 60 new academies by 2010 (DfES, 2004, pp 9, 51).

In an article in *The Guardian*, published on 9 July 2004, education journalist Francis Beckett pointed out that, while it might seem strange that New Labour education ministers should seek to resurrect the Conservatives' CTC project, which had come to a sudden end with the creation of only 15 schools, they were at least determined 'not to repeat some of the Conservatives' more obvious mistakes' (Beckett, 2004). Where funding was concerned, for example, Education Secretary Kenneth Baker had been unduly optimistic in believing that private sponsors would be prepared to pay 'all or most' of the estimated £10 million cost involved in setting up a CTC in the late 1980s. The Conservative government had soon found that businesses did not relish parting company with this sort of amount and Baker had been obliged to drastically revise his expectations downwards. In the event, he finally settled on the more realistic sum of just £2 million, which, coincidentally, was the figure New Labour decided on for its city academies in 2000, although £2 million was obviously worth far less by then and represented a far smaller proportion of the total cost. As time went by, New Labour was even prepared to allow new sponsors, particularly independent schools and universities, to dispense with any contribution towards the starting costs.

In a speech to New Labour's 2005 Labour Party Conference, Tony Blair confidently asserted that the new academies were helping children in some of the country's most deprived communities. 'The beneficiaries of these new schools are not fat cats', he said. 'They are, in fact, some of the poorest families in the poorest parts of Britain' (reported in *The Guardian*, 28 September 2005). Yet it was revealed a few weeks later that the percentage of pupils from 'less affluent families' in two thirds of the new academies had actually dropped, 'in some cases drastically', from the figure for 'poor children' in the so-called failing schools they replaced (*The Guardian*, 31 October 2005).

By September 2006, there were 46 academies in existence, and in a speech to the Specialist Schools and Academies Trust (SSAT) in November 2006, Tony Blair announced a doubling of the target figure to 400. It was also made clear that some of the new academies would be aimed at catering for pupils aged from three to 19. A total of 67 new academies were opened at the beginning of the school term in September 2009, bringing the total of these new schools to 200. The decision to scrap the £2 million sponsorship requirement for private schools and universities had clearly prompted a marked expansion in the numbers coming forward: of the 67 academies opening in 2009, 45 were either sponsored or co-sponsored by educational bodies.

Prospects for the future

The current Education Secretary Ed Balls has had to contend with criticisms of New Labour's education programme from a number of quarters. As we have already seen, the major Cambridge Primary Review, led by Professor Robin Alexander of the University of Cambridge, found that the government's emphasis on literacy and numeracy had had a largely detrimental effect on the creative and aesthetic aspects of the primary curriculum, with many pupils being bored and frustrated by the narrow and uninspiring curriculum diet on offer. At the other end of the age range, recent attempts to reform and broaden the 14–19 curriculum, effectively breaking the stranglehold of A-levels and GCSEs, were criticised for being both half-hearted and lacking in conviction, with the added problem of the new academic diplomas being launched in 2011 receiving a lukewarm response as suitable qualifications from many of the leading universities. Following all the difficulties over the marking of SATs (standard assessment tasks or tests) in the summer of 2008, Ed Balls announced the abolition of SATs tests for 14-year-olds in October 2008, and since then, the government has also announced the end of Key Stage 2 tests in science from 2010. These moves have been welcomed by many teachers and union leaders, but have also led to a demand for the scrapping of all tests and league tables.

Where the academies programme is concerned – surely the most controversial of all New Labour's education policies – government support seems to be assured, whatever the outcome of the 2010 General Election, in that it has the wholehearted support of the Conservative Party. (The Liberal Democrats would have 'sponsor-managed schools' instead of academies, and these would be under the strategic oversight of local authorities and not of ministers in Whitehall.) One of David Cameron's decisive moves as Conservative Party Leader was to let it be known that the academies were 'the schools of the future', while, at the same time, abandoning the party's long-standing commitment to the creation of new grammar schools throughout the country. Addressing a conference of the Confederation of British Industry (CBI) in May 2007, the then Shadow Education Secretary David Willetts said that the Conservatives would be happy to 'adopt Tony Blair's academies' and 'run them better than would be the case under Gordon Brown' (reported in *The Guardian*, 17 May 2007).

In a major extension of the academies project, Michael Gove, the current Shadow Schools Secretary, announced at the Conservatives' Spring Conference in Cheltenham at the end of April 2009 that all primary schools would be free to apply for academy status 'within two years of a Conservative election victory' (reported in *The Daily Telegraph*, 25 April 2009). And it emerged at the Conservative Party Conference in October 2009 that a Conservative government would encourage private companies to run state schools 'for profit', in 'a radical departure from commonly-accepted practice in England' (reported in *The Guardian*, 9 October 2009).

We have long reached the stage in this country where the education policies of the two main parties are so similar that they are virtually interchangeable. As we have seen, both parties are committed to the continued privatisation of education, with a key role envisaged for privately sponsored schools. There seems to be a consensus within the education establishment that the National Curriculum cannot be scrapped, although the Liberal Democrats would abolish the existing, overly prescriptive, 600-page National Curriculum document, and replace it with a 'light touch' Minimum Curriculum Guarantee of just 20 pages. Both major parties show little respect for teachers, and the proper accountability of professionals to the public is increasingly being replaced by accountability to regulators, private sponsors and government departments. There seems to be scant realisation of the fact that schools and teachers function best in a civilised environment where intelligent accountability is balanced by the promotion of professional initiative and autonomy.

References

Alexander, R. (ed) (2009) *Children, their world, their education, Final report and recommendations of the Cambridge Primary Review*, London: Routledge.

Beckett, F. (2004) 'Business class', *The Guardian*, 9 July.

Benn, C. and Chitty, C. (1996) *Thirty years on: Is comprehensive education alive and well or struggling to survive?*, London: David Fulton.

Blair, T. (1994) *Socialism*, London: Fabian Society, July.

Bogdanor, V. (1979) 'Power and participation', *Oxford Review of Education*, vol 5, no 2 (June), pp 157–68.

Chitty, C. (1988) 'Two models of a national curriculum: origins and interpretation', in D. Lawton and C. Chitty (eds) *The National Curriculum*, Bedford Way Paper 33, London: Institute of Education, pp 34–48.

Chitty, C. (2007) 'Aptitude and ability', in *Fair enough: School admissions – The next steps*, London: Comprehensive Future, pp 18–20.

Chitty, C. and Dunford, J. (eds) (1999) *State schools: New Labour and the Conservative legacy*, London: Woburn Place.

DfEE (Department for Education and Employment) (1997) *Excellence in schools*, Cm 3681, London: The Stationery Office.

DfEE (2001) *Schools: Building on success: Raising standards, promoting diversity, achieving results*, Cm 5050, London: The Stationery Office.

DfES (Department for Education and Skills) (2002) *14–19: Extending opportunities, raising standards*, Consultation document, Cm 5342, London: The Stationery Office.

DfES (2004) *A five-year strategy for children and learners: Putting people at the heart of public services*, Cm 6272, London: The Stationery Office.

Giddens, A. (1998) *The third way: The renewal of social democracy*, Cambridge: Polity Press.

Giddens, A. (2000) *The third way and its critics*, Cambridge: Polity Press.

Labour Party (1995) *Diversity and excellence: A new partnership for schools*, London: Labour Party.

Maclure, S. (1987) 'Leading from the centre', *The Times Educational Supplement*, 3 April.

Marquand, D. (2000) 'Revisiting the Blair paradox', *New Left Review*, no 3, May/June, pp 73-9.

Patten, J. (1992) 'Who's afraid of the "s" word?', *New Statesman and Society*, 17 July, pp 20-1.

Rogers, M. and Migniulo, F. (2007) *A new direction: A review of the school academies programme*, London: Trades Union Congress.

Woodhead, C. (2002) *Class war: The state of British education*, London: Little, Brown.

TWO

Children's social care under New Labour

Mary Langan

Introduction

In the early years of the New Labour government after 1997, modernisation through the extension of market and managerial principles was the central theme of policy in relation to social services as in other areas of the public sector (Clarke et al, 2000; Harris, 2003). However, looking back after more than a decade, we can identify a more fundamental transformation in welfare policy in Tony Blair's third term (2005–07), continuing under Gordon Brown's premiership after the summer of 2007.

The distinctive feature of New Labour's social policy is a shift away from the collectivist, redistributive approach of the post-war welfare state to a more individualistic, therapeutic ethos. While the ideological groundwork for this shift was central to the emerging New Labour project in the mid-1990s, it came to dominate government policy a decade later. By contrast, the marketisation agenda, directly inherited from the Thatcher–Major era, appeared to lack any entrepreneurial impetus and rapidly became mired in bureaucracy.

In its shift away from material redistribution towards a concern with the moral and spiritual welfare of the individual, New Labour social policy came to focus on the section of society that appeared to be both most vulnerable to the threats of the post-modern world and most susceptible to state intervention: children. Transforming children's social care into an effective means of tackling social exclusion and improving well-being has become a central policy commitment over the past decade. Key innovations, including Sure Start programmes and children's trusts, have sought to cut across established modes of governance and professional boundaries, at national and local levels. Inspired by theories of 'positive psychology' and US practice models, these initiatives are forging a new pattern of relationships between the state and the family. Yet, although promoters of these methods claim the legitimacy afforded by scientific evaluations, the evidence remains contentious and the question of 'what works?' in the long term remains uncertain.

Positive welfare

The protection and care of children is the single most important thread that should guide family policy. (Giddens, 1998, p 93)

For most parents, our children are everything to us: our hopes, our ambitions, our future. Our children are cherished and loved. (Blair, 2003)

For Anthony Giddens, an important academic influence on the dramatic revision of New Labour social policy in the 1990s, welfare was 'not in essence an economic concept, but a psychic one, concerning as it does "well-being"' (Giddens, 1998, p 117). He emphasised that 'welfare institutions must be concerned with fostering psychological as well as economic benefits', arguing that, for example, counselling 'might be more helpful than direct economic support' (Giddens, 1998, p 117). Although this approach was not entirely novel – Margaret Thatcher's government had provided counselling for industrial workers who lost their jobs in the early 1980s recession – it was pursued in a much more systematic way after 1997. Some years earlier, in a call for 'rethinking the welfare state', Giddens had proposed an 'escape from reliance on the precautionary aftercare' provided by the Beveridge framework (Giddens, 1994, p 185). Instead of a system based on provision for the vicissitudes and crises of life (illness, disability, loss of work, retirement), he suggested a 'new ethics of individual and collective responsibility' (1994, p 185). Anticipating a later New Labour theme, he argued that 'the aim of good government' should be the 'happiness' of its citizens, understood in terms of the 'security of mind and body' and 'self-respect'. He advocated a concept of 'positive welfare' that emphasised 'health promotion' and coping with the risks of the post-modern world (1994, p 183).

Supporters of New Labour's therapeutic turn welcomed the government's adoption of 'a social policy which aims at meeting the emotional as well as physical needs of human beings' (Hoggett, 2000, p 144). From this perspective, the concept of well-being provided a 'core principle around which a new vision of positive welfare could be organised' (Hoggett, 2000, p 145). After 1997, 'children emerged as key figures in New Labour's nascent social investment state' (Lister, 2004, p 175). In his 1999 Beveridge lecture commemorating the founder of the welfare state, Blair proclaimed that children – '20% of the population, but 100% of our future' – were his government's top priority and pledged to abolish childhood poverty within two decades (1999, p 16). Childhood moved to the centre of policy priorities because it was regarded as 'the fulcrum of attempts to tackle social exclusion and invest in a positive, creative and wealth-creating future' (Parton, 2006, p 98).

In Tony Blair's first term in office as Prime Minister the drive to reform personal social services, as in other areas of the welfare state, proceeded hesitantly and unevenly. The 1998 White Paper *Modernising social services* (DH, 1998) indicated the government's determination to persist with the promotion of a mixed economy of welfare provision that had been initiated by the previous Conservative government. However, following Blair's second general election victory in June 2001, the pace of reform accelerated, and the focus shifted towards measures to improve parenting and early intervention to prevent later difficulties. The 2003 Green Paper *Every Child Matters* (Chief Secretary to the Treasury, 2003) proclaimed a 'new approach to the well-being of children and young people from birth to age 19', specifying as its aims and objectives that 'every child, whatever their background or their circumstances' should have the support they needed to 'be healthy; stay safe; enjoy and achieve; make a positive contribution; achieve economic well-being' (Chief Secretary to the Treasury, 2003, pp 6-7). The pursuit of these five *Every Child Matters* outcomes became a central policy commitment. It would not only bring about major organisational change but 'would also reconfigure the relationship between children, parents, professionals and the state well beyond concerns about child abuse' (Parton, 2006, p 2).

The government's programme of intervention in childhood was driven by a plethora of reports, guidelines, spending reviews, action plans and 'toolkits' emerging from diverse ministries (HM Treasury, Health, Education, Home Office) as well as from the Cabinet Office and the Downing Street Policy Unit. It was supported by quasi-governmental bodies such as the Social Exclusion Unit and the Audit Commission, by influential voluntary groups and think-tanks (National Centre for Social Research, Joseph Rowntree Foundation, National Children's Bureau, Family Policy Study Centre, Family and Parenting Institute, Institute for Public Policy Research, Demos and others).

Increased therapeutic intervention in children's lives through social care services was accompanied by parallel initiatives in other areas:

in education (Early Years, extended schools and social and emotional aspects of learning [SEAL] programmes), in criminal justice (through the wider use of Anti-social Behaviour Orders [ASBOs] and the Respect agenda) and in health (through campaigns against teenage pregnancy and obesity, such as the Change4Life programme to promote healthy lifestyles) (Earnshaw, 2008). The common theme was that 'linked-up' government agencies and appropriately qualified professionals could work with children and their families to enhance individual well-being and promote social cohesion. The key assumptions underlying New Labour social policy were that children were uniquely at risk in contemporary society, that they had been betrayed by existing services and professions and that early intervention was the key to their future happiness (and to the stability of society). We will now look at these more closely.

Children in danger

Life is more complex than it ever was. (DCSF, 2007b, p 19)

The profound and menacing character of the social changes impinging on children's lives are recurrent themes of New Labour policy documents from the mid-1990s onwards (CSJ, 1994). These acknowledge the effects of globalised market forces in causing the collapse of traditional manufacturing industries with destructive consequences for working-class communities and family life. Globalisation is regarded as a destructive force, increasing insecurity in employment and inequalities in income, with the result that a substantial proportion of children have remained persistently below the poverty line. Policy makers take a gloomy view of changes in family life, noting that both fathers and mothers now often combine full-time and part-time work with childcare and responsibilities for elderly dependants. They accept that the breakdown of the nuclear family is confirmed by the high proportion of children who now live in more precarious single-parent or step-families. While Conservatives identify 'the broken society' and the collapse of traditional moral values, radical critics recall the 'profound damage, material and spiritual' inflicted on working-class communities by the governments of Margaret Thatcher in the 1980s (Davies, 1998; Ferguson and Lavalette, 2009, p 30). Other commentators point to the influence of consumer values and celebrity culture on young people, their ready access to alcohol and drugs and the pressures of bullying, abuse and premature sexual experimentation.

A series of high-profile criminal cases had an important influence on the climate of opinion in which New Labour's social care policies for children were developed and introduced. The murder of two-year-old James Bulger in Liverpool by two 10-year-old boys in Liverpool in 1993 provoked a populist backlash in which the perpetrators were widely demonised in the media. Tony Blair, then a rising Labour politician, advanced the slogan 'tough on crime, tough on the causes of crime', which subsequently became a theme of New Labour policy. The emerging 'third way' approach combined 'intensive inclusionary strategies' to integrate marginalised individuals with 'strong exclusionary strategies' for those who refused to conform and who engaged in the expanding category of 'anti-social behaviour' (Parton, 2006, p 89; Waiton, 2008). The murders of Sarah Payne (aged nine) in West Sussex in 2000 and of Jessica Chapman and Holly Wells (both aged 10) in Soham in 2002, and the subsequent convictions of two known sex offenders, led to an upsurge of public anxieties about paedophiles and to the establishment of a national vetting scheme which implicitly placed all adults under suspicion as potential abusers. The deaths of Victoria Climbié in 2000 and Peter Connelly (formerly known as Baby P) in 2007 resulted in inquiries that were highly critical of local child protection services in Haringey and provoked national furores. The abduction of nine-year old Shannon Matthews by her own mother and another relative in the northern town of Dewsbury in 2008, in an abortive extortion scheme, was widely interpreted as confirming the existence of a feckless underclass in which incompetent and abusive parenting were commonplace.

These grim cases appeared to provide dramatic confirmation of children's vulnerability to a wide range of malign forces both within and beyond their own homes, and of their potential for criminal behaviour. From the perspective of New Labour policy makers the 'child as victim and the child as villain are both seen as in need of attention, because for both, it is their health and development which should be the focus' (Parton, 2006, p 169). Indeed, children's health and development became a national preoccupation, most notably in the controversy around television chef Jamie Oliver's crusade to improve school meals, probably the most prominent issue in the 2005 General Election campaign. The US public health academic Philip Alcabes links popular concerns about obesity with the increased recognition of autistic spectrum disorders among children (Alcabes, 2009). For Alcabes, the fact that both are widely – if contentiously – depicted as 'epidemic' conditions reveals deep anxieties in contemporary society, about personal and social behaviour, individual and communal failure, fears about childhood and parenting, performance at school and work, worries about the future health of individuals and society. It appears that children who are overweight or whose behaviour is unusual have 'suddenly become exemplars of the threat of modern life, unprecedented and uniquely dangerous' (Alcabes, 2009, p 213).

In many respects the perception that children are gravely disadvantaged in modern British society is counter-intuitive. By objective criteria, they enjoy higher standards of living and health (judged, for example, by the very low rates of perinatal and infant mortality, even among poorer children, and the rapidly increasing duration of life expectancy from birth) than any children in human history. Yet the sentiment of 'doing better and feeling worse' dominates in the prevailing climate of pessimism and insecurity (Wildavsky, 1977). Hence a Unicef report in 2007, which rated the UK at the bottom of the league table on the status of children in developed countries according to a series of six dimensions of well-being, appeared merely to confirm a familiar gloomy picture (Unicef, 2007, p 2). The measures used included material and educational well-being, health and safety, family and peer relationships, behaviour and risks and subjective well-being; the UK was consistently rated lowest on the last three (more subjective) indicators.

In the early days of the New Labour government, the newly established Social Exclusion Unit (SEU) took the lead in advancing Giddens' 'positive welfare' agenda, aiming to promote economic growth and individual well-being through positive prevention and early intervention in family life. For the government's pioneering welfare initiative, 'social exclusion' occurred when 'people or areas suffer from a combination of problems such as unemployment, poor skills, low income, poor housing, high crime, bad health and family breakdown' (SEU, 2001, p 11). While recognising that it was difficult to distinguish risk factors that were causes or effects, for New Labour, 'the primary and original cause of many problems associated with crime, education and employment is seen to reside with poor parenting' (Parton, 2006, p 93). New Labour's focus on the risks facing children and young people led inexorably to its policy focus on professional intervention to improve parenting.

Government family policies now assumed the breakdown of the family and the divergent needs of different family members:

No longer was the traditional patriarchal nuclear family seen as an adequate instrument of government. Increasingly the interests and identities of children and parents (both mothers and fathers) were disentangled and disaggregated. (Parton, 2006, p 5)

Parenting now became a public concern. For New Labour parents, both mothers and fathers, needed professional support to help them to grasp and fulfil their parental responsibilities and children relied on professionals to guarantee their safety and well-being.

Children betrayed

The public and political image of social workers by the late 1990s was inextricably interrelated with failures in relation to children, particularly in terms of child abuse. (Frost and Parton, 2009, p 159)

The defining trope of New Labour was the self-conscious contrast with Old Labour, and nowhere was this more forcefully deployed than in relation to children's social care. In its first term New Labour embarked on 'modernising' social services and in its second term raised the rhetorical stakes with the 'transformational reform agenda' promoted with *Every Child Matters*. Any opposition to these measures was by definition reactionary and defensive, as the government claimed the ideological high ground through its commitment to challenging obsolete structures and practices in the quest to advance children's interests (Garrett, 2009).

The government faced little resistance to its reform programme from a social care workforce demoralised by public condemnations arising from failures of child protection and from revelations of long-term institutionalised abuse in children's homes. Child protection scandals have cast a long shadow over social work with children, from the case of Maria Colwell in the early 1970s, through the controversies about child sexual abuse in Cleveland and elsewhere in the 1980s, to the recent Climbié and Connelly deaths. The inquiry into the Climbié case by Lord Laming documented a familiar list of failures of professional practice and interagency coordination (Laming, 2003). Reports by Sir William Utting in the 1990s revealed the scale of abuse in the childcare system; these were complemented by Ronald Waterhouse's subsequent investigation of abuses in children's homes in Wales over three decades (Utting, 1991, 1997; Waterhouse, 2000). The depiction of the past in terms of scandal and failure (compounded by reports showing poor outcomes for children emerging from residential care) provided the context for the 'Care Matters' reform programme introduced in 2006 (Frost and Parton, 2009, pp 105-12).

The key targets for New Labour's reforming zeal were the twin symbols of the old order: the local authority social services department, established in the early 1970s following the radical Seebohm report of

1968, and the generic social worker as the leading professional of the old social care system. For Tony Blair and his colleagues, local councils were too often associated with the so-called 'loony left' around Ken Livingstone and Tony Benn in Labour's internal squabbles of the 1980s. Social workers too carried an aura of radicalism, of past associations with feminism, trades union militancy and liberal causes. In a widely reported speech to a national social services conference in Cardiff in 2002, Health Secretary Alan Milburn denounced the 'old monolithic single social services' (Milburn, 2002). He declared the government's intention to get rid of 'traditional service boundaries which get in the way of good care for children' in favour of 'specialised local organisations' aiming to 'provide a more seamless service for children'. The failures of the past provided New Labour with an opportunity to organise its interventions in social care for children through new structures and to bring in new professionals in place of the discredited social workers. The lesson that New Labour's policy advisers drew from the series of abuse inquiries culminating in the Laming Report on Victoria Climbié was that the key failing of the past was 'a failure to intervene early enough' – this now became the guiding principle of the *Every Child Matters* programme (Parton, 2006, p 152).

Get them early

We better understand the importance of early influences on the development of values and behaviour....We have a good idea what factors shape children's life chances. Research tells us that the risk of experiencing negative outcomes is concentrated in children with certain characteristics. (DCSF, 2003, pp 15-17)

Back in the early 1990s, Conservative Prime Minister John Major had attempted to take advantage of the revulsion over the killing of James Bulger by launching his 'back to basics' moral crusade. The fact that this provoked only ridicule confirmed that in pre-millennial Britain there was no longer any scope for backward-looking appeals to traditional moral certitudes. In fact, Major's predecessor Margaret Thatcher had, in her government's response to the emergence of HIV/Aids in the late 1980s, pragmatically discovered the way forward, through the promotion of the new morality of safety (Waiton, 2008). The doctrine of 'safe sex' sought to influence behaviour through the self-consciously non-judgemental strategy of promoting awareness of the risks of infectious disease. In future, social policy too would seek legitimacy through appeals to scientific evidence rather than trying to justify itself in ethical or political terms. Hence, *Every Child Matters* emphasised that 'research' had provided the knowledge on which the policy of early intervention was based. It advanced an approach familiar in the world of public health, identifying risk factors (the familiar list of characteristics contributing to social exclusion) predictive of adverse outcomes as the targets for preventive interventions.

The ascendancy of an 'evidence-based' approach in social policy had already been signalled in the title of the 1995 Department of Health report *Child protection: Messages from research* (DH, 1995). Largely derived from studies undertaken in the aftermath of the Cleveland child sexual abuse scandal of the late 1980s, this report emphasised the importance of emotional neglect and parenting style in terms of long-term outcomes. It suggested a wider developmental and preventive approach to families, rather than a narrow focus on child protection.

Expert report after expert report provided apparently irrefutable scientific evidence that early childhood experiences determined not only performance in school, but also success in later life. Thus, according to *Every Child Matters*, 'research suggests that parenting appears to be the most important factor associated with educational attainment at age ten, which in turn is strongly associated with achievement in later life' (Chief Secretary to the Treasury, 2003, p 18). A later joint study supported by the Family and Parenting Institute and the Institute of Education and published by the National Children's Bureau emphasised that cultivating emotional literacy was more important than cognitive skills:

> The single best predictor of a 10-year old child going on to fare poorly as an adult in their early thirties turns out not to be their reading or mathematical ability, as might be supposed, but their lack of capacity for self-restraint in response to distress – "externalising behaviour" as it is termed. (Feinstein et al, 2007, p 16)

Every Child Matters confidently claimed that increased knowledge and expertise in relation to early childhood development provided a ready guide to expert intervention. In fact, there is considerable controversy in neuroscience about the notion of neuroplasticity in the early years of life and also among psychologists about the claims of the effectiveness of intensive early behavioural interventions (Bruer, 1999). Yet these uncertainties have not deterred the drive for early intervention in families. Nor have they deterred the expanding range of expert intervention. The notion of providing 'protection' of children considered to be 'at risk' has widened into the concept of offering 'safeguarding' for all children; the aim is not merely to ensure children's physical survival but to guarantee their well-being and development.

Sure Start

> The jewel in New Labour's policy crown.' (Mary MacLeod, Chief Executive, Family and Parenting Institute, in McLeod, 2003)

The Sure Start programme for parents and young children is New Labour's flagship social policy initiative. Modelled on the US Head Start program – part of President Lyndon Johnson's 'great society' and 'war on poverty' policies of the 1960s – Sure Start began with 250 local programmes in the most deprived neighbourhoods in 1999 and subsequently expanded to cover the entire country. Sure Start was consolidated in 2004 with the establishment of a network of children's centres, offering 'seamless integrated services and information' (Frost and Parton, 2009, p 123) for parents and children of all ages, at first in the poorest areas, but rapidly spreading outwards, with a target of 3,500 centres throughout the country by 2010. Children's centres offer a combination of early education and childcare (incorporating elements of health as well as education and social care) together with support for parents, including help to get paid employment, and advice of a more or less systematic character on parenting. With a budget of £1.8 billion a year in 2006, the Sure Start programme amounted to a 'massive state investment in parenting and childhood' (Frost and Parton, 2009, p 125).

There were some tensions within the Sure Start programme between different aspects of the New Labour social policy agenda, tensions that unfolded as the programme expanded in scope (Glass, 2005; Hodge, 2005). On the one hand, they had a role to play in the welfare to work policy of encouraging parents, mothers in particular, to participate in the labour market rather than relying on benefits, in part by providing affordable childcare. On the other hand, they provided the opportunity for early intervention in childhood development and for the promotion of approved styles of parenting. The fact that the maternal employment rate remained almost static between 1994 and 2004 suggests that the latter policy remained the dominant influence (Lloyd, 2008). For authorities in social services preoccupied with failures of child protection, Sure Start programmes provided a means of targeting children at risk and pursuing preventive strategies; for those taking a wider view of child development, a universal service appeared to offer a less stigmatising and more comprehensive approach.

In practice, internal tensions in Sure Start were largely resolved by wider developments. On the one hand, the vogue for formal instruction in parenting popularised by successful television programmes such as Channel 4's 'Supernanny' and numerous popular books and internet sites meant that government initiatives in this area were more likely to be welcomed than regarded as intrusive (Bristow, 2009). On the other hand, the success of Sure Start in the context of the parallel government campaign against anti-social behaviour paved the way for parenting initiatives that were explicitly authoritarian (Waiton, 2008). For example, Family Intervention Projects, launched in 2006 within the framework of the Respect Action Plan designed to tackle anti-social behaviour, offered an approach described as 'assertive' and 'persistent' to improve parenting skills in targeted families (White et al, 2008). These projects involve support workers engaging with parents in intimate family activities such as washing, dressing and feeding children, either through outreach teams or in residential units. Although disparaged as 'sin-bins' in the tabloid press, these programmes were welcomed by broadsheet social commentators (Gentleman, 2009). Within three years of their launch, some 2,600 families had voluntarily attended schemes in 170 centres, in which they were treated 'primarily as victims' (Gentleman, 2009) even though they may have displayed anti-social behaviour. According to a senior project worker in a pioneering unit in Dundee, 'a lot of residents find it prison-like to begin with, initially they find it quite intrusive' (quoted in Gentleman, 2009).

In 2007 the government launched the Family Nurse Partnership, through which specialist nurses (linked to local Sure Start programmes/ children's centres) visit vulnerable, first-time, young parents from early pregnancy until the child is two years old (DCSF, 2007a; Cabinet Office, 2009). Immediately dubbed 'foetal asbos' in the tabloids, this programme is directly derived from the US Nurse Family Partnership scheme, an anti-poverty initiative developed more than 30 years ago in Colorado. The idea is that 'through building a close, supportive relationship with the whole family', the nurse guides the mother 'to adopt healthier lifestyles, improve their parenting skills and become self-sufficient' (Cabinet Office, 2009, p 1).

Following the transfer of power from Tony Blair to Gordon Brown in June 2007, the government pressed ahead with its radical early childhood intervention agenda. Brown immediately signalled his priorities with the establishment of a new ministry, the Department for Children, Schools and Families, headed by his long-standing ally Ed Balls. In December 2007 Balls launched *The Children's Plan*, to be implemented by newly established local children's trusts, bringing together education and social care and incorporating some community health services (and in some areas, youth offending teams). Extended schools are a key part of the programme for delivering the *Every Child Matters* outcomes of improved well-being (Teachernet, 2009). Open from 8am to 6pm, 48 weeks a year, these offer a varied menu of activities for children as well as parenting support and access to specialist services. By 2008 some 2,500 such schools were in operation. Children's trusts were given a new leadership role in coordinating children's services 'so that together they can engage parents and tackle all the barriers to the learning, health and happiness of every child' (DCSF, 2007b, p 3). The key themes in this ambitious programme were early intervention, multiagency working, integration of services and sharing of information.

A new way of doing things

> The Plan and the New Department mean that more than ever before families will be at the centre of excellent, integrated services that put their needs first, regardless of traditional institutional and professional structures. (DCSF, 2007b, p 3)

Sure Start, the children's centres and children's trusts were pioneering initiatives in a number of respects. At every level, from development to implementation, New Labour's policies for children were distinguished by its commitment to doing things differently, to 'joined-up' thinking and working, in defiance of established governmental frameworks and professional hierarchies. The driving force behind Sure Start was the late Norman Glass, formerly a civil servant in the Treasury, and the Treasury played a pivotal role in developing the programme (together with the associated changes in taxation and benefit arrangements) (Lloyd, 2008). Sure Start was at first funded from the education budget; the Department of Health, the traditional source of social policy, played a relatively minor role. More significantly, local authorities were marginalised, as Sure Start programmes were introduced under central direction, marking the 'death of the post-Seebohm local authority social services department' (Parton, 2006, p 148). Although local councils were later accorded a 'strategic' role in relation to the new children's trusts, these were now dominated by the education sector (only 20% of the newly appointed directors had a background in social services) (Churchill, 2007; Frost and Parton, 2009).

The therapeutic content of New Labour's interventions in childhood is a synthesis of the positive psychology and cognitive behavioural therapies associated with the programmes that have been imported from the US for deployment in UK schools and children's centres. A major influence is Martin Seligman, the author of numerous popular self-help and motivational books such as *Authentic happiness: Using the new positive psychology to realize your potential for lasting fulfilment* (Seligman, 2004) and *The optimistic child: A proven program to safeguard children against depression and build lifelong resilience* (Seligman, 1996). Seligman's Penn Resiliency Program, developed in Pennsylvania, has been promoted in the UK by New Labour's 'happiness tsar' Richard Layard as part of his drive to cultivate 'emotional literacy' (Layard, 2007). This programme has been translated (apparently with some difficulty) into British English and piloted in schools in Tyneside, Manchester and Hertfordshire (Challen et al, 2009). Another influential US model is the Incredible Years Program, developed by the nurse and clinical psychologist Carolyn Webster-Stratton in her Seattle parenting clinic. This has been widely implemented in parenting programmes in Wales (Hutchings et al, 2007; Bywater et al, 2009).

A new approach requires new professionals, especially given the recent damage to the reputation of professional social work. Layard is explicit on the need for a new cadre of specialist teachers 'acting as standard bearers of the movement' struggling to achieve an 'educational revolution' (Layard, 2007, p 4). New cohorts of specially trained Early Years teachers and family support workers are emerging as the 'barefoot doctors' of the Sure Start revolution. For the more specialised tasks of intensive family intervention, nurses, midwives and health visitors are preferred. According to a report on parenting policy by the think-tank Demos, health visitors are 'trusted and liked' (unlike social workers) and are an 'under-used resource' (Lexmond and Reeves, 2009, p 63). However, the authors insist that they will need 'more training on parenting styles' and 'motivational interviewing' (p 63).

The government has rapidly introduced a range of new qualifications and training courses for its staff at children's centres. These extend from the basic Early Years Professional Status qualification to the National Professional Qualification in Integrated Centre Leadership (NPQICL), required for heads of children's centres and achieved through a one-year MA-level course, developed at the Pen Green Centre in Corby, Northamptonshire. The course is 'based in feminist and transformational values, and aspires to the development of individuals, drawing deeply on self-reflection and personal change' (Frost and Parton, 2009, p 125).

The influences of US corporate psychology and new age therapy have been brought together by New Labour to create a cohort of new leaders willing and motivated to take forward the children's centres movement, while also creating an influential lobby group (Aubrey, 2007). Of the 354 people who embarked on the NPQICL course in 2005 nearly one third were teachers, around a quarter nursery nurses and less than 20% social workers (Frost and Parton, 2009, p 126).

If it doesn't work, try harder

> I am forced to admit that I doubt that [the government] has the slightest interest in research evidence when dealing with its own policies. (Rutter, 2007, p 207)

> It is reasonable to conclude that both longer exposure to Sure Start local programmes, and the continuing development of such programmes in response to the growing body of evidence, has been responsible for more positive results. (DCSF, 2008, p 7)

As noted, one of the distinctive features of New Labour's social policy was its commitment to 'what works' according to the results of scientific research. Thus the establishment of Sure Start was accompanied by the appointment of a special academic unit at Birkbeck to carry out an ongoing national evaluation of Sure Start, the largest social science evaluation ever undertaken in the UK (Frost and Parton, 2009, p 118). When the results turned out to be, at best, equivocal, the government's commitment to 'evidence-based policy' turned out to be a hostage to fortune (as Professor Sir Michael Rutter's comment indicates: see above).

Problems emerged when the findings of the first phase of evaluation were published in 2005 (Belsky et al, 2007). These revealed that Sure Start had failed to deliver on any of its major goals: it had failed to boost pre-schoolers' development, language or behaviour. Worse, it had had an 'adverse impact' on 'children from more deprived backgrounds' (Rutter, 2006, p 137). According to Rutter in his comprehensive review, 'a prudent reading of the evidence suggests that it would be wise to pay at least attention to possible adverse effects as to possible beneficial ones' (Rutter, 2006, p 135). He concludes that, given the diversity of Sure Start programmes, it is difficult to make any sense at all of 'what works'.

However, as Rutter recognised, the government was determined to continue with the implementation of the Sure Start policy. More targeted studies focusing on more intensive parenting interventions – for example in relation to children manifesting 'conduct disorder' – showed modest positive effects, at least in Wales (Hutchings et al, 2007; Edwards et al, 2007; Bywater et al, 2009). Defenders of the wider Sure Start programme emphasised some positive outcomes, such as 'warmer parenting' or the fact that parents were making greater use of support services (Toynbee, 2005). The government's own 'summary of the evidence' in 2008 that led to the positive spin quoted above claimed that, as a result of Sure Start, 'parents of three year old children now show less negative parenting and provide their children with a better home learning environment' (DCSF, 2008, p 7).

Evidence of the efficacy of Sure Start programmes seems destined to follow the pattern revealed by James Nolan in his well-known study of the outcomes of therapeutic alternatives to incarceration for drug offenders in Florida (Nolan, 1998). Early studies conducted by professionals engaged in these programmes or academics closely involved with them, using scaled-down outcome measures, yielded favourable results. However, when more rigorous long-term studies were carried out by independent observers, using strict outcome measures, the benefits evaporated. This evidence of failure has not deterred the pursuit of therapeutic drug treatment programmes in Florida and far beyond, including in the UK. Indeed claims for the positive achievements of US child intervention schemes on which UK initiatives were modelled were also contested: a survey of 'area-based' anti-poverty initiatives in the US and the UK found that they had only a minor impact (Alcock, 2005). In its 2008 assessment of children's trusts, the Audit Commission found confusion all around and concluded that there was 'little evidence that the trusts had improved outcomes for children' or that they offered better value for money in the provision of children's services (Audit Commission, 2008, p 2). But, whatever the evidence about 'what works', New Labour's policies for children had acquired a momentum of their own.

Conclusion

The term 'nanny state' is used pejoratively to describe government meddling in the private concerns of citizens. But if there is one area where government intervention is justified, it is in precisely the area of life signalled by the term 'nannying' – the development of children's capabilities. (Lexmond and Reeves, 2009, p 58)

Although the rhetoric of modernisation, reform and transformation has been a pervasive feature of New Labour policy making, in the sphere of social care for children the scale of change was indeed dramatic. Welfare policy shifted decisively from the provision of impersonal services and benefits to an intimate involvement in encouraging approved styles of parenting and in fostering the emotional (as well as the cognitive and physical) development of children. Within a decade the old order established around local authority social services departments was replaced by new structures and institutions, incorporating educational and health services and staffed by new professionals (or at least old professionals with new titles and qualifications), organising systematic interventions in the lives of children and their parents.

There can be no doubt that the massive investment in children's services produced some benefits, particularly for 'looked-after children' and other children with special needs. However, the apparently inexorable trend of the New Labour years has been to expand the scope of intervention from children 'in need' or 'at risk' to children in general, who became the target of professional activity aiming to prevent adversity and promote beneficial outcomes, from an earlier and earlier age (indeed, the Family Nurse Partnerships, in extending back into antenatal life). Children may now receive professional assistance with all aspects of their development, in 'wraparound' facilities covering all the spaces between home and school, at every stage of their lives from infancy to further education. Parents too are offered professional support in carrying out their parenting responsibilities, and everybody is therefore exposed to the possibility of monitoring and surveillance.

As seen, the question of whether early childhood intervention 'works' remains controversial. Yet, as critics point out, the controversy over 'outcomes' misses the point: 'when it comes to Sure Start, what counts is not the outcome but the process' (Bristow, 2009, p 76). The Sure Start process puts parenting style at the heart of the policy agenda, 'popularising the idea of parental causality as the only way of keeping children in work and out of jail' (Bristow, 2009, p 76). The most important outcome of New Labour's early intervention programme is 'to transform the relationship between the family and the state' (Bristow, 2009, p 77). The process of what Jürgen Habermas described as the 'colonisation of the life world' of the private citizen by public authorities is made possible by the disorganisation of the public sphere and the weakening of informal relationships (Habermas, 1987, p 364). He warned that the 'juridification of everyday life' – which has advanced much further with New Labour's positive welfare policies –

could cause the 'disintegration of life relations' and the consolidation of dependence on state services (Habermas, 1987, p 369). Writing in 1998, about government proposals for extending the scope and application of formalised assessment and monitoring procedures beyond 'looked-after children' to a much wider category of children deemed to be 'in need', Harriet Ward commented that these plans raised 'far reaching ethical questions concerning issues of control, authority and the relationships between public and private responsibilities for children' (Ward, 1998, p 211). It is perhaps unfortunate that, although the scope of such interventions has widened and deepened in the succeeding decade, these ethical questions have often been neglected.

References

Alcabes, P. (2009) *Dread: How fear and fantasy have fuelled epidemics from the Black Death to avian flu*, New York, NY: Public Affairs.

Alcock, P. (2005) 'Maximum feasible understanding – lessons from previous wars on poverty', *Social Policy and Society*, vol 4, no 3, pp 321-9.

Aubrey, C. (2007) *Leading and managing Early Years settings*, London: Sage Publications.

Audit Commission (2008) *Are we there yet? Improving governance and resource management in children's trusts*, Local Government National Report, October, London: Audit Commission.

Belsky, J., Barnes, J. and Melhuish, E. (eds) (2007) *The national evaluation of Sure Start: Does area-based early intervention work?*, Bristol: The Policy Press.

Blair, T. (1999) 'Beveridge revisited: a welfare state for the 21st century', in R. Walker (ed) *Ending child poverty: Popular welfare for the 21st century*, Bristol: The Policy Press.

Blair, T. (2003) 'Foreword', in Department for Children, Schools and Families, *Every Child Matters*, Cm 5860, London: The Stationery Office (www.dcsf.gov.uk/consultations/downloadableDocs/EveryChildMatters.pdf).

Bristow, J. (2009) *Standing up to supernanny*, Exeter: Societas.

Bruer, J. T. (1999) *The myth of the first three years: A new understanding of early brain development and lifelong learning*, New York, NY: Free Press.

Bywater, T., Hutchings, J., Daley, D. and Whitaker, W. (2009) 'Long-term effectiveness of a parenting intervention for children at risk of developing conduct disorder', *The British Journal of Psychiatry*, vol 195, pp 318-24.

Cabinet Office (2009) *Family Nurse Partnership* (www.cabinetoffice.gov.uk/social_exclusion_task_force/family_nurse_partnership.aspx).

Challen, A., Noden, P., West, A. and Machin, S. (2009) *UK resiliency programme evaluation*, Interim report, Research Report No DCSF-RR094, London: Department for Children, Schools and Families/London School of Economics and Political Science.

Chief Secretary to the Treasury (2003) *Every Child Matters*, Cm 5860, London: The Stationery Office.

Churchill, H. (2007) 'Children's services in 2006', in K. Clarke, T. Maltby and P. Kennett (eds) *Social Policy Review 19*, Bristol: The Policy Press for the Social Policy Association, pp 85-105.

Clarke, J., Gewirtz, S. and McLaughlin, E. (eds) (2000) *New managerialism new welfare?*, London: Sage Publications.

CSJ (Commission on Social Justice) (1994) *Social justice: Strategies for national renewal*, London: Institute for Public Policy Research.

Davies, N. (1998) *Dark heart: The shocking truth about hidden Britain*, London: Vintage.

DCSF (2007a) 'Government's parenting strategy – putting parents in control', Press Release 2007/0020, 8 February.

DCSF (2007b) *The Children's Plan: Building brighter futures*, London: The Stationery Office.

DCSF (2008) *The Sure Start journey: A summary of the evidence*, London: The Stationery Office.

DH (Department of Health) (1995) *Child protection: Messages from research*, London: HMSO.

DH (1998) *Modernising social services: Promoting independence, improving protection, raising standards*, Cm 4169, London: The Stationery Office.

Earnshaw, M. (2008) 'Communities on the couch', in D. Clements, A. Donald, M. Earnshaw and A. Williams (eds) *The future of community: Reports of a death greatly exaggerated*, London: Pluto Press

Edwards, R.T., Geilleachair, A., Bywater, T., Hughes, D.A. and Hutchings, J. (2007) 'Parenting programme for parents of children at risk of developing conduct disorder: cost effectiveness analysis', *British Medical Journal*, vol 334, p 682.

Feinstein, L., Hearn, B. and Renton, Z. (2007) *Reducing inequalities: Realising the talents of all*, London: National Children's Bureau.

Ferguson, I. and Lavalette, M. (2009) *Social work after Baby P: Issues, debates and alternative perspectives*, Liverpool: Liverpool Hope University.

Frost, N. and Parton, N. (2009) *Understanding children's social care: Politics, policy and practice*, London: Sage Publications.

Garrett, P.M. (2009) *Transforming children's services? Social work, neoliberalism and the 'modern' world*, Maidenhead: Open University Press.

Gentleman, A. (2009) 'How do you solve a problem like 50,000 chaotic families?', *The Guardian*, 2 November.

Giddens, A. (1994) *Beyond Left and Right: The future of radical politics*, Cambridge: Polity Press.

Giddens, A. (1998) *The third way: The renewal of social democracy*, Cambridge: Polity Press.

Glass, N. (2005) 'Some mistake surely', *The Guardian*, 8 January.

Habermas, J. (1987) *The theory of communicative action. Vol 2. Lifeworld and system: A critique of functionalist reason*, Cambridge: Polity Press.

Harris, J. (2003) *The social work business*, London: Routledge.

Hodge, M. (2005) 'A reply to Norman Glass', *The Guardian*, 8 January.

Hoggett, P. (2000) 'Social policy and the emotions', in G. Lewis, S. Gewirtz and J. Clarke (eds) *Rethinking social policy*, London: Sage Publications.

Hutchings, J., Bywater, T., Daley, D., Gardner, F., Whitaker, C., Jones, K., Eames, E. and Edwards, R.T. (2007) 'Parenting intervention in Sure Start services for children at risk of developing conduct disorder: pragmatic randomised controlled trial', *British Medical Journal*, vol 334, p 678.

Laming, H. (2003) *The Victoria Climbié Inquiry: Report of an inquiry by Lord Laming*, Cm 5730, London: The Stationery Office.

Layard, R. (2007) 'The teaching of values', Ashby Lecture, University of Cambridge, *CentrePiece*, Summer.

Lexmond, J. and Reeves, R. (2009) *Building character*, London: Demos.

Lister, R. (2004) 'The third way's social investment state', in J. Lewis and R. Surender (eds) *Welfare state change: Towards a third way?*, Oxford: Oxford University Press.

Lloyd, E. (2008) 'The interface between childcare, family support and child poverty strategies under New Labour', *Social Policy and Society*, vol 7, no 4, pp 479-94.

MacLeod, M. (2003) 'Drawing the boundaries between the state and the family', ESRC, *The Edge*, vol 13, June.

Milburn, A. (2002) 'Reforming social services', Speech at Annual Social Services Conference, Cardiff, 16 October (www.dh.gov.uk/en/News/Speeches/SpeechesList/DH_4031620).

Nolan, J. (1998) *The therapeutic state*, New York, NY: New York University Press.

Parton, N. (2006) *Safeguarding childhood: Early intervention and surveillance in late modern society*, Basingstoke/New York, NY: Palgrave Macmillan.

Percy-Smith, J. (2006) 'What works in strategic partnerships for children: a research review', *Children and Society*, vol 20, no 4, pp 313-23.

Rutter, M. (2006) 'Is Sure Start an effective intervention?', *Child and Adolescent Mental Health*, vol 11, no 3, pp 135–41.

Rutter, M. (2007) 'Sure Start local programmes: an outsider's perspective', in J. Belsky, J. Barnes and E. Melhuish (eds) *The national evaluation of Sure Start: Does area-based early intervention work?*, Bristol: The Policy Press.

Seligman, M. (1996) *The optimistic child: A proven program to safeguard children against depression and build lifelong resilience*, New York, NY: Harper.

Seligman, M. (2004) *Authentic happiness: Using the new positive psychology to realize your potential for lasting fulfilment*, New York, NY: Simon and Schuster.

SEU (Social Exclusion Unit) (2001) *Preventing social exclusion*, London: The Stationery Office.

Teachernet (2009) *Extended services* (www.teachernet.gov.uk/wholeschool/extendedschools/).

Toynbee, P. (2005) 'We must hold our nerve and support deprived children', *The Guardian*, 13 September.

Unicef (2007) *Child poverty in perspective: An overview of child well-being in rich countries*, Report Card 7, Florence: Innocenti Research Centre.

Utting, W. (1991) *Children in the public care: A review of residential child care*, London: HMSO.

Utting, W. (1997) *People like us: The report of the review of the safeguards for children living away from home*, London: The Stationery Office.

Waiton, S. (2008) *The politics of anti-social behaviour*, Abingdon: Routledge.

Ward, H. (1998) 'Using a child development model to assess the outcomes of social work interventions with families', *Children and Society*, vol 12, no 3, pp 202–11.

Waterhouse, R. (2000) *Lost in care: Summary of the report*, London: The Stationery Office.

White, C., Warrener, M., Reeves, A. and La Valle, I. (2008) *Family Intervention Projects: An evaluation of their design, set-up and early outcomes*, Research Report No DCSF-RW047, London: National Centre for Social Research.

Wildavsky, A. (1977) 'Doing better and feeling worse: the political pathology of health policy', *Daedalus*, vol 106, Winter.

THREE

Health policy under New Labour: not what it seems?

Sally Ruane

Introduction

This chapter discusses some of the key elements of health policy since 1997 and argues that there is a discrepancy between the appearance of health policy as presented by government during New Labour's period in office and the reality of its character and significance. New Labour's approach to communication has drawn considerable attention to the use of 'spin' in the management of party and governmental initiatives. Previous experience of damaging newspaper coverage, the 24-hour news media and the insecure position of the Labour Party electorally have all contributed to a discernible shift towards the more cautious and studied management of information about government policy in relation to different audiences or 'publics'. No doubt the significant connections between New Labour and the public relations industry have further fuelled this drift (Dinan and Miller, 2007).

'Spin' can be understood as the defining and exposition of political issues in order to shape public understanding in a manner consistent with one's own interests, and can entail manipulation, ambiguity, euphemism and selective presentation. This chapter is not about the use of spin or the management of information per se but about how selected aspects of health policy have been developed and implemented without adequate democratic determination despite reiterated promises to give patients and public a greater say in the National Health Service (NHS).

Labour's record is worth examining because of two connected facts: first, the policies implemented in the NHS have been very radical, more far-reaching than at any previous point in the institution's 60-year history; and second, there has been relatively little public debate about these policies at a national level. This could well be taken as evidence that the public supports the government's reforms and considers them to be bringing about desired improvements. On the other hand, relative public silence, or even acquiescence, could be interpreted as reflecting a lack of understanding of the nature and long-term consequences of the reforms. Such a lack of understanding could result from a disengagement from politics, an uncritical trust in the government's stance or a lack of relevant information by which to make a judgement.

Immediately, this representation requires elaboration and qualification. To elaborate, a very socialised institution – nationalised hospitals and well over a million state employees – has been opened up to commercial penetration and the increasing use of public–private partnerships (PPPs) and contracting out for the provision of an ever-growing range of health services. An internal market, which the incoming Labour government claimed in its general election manifesto of 1997 would be abolished, has been fortified, augmented and broadened into an open market in healthcare in which, with provisos, 'any person' (and any company) can be contracted to provide services. This has been accompanied by a system of patient choice and stands alongside a complex array of targets and inspection arrangements. In addition, scores of new hospitals have been built under a scheme known as the private finance initiative (PFI) that means these facilities are no longer publicly owned or managed. A programme of widespread reconfiguration is under way, characterised by the centralisation of some hospital services, resulting in closures of major hospital departments and the transfer of some services from acute hospitals into the 'community'.

To qualify, it is not entirely true to say the public have remained completely silent or acquiescent. Some of these policies have faced significant and loud opposition: for example, from trades unions in the case of PFI and from local popular 'save our hospital' campaign groups in the case of the threatened closure of maternity units and accident and emergency (A&E) departments (Lister, 2008). Nonetheless, despite the radical character of Labour's health reforms, there has been no mass public reaction as there was in the case of the invasion of Iraq or the Members of Parliament (MPs') expenses scandal. The British public are known for their emotional attachment to the NHS. Thus, acquiescence is significant and could indicate a belief that the 'NHS is safe in Labour's hands'. Labour has been exposed to accusations of privatisation and even destroying the NHS (see, for example, Dobson, 2003), but this has not led to or translated into any sustained debate or coherent and organised widespread public opposition.

This chapter argues that one of the main reasons for this paradox lies in policy presentation: the effectiveness of the presentation has been critical to the successful implementation of the reforms. First, the presentation of the reforms as constitutive of the 'modernisation' of the service has been an important counter-discourse to the anticipated (and actual) accusations of privatisation. Second, the distinction between funding healthcare on the one hand and providing it on the other has been instrumental in allowing the government to insist its policies do not amount to privatisation. Third, the large increases in spending on the NHS from 2000 deflect criticism that the NHS is not 'safe' with Labour. These have become a mantra, repeated in many announcements and ministerial speeches, and they have provided a convincing enough version of government initiatives and intentions. Finally, Labour ministers have emphasised and reiterated a pledge to 'give patients and citizens a greater say in the NHS' (DH, 2000) and it is this theme that is developed here. This chapter does not offer a comprehensive assessment but illustrates through a discussion of selected key policies how this claim has been repeatedly contradicted by the reality of policy development and implementation.

Expanding healthcare and improving quality

Labour came into office in a context of very high public expectations in relation to policy for the NHS. Tony Blair announced on the eve of the election that Labour had '24 hours to save the NHS' (BBC, 2007). In fact, the new Labour government had to rein in these expectations somewhat as it had pledged, when in opposition, to follow Conservative spending plans for the first two years in office. This meant relatively low levels of spending on public services initially. Instead, the Secretary of State concentrated on reorganising the service through the creation of primary care groups (PCGs) (and later primary care trusts [PCTs]) as the means by which health services would be commissioned and the establishment of national service frameworks which specified nationally applicable standards in a range of areas of healthcare (see, for example, DH, 1997, 1998). The reorganisation and centrally set targets evident in these policies became recurrent motifs for New Labour's approach to health policy during the subsequent years and a source of criticism both within and outside the service.

Nonetheless, ministers could claim, with some justification, that this had been the first government to establish and enforce national quality standards. A legal duty of quality was imposed and a new system of clinical governance aimed to ensure implementation of quality standards. A system of inspection was established (and then frequently reorganised), initially (1999) through the Commission for Health Improvement and most recently (2009) the Care Quality Commission, and for the first time a system for inspecting services in the independent sector was established. Alongside this, a system for evaluating the effectiveness and cost-effectiveness of treatments was also set up in the shape of NICE (the National Institute for Clinical Excellence, which later evolved into the National Institute for Health and Clinical Excellence).

By the end of Labour's first term in office, it was possible to promise substantial increases in spending on healthcare for the forthcoming years although the government insisted that additional finances alone could not address the long-standing problems of the NHS and that significant reform was also required. *The NHS Plan* (DH, 2000) was published less than a year before the 2001 General Election. It promised the continuation of funding through taxation and access to healthcare on the basis of need and free at the point of use; a hospital building programme through PFI; services designed around the needs and preferences of individual patients; better quality care; attention to the needs of different populations; greater collaboration across different sectors; a greater and more constructive role for the private sector; and a greater say for patients and citizens in the NHS.

In the same year as *The NHS Plan* was published, one of the most significant reforms relating to healthcare came into effect. This was not a health reform per se but a constitutional reform which established a Scottish Parliament and Welsh Assembly, alongside the Northern Ireland Assembly, which assumed responsibilities under devolution for health policy (although not revenue raising). This constitutional reform was a key plank of Tony Blair's 'deepening democracy' initiative, one of the themes by which 'New Labour' struggled to define itself in its early years in power (Powell, 1999). This has had profound consequences, not least because it has enabled the NHS in Wales and Scotland particularly to evolve in different directions and to escape some of the commercialising reforms imposed on the NHS in England. The remainder of this chapter focuses on policy in the English NHS.

Some of the most important dimensions of Labour's footprint in health can be captured in figures. During the Conservative period of 18 years in office, there had been an average annual growth in spending on the NHS of roughly 3%. By contrast, expenditure on the NHS has much more than doubled in cash terms since Labour came into power: from £34.5 billion in 1997/98 to over £100 billion in 2009/10. Between

2000/01 and 2007/08 annual real terms increases fluctuated between 6.5% and 11.6% (DH, 2007) and public expenditure on healthcare rose from roughly 7% of GDP in 1997 to about 9% by 2007. This has led to a notable expansion of the service both in terms of higher numbers of staff and in terms of more and faster healthcare, although criticisms of the use of additional resources are plentiful (see, for example, Wanless et al, 2007).

The NHS in England employed a little under 1.1 million people in 1998 and well over 1.3 million people in 2008 (NHS Information Centre, 2009). Roughly one million patients are seen every 36 hours. Waiting times have reduced impressively and are now lower than at any point in the NHS's history, with all strategic health authorities (SHAs) meeting the 18-week target (maximum time between GP referral for further treatment and start of treatment) by the set deadline (1 January 2009). The average wait for hospital treatment was just 8.6 weeks (NHS Choices, 2009). Particular attention was focused on improving cancer services that were seen to compare very unfavourably with those provided by other health systems in Europe. As in other areas of policy, this improvement was characterised by new ways of working and greater collaboration or partnerships among service providers.

Labour have also undertaken the 'biggest hospital building programme the country has ever seen' (Milburn, 2001). Department of Health figures issued in October 2009 for hospital capital investment in England reveal 110 PFI schemes worth more than £13 billion either in the pipe line or already operational since May 1997 (DH, 2009).

However, these bald figures belie a deeper process of reform and a more profound dimension of Labour's legacy in health. The most radical reforms are not the expansion of treatment or establishment of a system of inspection, significant though these are. They are reforms to the underpinning dynamic of the service through the creation of a market system and embracing of commercial providers. The remainder of this chapter considers a selected number of examples that illustrate contradictions between the claim to give patients and citizens a greater say in the NHS and the undemocratic character of some of Labour's fundamental reforms. Examples have been chosen which concern some of the main dimensions of Labour's health policy: the introduction of the market; the use of commercial providers; greater local freedoms; and service reconfiguration.

Deepening democracy? The absence of effective electoral, party and parliamentary checks on Labour's reforms

One of the wider contradictions in the New Labour government's position in policy making is the very early pledge to 'deepen democracy' versus its own precarious position with regard to an electoral base. This concerns the mismatch between the limited extent of electoral endorsement for the Labour Party as the party of government and the very large majorities enjoyed by Labour in the House of Commons. This mismatch can be seen in Table 3.1.

Table 3.1: UK electoral facts – Labour's wins

Year	Number of votes (million)	% turnout	Labour's % share of vote	% share of electorate backing Labour	Number of votes for Labour (million)	Parliamentary seat majority
1997	30.5	71.4	43.2	30.8	13.5	177
2001	26.4	59.2	40.7	24.2	10.7	165
2005	27	61.3	35.2	21.6	9.5	64

Source: Mellows-Facer (2005); Morgan (1997, 2001)

These figures reveal first, that the electoral endorsement of Labour as government has declined with succeeding elections, and second, that the modesty of the electoral support for Labour is ignored in, even denied by, the distribution of seats in the House of Commons following election. For example, in 2001 Labour received the backing of only 25% of the electorate and 40% of the vote, but secured over 62% of seats in Parliament, a majority of 165. By 2005, Labour's support from the electorate had further declined to barely a fifth while the party still had well over half the seats in the Commons. The development of a more scientific approach to campaigning and canvassing, with the greater use of 'market' analysis and targeting of key marginal constituencies (or more specifically, certain demographic groups within those selected marginal constituencies) has become a defining feature of modern, professional electioneering (Kavanagh, 1995; Todd and Taylor, 2004). Rather than seeking to persuade as many voters as possible that their political manifesto is the right one, politicians instead try to persuade those relatively few (just several hundred thousand out of an electorate of more than 40 million) who are calculated to determine the outcome in specified constituencies. Securing the right to govern has thus become somewhat divorced from the need to establish a strong or broad electoral base. This has been particularly important for Labour which, in common with some other social democratic parties in Europe, has seen its traditional core base, the organised industrial working class, eroded through economic restructuring and the changing international division of labour (Crouch, 2000).

In order to achieve this, Labour altered its policies and its policy-making processes, eventually removing the policy-making powers of Conference. This has gone a long way to removing the influence of the grassroots over policy and sets up the contradiction or paradox of New Labour's period in office under scrutiny here: the enormity of the health service's transformation versus the limited extent of popular demand for or popular engagement with it. The style of the Prime Minister became ever more 'presidential' (Hennessy, 2000; Ham, 2009) and backbench MPs increasingly disciplined and managed. Overall, through both the weakness of democratic mechanisms within the party and absence of effective checks and balances in Parliament, the government, more widely, and Prime Minister, more specifically, have increased their ability to define and drive through their chosen policies.

This is seen in the creation of the market itself where the paucity of parliamentary activity, relative to the scale and depth of the reforms at hand, is evident with hindsight. It is thought that the legislative basis for the service's restructuring as an open competitive market, which established the framework through which a highly, if not exclusively, socialised service can bring transnational corporations and other profit-making providers into mainstream provision, is an obscure phrase in an obscure paragraph in the 2003 Health and Social Care Bill (Section 175, para (2), subsection (b)) (D. Price, personal communication, 2007). This clause attracted no particular debate in committee and its implications were not recognised until subsequently. There was no explicit mention of the creation of a market in the 2001 General Election Labour Party manifesto, *The NHS Plan* of the year before or numerous public speeches by ministers in the previous months. Radical redesign is referred to, making services more responsive to the preferences of patients is referred to, but not the creation of an open competitive market. This most radical of reforms appears to have been introduced with barely any democratic scrutiny or democratic determination whatsoever.

Enhancing local accountability: the case of foundation trusts

The Health and Social Care Bill, which received its final vote in the Commons in November 2003, *did* attract a lot of controversy, but around its clauses relating to the establishment of foundation trusts (FTs). This was a significant, but in comparison with the creation of the market, more modest reform. FTs, too, had been omitted from the Labour Party manifesto. Ministers claimed FT status would make available greater freedoms to local managers and would secure enhanced accountability outwards to the local community. Managers expected to secure significant financial autonomy, reporting to a quasi-autonomous regulator, known as Monitor. An FT does not have the same legal form as an NHS hospital trust but is a public benefit corporation in which local people, patients and staff can become members and governors and, it is claimed, hold the trust to account.

Concerns surrounding FT status were expressed following their announcement in 2002 and continually to their passage through Parliament in late 2003. For instance, although accountability outwards to the local community was claimed to be stronger under FT status, accountability upwards to the Secretary of State, an elected MP, was removed. However, the Health Select Committee of the House of Commons at the time claimed there was confusion surrounding arrangements for local accountability and the danger of growing inequity in the distribution of health services and the distribution of high-quality staff (Health Committee, 2003). Even in Cabinet, division was evident, with the Secretary of State arguing for greater, and the Chancellor arguing for more restricted, freedoms (Seldon et al, 2007). In the event, FTs were very unpopular with a significant minority in the parliamentary Labour Party such that the government's majority in the House of Commons was cut to a fraction of what it had been.

Six years later, it is possible to offer a preliminary assessment of the policy. By December 2009 there were 125 FTs, of which 37 were mental health trusts (Monitor, 2009). While the wishes of hospital managers to escape overweening micro-management from the Department of Health were understandable, the extent to which autonomy has been achieved – or can be achieved – is questionable. There have been tensions between Monitor and the Department of Health over the boundaries of accountability, with the Department seeking to direct policy in areas Monitor believes lie within its own domain (Health Committee, 2008). This points to the near inescapability of health service provision from political control because of the centrality of healthcare to electoral concerns. A House of Commons Select Committee Inquiry in late 2008 (Health Committee, 2008, pp 41-3) addressed two of the main advantages imputed to FTs. It concluded, first, that many of the financial freedoms theoretically assumed by FTs had been difficult to realise because of uncertainties created by the newly developing market in healthcare. Second, the Select Committee found that governance provisions for effective accountability to the local community and involvement of the local community were weak. This suggests either that greater autonomy and genuine outward accountability were not the key drivers of the policy, as claimed by politicians, or that the policy was ill designed to meet those objectives.

There is no systematic assessment of the contribution of FTs to reducing or widening health inequalities through their formal ability to borrow on the private market and pay higher wages. There are instances, however, where the surpluses retained by FTs do appear to have a knock-on effect on nearby communities. For instance, in outer South East London, a non-PFI hospital, Queen Mary Hospital in Sidcup, is threatened with closure as a district general hospital (DGH) because of mounting deficits in the hospital sector arising to a considerable extent from the long-term PFI commitments in the three other DGHs that reduce flexibility in hospital policy. A King's Fund seminar in 2007 noted that the surpluses retained by the two inner South East London FTs, which were nominally in the reconfiguration area, exceeded the aggregate deficit across the four non-FT hospitals. However, as FTs, their surpluses were no longer available to the wider health economy and would not be used to retain the threatened local services (cited by Lister, 2007). It is debatable whether this can be considered an example of a two-tier NHS – Sidcup patients, as consumers, can 'choose' to be treated by one of the FT hospitals although would obviously need to travel to inner London. However, it certainly does seem to illustrate that the weakening of the cross-subsidy mechanism underpinning the NHS as a universal service can have damaging consequences since the efforts of Sidcup residents, as citizens, to 'choose' to retain their services locally look doomed.

What does local consultation mean? An instance of service reconfiguration

The creation of the market and the establishment of the first NHS hospitals no longer accountable to the Secretary of State inevitably raise the question of patient and public involvement. Three years prior to the Health and Social Care Bill, *The NHS Plan* had promised a greater say in the NHS for patients and citizens and the deepening democracy theme has been developed in healthcare through the policy of 'public and patient involvement' (PPI). Community health councils (CHCs) were established in the 1970s in part to address the absence of mechanisms for democratic accountability. This generally collective approach was supplemented by the more individualist and consumerist Patient's Charter introduced by John Major in 1992.

New Labour have made PPI a key facet of their approach to health. The Department of Health claims that its new mechanisms can help drive up service quality, secure better value for money in commissioning and reduce health inequalities. However, quite what 'involvement', or the more recent 'empowerment', amount to and the extent to which the public and patients can influence the design and delivery of the service, or health policy and healthcare more broadly, are the subject of contentious debate.

Labour's decision to abolish CHCs astonished almost everyone, including members of what might be described as the 'public involvement community' at the time, and was so bitterly and widely opposed that securing parliamentary approval had to be delayed until after the 2001 General Election. Abolition was justified on the grounds that CHCs offered a model of patient representation in which patients were on the *outside* of the service, whereas an alternative approach could secure patient, carer and public views throughout the service. Their replacements were established in late 2003: the Commission for Public and Patient Involvement in Health (CPPIH); public and patient involvement forums attached to PCTs; and a patient advice and liaison service (PALS) in every trust. However, with the exception of PALS, these new structures did not last the course; in 2004 the Commission's abolition was announced and in 2006, that of the forums. That the forums and Commission were so short-lived and under-resourced has tended to reinforce the suspicions of those who believed from the outset that the motivation to abolish the CHCs was not a technical objection to their weaknesses and desire to find something stronger, but a political wish to fragment and reduce organised opposition to government policy (see, for example, Milewa et al, 2003), since the removal of the latter effectively eliminated the local watchdog. This is particularly significant in the context of the radical transformation of the service that ensued over the next few years.

In addition to the Commission, forums and FTs, a myriad of new mechanisms of involvement have been established over the past few years, including GP practice-based patient groups, e-consultations and petitions, public involvement meetings between PCT representatives or hospital staff and local residents and formal public consultation exercises. More substantially, at the PCT level, local involvement networks (LINks) were established in 2008 to replace forums. They have a geographical territory, cover health and social care and are expected to focus on commissioning. However, they too have few resources and limited powers. Critics have pointed out that several policy aims are identified under the loose heading of PPI and that these aims are in tension. For instance, PPI can be seen as a means to secure representativeness, to aid in the implementation of national policy such as reducing inequalities, to inform priority setting by drawing on patient expertise or to improve the take-up of services, to mention a few (Martin and Parry, 2009). Hogg (2009) suggests that, in any case, local involvement may have limited impact where NHS bodies are following top-down, prescribed policies. This is surely the case in the current NHS where PCTs are charged with creating a market in primary care and community services and are being performance-managed by SHAs to achieve this.

David Chandler (2001) and Christine Hogg (2009) distinguish participation from democracy, and Hogg suggests that 'the many new means of communication established between government, users, community groups and individuals may have given people less rather than more control over policy-making' (2009, p 177). Certainly, current mechanisms seem to emphasise the incorporation of the patients and local people into the details of implementation rather than to empower them to shape or challenge the direction of government policy. This can be seen, for instance, in relation to two significant dimensions of current health policy: the reconfiguration of services (for example concentrating some hospital departments into fewer units or transferring some hospital-based services into community settings); and the creation of a market in primary and community services through contracting out. Here, public experiences of formal consultation exercises conducted by NHS bodies at a local level have not so far succeeded in convincing the sceptics that the government – or NHS managers – really do want the public to influence the development of local services in anything other than relatively modest matters of detail at the implementation stage.

A duty to consult the public in relation to a substantial variation in service provision was introduced first in the 2001 Health and Social Care Act. I have not so far come across a single instance in which a lack of public endorsement or outright public opposition expressed through a formal consultation has resulted in the withdrawal or radical rewriting of local NHS proposals for change. There certainly have been reversals on the part of local NHS bodies – for example, in the case of the planned downgrading of the Horton General in Banbury or the centralisation of maternity services in Eastbourne and Hastings – but these reversals have resulted from a broad-based popular campaign waged in each town over a period of several years and not from responses to a particular consultation exercise (Ruane, 2009). A high profile campaign to challenge the local PCT's decision to contract out GP services in Langwith and Cresswell to a US-based company in Derbyshire on the grounds of inadequate consultation was won at the High Court on appeal. After this, the PCT consulted again and then contracted out the service to another commercial provider and the law governing duty to consult was re-drawn (see the 2006 NHS Act) in a way perceived by campaigners to *curb* popular powers (Pearce, 2008).

One East Midlands consultation on transferring some acute hospital-based services into the 'community' offers another case study. A report (HaCIRIC, 2008) commissioned by the PCT to assess the consultation revealed a number of sobering points. The proposals were radical, involving a significant reorganisation of health services and the closure and selling off of several hospitals across the area. However, engagement by local residents either individually or through civil organisations was modest – just 0.15% of those aged over 16 completed a questionnaire, for instance. This meant that although agreement with the proposals scored higher percentages than disagreement, the numbers of residents endorsing the proposals were tiny (for example, out of an over-16s population of almost 70,000 in Harborough District, only 130 people agreed to the establishment of a 'one-stop hub' and only 85 agreed to the sale of the district hospital and removal of the war memorial). Second, in every case across the county, the numbers endorsing the sale of local hospitals fell well below the numbers of those who 'did not know', which constituted a steady 42% of questionnaire respondents in the three affected locales. This draws attention to a third point, which is the difficulty of even those willing to participate in assessing the formal proposals.

Some preliminary explanations for this may lie in the qualitative comments respondents made of the consultation process itself. These comments included a belief that those formulating the proposals had ignored public input in prior involvement exercises; that the consultation exercise was flawed since it had assumed a higher level of knowledge and understanding among the public than was the case; that invitations to the PCT to attend meetings to explain and discuss the proposals had been declined; that 'information events' had provided insufficient information; and that there was a lack of information regarding the financial case and current patterns of usage and even about which services would be located in which locales. Although these comments came from a minority of participants, they hint at distrust and point to significant frustrations regarding the nature of public consultation itself.

Two other observations are worth noting. First, although there was no formal statement to the effect that questionnaire responses would be considered of superior value to other forms of engagement, in practice the collection of 476 signatures against the proposals in Hinckley, outweighing by several hundred those registering their support, counted for little in the presentation of results. Second, the PCT declined to hold a series of public meetings during the consultation period. Instead, they staged 'information events' at which members of the public could see written information and ask questions on an individual basis but at which they could not participate in a collective, public discussion and debate. Despite this, the PCT erroneously reported in its follow-up newsletter that it had held 10 public meetings.

Formal consultation events are often regarded with scepticism and even inspire satire. It is important when assessing them not simply to fall into cynicism. However, there are other features of consultation events that reinforce the notion that they do not offer the public a genuine opportunity to reject a set of proposals. The lack of publicity for some 'public' meetings, with PCTs in some instances declining to publish a schedule of meetings even when asked to do so, adds to a sense that involvement is being managed. Another limitation is the fairly narrow range of issues the public are allowed to judge. For instance, although there is much emphasis on public involvement to influence commissioning, decisions to switch to commercial providers or to consider tenders from commercial providers are typically not decisions the public are invited to comment on despite the fact that commercial provision introduces a new dynamic into the health system and the public could reasonably be expected to have a view.

Evading effective scrutiny: independent sector treatment centres

At the time that CHCs were being closed down and forums were trying to establish themselves, the Department of Health was pushing ahead with a radical departure in NHS policy. The Department invited private companies to tender to run 'treatment centres' to provide routine surgery and diagnostics for NHS patients on a contractual basis. Some £1.7 billion was set aside for financing five years' worth of healthcare from these providers. Companies were invited to set up treatment centres either in adapted existing premises or in their own new premises, ostensibly to drive waiting times down and thus help achieve a government pledge on this. The Department of Health selected a number of firms, all of which happened to be based overseas, and negotiated contracts for procedures in the field principally of ophthalmic, orthopaedic and general surgery. Affected PCTs were pressured (HSJ, 2005; Hanna, 2006) to sign up to these centrally negotiated contracts, that is, to commit in advance a specified sum of their budget to paying for NHS patient treatment from these centres. First wave independent sector treatment centres (ISTCs) came on stream from 2003 onwards and, by January 2006, 25 ISTCs were either already up and running or shortly to be operational, with a further four under negotiation. In contrast to NHS 'providers' (for example, NHS hospitals) in the new market context of payment by results, first wave ISTCs were paid above the NHS national tariff and were guaranteed their income for the five-year period of the contract regardless of whether they performed the procedures purchased.

The policy was executed and implemented without transparency either from the point of view of the public or from the policy analyst's perspective.

Governance processes within the local NHS failed to secure proper accountability. For example, in some instances, the Department of Health, through the SHA, ran roughshod over the normal accountability processes. Jane Hanna, a non-executive director of South West Oxfordshire PCT at the relevant time, submitted to the Select Committee (Hanna, 2006) a detailed account of SHA bullying and intimidation of board members. Their objections to the contract, that the ISTC contract did not represent good value for money since the (NHS) Oxford Eye Hospital offered a very high quality service without waiting list problems, counted for nothing. Hanna stood down, she claimed, after several instances of the PCT being required to rubber-stamp Department of Health decisions while presenting them as their own. The request of the non-executive directors for an inquiry into a number of governance anomalies was denied. The imposition of the contract cost the taxpayer £255,000 for £40,000 worth of work in the first six months of the contract. That is, for every patient treated, another five could have been treated had the NHS budget been expended on NHS provision. The financial sums may be at the extreme end of profligate waste of public money but concerns about the way in which the policy was being driven through were certainly not unique. Debbie Abrahams, then chair of Rochdale PCT, objected, as had other local PCT chairs, to a new treatment centre in the Greater Manchester area on the grounds of lack of demand. She subsequently resigned following a decision by the SHA not to undertake a comprehensive evaluation of the centre that she believed had been promised (BBC, 2006).

Academic scrutiny, too, has suffered: even quite basic information – about the number of procedures contracted, number of procedures performed, price paid per procedure, numbers of staff employed, numbers of beds available, quality of treatment given and details of contract – have been difficult or impossible for policy analysts to obtain (Player and Leys, 2008). Democratic scrutiny did not fare much better. The Health Select Committee was refused detailed information regarding the contracts and the Department of Health's value for money calculations, even in private session, on the grounds of commercial confidentiality, clearly considered by the government more important to safeguard than public accountability (Health Committee, 2006).

The formal democratic scrutiny process that did take place did not give the ISTCs a clean bill of health. The ISTC programme was justified largely on the grounds that it would drive down waiting times, partly by separating planned routine surgery from emergency admissions that could disrupt a schedule of planned care. That this had been their chief effect was strongly disputed in evidence to the Select Committee. The Oxfordshire case above is one instance of many centres located in places where they were not needed for capacity reasons, and thus offered competitive rather than supplementary capacity. While presented as introducing greater choice and faster treatment, an alternative interpretation is that they constituted a major element in Labour's plan to create a market in secondary care (Player and Leys, 2008), to be secured whatever the opposition. Claims by the Department that they would lead to innovation in healthcare and, through competition, more efficient healthcare, were dismissed by the Select Committee as unsubstantiated. ISTCs were introduced on the basis of an unclear and shifting rationale. The Select Committee, unable to discern clear evidence for many of the Department's claims, concluded that the policy had been a 'leap in the dark' and that the Department's 'changing objectives for the programme pointed to a policy that had not been carefully thought-out' (Health Committee, 2006, p 38).

Perhaps most perplexing is the situation of the patient. In Labour's healthcare market and in the absence of strong institutions able to express a collective 'voice', accountability is to be effected largely through choice and competition. Rival providers compete for patients who are empowered through the market to choose which provider they want. However, this is not what has happened. Although lauded by ministers as enhancing patient choice, if anything, ISTCs damaged patient choice (Player and Leys, 2008; Ruane, 2008). Since PCTs were required to transfer a portion of their budget away from traditional NHS providers to the new ISTCs and since this payment to ISTCs was guaranteed regardless of whether treatments were performed or not (the so-called 'take or pay' element), PCTs came under pressure to find ways to shepherd patients towards the ISTCs, as fewer funds remained in the PCT budget to commission these procedures from NHS providers. Financial incentives to influence the referral practices of GPs were used in some instances. Thus, patient choice may well have been constrained.

Second, patients are not told that these treatment centres are privately owned and are not part of the permanent structure of the NHS. ISTCs, which are profit-making organisations, are allowed to bear the NHS logo and to describe themselves as 'NHS treatment centres'. There is no reason why a patient entering the premises of an ISTC should know the provider is a commercial one. Further, many of these centres are located on NHS property or adjacent to NHS property. The ISTC in Nottingham, for instance, is next to the Queen's Medical Centre and is accessed via a corridor that adjoins the two. Third, the NHS Choices website, itself run by Capita since August 2008, does not inform the visitor that some of the providers listed are commercial or that a particular provider is commercial. NHS patients are simply unaware that some of their treatment is provided on a profit-making basis. Like public consultation exercises, this highly sensitive aspect of NHS reform has been airbrushed out of the picture. NHS patients are being trained to behave like consumers and obstacles are being put in place to prevent them from behaving like citizens.

So neither patient nor citizen has done particularly well. Moreover, apart from the opportunity cost ISTCs represent in terms of the use to which public money is put and apart from the failure of the Select Committee to function more robustly in its scrutiny of this policy, citizens have not been consulted on their establishment despite the fact that they represent a significant change in the delivery of services. As mentioned above, they arguably should have been considered in relation to the 2001/2006 duty to consult in the event of a substantial variation to health services.

Conclusion

This chapter has shown that despite claims of deepening democracy and giving patients and the public a greater say in the NHS, this has not been the case in a number of key policies. These policies have been driven through despite strong and considered opposition from, variously, the parliamentary Labour Party, affiliated trades unions, local citizens, PCT board members and participants in the former public involvement structures. At the same time, 'checks and balances' designed to ensure accountability have not always functioned effectively. While it is true that the number of channels through which patients (especially) can shape services has multiplied, this does not amount to democracy, as Hogg (2009) points out. The timing of the abolition of CHCs with no *effective* replacement, disrupting the infrastructure of public involvement at the outset of a sustained period of radical restructuring – switching the NHS decisively away from being an integrated service towards a marketised, part-privatised one – can be interpreted as an attempt to sidestep and outwit public feeling and possible public opposition rather than engage with it.

The views of the 'public' are complex, qualified and multifaceted (see, for example, Opinion Leader Research, 2006). They are difficult to measure and interpret and reducing public views to single dimensions is of limited usefulness.

This must be borne in mind when examining the findings of the *British social attitudes* report, published in early 2009 but based on survey data collected in 2007 (Park et al, 2009). This revealed the highest levels of satisfaction with the NHS since 1984. Fifty-one per cent of people were 'very satisfied' or 'quite satisfied' with the NHS, up 17 percentage points since 1997. The authors of the report interpret this as related to the massive increase in spending on the NHS over the previous seven years, increases in staffing and reduced waiting times. At the same time, the report revealed that while the public support 'choice' in accessing public services, they do not support the provision of services by private companies or charities. Seventy-five per cent believe people should be able to exercise 'a great deal' or 'quite a lot' of choice as to which hospital to attend, but only 22% believed private companies should run NHS hospitals and 57% actively opposed this. The figures for England, where radical reforms have been most extensively implemented, are not appreciably different from those for Britain as a whole. The authors conclude that the public do not necessarily accept the link between choice and competitive quasi-markets involving private providers.

In the event, the public were not consulted either on the introduction of the market or on the mainstreaming of private provision. It remains to be seen how effectively they can influence the ongoing reconfiguration of local services.

References

BBC (British Broadcasting Corporation) (2006) 'File on 4 – Private corporations in the NHS', Transcript, transmission 17 October.

BBC (2007) 'Blair's legacy: health', BBC News, 10 May.

Chandler, D. (2001) 'Active citizens and the therapeutic state: the role of democratic participation in local government reform', *Policy & Politics*, vol 29, no 1, pp 2-14.

Crouch, C. (2000) *Coping with post democracy*, London: Fabian Society.

DH (Department of Health) (1997) *The new NHS: Modern, dependable*, Cm 3807, London: DH.

DH (1998) *A first class service: Quality in the new NHS*, London: DH.

DH (2000) *The NHS plan: A plan for investment, a plan for reform*, Cm 4818-I, London: DH.

DH (2007) *Departmental report 2007*, Cm 7903, London: DH.

DH (2009) *Prioritised capital schemes approved to go ahead since May 1997 (England)*, London: DH, October.

Dinan, W. and Miller, D. (2007) *A century of spin: How public relations became the cutting edge of corporate power*, London: Pluto Press.

Dobson, F. (2003) 'Labour threat to NHS', Speech to Catalyst fringe meeting at TUC Congress, 9 September.

HaCIRIC (Health and Care Infrastructure Research and Innovation Centre) (2008) *Community health services review: Public consultation feedback report*, London and Loughborough: HaCIRIC and Loughborough University, November.

Ham, C. (2009) *Health policy in Britain* (6th edn), Basingstoke: Palgrave Macmillan.

Hanna, J. (2006) 'Memorandum' submitted by Jane Hanna, former non-executive director of South West Oxfordshire Primary Care Trust, written evidence, House of Commons Health Committee, *Fourth report of session 2005–06: Independent sector treatment centres, Vol II*, London: The Stationery Office.

Health Committee (2003) *Second report of session 2002–03: Foundation trusts, Vol I*, House of Commons Health Committee, London: The Stationery Office.

Health Committee (2006) *Fourth report of session 2005–06: Independent sector treatment centres, Vols I––III*, House of Commons Health Committee, London: The Stationery Office.

Health Committee (2008) *Sixth report of session 2007–08: Foundation trusts and Monitor, Vol I*, House of Commons Health Committee, London: The Stationery Office.

Hennessy, P. (2000) *The prime minister*, Harmondsworth: Penguin.

Hogg, C. (2009) *Citizens, consumers and the NHS: Capturing voices*, Basingstoke: Palgrave Macmillan.

HSJ (*Health Service Journal*) (2005) 'Target pressure threatens services', 20 January.

Kavanagh, D. (1995) *Election campaigning: The new marketing of politics*, Oxford: Wiley-Blackwell.

Lister, J. (2007) *Under the knife: An analysis of the planned changes in hospital and health services South East London*, London: London Health Emergency.

Lister, J. (2008) *The NHS after 60: For patients or profits*, London: Middlesex University.

Martin, G. and Parry, R. (2009) 'Patient and public involvement keys to success', *Health Service Journal*, 29 January.

Mellows-Facer, A. (2005) *General Election 2005, House of Commons Research Paper 05/33* (www.parliament.uk/commons/lib/research/rp2005/RP05-033.pdf).

Milburn, A. (2001) 'Shifting the balance of power to frontline services', Speech at the launch of the NHS Modernisation Agency, April.

Milewa, T., Harrison, S. and Dowswell, G. (2003) 'Public involvement and democratic accountability in primary care organisations', in B. Dowling and C. Glendinning (eds) *The new NHS, modern, dependable, successful?*, Buckingham: Open University Press, pp 179-95.

Monitor (2009) *NHS foundation trust directory*, London: Monitor.

Morgan, B. (1997) *General election results 1 May 2007, House of Commons Research Paper 01/38* (www.parliament.uk/commons/lib/research/rp2001/rp01-038.pdf).

Morgan, B. (2001) *General election results 7 June 2001, House of Commons Research Paper 01/54* (www.parliament.uk/commons/lib/research/rp2001/rp01-054.pdf).

NHS Choices (2009) *NHS waiting times Q&A*, March.

NHS Information Centre (2009) *NHS staff 1998–2008 overview*, March (www.ic.nhs.uk/statistics-and-data-collections/workforce/nhs-staff-numbers).

Opinion Leader Research (2006) *Your health, your care, your say*, Research Report, London: Opinion Leader Research.

Park, A., Curtice, J., Thomson, K., Phillips, M. and Clery, E. (2009) *British social attitudes: The 25th report*, London: Sage Publications.

Pearce, U. (2008) *Public consultation in the NHS*, November (www.keepournhspublic.com/pdf UrsulaPearcePublicConsultationNHSNov2008-2.pdf).

Player, S. and Leys, C. (2008) *Confuse and conceal: The NHS and independent sector treatment centres*, Monmouth: Merlin Press.

Powell, M. (1999) 'Conclusion', in M. Powell (ed) *New Labour, new welfare state: The 'third way' in British social policy*, Bristol: The Policy Press, pp 281-300.

Ruane, S. (2008) 'One modest brick: independent sector treatment centres and the re-commercialisation of the NHS', *Radical Statistics*, issue 96.

Ruane, S. (2009) '"Save our hospital" campaigns in England', Unpublished paper, presented at the International Association of Health Policy in Europe Conference 'Condition Critical Healthcare, Marketising Reforms and the Media', Coventry, June.

Seldon, A. with Snowdon, P. and Collings, D. (2007) *Blair unbound*, London: Simon and Schuster.

Todd, M. and Taylor, G. (2004) 'Introduction', in M. Todd and G. Taylor (eds) *Democracy and participation*, London: Merlin, pp 1-28.

Wanless, D., Appleby, J., Harrison, A. and Patel, D. (2007) *Our future health secured? A review of NHS funding and performance*, London: King's Fund.

FOUR

Towards a social democratic pension system? Assessing the significance of the 2007 and 2008 Pensions Acts[1]

Paul Bridgen

Pension policy over the last few years has been dominated by the debates and legislative agenda that have followed the publication of the Pensions Commission's final report in 2005. Established in 2002 to 'report on how the current voluntarist approach [to private savings] is developing', the Pensions Commission interpreted its brief broadly to produce a wide range of recommendations for both the public and non-state pension sectors (2005, pp 18-22). These will be outlined in more detail below, but the most noteworthy were the suggestion that the basic state pension (BSP) should return to uprating in line with earnings from 2010 and that entitlement should shift to a residence basis for future accruals. In the non-state sector, the Commission recommended the establishment of a National Pensions Saving Scheme (NPSS) to which all employees not already covered by adequate occupational provision would be auto-enrolled on the basis of contributions from their employer (3% of pensionable earnings[2]), themselves (4%) and the state (1%). After intense negotiations in Whitehall between HM Treasury and the Department for Work and Pensions (DWP), the government accepted many of the Commission's recommendations in two White Papers (DWP, 2006a, 2006b), which were then implemented in the 2007 and 2008 Pensions Acts. Earnings uprating was accepted but from 2012 at the earliest, rather than 2010,[3] and a delivery authority was put in place to establish an NPSS, rebranded as 'Personal Accounts',[4] by 2012, with the 2008 Act legislating for the phased introduction of quasi-employer compulsion from this date (DWP, 2006b). However, the government rejected residency-based entitlement for state provision. Instead, a range of measures was taken to ease access to basic state provision for carers.

Assessments of this reform have focused, at one level, on its individual components, most particularly those areas where the government went less far than the recommendations of the Pensions Commission (see, for example, Pemberton et al, 2006; Price, 2007; Pemberton, 2010), but underlying much of this analysis is the more general conclusion that because of the individual limitations of the reform the Acts continue to support the existing liberal policy paradigm, that they have largely failed to give the British pension system a more social democratic character. Thus while various elements of the Acts have been welcomed, particularly those relating to the state pension, overall judgements about the reform have been framed in relation to the continuing inadequacy of the reformed system compared with social democratic ideal types (see below). 'Pragmatism' has trumped 'ideology', according to Pemberton (2010); 'neoliberal policies' continue, according to Price (2008, p 65).

This chapter raises doubts about the claim that the essence of the British liberal pension regime has been unaffected by the recent reforms. First, on the basis of recent theoretical debates on institutional change (see, for example, Thelen, 2004; Ebbinghaus, 2005; Streeck and Thelen, 2005), it suggests that significant individual reforms can happen without immediate evidence of paradigmatic change. To substantiate this claim, an alternative framework for assessing the Acts is constructed which captures the extent of incremental change. Second, it is argued that the apparent failure of recent reforms to significantly alter the British liberal regime may be explained by an over-emphasis on statist conceptions of social democracy. As Esping-Andersen (1990, pp 81-3) and others (Hyde et al, 2003; Trampusch, 2007a, 2007b) have recognised, models of social democracy in pensions sometimes involve a substantial non-state sector; this is true, for example, in the Netherlands and Denmark (Goodin et al, 1999; Anderson, 2007; Bannink and de Vroom, 2007). On this basis the scale of change in Britain is assessed by including the reforms of the public sector and regulation and compulsion in the non-state sector. From this perspective this chapter argues that the 2007 and 2008 Pensions Acts represent an unambiguous and significant movement of the British pension system in a social democratic direction.

This chapter is organised in the following way. The next section provides a brief summary of the policy problems with which Labour was faced when it came to power in 1997, and its responses up to 2008. In the following section, an analytical framework is established which is used in the final three sections to assess the 2007 and 2008 Acts on the basis of secondary data from previous analysis and policy simulations.

Pension policy context in 1997

When Labour came to power in 1997 poverty[5] among current pensioners stood at over a quarter of the pensioner population; inequality had risen (Evandrou and Falkingham, 2005, p 168); and the occupational pensions sector, which had since the 1930s always played an important role in the British system, was beginning to retrench in the face of a range of cost pressures (Bridgen and Meyer, 2005). Poverty rates were largely a product of the low BSP, which for those reliant entirely on the state was only supplemented to a limited extent by state earnings-related pensions (SERPs).[6] Women were disproportionately represented among poor pensioners, and became particularly vulnerable as they got older (Evandrou and Falkingham, 2005, p 172). The rise in inequality had much to do with restricted access to occupational pensions. Coverage stood at just over 40% in 1997 (Pensions Commission, 2004, p 71), boosted substantially by universal provision in the public sector. In the private sector, coverage favoured middle-class professionals and men, with access outside these groups largely a matter of chance related to job type and sector of employment (Meyer and Bridgen, 2008). The take-up of means-tested benefits was far from 100% and in any case the amount provided was below the poverty line (Evandrou and Falkingham, 2005, p 168). The future prospects looked grimmer still, given the abolition of the earnings link for the BSP, which was consequently projected to fall to 7.5% of average male earnings by 2050 (Evandrou and Falkingham, 2005, p 184).

New Labour's response for current pensioners was to focus on means testing. Income support for pensioners was rebranded, first as Minimum Income Guarantee and then as Pension Credit. This involved a one-off above-inflation increase in benefit levels and then uprating in line with earnings rather than prices. For future pensioners, SERPs, renamed as state second pension (S2P), was made more redistributive towards lower-paid workers (Agulnik, 1999), companies were required to guarantee workers access to a personal pension with insurance companies encouraged to offer 'stakeholder' pensions[7] to serve this potential new market and attempts were made to encourage greater private saving not least through occupational provision (DWP, 1998, 2002; Pickering, 2002).

However, by the early 2000s it was clear that the desired expansion of personal pensions was not happening (ABI, 2003),[8] and that the closure by companies of their defined benefit schemes to new members was accelerating (Bridgen and Meyer, 2005). Against this background the Pensions Commission recommendations amounted to a reconfiguration of the relationship in pension provision both between the individual and the state, and the public and the private sector. The state should do more but its role should be limited to ensuring that pension entitlement was as inclusive as possible, particularly for women, thus reducing the disincentive effects caused to private savings by means testing and the complexity of the state system. The Commission proposed that:

- future entitlement to the BSP should be based on residency, rather than contributions and credits, and entitlements to the S2P should be broadened, particularly for carers
- BSP uprating should revert to an earnings basis from 2010
- the shift of the S2P to a flat rate basis should be accelerated
- the indexing of the savings credit part of Pension Credit should be frozen in real terms.

To pay for these reforms, the state pension age would rise incrementally to 68 between 2020 and 2050, a change that could be justified given increasing longevity.[9] Even with these changes the Commission concluded that sufficient private savings would only occur with the introduction of an NPSS on an automatic enrolment basis and a minimum employer contribution. The national and centralised nature of the NPSS was justified on the basis that is was more likely than a more market-based solution to ensure that charges were low and thus individual returns maximised. As has been seen, it was largely on the basis of the Pensions Commission's recommendations that the 2007 and 2008 Pensions Acts were constructed, although in most cases the government was not prepared to accede fully to the Commission's recommendations.

Paradigm shifts and the significance of incremental reform

In assessing these reforms social policy commentators have generally focused on their limitations (Pemberton et al, 2006; Price, 2006, 2007, 2008; Pemberton, 2010). Thus, while Price, for example, accepts that the reform, particularly to state provision, moves the system in a 'welcome direction', she is dismissive of its overall significance: 'Lobbying for incremental change has resulted in incremental change. This will improve the financial situation for many women, but it does not represent paradigmatic reform of a kind that will have a substantial impact on gendered outcomes in later life...' (Price, 2007, p 580). On the reforms in the non-state sphere she is even stronger: the reform amounts to a 'fundamental ideological commitment to the private sector.... [It] continues neo-liberal policies that have led in the past to gender, class and ethnic inequalities in pension provision' (Price, 2008, p 64). These latter views typify a more general approach to social democratic ideology in recent assessments that view it as inconsistent with a large role for non-state provision. Thus unfavourable comparisons have been drawn between the reformed British arrangements and a range of systems in which state provision is predominant, that is, 'continental systems' (Pemberton et al, 2006, p 261), Labour's 1957 plan for pension reform, *National Superannuation* (Pemberton, 2008) and more generally, a 'public earnings-related' system (Price, 2008, p 64). Thus, similarly to Price, Pemberton has concluded that New Labour, by embracing 'a private sector solution' on the grounds that 'what matters is what works', has so diluted its ideological commitment to social democracy that pragmatism has effectively trumped ideology (2010).

These conclusions rest, sometimes quite loosely, on theories of institutional change which have developed over the past two decades to analyse welfare state retrenchment (see, for example, Hall, 1993; Pierson, 1993, 2000a, 2000b, 2001), and which seek to differentiate between paradigmatic and incremental change. This type of analysis involves the assessment of welfare state reforms in relation to existing policy paradigms or policy paths, which in welfare state research have generally been understood in terms of regime types: social democratic, conservative and liberal (see, for example, Esping-Andersen, 1990). Thus most recent assessments of British pension reform have focused on the apparent absence of paradigmatic change, with individual components of the reform viewed as essentially incremental and thus of limited significance in terms of the overall configuration of the British pension regime. Implicit in much of this analysis is Hall's categorisation of policy change into three types (1993). First order change occurs when *levels* are changed, such as increases in contribution rates for social insurance, or reductions in benefits. Second order change involves a change in *instruments*, such that the structure of the scheme is altered by, for example, amending the indexation method. Third order or paradigmatic change constitutes goal shifts, where the basic philosophy on which the programme is based is altered. Crucially, first and second order change is generally regarded within this literature as a 'reactive and adaptive' strategy for preserving institutional continuity (Streeck and Thelen,

2005, p 8), not a potentially transformative step to third order change, and this is largely how it has been treated in the recent literature on British pension reform.

This chapter views recent reforms through a rather different lens. It does not seek to assess whether the reformed British system is social democratic, but how much recent reforms constitute a step in this direction. It is on this basis that it argues that the liberal essence of the British system has been significantly diminished. This approach is undertaken on the basis of recent critiques of institutional change theory and a growing acceptance that social democratic values and non-state provision are less in conflict than some social policy analysts have suggested.

With regard first to existing models of institutional change, as a number of commentators have suggested, while the three orders of change model provides a useful heuristic device for understanding reforms (see, for example, Hinrichs and Kangas, 2003), the boundaries between the three types have proved difficult to operationalise. These problems are related to a broader empirical and theoretical critique that has questioned whether policy systems ever rest stably on single, coherent ideological foundations (Streeck and Thelen, 2005), the overturning of which can be said to constitute paradigmatic change. Instead, it appears that policy frameworks are often based on ideological compromises (see, for example, Bridgen, 2006), with a range of principles sometimes working simultaneously in a policy system at any given time (Orren and Skowronek, 2004; Thelen, 2004; Crouch and Keune, 2005, pp 83-7; Streeck and Thelen, 2005). In such circumstances greater attention needs to be focused on incremental changes, which rather than merely generative of newer variations of old ideas and institutions (Streeck and Thelen, 2005, p 16), as implied by the concepts of first and second order change, can be transformative on the basis of 'creeping change' (Pierson, 2000b; Ebbinghaus, 2005, p 19). Conversely, given the ideational complexity of policy systems, a shift in underlying principles might occur without there being an overall change in the policy path (Ebbinghaus, 2005, pp 18-19).[10] Layering, for example, can occur when new institutions, operating on the basis of different principles from existing institutions, are introduced to – or rekindled in – a policy domain without the abolition of the older arrangements. In such circumstances, no immediate paradigm shift occurs but this might happen in time if the new institution builds up greater public support than the existing one (Thelen, 2004, p 35; Streeck and Thelen, 2005, p 23). Finally, and in a similar vein, Hinrichs and Kangas have shown that while some changes might have no immediate effect, say on pension levels, they might imply substantial changes in benefits further down the line; because the immediate impact of a reform is negligible it does not mean that the reform is not a large one (Hinrichs and Kangas, 2003, p 588).

In summary, incremental change can have more profound implications than the traditional institutional literature has suggested. It is on the basis of this insight that the following sections will argue that the latest British pension reform represents more than mere path stabilisation and instead constitutes an 'adaptation' of the existing liberal model involving some 'redirection of core principles' (Ebbinghaus, 2005, p 17; see also Streeck and Thelen, 2005, p 8). This analysis is structured by Esping-Andersen's criteria for judging regime types, enhanced in light of feminist critiques of his approach (Lewis, 1992; O'Connor et al, 1999). Changes in entitlement and benefit levels are considered in relation to class and gender, and alterations in the relationship between state and non-state provision are assessed. To judge the extent of change along each dimension Hall's three types are used but on the basis, as detailed above, that first and second order change can have transformative potential and that an alteration in underlying principles of a policy system can occur without this necessarily signifying a shift in the overall policy paradigm (see Ebbinghaus, 2005, p 17). In thinking about social democratic principles this chapter adopts a less statist approach than most recent assessments. Increased state *provision* is not the only route towards social democracy; greater regulation and compulsion of the non-state sector represents another one (Esping-Andersen, 1990, pp 81-3; Hyde et al, 2003; Trampusch, 2007a, 2007b). Thus, it is equally appropriate in assessing the British reform to compare the reformed system with less statist social democratic pension systems, such as those in the Netherlands and Denmark (Goodin et al, 1999). Data comes from secondary analysis and new projections of the individual impacts of the reform undertaken for this chapter.

Entitlement

Entitlement to benefits in a social democratic pension system is not tied to participation in the labour market but comes as a right to all citizens or residents. This is the case, for example, in the state systems in the Netherlands and Denmark. The British system in contrast has, since 1925, rested firmly on a contributory basis, with little allowance initially for periods of unemployment or unpaid work. The introduction of unemployment credits, Home Responsibilities Protection (HRP) –

which reduced the qualifying years required for a full BSP – and a Carer's Credit for those receiving Carer's Allowance, mitigated the effects of this contributory system but problems remained, especially for women. Only a small proportion of carers – those caring for more than 35 hours a week (7% in 2006) – received the credit, and individuals caring for two people for less than 35 hours each but more than this in total did not qualify (Hollis, 2006, pp 115-16).

The case for Britain to adopt a 'citizenship' or residency-based pension was strongly made during the reform process (NAPF, 2005; PPI, 2005; Hollis, 2006), and a move to entitlement on the basis was, as has been seen, recommended by the Pensions Commission for future accruals (2005, p 206). To pay for this and other recommended changes the Commission proposed an increase in the state retirement age, which of course would extend the period that citizens are reliant on labour market income.

The introduction of a residency-based pension would have represented a clear change of principle in the British system and on this basis could have been regarded as a third order change. The government's rejection of this option was at least partially on the grounds that such a change in principle was unwelcome: the government's view remained that 'it is right for people to receive state pensions in return for making economic or social contributions during their working lives' (DWP, 2006a, p 126).[11] However, in upholding the principle of a contributory pension, the government strongly reinforced its view that work should include unpaid caring work in the home. On this basis, further extensive changes have been made to entitlement conditions, particularly with regard to the BSP. Thus, the number of qualifying years required for a full BSP is reduced to 30 for men and women; HRP is converted into a system of credits payable on a weekly basis; a new Carer's Credit is introduced for those undertaking care for the sick and severely disabled for 20 hours or more a week; and the minimum contribution rule for entitlement – the *de minimis* rule – is abolished. The entitlement rules for S2P were also changed, but not by as much as for basic state provision. These followed significant changes made when S2P was introduced. Thus 49 qualifying years are still required to gain full access to S2P and only 7 of the 19 credits available for BSP also apply for S2P (PPI, 2006a). However, the Carer's Credit introduced for the BSP was extended to S2P, and the credit system as a whole is moved from a system of annual credits to weekly credits, enabling people to combine credited and paid contributions in order to accrue a year of entitlement to the S2P.

These reforms are projected to significantly improve women's entitlement. Thus, while under the existing system around 50% of women reaching state pension age in 2010 were expected to be entitled to a full BSP compared with around 90% of men, after the changes around 70% of women reaching state pension age in this year will have a full BSP entitlement. By 2025 over 90% of women and men reaching state pension age are expected to get full BSP entitlements compared with around 80% if nothing had been done (DWP, 2006a; Evandrou and Falkingham, 2009). Nevertheless, some individuals continue to lose out: those who retire before April 2010 will continue to be entitled to BSP on the basis of the old system, although the government has taken steps to ease the inequities for this transition group (DWP, 2008); and carers who care for less than 20 hours will still find their entitlement restricted. Likewise, those individuals, mainly women (600,000 in 2006), who earn less than the lower earnings limit, will not build up entitlement for each year that they are in this position (Fawcett Society, 2006, p 2). The more limited reforms to S2P provision mean that the impact on entitlement is less. According to the PPI, around one million extra individuals each year will build up entitlement for S2P, but 25% of working-age people (nine million individuals) will still be excluded each year (PPI, 2006a).

However, overall the changes made to entitlement conditions by the reforms strongly move the British pension system in a social democratic direction. While the BSP system remains ostensibly contributory, the extension of the credit system has, in fact, made it 'near-universal' for individuals who retire after 2010 (DWP, 2006a, p 127; PPI, 2006a), a situation which will become increasingly significant as the BSP begins to rise in line with earnings. A series of incremental shifts, of which the recent reform is the latest, has created what amounts to a third order change. The situation with regard to S2P lags behind, but second order changes have substantially extended entitlements over the past 10 years, such that overall 2.5 million individuals who were not entitled to an additional state pension before 1997 are entitled to it under the new system (DWP, 2006a, p 133). Moreover, these changes look set to have a significant impact on the pension levels of the affected groups, as will be discussed below.

Public/private mix

In social democratic pension systems responsibility for ensuring universal access to pension provision is expected to rest mainly with the state on the basis that it is not appropriate for 'essential human needs' to be 'relegated to private versus public responsibility' (Esping-Andersen, 1990, p 80). This does not mean that the state must be the monopoly, or even dominant, provider of pensions. In the Netherlands and Denmark, for example, state action takes the form of mandating occupational provision often on the basis of well-established corporatist arrangements at industry level (see Anderson, 2007; Bannink and de Vroom, 2007; Bridgen and Meyer, 2009). As has been seen, in Britain state responsibility has been comparatively light particularly with regard to provision. In the non-state sector, the situation is more complicated. Thus, while employer voluntarism has remained a central underpinning principle of the British pension system, links between the state and non-state sectors have increased over the past 20 years and regulation has become tighter (Blake, 2003; Meyer and Bridgen, 2010). Moreover, in the hybrid area of public sector occupational provision, where coverage is near universal, the state is responsible for employer contributions and unfunded liabilities in, for example, National Health Service (NHS) pensions.

The case for an increase in the state's role, either immediate or phased, was made strongly in the process that preceded recent reforms. A range of policy actors called for state provision to be unified in a single pension increased to the level of the Guarantee Credit, and its yearly uprating to be pegged to earnings (NAPF, 2002; ABI, 2003; TUC, 2003, 2004; CBI, 2004; PPI, 2005). The trades unions supplemented this demand with a call for a more compulsory occupational pension system, an option at least partially endorsed by the Association of British Insurers (ABI) (2003) but strongly opposed by the Confederation of British Industry (CBI) (2004). The acceptance of these demands would have made the British occupational system more like the Dutch and Danish systems, and thus constituted a clear break from the liberal system. The government was not prepared to go this far. Instead, it accepted the Pensions Commission's proposal for a more generous flat rate state provision pension using the BSP and S2P (2005, p 215; see above). While the case for more compulsion in the occupational sector was conceded, this was on the basis of an individual opt out.

The significance of these changes in the British public/private mix has generally been downplayed by social policy commentators, mainly on the basis that the increase in state provision will happen slowly, so will only have a noticeable impact over the longer term. Even then, it is suggested, the impact on the government's accounts will be slight, with any additional expenditure compensated for by cuts in other parts of the government's budget for pensioners[12] (PPI, 2006a, pp 8-9; see also Pemberton et al, 2006). Likewise, the government's emphasis on funded non-state provision has been regarded as a reflection of its continuing commitment to the private sector (Price, 2008, pp 64-5; Pemberton, 2010).

Certainly, these assessments are correct in their conclusion that the reforms have not created a strongly statist pension system in Britain. Yet, in important respects the significance, immediate or potential, of the reforms that have taken place has been underplayed: the state's role both as a provider and a regulator has increased markedly. Thus, while earnings uprating has been delayed, its reintroduction will mean that a mechanism is in place that has operated for the BSP for only four years since its introduction in 1946. Moreover, this move to earnings uprating strongly contrasts with developments in most other advanced pension systems, many of which have recently moved to price indexation (Hinrichs, 2009). Second, while projections for total public expenditure on pensions (that is, including state and non-state) as a proportion of gross domestic product (GDP) stay almost static overall (PPI, 2006a), this still represents an increase of 1% of GDP over that which had been projected to be spent under the pre-reform system. Moreover, there is a significant shift in the way this money is spent. Thus, government expenditure on its own contributory provision, rather than subsidisation of occupational provision, is projected to increase up to 2050 by around 1.5% of GDP in relation to planned expenditure before the reform (DWP, 2006a, 2009; PPI, 2006a, 2006b). More money is thus being spent on universal state provision and less on supplementing the contributions of those with defined contribution occupational pensions. These changes improve Britain's comparative performance, particularly if the state's liability for unfunded public sector pensions is included. Thus, while on this basis the projected level of public spending on pensions in Britain at 9.3% of GDP remains significantly behind the Bismarckian systems in France and Italy, it is broadly similar to that in Denmark (9.2%) and the Netherlands (10.5%) (European Commission [DG ECFIN] and the Economic Policy Committee [AWG], 2009a, pp 82, 196; 2009b, pp 34, 96, 138, 165).

Changes to the non-state sector as part of the British reforms are particularly ill served by a comparison with strongly statist variants of social democracy, either from the past or from elsewhere in Europe. In contrast, when compared with the less statist Dutch system, for example, where mandated non-state provision is the norm, the introduction of quasi-compulsion in Britain seems less clearly consistent with 'neoliberalism' (see Clark, 2006). The state is taking greater responsibility for ensuring access to non-state provision through the establishment of a national savings infrastructure and the introduction of an employer quasi-mandate. From a situation where employers had the final say on occupational pension contributions, this decision will now rest with employees. On this basis, Personal Accounts represent a clear shift in the underlying values of the British system and thus a form of third order change; the voluntarist principle for employers has been ended. The implications of this shift might grow over the longer term. In this respect, Personal Accounts can be regarded as a new institutional layer on top of the existing personal and occupational pensions system (Streeck and Thelen, 2005), which has the potential, due to its very low costs, to undermine the existing private market for those without – or with very limited – occupational provision, including the self-employed (Emmerson and Wakefield, 2009, p 2). This concern has certainly occurred to some in the insurance industry, who regard the NPSS model of quasi-compulsory saving as a potential threat (Bee, 2006; Timmins and Hall, 2006). The industry has tried hard to secure a greater role in the operation of Personal Accounts or alternatively to limit their scope by means of smaller maximum yearly contributions than those initially proposed by the government (that is, £5,000; see DWP, 2006b, p 141; Pemberton, 2008). On the former they have had little success: the NPSS model has largely been retained so far in implementation given the government's anxiety not to risk its low charge advantages (DWP, 2006b; Aboulian, 2009). They have been more successful on yearly contributions: the government has reduced the maximum to £3,600 (2005 prices) but this still leaves employees with considerable scope for contributions over and above the default level of 8%, which equates to a £1,600 annual contribution for an average earner (Personal Accounts Delivery Authority, 2009).

Benefit levels

In social democratic systems benefits are sufficient by themselves to lift all pensioners above the poverty line without recourse to means-tested provision. They do so by mitigating or dispensing with the link between lifetime earnings and benefit levels on the basis of horizontal redistribution between income and gender groups. This can occur either through a large state scheme or a combination of state provision and mandated occupational pensions. The British system, while providing a BSP that has been quite redistributive (Bridgen and Meyer, 2007b), has done so at a level consistently below the means-tested minimum. This situation has only begun to be rectified for some by the gradual maturation of SERPs/S2P, and for others was less problematic due to their access to occupational provision. It was to lift more pensioners out of poverty without recourse to means testing that those on the left pressed for the substantial increase in state provision outlined above, but this was not accepted either by the Pensions Commission or the government (see Bridgen and Meyer, 2006).

Assessment of the policy that *was* adopted has generally focused on two issues: the absence or slow pace of change for most of today's pensioners and those who will retire in the next 20 years; and the reliability of the government's estimate that the proportion of the population who will be entitled to means-tested support by 2050 will fall to around 30% rather than rise substantially, as projected under the old system. On the first point, there can be little doubt that the reform is future-oriented. Significant improvements are in line for some women from 2010, but the impact of the reintroduction of earnings relation will only be felt gradually. However, as we have seen, it is important, given the long time scales over which pensions policy operates, to also consider the long-term impact of the reforms (Hinrichs and Kangas, 2003). This is the ground on which the means-testing issue has been contested. Here, the PPI shows that the government's claims that means testing will fall up to 2050 is sensitive to the assumptions used, and on this basis argues that the level of means testing might stay static at around 40%–45% (PPI, 2006a, 2006b). The precise situation is uncertain, but there seems little doubt that means testing will continue to play a significant if probably diminishing role in the British pension system for the next few decades. This is largely because many pensioners in 2050 will have lived at least part of their working lives under a pension system in which entitlement to state provision was more restricted than the reformed one, and in which opportunities to build up occupational provision were more limited. Even so, most projections suggest that the new system is likely to increase the non-means-tested income of many of this group (particularly those without private savings), and those cohorts who retire between the Acts' full implementation and 2050 (see Price, 2007;[13] and DWP, 2009).

For younger cohorts, the situation is the most promising, particularly for low/moderate paid workers who would not have had access to occupational provision under the old system. The opportunities for this group to amass a pension above the means-tested minimum are much greater after the reform, and the state pension is more redistributive in their favour. This can be illustrated by simulations of the pension outcomes of a range of hypothetical biographies who start work

—

in 2007 (see Table 4.1; for more on this methodology see Meyer et al, 2007), most of whose wages are lower than average and whose attachment to the labour market is sometimes curtailed. Three of these biographies are 'female' and thus experience greater amounts of care-related employment gaps and part-time work in line with current social trends. A higher wage biography is also included to illustrate the relative consequences of the reform for individuals at different points on the income scale.

Table 4.1: Working life details of the illustrative biographies used in pension simulations

	Lifetime wage as % of average	Age at start of work	Age at retirement	Ages when out of paid workforce	Reason for absence
The mother and unqualified part-time worker in the retail sector	39	18	65	24–25, 27–29	Caring for children under 12
The mother and qualified part-time worker in the welfare sector	42	20	63	26–27, 30–31	Caring for children under 12
The married carer	22	18	68	23–29, 50–59	Caring for children under 12 (23–29) and relative (50–59) for less than 35 but more than 22 hours
The unqualified worker in the car industry	79	18	65	26	Unemployment
The middle manager in financial services	131	20	60	None	
The small business entrepreneur	84	18	65	None	

For each of these biographies the projected pension entitlements both before and after recent reforms are calculated under various plausible assumptions.[14] Once calculated in this way the pension entitlements of all biographies have been examined in relation to the projected old age poverty (that is, dependency on means-tested provision) and social exclusion (the latter defined as a pension that is less than 40% of average wages) thresholds. As with all simulations of this type, the results are sensitive to the assumptions used, but a quite pessimistic scenario has been adopted in relation both to the accumulation and decumulation phase of Personal Accounts.[15]

Table 4.2 shows that under the previous system the biographies had to rely solely on the state pension.[16] If we assume that under the reformed system individuals of this type accept auto-enrolment and pay the minimum contribution into Personal Accounts, quite substantial increases in pensions are evident in comparison to the old system. These increases are in and around the mid-30s percentage points for the retail worker and the welfare worker and are over 50% for the manufacturing worker.

The position of our biographies with less attachment to the formal employed labour market – the mother/carer and self-employed entrepreneur – also improves under the new system. Here the impact of the improvements in state provision are particularly evident: the mother/carer benefits from the more generous credit system and abolition of the *de minimis* rule, and both she and the self-employed individual benefit from the reintroduction of earnings relation to the BSP. The improvement in state provision for the higher paid employed workers is less substantial, particularly for the middle manager, whose state pension only rises by three percentage points. This is a product of the gradual move to a flat rate state system. The pensions of most of the biographies consequently move substantially above the level of the Guarantee Credit, such that they are also above the savings credit level (Table 4.3). The exception here is the self-employed entrepreneur whose pension would only move above the Guarantee Credit level if he/she opted into Personal Accounts.

These outcomes for the British biographies can also be compared with projected outcomes for the same biographies in the Netherlands (Table 4.4), each of whom would have mandated occupational provision.[17] As would be expected, the reform significantly improves the comparative performance of the British pension system, albeit that British provision is now only available from the age of 68.[18] Whereas before the reform the British biographies, excluding the middle manager, had pensions

Table 4.2: Comparison of pre-reform and post-reform projected outcomes on retirement for British biographies without voluntary occupational provision as percentage of social exclusion line

	State	Non-state	Overall		State	Non-state	Overall
The mother and unqualified part-time worker in the retail sector				The unqualified worker in the car industry			
Old system	47	0	47	Old system	54	0	54
New system	63	19	82	New system	65	45	110
Difference	16	19	35	Difference	11	45	56
The mother and qualified part-time worker in the welfare sector				The middle manager in financial services			
Old system	48	0	48	Old system	63	0	63
New system	63	23	86	New system	66	66	132
Difference	15	23	38	Difference	3	66	69
The married carer				The small business entrepreneur			
Old system	39	0	39	Old system	23	0	23
New system	63	1	64	New system	43	0	43
Difference	24	1	25	Difference	20	0	20

Table 4.3: Comparison of pre-reform and post-reform projected outcomes on retirement for British biographies without voluntary occupational provision as percentage of Guarantee Credit

Total pension		Total pension	
The mother and unqualified part-time worker in the retail sector		The unqualified worker in the car industry	
Old system	99	Old system	121
New system	165	New system	223
Difference	66	Difference	102
The mother and qualified part-time worker in the welfare sector		The middle manager in financial services	
Old system	101	Old system	161
New system	174	New system	266
Difference	73	Difference	105
The married carer		The small business entrepreneur	
Old system	82	Old system	49
New system	128	New system	88
Difference	46	Difference	39

Table 4.4: Comparison between pre-reform, post-reform and Dutch projected state and non-state pension outcomes of all biographies on retirement as a percentage of the social inclusion line

	The mother and unqualified part-time worker in the retail sector			*The mother and qualified part-time worker in the welfare sector*			*The married carer*		
	State	Non-state	Total	State	Non-state	Total	State	Non-state	Total
Netherlands	70	25	95	70	47	117	70	8	78
Pre-reform Britain	47	0	47	48	0	48	39	0	39
Post-reform Britain	63	19	82	63	23	86	63	1	64
	The unqualified worker in the car industry			*The middle manager in financial services*			*The small business entrepreneur*		
	State	Non-state	Total	State	Non-state	Total	State	Non-state	Total
Netherlands	70	90	160	70	188	236	70	7	77
Pre-reform Britain	54	0	54	63	0	63	23	0	23
Post-reform Britain	65	45	110	66	66	132	43	0	43

that were between 39 and 106 percentage points lower in relation to the national social inclusion line than their equivalent biography in the Netherlands, after the reform the gap is much lower – between 13 and 50 percentage points. The gap would be likely to be even lower for British biographies with company-provided occupational provision rather than Personal Accounts, given generally higher employer contributions. We also see that state provision in Britain becomes more universally available at a level which compares quite favourably with that provided in the Netherlands, although of course the residency basis for the Dutch first tier means that they are better at protecting the married carer and self-employed entrepreneur.

Conclusion

It is now largely accepted in the literature that most individual social policy reforms are not paradigm shifting, as this concept has been traditionally understood. Substantial institutional and interest-based obstacles lie in the way of regime-altering reforms, which have been well recognised as a factor in post-war British pension policy. Thus repeated efforts from the left to reform the Beveridgean pension system have faced a number of major obstacles in the form of policy legacies (see Fawcett, 1996; Bridgen, 2006; Pemberton et al, 2006) and established interests (Pemberton, 2008). The dominant role of the Treasury at the heart of the British policy-making process has also constituted a major obstacle to reform, given its continuing opposition to universal benefits (see, for example, Bridgen, 2006). In the face of these obstacles policy did change, often in the form of add-ons to the existing policy framework (see Pemberton et al, 2006), but this change was generally of a smaller scale than reformers had originally proposed. The most recent reform of the British pension system fits this pattern well.

However, because individual reforms rarely by themselves shift policy systems onto new paths this does not mean that they necessarily leave the fundamentals of existing arrangements untouched. Incremental change and paradigmatic change are not unrelated; the former can sometimes result in a partial adaption of the regime's founding principles that can lead in time to more thoroughgoing change. For this reason, analysis of reform needs to focus more closely on the nature and scale of incremental change rather than the limitations of the reformed system in relation to models of other regime types. This chapter has sought to analyse recent British pension reform on this basis. It has concluded that, assessed in relation to all the standard criteria for judging social democratic regimes, the reform represents a clear and significant shift of the British pension system in a social democratic direction. Entitlement has become less commodified and familial. Non-means-tested benefits will rise for many and outcomes are likely to become more equal. The role of the state both as a provider and as a facilitator of access to non-state provision has risen. Some of these changes will take time to have an impact but this does not by itself make them insignificant (Hinrichs and Kangas, 2003).

What remains in doubt is how the reform will develop should the Conservatives win the next election. They have indicated their willingness to reintroduce earnings uprating for the BSP, but their attitude towards S2P remains doubtful (Conservative Party, 2009), and they have also indicated that they will review Personal Accounts (Timmins, 2009). The latter issue will be an important test of the party's apparent re-positioning on social policy issues. One nation Conservatives have in the past accepted the need for state compulsion in the non-state sphere (Bridgen, 2000), but in a situation where employers' opposition shows signs of growing (Insley, 2010), will Mr Cameron?

Notes

[1] I am very grateful to Traute Meyer for her comments on an earlier draft of this chapter. I would also like to thank John Hills and Chris Curry for their helpful advice.

[2] Salary between the lower earnings limit and the upper earnings limit.

[3] This date was within the implementation period the Pensions Commission considered necessary for the BSP to play the role they envisaged for it in their integrated reform package (see Pensions Commission, 2006, p 29) but the Commission cautioned against further delay. In fact the slower growth in overall average wages since the Commission reported (from an average yearly rise of 3.9% between 1999 and 2005 to 3.2% between 2006 and 2009) has made this delay less important (ONS, 2009) given the government's commitment to raise annually the basic state pension by 2.5%.

[4] In January 2010 another rebranding was announced. Personal Account pensions will now be known as National Employment Savings Trust (NEST) pensions. See www.padeliveryauthority.org. uk/nest.asp

[5] This is measured as household income below 60% contemporary median household income after housing costs.

[6] Some pensioners also received an earnings-related supplement as a result of the 1961 Pensions Act, but this was very small.

[7] Charges for stakeholders were initially pegged to 1% in an effort to ensure maximum returns for the target market, but were later increased to 1.5%.

[8] Insurance companies were worried about selling such products to lower-income individuals, which they did not think was profitable. They also feared accusations of 'misselling'. This was because it was not clear that stakeholder savings would provide an overall pension for low-income individuals above the level of means-tested benefits.

[9] The Pensions Commission sought to stabilise the percentage of the adult life spent in retirement, a figure that had increased steadily since 1950 (2005, p 96).

[10] Ebbinghaus (2005) rather confusingly refers to such a development as 'path departure', which he contrasts with 'path switching' (that is, full-scale paradigmatic change).

[11] It also raised practical and expenditure concerns about the introduction of a residency-based system (DWP, 2006a, p 126), many of which have been contested (PPI, 2006a, pp 13-14).

[12] This includes the cost of the contracting out rebate for defined contribution occupational pensions that will be ended under the reform.

[13] The Pensions Commission's simulations for a similar system to that introduced by the Acts (as detailed by Price, 2007, p 572) show significant increase in non-means-tested benefit levels for current 40-year-olds of various types, particularly for those without private savings under the current system who decide to opt into Personal Accounts under the new system.

[14] Annual inflation, 1.9%; average wage rise, 3.9%; saving in Personal Accounts starts in 2012 when the biographies are 23 on the basis of the minimum level of contributions and continues until retirement; real rate of return of 3.5% after charges; annuity rate of 5%.

[15] On annuity rates in 2009 see www.fsa.gov.uk/tables/table/results_frameset.jsp; on real rates of return, the 20-year average annual return was 5.5% for gilts and 4.6% for the FTSE All Share, although figures for the last 10 years have been significantly lower (see Barclays Capital, 2009).

[16] Some might, of course, have had private savings but these were generally very low among individuals of this type (Pensions Commission, 2005, pp 157-60).

[17] The Dutch simulations were undertaken by Bert deVroom and Duco Bannink as part of an EU Fifth Framework-funded project (detailed in Meyer et al, 2007; see also Bannink and de Vroom, 2007). They use the same methodology and are based on the same assumptions as used in the British simulations. The only difference is that the starting year for the Dutch simulations is 2003 rather than 2007 in the British simulations. However, this does not affect the validity of the results because the Dutch pension system has remained generally stable during the intervening period.

[18] A similar move is being discussed in the Netherlands but has not yet been implemented (see Legorano, 2009).

References

ABI (Association of British Insurers) (2003) *Simplicity, security and choice: ABI response to the Green Paper*, London: ABI (www.abi.org.uk/).

Aboulian, B. (2009) 'UK's national pension scheme to favour passive strategies', *Financial Times*, 27 September.

Agulnik, P. (1999) 'The proposed S2P', *Fiscal Studies*, vol 20, no 4, pp 409-21.

Anderson, K.M. (2007) 'The Netherlands: political competition in a proportional system', in E.M. Immergut, K.M. Anderson and I. Schulze (eds) *Handbook of West European pension politics*, Oxford: Oxford University Press, pp 713-57.

Bannink, D. and de Vroom, B. (2007) 'The Dutch pension system and social exclusion', in T. Meyer, P. Bridgen and B. Riedmuller (eds) *Private pensions versus social inclusion? Non-state provision for citizens at risk in Europe*, Cheltenham: Edward Elgar, pp 79-106.

Barclays Capital (2009) *2009 Barclays Capital Equity Gilt Study* (www. barcap.com/Client+offering/Research/Global+Asset+Allocation/ Equity+Gilt+Study).

Bee, S. (2006) 'Royal London's views on the proposed National Pension Savings Scheme' (www.scottishlife.co.uk/scotlife/Web/Site/BeeHive/ PoliticalPapers/BHPPJan06Page1.asp).

Blake, D. (2003) *Pension schemes and pension funds in the United Kingdom*, Oxford: Oxford University Press.

Bridgen, P. (2000) 'The one nation idea and state welfare: the Conservative Party and pensions in the 1950s', *Contemporary British History*, vol 14, no 3, pp 83-104.

Bridgen, P. (2006) 'A straitjacket with wriggle room: the Beveridge Report, the Treasury and the Exchequer's pension liability 1942–1959', *Twentieth Century British History*, vol 17, no 1, pp 1-25.

Bridgen, P. and Meyer, T. (2005) 'When do benevolent capitalists change their mind? Explaining the retrenchment of defined benefit pensions in Britain', *Social Policy and Administration*, vol 39, no 4, pp 764-85.

Bridgen, P. and Meyer, T. (2006) 'Towards a "balanced" approach to pensions reform? Individuals, the state and employers in the restructuring of post-retirement income in the UK', Pension Institute Discussion Paper PI-0509 (www.pensions-institute.org/papers.html).

Bridgen, P. and Meyer, T. (2007a) 'Private pensions versus social inclusion? Three patterns of provision and their impact', in T. Meyer, P. Bridgen and B. Riedmuller (eds) *Private pensions versus social inclusion? Non-state provision for citizens at risk in Europe*, Cheltenham: Edward Elgar, pp 223-51.

Bridgen, P. and Meyer, T. (2007b) 'The British pension system and social inclusion', in T. Meyer, P. Bridgen and B. Riedmuller (eds) *Private pensions versus social inclusion? Non-state provision for citizens at risk in Europe*, Cheltenham: Edward Elgar, pp 47-75.

Bridgen, P. and Meyer, T. (2009) 'The politics of occupational pension reform in Britain and the Netherlands: the power of market discipline in liberal and corporatist regimes', *West European Politics*, vol 32, no 3, pp 584-608.

CBI (Confederation of British Industry) (2004) *Securing our future: Developing sustainable pension provision in the UK*, London: CBI.

Clark, G.L. (2006) 'The UK occupational pension system in crisis', in H. Pemberton, P. Thane and N. Whiteside (eds) *Britain's pensions crisis: History and policy*, Oxford: Oxford University Press, pp 145-68.

Conservative Party (2009) *Where we stand: Pensions* (www.conservatives. com/Policy/Where_we_stand/Pensions_and_Older_People.aspx).

Crouch, C. and Keune, M. (2005) 'Changing dominant practice: making use of institutional diversity in Hungary and the United Kingdom', in W. Streeck and K. Thelen (eds) *Beyond continuity: Institutional change in advanced political economies*, Oxford: Oxford University Press, pp 83-102.

DWP (Department for Work and Pensions) (1998) *Partnership in pensions*, London: The Stationery Office.

DWP (2002) *Simplicity, security and choice: Working and saving for retirement*, Cm 5677, London: The Stationery Office.

DWP (2006a) *Security in retirement: A new pensions system*, Cm 6841, London: The Stationery Office.

DWP (2006b) *Personal accounts: A new way to save*, London: DWP.

DWP (2008) 'Drive to help women boost their state pension' (www. dwp.gov.uk/newsroom/press-releases/2008/may-2008/pens066-060508.shtml).

DWP (2009) *Saving for retirement: Implications of pensions reforms on financial incentives to save for retirement*, DWP Research Report No 558, London: DWP (http://research.dwp.gov.uk/asd/asd5/report_abstracts/ rr_abstracts/rra_558.asp).

Ebbinghaus, B. (2005) 'Can path dependence explain institutional change? Two approaches applied to welfare state reform', Max-Planck-Institut für Gesellschaftsforschung Discussion Paper 05/2 (www.mpifg. de/pu/mpifg_dp/dp05-2.pdf).

Emmerson, C. and Wakefield, M. (2009) *Amounts and accounts: Reforming private pension enrolment*, London: Institute for Fiscal Studies (www.ifs. org.uk/publications/4541).

Esping-Andersen, G. (1990) *The three worlds of welfare capitalism*, Cambridge: Polity Press.

European Commission (DG ECFIN) and the Economic Policy Committee (AWG) (2009a) *2009 Ageing Report: Economic and budgetary projections for the EU-27 member states (2008–2060)* (http://ec.europa.eu/economy_finance/publications/).

European Commission (DG ECFIN) and the Economic Policy Committee (AWG) (2009b) *2009 Ageing Report: Economic and budgetary projections for the EU-27 member states (2008–2060): Statistical annex* (http://ec.europa.eu/economy_finance/publications/).

Evandrou, M. and Falkingham, J. (2005) 'A secure retirement for all? Older people and New Labour', in J. Hills and K. Stewart (eds) *A more equal society? New Labour, poverty, inequality and exclusion*, Bristol: The Policy Press, pp 167-88.

Evandrou, M. and Falkingham, J. (2009) 'Pensions and income security in later life', in J. Hills, T. Sefton and K. Stewart (eds) *Towards a more equal society? Poverty, inequality and policy since 1997*, Bristol: The Policy Press, pp 157-77.

Fawcett, H. (1996) 'The Beveridge straitjacket: policy formation and the problem of poverty in old age', *Contemporary British History*, vol 10, pp 20-42.

Fawcett Society (2006) *Fawcett Society response to the pensions White Paper 'Security in retirement: Towards a new pensions system'*, London: Fawcett Society.

Goodin, R., Headey, B., Muffels, R. and Dirven, H.-J. (1999) *The real worlds of welfare capitalism*, Cambridge: Cambridge University Press.

Hall, P.A. (1993) 'Policy paradigms, social learning and the state: the case of economic policymaking in Britain', *Comparative Politics*, vol 25, no 3, pp 275-96.

Hinrichs, K. (2009) 'Pensions in Europe: convergence of old-age security systems?', in J.-K. Petersen and K. Petersen (eds) *The politics of age: Basic pension systems in comparative and historical perspective*, Frankfurt am Main: Peter Lang, pp 119-43.

Hinrichs, K. and Kangas, O. (2003) 'When is a change big enough to be a system shift? Small system-shifting changes in German and Finnish pension policies', *Social Policy and Administration*, vol 37, no 6, pp 573-91.

Hollis, P. (2006) 'How to address gender inequality in British pensions policy', in H. Pemberton, P. Thane and N. Whiteside (eds) *Britain's pension crisis: History and policy*, Oxford: Oxford University Press.

Hyde, M., Dixon, J. and Drover, G. (2003) 'Welfare retrenchment or collective responsibility? The privatisation of public pensions in Western Europe', *Social Policy and Society*, vol 2, no 3, pp 189-97.

Insley, J. (2010) 'Government pensions policy "is failing"', *The Guardian*, 4 January.

Legorano, G. (2009) 'Dutch MPs discuss pension age reform', *Global Pensions*, 12 November (www.globalpensions.com/global-pensions/news/1562016/dutch-mps-discuss-pension-age-reform).

Lewis, J. (1992) 'Gender and the development of welfare regimes', *Journal of European Social Policy*, vol 2, no 3, pp 159-73.

Meyer T. and Bridgen, P. (2008) 'Class, gender and chance: the social division of occupational pensions in the United Kingdom', *Ageing and Society*, vol 28, no 3, pp 353-81.

Meyer, T. and Bridgen, P. (2010) 'The convergence of a liberal and a conservative pension regime?', in J. Clasen (ed) *Converging worlds of welfare? Towards new social policy settlements in Germany and the United Kingdom*, Oxford: Oxford University Press.

Meyer, T., Bridgen, P. and Riedmuller, B. (eds) (2007) *Private pensions versus social inclusion? Non-state provision for citizens at risk in Europe*, Cheltenham: Edward Elgar.

NAPF (National Association of Pension Funds) (2002) 'Radical new proposals will boost savings and slash red tape', NAPF Press Release, London: NAPF (www.napf.co.uk/documentArchive.asp).

NAPF (2005) *Towards a citizen's pension. Final report*, London: NAPF (www.napf.co.uk).

O'Connor, J.S., Orloff, A.S. and Shaver, S. (1999) *States, markets, families: Gender, liberalism and social policy in Australia, Canada, Great Britain and the United States*, Cambridge: Cambridge University Press.

ONS (Office for National Statistics) (2009) *2009 Annual Survey of Hours and Earnings (ASHE)* (www.statistics.gov.uk/cci/nugget.asp?id=285).

Orren, K. and Skowronek, S. (2004) *The search for American political development*, New York, NY: Cambridge University Press.

Pemberton, H. (2008) 'Forces of reaction? The cross-class alliance against earnings-related pensions in Britain in the 1950s', Paper delivered to the European Social Science History Conference, Lisbon, 26 February–1 March.

Pemberton, H. (2010) 'What matters is what works': Labour's journey from "national superannuation" to "personal acocunts"', *British Politics*, vol 5, no 1, pp 41-64.

Pemberton, H., Thane, P. and Whiteside, N. (2006) *Britain's pension crisis: History and policy*, Oxford: Oxford University Press.

Pensions Commission (2004) *Pensions: Challenges and choices. The first report of the Pensions Commission,* London:The Stationery Office (www. webarchive.org.uk/wayback/archive/20070801230000/http://www. pensionscommission.org.uk/index.html).

Pensions Commission (2005) *A new pensions settlement for the twenty-first century. The second report of the Pensions Commission,* London: The Stationery Office (www.webarchive.org.uk/wayback/ archive/20070801230000/http://www.pensionscommission.org.uk/ index.html).

Pensions Commission (2006) *Implementing an integrated package of pension reforms:The final report of the Pensions Commission,* London:The Stationery Office (www.webarchive.org.uk/wayback/archive/20070801230000/ http://www.pensionscommission.org.uk/index.html).

Personal Accounts Delivery Authority (2009) 'Myth buster' (www. padeliveryauthority.org.uk/documents/myth_buster_v3.pdf).

Pickering, A. (2002) *A simpler way to better pensions: An independent report,* London: Department for Work and Pensions.

Pierson, P. (1993) 'When effect becomes cause: policy feedback and political change', *World Politics,* vol 45, no 4, pp 595-628.

Pierson, P. (2000a) 'Increasing returns, path dependence, and the study of politics', *American Political Science Review,* vol 94, no 2, pp 251-67.

Pierson, P. (2000b) 'Not just what, but when: timing and sequence in political processes', *Studies of American Political Development,* vol 14, no 1, pp 72-92.

Pierson, P. (2001) 'Coping with permanent austerity: welfare state restructuring in affluent democracies', in P. Pierson (ed) *The new politics of the welfare state,* Oxford: Oxford University Press, pp 410-56.

PPI (Pensions Policy Institute) (2005) *Towards a citizen's pension: Final report,* London: PPI.

PPI (2006a) *An evaluation of the White Paper state pension reform proposal,* London: PPI (www.pensionspolicyinstitute.org.uk/news. asp?p=235&s=2&a=0).

PPI (2006b) *Will Personal Accounts increase pensions saving?,* London: PPI (www.pensionspolicyinstitute.org.uk/default.asp?p=12).

Price, D. (2006) 'The poverty of older people in the UK', *Journal of Social Work Practice,* vol 20, no 3, pp 251-66.

Price, D. (2007) 'Closing the gender gap in retirement income: what difference will recent UK pension reforms make?', *Journal of Social Policy,* vol 36, no 4, pp 561-83.

Price, D. (2008) 'Towards a new pension settlement? Recent pension reform in the UK', *Social Policy Review,* vol 20, pp 51-68.

Streeck, W. and Thelen, K. (eds) (2005) 'Introduction: institutional change in advanced political economies', in W. Streeck and K. Thelen (eds) *Beyond continuity: Institutional change in advanced political economies*, Oxford: Oxford University Press, pp 1-39.

Thelen, K. (2004) *How institutions evolve: The political economy of skills in Germany, Britain, the United States and Japan*, Cambridge: Cambridge University Press.

Timmins, N. (2009) 'Tories propose fast review of new pensions', *Financial Times*, 27 September.

Timmins, T. and Hall, B. (2006) 'Pensions plan defers crucial decisions', *Financial Times*, 15 June.

Trampusch, C. (2007a) 'Industrial relations as a source of solidarity in times of welfare state retrenchment', *Journal of Social Policy*, vol 36, no 2, pp 197-215.

Trampusch, C. (2007b) 'Industrial relations as a source of social policy: a typology of the institutional conditions for industrial agreements on social benefits', *Social Policy and Administration*, vol 41, no 3, pp 251-70.

TUC (Trades Union Congress) (2003) *TUC response to the pensions Green Paper: 'Simplicity, security and choice'*, London: TUC (www.tuc. org.uk/pensions).

TUC (2004) *Prospects for pensions*, London: TUC (www.tuc.org.uk/ pensions).

FIVE

Minimum income standards and household budgets

(Social Policy Association prize-winning paper)

Chris Deeming

Introduction

Securing an adequate diet is essential for the maintenance of our health and function in society. In the UK and other modern societies we have looked to the market to manage the risks associated with food supply, yet issues to do with food poverty as insufficient purchasing power at the household level continue to be discussed as a matter of concern (see, for example, Paton et al, 1901; Lindsay, 1913; Paton and Findlay, 1926; Boyd Orr, 1936; Titmuss, 1938; Townsend, 1962; Lambert, 1964; McKenzie, 1971; Shaw, 1999; Dowler et al, 2001; Nelson et al, 2007). One way to determine the adequacy of a household budget is to observe what people in practice secure with their existing patterns of household expenditure. In this inquiry we calculate minimum income standards or budget lines for the older UK population using data from a national survey of household expenditure and food consumption. The budget line calculations are anchored to national dietary standards for healthy living, but importantly they are also grounded in the consumption habits and market prices faced by ordinary people. We may see this as a semi-normative approach to poverty assessment following the classification of poverty measures by the 'Rio Group' (Expert Group on Poverty Statistics, 2006). 'Normative' is being used here in the sense of representing the cost of satisfying an externally imposed norm or expert recommendation; grounding the budget line in empirical expenditure data makes the calculation semi-normative.

The inquiry uses a variety of statistical methods to determine the budget line, while observing age- and sex-specific dietary standards for protein, energy, vitamins and minerals (shown in Table 5.1). UK data on household expenditure and food consumption are taken from the 2002-05 Expenditure and Food Survey (EFS) (Craggs, 2003; Gibbins, 2005; Gibbins and Georgina, 2006). The sample has been restricted to older person households, people aged 60 and above, and three years of data provides a combined sample of 4,300 households. Before describing the study methods and results, and discussing their implications; semi-normative approaches to poverty assessment are discussed in more detail.

A semi-normative approach to drawing a budget line

In the UK, and in the rest of Europe, poverty is measured using relative standards, 60% of the median is the official low-income measure and this is supported by indicators of material deprivation and exclusion (Wolff, 2009). The latest statistics by Eurostat (the European Statistical Office) shows that one in four people aged 60 or over in the UK were at risk of poverty in 2007; the figure was nearer one in three at age 65 and over. In Britain, the New Labour government has done much to help pensioners (Evandrou and Falkingham, 2009), but the issue over what might constitute a minimally adequate income in later life refuses to go away.

Family and household budget standards research in the tradition established by the Quaker industrialist Seebohm Rowntree continues to be a popular method for setting minimum income standards relating to adequacy. The challenge is to define standards for different types of personal expenditure in order to arrive at a total weekly budget. In the UK there has been considerable debate over how this should be done. Bio-medical scientists, for example, have devised budgets for safe healthy living (see, for example, Morris et al, 2000, 2005), social scientists have set budgets according to established patterns of household consumption (see, for example, Bradshaw, 1993; Parker, 2000), while others have turned to public opinion captured in focus group research (see, for example, Middleton, 2000; Bradshaw et al, 2008). The different approaches appeal to different traditions in the social and natural sciences (Deeming, 2005).

A semi-normative approach offers another way of determining a family budget. As the 'Rio Group' explains, a semi-normative measure of poverty observes expert recommendations for health and the poverty line is also empirically grounded in behavioural data. This may be seen to represent the rather absolute tradition of poverty measurement, as Bradshaw (2001) argues. The poverty line is drawn using family budget survey data and usually only covers basic essentials. A strictly normative approach, such as a budget set by experts, may not necessarily represent or reflect consumer behaviour as the 'Rio Group' suggests. Normative is being used here in the sense of representing the cost of satisfying an externally imposed norm or standard.

On the international stage it is common for food baskets to be constructed to meet the energy (calorie) requirements for defined populations and reference groups. However, there is no reason why food baskets cannot be constructed to meet other parameters of nutritional quality including vitamin and mineral requirements for good health (Svedberg, 2000). What usually happens is the basal metabolic rate (BMR) is initially calculated to be the minimum calorific requirement needed to sustain life at rest. Daily kilocalorie (kcal) requirements are next computed for different groups of the population, defined according to age, sex and level of physical activity. Food types and quantities can then be explicitly listed and priced to meet the standard requirements, as they were for the official US poverty lines (Citro and Michael, 1995) and more recently in Canada (Hatfield, 2002). Another way to determine the food basket is to estimate the cost per calorie directly from the reference population without listing the contents of the food basket. Standard calorie requirements are multiplied by the cost per calorie faced by the chosen reference population. Official poverty lines in Thailand, for example, were calculated this way (National Economic and Social Development Board, 2004). The non-food basket is usually much harder to enumerate in the poverty line calculations and is often contested (Boltvinik, 1998). When the cost of the food basket is known, the Engel-coefficient is usually used to calculate the cost of the non-food component. In the US, for example, food basket costs were multiplied threefold to set official poverty lines for three-person families and by 3.7 for two-person families (Orshansky, 1988).

Data and empirical strategy

Data on household expenditure and food consumption are taken from the UK's national budget survey, the EFS. The EFS is a survey of private households that began in April 2001 when two long-running UK surveys were combined: the Family Expenditure Survey (FES, established 1957) and the National Food Survey (NFS, established 1940). The UK family spending survey (FES/EFS) is particularly good at capturing household expenditure, including expenditure on food and drink (Banks and Johnson, 1998). Each member of the household uses two-week diaries to record all spending. The EFS tries to address the 'lumpiness' of major outlays like cars, holidays, furniture, utility bills and other irregular purchases by asking people to recall spending on such items over the last three or 12 months, and this information is then converted into weekly amounts. All food and drink acquired gets recorded, including any food eaten out or homegrown food entering the home. The weight of food is recorded in grams or, for other items such as eggs, the actual number is recorded. For drinks and other liquids, including oils and ice cream, volume is recorded in millilitres.

The budget line calculations in this inquiry relate to an older UK population living in private households. There were a number of reasons for choosing this group, in addition to the concern about poverty levels mentioned earlier. Among the older population there appears to be less variation in physical activity (Sproston and Primatesta, 2004), while observing nutrient intake for families with children is quite complicated and hard to measure. It would be quite a challenge to account for the nutritional value of school meals and packed lunches, for example (Burgess and Bunker, 2002).

The unit of analysis in this inquiry is the household. The non-household population is not covered; the nutritional status of older people in care homes raises a different set of issues for policy makers outside the framework for measuring poverty presented here (Leslie et al, 2006). The study sample, which was derived from the household reference person, comprised of single older people aged 60 or over living alone, as well as older couples living together on their own (male and female, both aged 60 or over). This approach is not the same as including all those aged 60 or over. If all those over 60 had been included it would have meant calculating household dietary requirements for everyone living with an older person, regardless of age. This could have included more unusual circumstances, where for example, there were three older people living together. Such decisions are largely pragmatic; with so many possible permutations it would have meant lots of additional dietary calculations for a relatively small number of cases. In the 2002-05 EFS data, for example, there were four households where two older men were living together.

The three years of EFS data (2002-05) provided a sample of 5,500 households, comprising 3,000 older singles and 2,500 older couples (ONS/Defra, 2006). Combining these datasets increased the sample size threefold; a large sample will allow small but statistically significant differences in the data to be detected compared with using data for a single year. Food eaten out at cafes and restaurants is included in the analysis, as is any homegrown food that is consumed. However, because we are interested in drawing a minimum budget line we exclude 200 households consuming large amounts of food out and/or large amounts of homegrown produce (anything contributing more than 10% of total energy over the two-week reference period). Also, there is no easy way to equivalise for the extra costs of disability in the data and so a thousand households in receipt of disability benefits were excluded from the analysis. Disability raises further issues for determining minimum income standards and should be the focus for further study (Zaidi and Burchardt, 2005). The total combining sample was therefore 4,300 households. All cases were weighted in the analysis to correct for non-response bias and to ensure study estimates relate to the national population (Crockett, 2006).

In this inquiry we determine budget adequacy by considering the total level of household expenditure required to meet the minimum dietary standards for good health. Many argue that household expenditure can provide a reliable measure of poverty; first, it represents household consumption much better than income, and second, research suggests that pensioners tend to save income (Banks et al, 1998; Brewer et al, 2006). To determine the budget line we use the total level of household expenditure, which includes all expenditure except certain housing costs. By convention, housing costs usually include rents, mortgage payments and local government council tax payments. This is an after housing costs (AHC) measure of poverty chosen to suit the UK social policy context; however, in other circumstances a before housing costs (BHC) measure of poverty may be more preferable. In Britain, many older people are homeowners, while those on low incomes can get help towards their housing costs after means testing. The EFS expenditure data for 2002/03 and 2003/04 were adjusted to be in line with the 2004/05 data using the UK's Retail Price Index (RPI) and the series CHAZ includes all items except housing (ONS, 2009). Adjustments were also made for regional variations in the cost of living observed in 2004; housing costs are not included (Wingfield et al, 2005).

National dietary standards for older people, published by the Department of Health (1991, 1992), are employed in the analysis (see Table 5.1). The standards are designed to meet the nutritional needs of practically all healthy people in the population. For couples, the nutritional requirements of the household unit were calculated according to the nutritional needs of each person within the household, observing the age- and sex-specific recommendations shown in Table 5.1. Care has been taken not to use recommendations and standards where nutrient levels are known to be low in the older population and dietary supplementation is recommended (DH, 1998; WHO/Tufts University School of Nutrition Science and Policy, 2002; Expert Group on Vitamins and Minerals, 2003; BNF, 2007). This effectively ruled out recommendations for vitamins B12 and D and there are no reference values for vitamin E in the UK national guidance (DH, 1991, 1992). Recommendations on levels of fat and sodium (salt) in the diet are also excluded, as are recommendations on the consumption of alcohol. These recommendations are primarily concerned with keeping consumption below a set level rather than anything to do with minimum standards. This inquiry is attempting to establish budget lines to guard against under-nutrition, not over-consumption and over-nutrition.

Table 5.1: National UK dietary recommendations for older people

| | | | Minimum daily requirements[a] | |
Nutrient	Unit	Age	Male	Female
Calcium	mg	60+	700	700
Copper	mg	60+	1.2	1.2
Energy	kcal	60–64	2,380	1,900
Energy	kcal	65–74	2,330	1,900
Energy	kcal	75+	2,100	1,810
Folate	ug	60+	200	200
Iron	mg	60+	8.7	8.7
Magnesium	mg	60+	300	270
Protein	g	60+	53.3	46.5
Riboflavin	mg	60+	1.3	1.1
Vitamin A[b]	ug	60+	700	600
Vitamin C	mg	60+	40	40
Zinc	mg	60+	9.5	7.0

Notes: mg: milligram; ug: microgram; kcal: kilocalorie.

[a] Where there is a recommended range, the lowest values have been used to represent the minimum standards for health.

[b] Retinol equivalents.

Source: Department of Health (1991, 1992)

The nutritional value of household food was evaluated using conversion factors developed by the UK's Food Standards Agency (FSA), covering the period 2002–05. The conversion tables are under regular review as the nutrient density of food can change, reflecting, for example, new methods of food production, handling and fortification. All of this information may be accessed online at the UK Data Archive, along with EFS data: interested readers should refer to FSA (2002) for the latest major revision in the series looking at the composition of UK food. FSA conversion factors did not cover all aspects of nutrition when applied to the EFS data, for example, standards for vitamin K, chromium and selenium could not be included here. Allowances are made in the study calculations for waste and for the loss of nutrients during the cooking process; there are also allowances for the seasonal variations in the nutrient content of fresh fruit and vegetables (MAFF, 1991). In the study calculations, average daily household nutritional values were obtained for each household by taking the mean of the 14-day reference period in order to compare against the recommended minimum daily requirements set out in Table 5.1.

Logistic regression and discriminant function analysis (DFA) are statistical techniques which belong to the theoretical framework of the General Linear Models (GLM) set out by Nelder and Wedderburn (1972). Logistic regression allows a discrete outcome, like meeting a minimum standard of nutrition, to be predicted from a continuous variable such as level of household expenditure. DFA can be used to determine which variables discriminate between two groups or more. These methods are ideal in this situation where a continuous response variable, such as the nutritional value of household food, has been categorised as a dichotomy with binary coding. In this inquiry a household was coded one if it met a dietary standard and zero if it did not. This was done for each of the dietary standards in Table 5.1. Next, those households meeting all of the standards were coded one to show that they meet the minimum standards of a healthy diet and the rest were coded zero. Statistical models predict whether a household achieves the dietary standard according to the level of household expenditure. Other socio-demographic variables that make a significant contribution are held constant in the model. Lachenbruch (1975) provides further information on DFA and Hosmer and Lemeshow (2000) consider logistic regression. Interested readers may also refer to Townsend and Gordon's work on poverty measurement using these statistical techniques. The analysis presented here develops some of their ideas (see, for example, Townsend and Gordon, 1991; Townsend, 1993; Gordon et al, 2000).

Results

A first step was to examine the household data relating to nutrition. The data for vitamin A and vitamin C were positively skewed and have been corrected by taking the square root of each observation; the rest appear normally distributed. See, for example, the data for single-person households shown in Figure 5.1. Average nutrition levels per person, per day were also found to be comparable with the figures reported by UK government officials for the same period (see Table 5.2). With this observation we can be fairly confident that the FSA conversion factors were correctly applied to the EFS data in this inquiry.

Figure 5.1: Nutrient distributions (singles)[a]

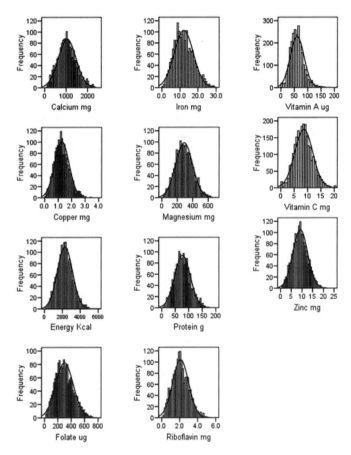

Note: [a]The data for Vitamin A and Vitamin C have been corrected by square-root transformation.

Table 5.2: Average nutrition levels per person per day (study and official estimates)

		Study calculations 2002–05 60+	Official figures 2002–05[a] 65–74
Calcium	mg	1,168	1,171
Copper	mg	1.5	–
Energy	kcal	2,628	2,663
Fat	g	108	110
Folate	ug	351	350
Iron	mg	14.1	14.2
Magnesium	mg	329	332
Protein	g	89.3	91.4
Riboflavin	mg	2.4	2.4
Vitamin A[b]	ug	4,496	4,442
Vitamin C	mg	86	86
Zinc	mg	10.6	10.9

Notes: [a] ONS (2006, p 84); [b] Retinol equivalents.

Next we evaluate the household data against the dietary standards, a necessary step in determining the budget lines. The findings shown in Table 5.3 observe age- and sex-specific recommendations. For more than half the sample the food acquired during the reference period fails to meet the minimum standards of nutrition and there is a clear relationship with expenditure, shown by quintile group (each group will include approximately 20% of the households within the sample). Less than 20% of singles meet the minimum standards in the bottom quintile group compared to 60% in the top quintile group. For couples the figures are 32% and 53% respectively.

Table 5.3: Households meeting the minimum standards of nutrition

	Singles (%)	Couples (%)
Minimum standard	44	47
Calcium	82	87
Copper	59	67
Energy	68	65
Folate	78	88
Iron	76	84
Magnesium	58	63
Protein	85	91
Riboflavin	86	91
Vitamin A	95	98
Vitamin C	74	84
Zinc	69	73

Further analysis shows a positive relationship between household nutrition and expenditure. Figure 5.2 shows the results for singles by quintile group and Figure 5.3 provides the results for couples. Error bars represent 95% confidence intervals from the mean. Virtually all of the nutrients, including energy, show a low but significant relationship with expenditure and are retained for the budget calculations (see Table 5.4).

A multivariate logistic regression model established the independent effect of a number of socio-economic and demographic factors relating to meeting the minimum dietary standard. This is important with surveys of food and diet in Britain reporting variations in nutrient intake by certain sections of the population (Finch et al, 1998). The relative odds of meeting the minimum dietary standard are shown for each factor; the 'base case' is always one (1.00). Table 5.5 shows strong negative

Figure 5.2: The relationship between household nutrition and expenditure (£ per week singles)

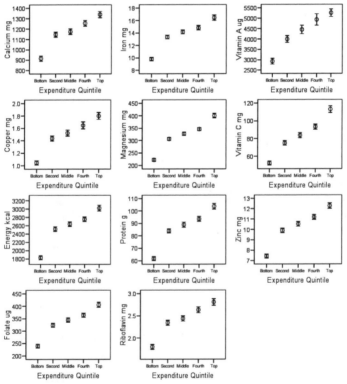

expenditure gradients; older people in the lowest expenditure groups have less chance of meeting the dietary standard. The effects are stronger in the singles data; those in the highest expenditure groups are at least five times as likely to meet the minimum standard as those in the lowest group. There are also significant differences in the expenditure data for couples; those in the highest expenditure groups are twice as likely to meet the minimum standard compared to those in the lowest group.

Figure 5.3: The relationship between household nutrition and expenditure (£ per week couples)

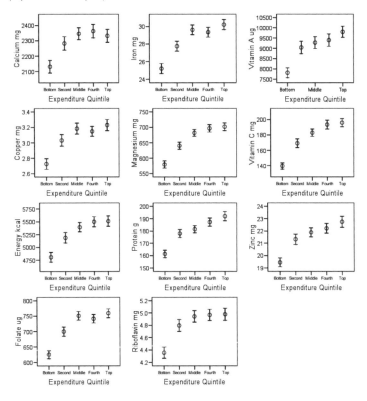

Table 5.4: The relationship between household nutrition and expenditure (£ per week)

	Singles		Couples	
	Pearson correlations	Significance	Pearson correlations	Significance
Calcium	0.162	***	0.041	*
Copper	0.191	***	0.077	***
Energy	0.203	***	0.071	***
Folate	0.199	***	0.103	***
Iron	0.206	***	0.97	***
Magnesium	0.273	***	0.118	***
Protein	0.224	***	0.108	***
Riboflavin	0.168	***	0.069	***
Vitamin A	0.148	***	0.082	***
Vitamin C	0.246	***	0.137	***
Zinc	0.220	***	0.090	***

Note: Key to significance levels (1-tailed): *<0.05; **<0.01; ***<0.001

Single women have more chance of meeting the dietary standard compared to single men. In the data for couples, ethnicity and the age at which the household reference person ceased full-time education were important. The data also suggest that more food is consumed around Christmas time, in the month of December, as might be expected. Geographical region, however, did not appear to have a strong influence on diet in this study.

Drawing a budget line is an exercise in demarcation. Lines need to be drawn and they have to be made clear and precise. The results from the logistic regression in Figure 5.4 shows the predicted probability of meeting the dietary standard based on continuous household expenditure data. Here the budget line for singles appears to correspond to the point where over 90% are expected to meet the dietary standard, a significant break occurs in the expenditure data at £110.00 per week. For couples, the budget line corresponds to a point where nearly 80% are predicted to meet the minimum standard, again a significant break can be observed in the expenditure data at £170.00 per week.

Table 5.5: Logistic regression model predicting the odds of meeting the dietary standard

	Singles	Couples[a]
Expenditure quintile		
Top	1.00	1.00
Second	0.71*	1.08
Middle	0.64**	1.09
Fourth	0.44***	0.75***
Bottom	0.15***	0.49***
Age		
60-69	1.00	1.00
70-79	0.84	0.94
80+	0.62***	0.64***
Sex		
Male	1.00	–
Female	1.31**	–
Ethnicity		
White	1.00	1.00
Black and minority ethnic	0.84	0.81**
Sample month		
January	1.00	1.00
February	0.84	1.06
March	0.78	0.83
April	1.07	1.02
May	0.86	0.96
June	1.15	0.92
July	0.84	1.43**
August	0.82	1.00
September	0.85	1.14
October	0.98	1.25
November	0.84	1.14
December	1.05	1.73***
Region of residence		
Northern Ireland	1.00	1.00
Scotland	0.84	1.01
Wales	1.24	1.16
South West	1.02	0.88
South East	1.29	1.26
London	1.19	1.24
East of England	1.10	0.86
West Midlands	1.12	1.20
East Midlands	1.20	1.00
Yorkshire and the Humber	1.50	1.04
North West	1.14	1.25
North East	1.20	1.29
Education[b]		
Left at school-leaving age	1.00	1.00
Continued in education	1.06	1.12*
Correctly classified (%)	63.6	64.9

Notes: Key to significance levels: *<0.05; **<0.01; ***<0.001
[a] For couples, personal data relate to the household reference person.
[b] Note that in 1947 the school-leaving age was raised from 14 to 15.

Figure 5.4: Predicted probabilities of meeting the dietary standard

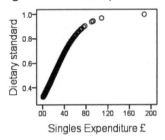

Singles Expenditure £

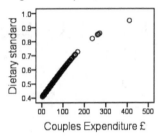

Couples Expenditure £

It is interesting to note that the estimated poverty line for couples is around 50% higher than for singles, which corresponds to the usual equivalence scale estimates (see, for example, the review by the OECD, not dated). DFA can also be used to test the reliability of the findings. In the next stage of the analysis discriminant models are used to predict whether a household meets the dietary standard according to its level of household expenditure. Household expenditure was entered into the model using a banding scheme that increased by £5.00. Other significant predictor variables are held constant in the model (eg, age, sex, etc). For example, single-person households were assigned to one of the two dietary groups if their household expenditure was greater or less than £50.00, greater or less than £55.00 and so on. The model predicts whether a household meets the dietary standard according to the level of expenditure. We are interested in the best fitting model that may help to confirm the budget line in this inquiry. In Table 5.6 we see the optimum classification in the singles sample was 63%, indicating a poverty threshold of £110.00 per week, for couples it was 59% indicating a threshold of £175.00 per week.

The discriminant models classify 62% of all households correctly. This prediction is certainly better than results expected by chance. If we assume all households meet the standard we would classify 45% correctly by chance or 55% if we assumed all households fail to meet

Table 5.6: Semi-normative budget line 2005 prices

	Expenditure (£)	Chi^2	Wilks' lambda	Eigenvalue	Canonical correlation	Correctly classified (%)
Singles	110.00	172.3***	0.93	0.080	0.272	63.0
Couples	175.00	323.9***	0.96	0.039	0.195	58.9

Note: Key to significance levels: *<0.05; **<0.01; ***<0.001

the standard. We might therefore conclude that the overall hit rate was, at best, 17% better than chance or 7% at worst. The findings suggest that the expenditure variable in the calculation is able to discriminate to a degree that is unlikely to be due to chance. We know this because the chi-square results are all significant. The model fails to account for 95% of the variance in dietary status (the Wilks' lambda scores are around 0.95); however, this should not concern us too much as we are not trying to explain people's behaviour here.

The number of older people with 'disposable income' below the estimated budget line can be calculated ('disposable income' here means total household income after deductions for housing costs). About a quarter of the older population were at risk of 'absolute poverty' as defined for this inquiry. 'Absolute poverty' may be defined in a number of different ways, however. Another measure, for example, suggests a pensioner poverty rate of 9% for 2006/07. Here 'absolute poverty' is based on a poverty line that is fixed in real terms at 60% of 1996/97 median income and has then been up-rated in line with prices each year (Brewer et al, 2009).

Conclusion

The inquiry has attempted to determine food poverty lines for an older population. In so doing it helps to shed more light on the levels of household expenditure required to secure a healthy standard of living in practice. In the logistic regression model the budget line of £110.00 per week for singles corresponds to the point where over 90% are expected to meet the minimum dietary standard and the budget line for couples of £170.00 per week corresponds to the point where nearly 80% are predicted to meet the standard. Further modelling with DFA helped to confirm these findings.

Setting a poverty standard purely in relation to the tendency of people below that line to have inadequate diets is just one feature of 'poverty' however, and thus most useful if looked at alongside other research-based income standards for older people. In this sense the semi-normative budgets are striking in terms of the similarity to other best estimates of minimum income thresholds shown in Table 5.7. The Pension Credit guarantee, the official welfare safety-net for pensioners in the UK, also compares favourably against the semi-normative budgets. This suggests that the government's guarantee is probably sufficient to keep most pensioners with low incomes out of 'absolute' poverty, if the entitlement is claimed in full. The problem is that many pensioners fail to claim the money to which they are entitled; the latest figures suggest at least one fifth (DWP, 2008).

Table 5.7: Comparable budget standards for older people in the UK[a]

	Single (£)	Couple (£)
Semi-normative budget line 2005 prices	110.00	170.00
Pension Credit guarantee April 2005	109.45	167.05
Minimum Income for Healthy Living (MIHL) April 2005[b]	122.70	192.10
Low Cost but Acceptable (LCA) April 2005[c]	116.03	169.94
Semi-normative budget line up-rated to April 2008 prices[d]	120.00	186.00
Minimum Income Standard (MIS) April 2008[e]	123.27	183.72

Notes: [a] Disposable household incomes, AHC, that is, excluding housing costs.
[b] English households, people aged 65 or more, budgets exclude housing costs (Morris et al, 2005).
[c] UK households, people aged 65–74, budgets exclude alcohol and housing costs (Family Budget Unit, 2006).
[d] Inflation adjusted to the nearest pound using the UK's non-housing RPI (CHAZ) (ONS, 2009).
[e] British households, pensioners, budgets exclude housing costs (Bradshaw et al, 2008).

We might wish to raise concern to the extent that some lower poverty thresholds might de facto under-estimate the number of people who miss out on an important feature of life (good diet) as a result of low income, and a clear statement of this limitation would indeed be pertinent. However, it would also seem appropriate to draw attention only to differences that are fairly substantial and with all but the MIS comparisons within 5% of the semi-normative figures, and the MIS ones about 10% different, such concerns may not be warranted.

In summary, the additional information that the inquiry provides is not a measure of whether a level of income (defined here by expenditure) *can* secure a healthy standard of living but rather whether it *does* so in practice, given the spending choices made by individuals. Family and household budget standards research in the Rowntree tradition can claim the former, that is, they are able to show what families and households are able to secure, whereas the current research is about the latter, that is, demonstrating what families and households succeed in securing in practice.

Future work might consider family households with children. The nutritional needs of the household unit can be calculated by summing the nutritional requirements for each person within the household, like the calculations for couples in this inquiry. Additional research might also explore the relationship between food poverty and other forms of deprivation using data emerging from the new Integrated Household Survey (IHS).The UK Office for National Statistics (ONS) is currently in the process of integrating a number of national surveys, including the EFS, into a single household survey. Soon detailed information on poverty and living conditions will become available from the new IHS, which should allow us to examine aspects of poor nutrition and other forms of material deprivation in further detail. ONS are also planning to include firm measures of educational status, including highest qualification, which would benefit any future work of this kind (ONS, 2008).

References

Banks, J. and Johnson, P. (eds) (1998) *How reliable is the Family Expenditure Survey? Trends in incomes and expenditure over time*, London: Institute for Fiscal Studies.

Banks, J., Blundell, R. and Tanner, S. (1998) 'Is there a retirement savings puzzle?', *American Economic Review*, vol 88, no 4, pp 769-88.

BNF (British Nutrition Foundation) (2007) *Healthy eating, nutrition through life, older adults*, London: BNF.

Boltvinik, J. (1998) *Poverty measurement methods – An overview*, Poverty Reduction Series Working Paper No 3, New York, NY: United Nations Development Program, Social Development and Poverty Elimination Division.

Boyd Orr, J. (1936) *Food health and income: Report on a survey of adequacy of diet in relation to income*, London: Macmillan.

Bradshaw, J. (ed) (1993) *Budget standards for the United Kingdom*, Avebury: Ashgate.

Bradshaw, J. (2001) 'The measurement of absolute poverty', in E. Schokkaert (ed) *Ethics and social security reform*, Aldershot: Ashgate, pp 105-39.

Bradshaw, J., Middleton, S., Davis, A., Oldfield, N., Smith, N., Cusworth, L. and Williams, J. (2008) *A minimum income standard for Britain: What people think*, York: The Joseph Rowntree Foundation.

Brewer, M., Goodman, A. and Leicester, A. (2006) *Household spending in Britain: What can it teach us about poverty?*, Bristol: The Policy Press.

Brewer, M., Muriel, A., Phillips, D. and Sibieta, L. (2009) *Poverty and inequality in the UK: 2009*, IFS Commentary No 105, London: Institute for Fiscal Studies.

Burgess, A.L. and Bunker, V.W. (2002) 'An investigation of school meals eaten by primary schoolchildren', *British Food Journal*, vol 104, no 9, pp 705-12.

Citro, C.F. and Michael, R.T. (eds) (1995) *Measuring poverty: A new approach*, Washington, DC: National Academy Press.

Craggs, A. (ed) (2003) *Family spending: A report on the 2002–2003 Expenditure and Food Survey*, London: The Stationery Office.

Crockett, A. (2006) *Weighting the social surveys*, Colchester: Economic and Social Data Service (www.esds.ac.uk/government/docs/weighting.pdf).

Deeming, C. (2005) 'Minimum income standards: how might budget standards be set for the UK?', *Journal of Social Policy*, vol 34, no 4, pp 1-18.

DH (Department of Health) (1991) *Dietary reference values for food energy and nutrients for the United Kingdom. Report of the Panel on Dietary Reference Values of the Committee on Medical Aspects of Food Policy*, Report on Health and Social Subjects 41, London: HMSO.

DH (1992) *The nutrition of elderly people. Report of the Working Group of the Committee on Medical Aspects of Food Policy*, Report on Health and Social Subjects 43, London: HMSO.

DH (1998) *Nutrition and bone health: With particular reference to calcium and vitamin D*, Report on Health and Social Subjects 49, London: The Stationery Office.

Dowler, E., Turner, S. and Dobson, B. (2001) *Poverty bites: Food, health and poor families*, London: Child Poverty Action Group.

DWP (Department for Work and Pensions) (2008) *Income related benefits: Estimates of take-up in 2006–08*, London: DWP Analytical Services Division.

Evandrou, M. and Falkingham, J. (2009) 'Pensions and income security in later life', in J. Hills, T. Sefton and K. Stewart (eds) *Towards a more equal society? Poverty, inequality and policy since 1997*, Bristol: The Policy Press, pp 157-77.

Expert Group on Poverty Statistics ('Rio Group') (2006) *Compendium of best practices on poverty measurement*, Rio de Janeiro: United Nations.

Expert Group on Vitamins and Minerals (2003) *Vitamin D*, London: Food Standards Agency.

Family Budget Unit (2006) *Low Cost but Acceptable budget for pensioners April 2006*, York: Family Budget Unit.

Finch, S., Doyle, W., Lowe, C., Bates, C.J., Prentice, A., Smithers, G. and Clarke, P.C. (1998) *National diet and nutrition survey: People aged 65 years and over, Volume 1: Report of the diet and nutrition survey*, London: The Stationery Office.

FSA (Food Standards Agency) (2002) *McCance and Widdowson's The composition of foods*, Cambridge: Royal Society of Chemistry.

Gibbins, C. (ed) (2005) *Family spending: A report on the 2003-04 Expenditure and Food Survey*, Houndmills: Palgrave Macmillan.

Gibbins, C. and Georgina, J. (eds) (2006) *Family spending: A report on the 2004–05 Expenditure and Food Survey*, Houndmills: Palgrave Macmillan.

Gordon, D., Adelman, L., Ashworth, K., Bradshaw, J., Levitas, R., Middleton, S., Pantazis, C., Patsios, D., Payne, S., Townsend, P. and Williams, J. (2000) *Poverty and social exclusion in Britain*, York: The Joseph Rowntree Foundation.

Hatfield, M. (2002) *Constructing the revised market basket measure*, Québec: Applied Research Branch, Strategic Policy, Human Resources Development Canada.

Hosmer, D.W. and Lemeshow, S. (2000) *Applied logistic regression* (2nd edn), New York, NY: John Wiley & Sons.

Lachenbruch, P.A. (1975) *Discriminant analysis*, New York, NY: Hafner Press.

Lambert, R. (1964) *Nutrition in Britain, 1950–60: A critical discussion of the standards and findings on the National Food Survey*, Welwyn: The Codicote Press.

Leslie, W.S., Lean, M.E.J., Woodward, M., Wallace, F.A. and Hankey, C.R. (2006) 'Unidentified under-nutrition: dietary intake and anthropometric indices in a residential care home population', *Journal of Human Nutrition and Dietetics*, vol 19, no 5, pp 343-7.

Lindsay, D.E. (1913) *Report upon the Study of the Diet of the Labouring Classes in the City of Glasgow carried out under the auspices of the Corporation of the City*, Glasgow: Glasgow Corporation.

McKenzie, J.C. (1971) 'Poverty: food and nutrition indices', in P. Townsend (ed) *The concept of poverty*, London: Heinemann, pp 64-85.

MAFF (Ministry of Agriculture, Fisheries and Food) (1991) *Household food consumption and expenditure 1990 with a study of trends over the period 1940–1990*, London: HMSO.

Middleton, S. (2000) 'Agreeing poverty lines: the development of consensual budget standards methodology', in J. Bradshaw and R. Sainsbury (eds) *Researching poverty*, Ashgate: Aldershot, pp 59-76.

Morris, J.N., Dangour, A., Deeming, C., Fletcher, A. and Wilkinson, P. (2005) *Minimum income for healthy living: Older people*, London: Age Concern England.

Morris, J.N., Donkin, A.J.M., Wonderling, D., Wilkinson, P. and Dowler, E. (2000) 'A minimum income for healthy living', *Journal of Epidemiology and Community Health*, vol 54, no 12, pp 885-9.

National Economic and Social Development Board (2004) *Thailand's official poverty lines*, Makati City: National Statistical Coordination Board.

Nelder, J.A. and Wedderburn, R.W.M. (1972) 'General linear models', *Journal of the Royal Statistical Society Series A (General)*, vol 135, no 3, pp 370-84.

Nelson, M., Erens, B., Bates, B., Church, S. and Boshier, T. (2007) *Low income diet and nutrition survey: Summary of key findings*, London: The Stationery Office.

OECD (Organisation for Economic Co-operation and Development) (not dated) *What are equivalence scales?*, OECD Social Policy Division (www.oecd.org/dataoecd/61/52/35411111.pdf).

ONS (Office for National Statistics) (2006) *Family food in 2004–05: A report on the 2004–05 Expenditure and Food Survey*, London: The Stationery Office.

ONS (2008) *Integrated Household Survey update May 2008*, London: ONS (www.statistics.gov.uk/articles/nojournal/IHS_web_update_May08.pdf).

ONS (2009) *Retail Prices Index: Monthly index numbers of retail prices 1948–2009*, Update 5/5/09, London: ONS.

ONS/Defra (Department for Environment Food and Rural Affairs) (2006) *Expenditure and Food Survey 2002–2003, 2003–2004, 2004–2005*, Colchester, Essex: UK Data Archive, Computer files SN: 5003, 5375, 5210 (www.esds.ac.uk).

Orshansky, M. (1988) 'Counting the poor: another look at the poverty profile (reprint)', *Social Security Bulletin*, vol 51, no 10, pp 25-51.

Parker, H. (ed) (2000) *Low Cost but Acceptable incomes for older people: A minimum income standard for households aged 65–74 years in the UK*, Bristol: The Policy Press.

Paton, D.N., Dunlop, J.C. and Inglis, E.M. (1901) *A Study of the Diet of the Labouring Classes in Edinburgh, carried out under the auspices of the Town Council of the city of Edinburgh*, Edinburgh: Otto Schulze.

Paton, N. and Findlay, L. (1926) *Poverty, nutrition and growth*, London: HMSO.

Shaw, M. (1999) 'Measuring eating habits: some problems with the National Food Survey', in D. Dorling and S. Simpson (eds) *Statistics in society: The arithmetic of politics*, London: Arnold, pp 140-7.

Sproston, K. and Primatesta, P. (eds) (2004) *Health Survey for England 2003. Volume 2: Risk factors for cardiovascular disease*, London: The Stationery Office.

Svedberg, P. (2000) *Poverty and undernutrition: Theory, measurement, and policy*, Oxford: Oxford University Press.

Titmuss, R.M. (1938) *Poverty and population: A factual study of contemporary social waste*, London: Macmillan and Co.

Townsend, P. (1962) 'The meaning of poverty', *British Journal of Sociology*, vol 13, no 3, pp 210-27.

Townsend, P. (1993) *The international analysis of poverty*, London: Harvester Wheatsheaf.

Townsend, P. and Gordon, D. (1991) 'What is enough? New evidence on poverty', in M. Adler, C. Bell, J. Clasen and A. Sinfield (eds) *The sociology of social security*, Edinburgh: Edinburgh University Press, pp 35-69.

WHO (World Health Organization)/Tufts University School of Nutrition Science and Policy (2002) *Keep fit for life: Meeting the nutritional needs of older persons*, Geneva: WHO.

Wingfield, D., Fenwick, D. and Smith, K. (2005) 'Relative regional consumer price levels in 2004', *Economic Trends*, vol 615, pp 36-46.

Wolff, P. (2009) *79 million EU citizens were at-risk-of-poverty in 2007, of whom 32 million were also materially deprived*, Eurostat Statistics in focus 46/2009, Luxembourg: Office for Official Publications of the European Communities.

Zaidi, A. and Burchardt, T. (2005) 'Comparing incomes when needs differ: equalization for the extra costs of disability in the UK', *Review of Income and Wealth*, vol 51, no 1, pp 89-114.

Part Two
Current issues and debates

Chris Holden

Re-connecting with 'what unemployment means': employability, the experience of unemployment and priorities for policy in an era of crisis

Colin Lindsay

Introduction

To plan for a society that involves all its members and actively promotes their participation in its work, we have to recognise more fully what unemployment means and how it affects not only those who are forced to waste substantial parts of their working lives, but also the great majority of the population. Until we do, the heaviest costs are borne by many of the poorest members of society, and that whole society is diminished. (Sinfield, 1981a, p 157)

"In the old days, the problem may have been unemployment, but in the next decades it will be employability. If in the old days lack of jobs demanded priority action, in the new world it is lack of skills." (Remarks by the Prime Minister, Rt Hon Gordon Brown MP, 2 January 2008)

It has been more than 40 years since Sinfield's (1968, p 13) seminal cross-national study highlighted the costs and consequences of long-term unemployment – the 'national and individual misfortune' of 'lost productivity and life wasted'. Writing at a time when long-term unemployment was generally low in OECD (Organisation for Economic Co-operation and Development) countries, he was then sharply critical of policy makers' lack of concern over the less acknowledged social and individual consequences of labour market exclusion. While economists were able to estimate the cost in lost taxation revenue of rising joblessness, Sinfield noted that the personal and psychological impacts of long-term unemployment on individuals appeared to be of less concern – 'it is easier to discover that a man's income has dropped by fifty percent ... than what it means to him to be unemployed after fifteen years of regular work' (Sinfield, 1968, p 52). Writing some years later, as the UK entered a period of deep recession and high unemployment in the early 1980s, the same author returned to the theme of how we need to 'understand more fully what unemployment means' and attack the full range of causes and consequences, supply-side and demand-side factors linked to long-term unemployment (Sinfield, 1981a, p 157). As the UK again faces the impact of a period of severe recession, and policy makers grapple with the consequences of increasing job losses, there is a need to renew our efforts to understand the impacts on individuals, and offer advice on what works in supporting long-term unemployed people to cope and move towards work.

This chapter reviews the evidence on the nature and extent of barriers to work faced by long-term unemployed people and critically assesses whether current policies (and indeed thinking) are fit for purpose in combating long-term unemployment in an era of economic crisis. The starting point for this discussion is the concept of employability, which has arguably provided the dominant framework for both UK and EU policy makers' approaches to unemployment and labour market policy for more than a decade. I want to argue that employability, as understood by UK policy makers in recent times, represents a 'hollowed out' concept that focuses almost solely on a small sample of the individual's assumed failings (with the emphasis usually on gaps in motivation and 'generic' skills) rather than acknowledging that a person's employability, and vulnerability to unemployment, is inevitably defined by their interaction with the labour market, public policy and other external forces. This matters, because such a (mis-)understanding of what unemployment and employability mean has led to a policy agenda, now endorsed by both major political parties in the UK, that: (a) prioritises 'Work First' employability programmes that offer few long-term benefits in terms of the sustainability of work and individuals' human capital development; (b) neglects the importance of job destruction and area-based disadvantage in explaining the tenacity and concentration of unemployment in some communities; and (c) buys into a 'hysterisis' thesis that sees long-term unemployment as the problem in itself, rather than seeking to target the combination of individual, personal and external/labour market factors that leave some people at greater risk of becoming long-term unemployed.

Following this introduction, the chapter discusses how a narrowly defined, hollowed out concept of employability has been deployed in recent policy debates in the UK, and then how this has fed into thinking on how to combat long-term unemployment. The chapter then offers a critique of the current Work First, supply-side focus of UK employability strategies. A more holistic model for understanding employability is deployed to consider evidence on the range of barriers faced by long-term unemployed people (including local/regional labour market conditions in times of both recession and growth). Finally, options for future policy development are briefly discussed.

Employability and labour market policy

The concept of employability has been around for more than a century, but was relatively obscure in the social and labour market policy literature until just over a decade ago (see McQuaid and Lindsay, 2005, for a review of the concept's development and use). Yet since the late 1990s, employability has emerged as one of the intellectual pillars of social and labour market policies in the UK, and for some time it was (and less explicitly remains) *the key element* in the European Employment Strategy (Serrano Pascual and Magnusson, 2007). But how employability is understood and operationalised remains contested territory. For UK policy makers, employability often continues to be defined narrowly, in terms of a specific set of individual characteristics (usually focused on motivation, 'adaptability' to employers' needs and generic skills). Soon after the newly elected Labour government entered power in 1997, it unveiled a range of employability-focused policies, where 'employability means the development of skills and adaptable workforces in which all those capable of work are encouraged to develop the skills, knowledge, technology and adaptability to enable them to enter and remain in employment throughout their working lives' (HM Treasury, 1997, p 1). Successive policy documents continued to define employability narrowly, with reference to improving individuals' basic skills and 'confidence in working' (DWP, 2006, p 43), and as we have seen above, 10 years after the introduction of his government's flagship New Deal programmes, Prime Minister Gordon Brown re-emphasised the centrality of the supply-side analysis within his approach to employability.

Thus, the Labour Party replaced its historic commitment to full employment with a promise of 'full employability' (Finn, 2003) – equality of outcome in the immediate term was less the objective than equality of opportunity, with more general benefits in the longer term (Lister, 2001). The objective of the employability agenda as formulated here was the creation of a higher skilled labour force and a more inclusive and competitive active labour market, leading to the combined benefits of social inclusion on the one hand, and downward pressures on wage inflation and improved productivity and competitiveness on the other. One of the obvious weaknesses of such an approach is its reinforcement of supply-side orthodoxies that fail to reflect how differences in local and regional labour demand (and job quality) impact on individuals' employability (Theodore, 2007). As Macnicol (2008, p 592) succinctly summarises: 'improving employability does not by itself create jobs'.

Employability and long-term unemployment

A similar dynamic defines debates around the specific issue of long-term unemployment. Supply-side labour economists have been successful in convincing policy makers that 'duration dependency' – the increased likelihood of continued unemployment among the long-term jobless due to the deterioration of skills, work habits and commitment over time – has a major role to play in explaining high levels of structural unemployment. This approach argues that hysterisis effects associated with long-term unemployment can artificially ratchet up the overall 'natural' rate of unemployment within a given economy. Accordingly, it is suggested that targeting activation on long-term unemployed people can impact on the employability of individual clients, and ratchet down the overall rate of unemployment. This reflects the broader analysis at the heart of much orthodox supply-side labour market economics. For de Koning et al (2004, p 4), 'The starting point is that, if we increase the supply of labour, we will increase employment'. Such thinking has been popular with recent UK governments, as have been the fundamentally supply-side policies that it has informed, from keeping benefit replacement rates relatively low (Nickell, 2001) to increasing compulsion on the unemployed to re-engage in the labour market, for example through Work First activation (Layard, 2000).

As noted above, those criticising such supply-side approaches to employability have pointed to the structural labour market problems (for example, limited demand following recession or industrial restructuring) that appear to contribute to the tenacity of long-term unemployment in some areas. For Macnicol (2008, p 587) 'supply-side optimism cannot obscure some very real underlying structural problems … to be sure, more people working is associated with an expanding economy; but is likely that economic growth is the cause of employment growth, rather than the other way around. An economy cannot grow without a supply of labour, but labour supply does not of itself guarantee economic growth'. Webster (2000, 2005) has offered compelling evidence that hysterisis effects are less likely to explain concentrations of long-term unemployment than are processes of mass job loss and deficient or inappropriate demand in post-industrial labour markets – as we will see below, this position appears to be backed by evaluation evidence on the impact of programmes seeking to tackle unemployment.

Yet despite the evidence, there seems little hope of a shift in approaches to explaining or tackling long-term unemployment in the short term. The Conservatives see long-term unemployment as a problem of individuals' declining value in the labour market. Indeed for David Cameron, concentrations of long-term unemployment are explained by way of a familiar-sounding homily: 'Cyclical unemployment becomes structural unemployment. There's a clever term for this – hysterisis…. When someone loses their job, they very often lose their self-esteem and from there it's very easy to lose hope. The longer they are out of a job, the more their social and economic skills diminish, and the harder it is to get work' (Cameron, 2008).

Of course, any criticism of such a position is not to deny that combating long-term unemployment should be a priority for employability and labour market policies. As we will see below, long-term unemployed people (like members of other disadvantaged groups) are more likely to face multiple barriers to work that will affect their future employability, including low levels of occupational and technical skills, limited recent and relevant work experience, a lack of formal qualifications, a lack of awareness of, and connection to, growing sectors of the economy and limited geographical mobility (Dex and McCulloch, 1997; Hasluck et al, 1997; McQuaid and Lindsay, 2002; Dean, 2003). There is also ample evidence that the experience of long-term unemployment can have a range of negative consequences in relation to the risk of poverty (Sinfield, 1968, 1981a; Clasen et al, 1997; Green and Owen, 2006), declining health (Waddell and Burton, 2006) and increasing social isolation (Julkunen, 2002; Lindsay et al, 2005; Lindsay, 2010). The problem is that UK employability policy has become locked into an analysis that sees long-term unemployment as its own cause and largely explained by individuals' failings in relation to a narrowly defined set of skills and attributes. The logical conclusion of such an analysis has been that long-term unemployed people should be subject to compulsory Work First activation programmes, and this agenda has indeed increasingly dominated the UK policy landscape (see below).

This error always matters, but particularly in an era of economic crisis, where rises in long-term unemployment are certain to follow from increased general unemployment as a result of job destruction (Webster, 2005). The solution cannot be found in Work First programmes that impose compulsory supply-side activation on the victims of a demand-side crisis. Yet the 'steady drift in the emphasis in economic thinking from the demand-side to the supply-side' (Krugman, 2009, p 182) has left us with few strategies to coherently link services for the long-term unemployed to the macro-economic interventions required to simulate jobs growth. Rather, policy makers have demonstrated their loyalty to an increasingly inadequate Work First approach to employability.

The UK's Work First approach to employability

The Labour government elected in 1997 described its employability and labour market policy as a 'Work First approach to moving people from welfare into work' (DWP, 2003, p 3). For ministers, establishing 'a Work First service for all people of working age' (HM Treasury, 2001, p 32) was central to early reforms such as the introduction of programmes like the New Deals, while the need 'to reinforce the Work First principle' (DWP, 2007, p 82) has more recently informed increasingly aggressive activation soon after job seekers make a claim for benefit. Lindsay et al (2007) suggest that the precise definition of Work First is unclear from policy documents, but that there was and remains an obvious emphasis on job seekers, wherever possible, moving quickly towards any kind of work. As Peck and Theodore (2000a) note, and as argued above, the roots of UK policy makers' Work First thinking are somewhat different from the superficially similar workfare ideology in the US. In the US, workfare polemicists are strongly attached to the idea that a dependency culture among the poor explains persistent unemployment and disadvantage (Murray, 1990; Mead, 2001). Such thinking still leads to its believers advocating Work First policies. For example, Mead (2001) sets up a false dichotomy between Work First activation and a sort of aimless (and probably apocryphal) 'education for education's sake' in order to justify punitive workfare measures. Yet while there are echoes of these arguments in the UK debate, here Work First employability strategies are more clearly rooted in the sort of supply-side labour economics described above – an analysis of long-term unemployment that leads to a belief in 'Work First over training first' as a means of improving labour market outcomes (Layard, 2004, p 5). 'As a result policies seek to address the problem of unemployment at the level of the individual; personal failings rather than a lack of labour market opportunities tend to be used by way of explanation; and Work First programmes have become, in many cases, the new orthodoxy in labour market policy' (Lindsay and Serrano Pascual, 2009, p 952).

Whatever their roots, international reviews have noted a number of common features of Work First employability programmes. Such programmes are short term and often focus on improving the individual's motivation and generic skills (Daguerre, 2007). They tend to restrict access to vocational training and human capital development, so that 'a Work First approach means that workers are allowed to access intensive services such as training only after they prove they cannot find a job without additional skills' (European Foundation, 2004, p 9). Work First measures often operate alongside strong levels of compulsion and conditionality in access to benefits (Daguerre, 2008). And crucially, Work First focuses on 'immediate labour market entry' (Mitchell et al, 2007, p 294), with job search itself often a key activity (if not the only activity) in these programmes (Bruttel and Sol, 2006). Finally, as Bellamy and Rake (2005, p 27) note, Work First programmes 'have targeted participation in employment above and beyond access to quality employment'. 'A Work First strategy ... encourages recipients to take any job, even a low-wage entry-level job' (Handler, 2006, pp 119-20). For Sol and Hoogtanders (2005, p 147), 'the aim is not to establish a long-term career goal but to reinforce the belief that any job is a first career step, no matter how precarious this employment might be'. Work First programmes also tend to offer little by way of engagement with the 'geographically uneven labour market in which people are searching for work' (Grant, 2009, p 331).

Sol and Hoogtanders (2005), and others, distinguish between Work First and human capital-oriented approaches, which conversely prioritise more gradual progress towards employment and long-term skills development, offer a range of other holistic services and support in-work progression. Lindsay et al (2007) have suggested that the policy agenda since 1997 has retained hybrid elements of both approaches. The strengthening of personal adviser provision under the New Deal and its successor Flexible New Deal has been seen as a positive move (Green and Hasluck, 2009). More generally, the inclusion of a wider range of providers and arguably an element of choice in the sort of activities open to job seekers may have resulted in a more 'client-centred experience' for some (Finn, 2003, p 721). The roll-out of Pathways to Work, while extending compulsory activity to those claiming incapacity benefits, has allowed for the development of innovative, voluntary health interventions and new forms of partnership working with the National Health Service (NHS) (DWP, 2008). And area-based policies such as City Strategy Pathfinders have sought to tailor employability provision to reflect the needs of disadvantaged communities and depressed labour markets (Green and Orton, 2009).

However, these inconsistent and halting attempts to incorporate a more holistic, human capital-oriented model of employability provision have been contradicted by a recent increasing focus on contracting out and Work First activation. A reliance on work-focused interviews and structured job search activities has been reinforced by 'payment-by-results' contracting that feeds into the prioritisation of 'quick wins', that is, promoting entry into paid employment for those closest to the labour market. Processes of 'creaming and parking' (targeting the easiest to help rather than those with substantial barriers) have arguably followed (van Berkel and Borghi, 2008). Meanwhile, the intensive, flexible and (if necessary) long-term interventions required by people facing severe health, personal or social problems have not fully materialised (Dean, 2003). Vocational skills development activities remain under-developed, and indeed in some cases prohibited by 'availability for work' rules that job seekers are required to comply with (Smith et al, 2008). For Lindsay et al (2007, p 558), 'there has been limited progress towards the kind of well-resourced, vocational training that is arguably the cornerstone of any genuinely human capital-oriented labour market strategy'.

Nor have these 'schizophrenic attempts to combine Work First and human capital approaches' (Lindsay, 2009, p 182) been able to produce a model of provision that effectively engages with employers or provides adequate in-work progression routes for those gaining entry-level employment. Job seekers are expected to find their way into sectors that may be unfamiliar and that sometimes offer few opportunities for development and progression into better paid work (Lindsay and McQuaid, 2004; Warhurst and Nickson, 2007; Ray et al, 2009). Meanwhile, many employers 'see themselves as the passive recipients of appropriate candidates for job vacancies' (Lindsay and Serrano Pascual, 2009, p 954) – it has proved difficult to persuade them that they have a role to play in providing decent opportunities and support for those entering work after a period of unemployment (Danson and Gilmore, 2009).

In conclusion, it is understandable that for Peck and Theodore (2000a, p 132) little can be achieved by Work First 'in terms of the alleviation of poverty, skill shortages or structural unemployment. Work First programmes are pitched in such a way that ... interventions are far too brief and modest in scope to allow participants an opportunity to move into stable, high-quality jobs'. Given these failings, it is unsurprising that the 'modest and contradictory results' (Lindsay and Serrano Pascual, 2009, p 952) that have been common to Work First programmes across the EU have similarly defined the outcomes achieved for job seekers in the UK. While initial job entry figures were encouraging, the New Deal programmes soon faced an increasing problem of 'revolving door' participation, with clients moving from activation into short-term employment, and then back into unemployment, eventually repeating their participation in activation (Lindsay, 2007). Sunley et al (2001, 2006), McVicar and Podivinsky (2009) and others have also shown that the impact of policies such as the New Deal (in its different forms) has varied significantly across regions of the UK. In areas where mass job losses followed from the decline of traditional industries in the 1980s and 1990s, the performance of such programmes has been least effective: 'In such areas the "recycling and churning" of participants through the programme are more significant, and suggest that local labour market structures play a significant role in shaping policy outcomes' (Sunley et al, 2001, p 484). As MacLeavy (2008, p 1663) concludes: 'In failing to take account of demand-side causes of structural unemployment ... the New Deals can have few positive outcomes in parts of the country and sectors of the population where the need for reform is greatest'. Moreover, the impact of Work First activation in general has been demonstrated to be subject to substantial deadweight effects (Blundell et al, 2003), with local levels of poverty and labour demand the clearest predictors of higher rates of job entry in some areas (GHK, 2004). The emergence of such Work First programmes, and their association with the concept of employability, has led some to question whether the language of employability can be usefully deployed by those seeking a more holistic understanding of the barriers to work faced by unemployed people (Serrano Pascual and Magnusson, 2007). Peck and Theodore (2000b, p 729) suggest that while the concept of employability may seem relatively new, 'the kind of supply side fundamentalism that it signifies most certainly is not'. Similarly, for Haughton et al (2000, p 670): 'the employability agenda taps into the orthodox strain of economic thinking which has it that both the underlying causes of, and the appropriate remedies to, unemployment essentially lie on the supply-side of the labour market'. There is apparent agreement among such critics that 'employability-based approaches, which locate both the problems and the solutions in labour market policy on the supply-side of the economy, are not sufficient to the task of tackling unemployment' (Peck and Theodore, 2000b, p 731).

Nevertheless, others who have sought to use the concept of employability as a means of analysing barriers to work among the unemployed have stressed the need to avoid policies that offer solely narrowly defined supply-side solutions (Hillage and Pollard, 1998; McQuaid and Lindsay, 2005). Indeed, there is a danger that in seeking to move 'beyond employability' (Peck and Theodore, 2000b) – that is, to reject the current supply-side orthodoxy in labour market policy – we risk eliminating a highly useful concept that has the capacity to inform holistic approaches to analysing labour market issues. For McQuaid and Lindsay (2005, p 2150):

> Employability deployed as a broad concept, enabling us to analyse and describe the multi-dimensional barriers to work faced by many unemployed people, offers an opportunity to transcend the orthodoxies of the supply-side *versus* demand-side debate, and arrive at explanations and policy solutions that reflect the multi-faceted and complex combination of factors affecting the labour market interactions of those in and out of work.

The remainder of this chapter reviews some of the key sources of evidence on factors affecting individuals' risk, and experiences, of long-term unemployment. Deploying a holistic 'framework for analysing employability', I hope to demonstrate that the concept of employability is worth retaining, *if* it is formulated so as to help identify the full range of individual factors, personal circumstances and external/labour market issues that help to explain why some individuals are more likely to become long-term unemployed (especially in an era of economic crisis), and what unemployment means in these people's lives.

Beyond Work First: towards a framework for understanding employability and the experience of unemployment

McQuaid and Lindsay (2005) have provided one of a number of holistic models for analysing employability. The McQuaid-Lindsay framework need not be reproduced here in full, but perhaps its defining feature is the manner in which it seeks to clarify and acknowledge the status of *individual factors* (taking in a range of skills sets, personal attributes, qualifications and indicators of labour market attachment) that can be addressed through supply-side policies targeted at job seekers, from *personal circumstances* (health, family and household circumstances, and access to economic and social capital) that may require different policy interventions or may inherently limit individuals' labour market participation. Both of these groups of factors are in turn distinguished from *external factors* (the location, nature and level of labour demand, the actions of employers and other employment/social policy factors that shape people's experiences in and out of the labour market). A review of evidence on the characteristics and experiences of long-term unemployed people suggests that policy interventions in all three of these domains of the McQuaid-Lindsay employability framework will be required at different times and locations by different job seekers. By definition, narrowly focused Work First employability programmes are not equal to the task.

Individual factors and employability

As we have seen above, many definitions of employability concentrate largely or entirely on the *personal attributes* of the individual. For some job seekers, such an approach will be justified in certain circumstances. At the most basic level, it must be acknowledged that essential attributes, self-efficacy and personal competencies, what might be called 'life skills' (Halliday and Hanson, 2004; Taylor, 2005; James, 2007), form part of the foundation for individual employability. *Basic skills* also appear to be important – there is strong evidence to suggest that literacy and numeracy problems increase the risk of repeat and long-term unemployment (Sanderson, 2006; Carpenter, 2007). There are also numerous studies pointing towards the relationship between *qualifications, occupational skills*, employability and experiences of unemployment. For example, Berthoud's (2003) study found that those previously employed in unskilled occupations were more than six times as likely to be out of work as those in higher skilled occupations. Similarly significant differences exist between the lowest and highest qualified (Begum, 2004; Berthoud, 2007). Additionally, job seekers' *labour market attachment* – their work record (including and beyond their most recent work experience) – can have a profound impact on later labour market trajectories (Devins and Hogarth, 2005). Individuals' broad experience in the labour market – for example, whether they consider themselves to have had a 'mostly stable' working life – has been shown to be an effective predictor of long-term unemployment (Lindsay et al, 2003).

Personal circumstances and employability

An emerging literature on employability problems in the UK has focused on the importance of *workless households*, in part echoing some of the concerns of the dependency culture thesis. Related ideas around intergenerational transmitted worklessness, where parents' unemployment transmits a lack of work ethic to their children, have not been supported by evidence, partly because of the difficulty in separating out structural factors such as poverty and low educational attainment from attitudinal and parenting issues, and partly because the majority of children from the most deprived families and neighbourhoods move ahead of their parents in terms of labour market status (Such and Walker, 2002).

However, beyond the 'workless household' issue, family *caring roles* can limit the ability of some job seekers to take on full-time and/or time- and place-specific work. Research with unemployed parents has consistently highlighted how parents' commitment to caring, combined with weaknesses in childcare provision, can reduce the range of opportunities that are accessible (Smith et al, 2008). Similar issues are often faced by people with adult caring responsibilities, whose opportunities can be limited by the scope for flexibility allowed by caring roles, gaps in local support services and employers' willingness to accommodate carers' needs (Arksey and Glendinning, 2008).

Those experiencing *ill health* will inevitably face additional problems in finding and sustaining work (Berthoud, 2007). One in five repeat claimants of Jobseeker's Allowance have been shown to have health problems (Carpenter, 2007). Green and Owen (2006) highlight how health and other factors can combine to severely limit opportunity, so that, for example, those job seekers with low educational attainment and health problems are significantly less likely to make transitions to work. Of course, the experience of unemployment may impact on the individual's health, but Waddell and Burton (2006) argue that any health benefits associated with employment depend on a range of issues including job security and quality, and the individual's capacity for work.

There is evidence that access to *social capital* (in the form of social networks) can facilitate effective job seeking, and therefore contribute to a return to work (Hannan, 1999; Lévesque and White, 2001). But there is also evidence that long-term unemployed people can struggle to access such networks (Julkunen, 2002; Lindsay et al, 2005; Gore and Hollywood, 2009; Lindsay, 2010). Gallie et al (2003) make the link between long-term unemployment, poverty and experiences of social exclusion. They suggest that the isolation experienced by some job seekers 'may seriously accentuate the psychological deprivations arising from unemployment', and identify a vicious circle created by a benefits system that forces the unemployed into poverty and social exclusion – 'unemployment heightens the risk of people falling into poverty, and poverty in turn makes it more difficult for people to return to work' (Gallie et al, 2003, pp 28-9).

External factors and employability

In line with the discussion above, the McQuaid-Lindsay framework highlights how employability cannot be understood without reference to the extent, nature and location of labour demand. We know that living in an area of strong local labour demand increases the likelihood of exits from unemployment, especially for those with fewer skills (Green and Owen, 2006). Yet despite claims of unfilled vacancies during the UK's 'long boom' of the 1990s and 2000s, job loss in some cities and regions during the 1980s was never fully matched by 'new economy' growth (Shuttleworth et al, 2005; Sanderson, 2006). There is a clear relationship between processes of industrial decline and job destruction on the one hand and rates of claiming of a range of working-age benefits, including incapacity benefits on the other (Beatty et al, 2009). Indeed, the diversion of job seekers to incapacity benefits has been identified as substantially reducing 'official' unemployment in declining former mining areas (Gore and Hollywood, 2009), major cities (Turok, 2007), rural areas (Beatty and Fothergill, 1997) and seaside towns (Beatty and Fothergill, 2003). Clearly, broader macro-level demand deficiency is a key problem thrown up by economic crises like the one that began in 2008. Local, regional and national labour markets have been affected. In an era of crisis, increases in both general and long-term unemployment are primarily explained by the weakness of labour demand, and strategies to improve the employability of the long-term unemployed will make little sense (or progress) if they are not linked to a plan to stimulate the growth of new jobs.

Even where local labour demand has remained relatively strong, there can still be problems fitting unemployed people to jobs. Devins and Hogarth (2005) note that individuals' employability can be affected by problems of mismatch between the mainly service-oriented opportunities that are growing in local, especially urban, labour markets and the large numbers of redundant workers who would prefer manual jobs (see also Ray et al, 2009). To this end, Houston (2005, p 225) provides a strong critique of 'one size fits all' Work First policies that assume that job seekers are able to search for jobs across sectors and commute across urban labour markets when in fact 'skills and spatial mismatches interact and can be expected to reinforce one another', severely limiting opportunities. More generally, much of the UK's jobs growth during the 1990s centred on low-quality, temporary and poorly paid positions at the margins of the labour market (Dieckhoff and Gallie, 2007), a situation that limits both the opportunity for people with financial or family responsibilities to pursue these opportunities, and the career benefits for those moving into employment.

As noted above, *the role of employers* has often been overlooked by UK employability policy. Yet the recruitment methods used by some employers, such as informal word-of-mouth networking, can disadvantage long-term unemployed people. Survey work has also confirmed that there can be negative attitudes towards recruiting the unemployed (Lindsay et al, 2003). Atkinson and Williams (2003) note that many employers can 'have an issue' with long-term unemployed people, even though the majority express satisfaction with those that they have recruited. There remains a fear that long-term unemployed people experience a decline in motivation and are more likely to have gaps in basic skills (Devins and Hogarth, 2005; Danson and Gilmore, 2009).

Finally, to return to the issues highlighted at the start of this chapter, policy clearly matters. The absence of a coherent policy agenda linking regional and local economic development with employability programmes means that supply-side initiatives such as the New Deal have reported widely varying outcomes according to labour market geography (McVicar and Podivinsky, 2009). There is also evidence to suggest that this type of Work First activation will only ever be effective in 'churning' many unemployed people from short-term, compulsory employability programmes to low-paid, insecure work (as a best case outcome) and then back into unemployment (Lindsay, 2007). Post-recession initiatives such as the Young Person's Guarantee, which directs people under 25 who have been unemployed for six months towards short-term college courses or sector-specific training, do little to challenge this basic model, and in fact largely involve merely the targeting of stretched resources on specific groups and in disadvantaged areas (DWP, 2009).

One deviation from the UK's Work First approach is the Future Jobs Fund, which was established by the Labour government to create new, additional jobs lasting at least six months in the public and third sectors (HM Treasury, 2009). However, the Fund fails to reflect the scale of the problem posed by the recession and its aftermath. It is estimated that between 100,000 and 150,000 (often temporary) jobs will be created, but with Jobseeker's Allowance claims rising by more than 700,000 in the year preceding the announcement of Future Jobs Fund in the 2009 Budget, its impact is likely to be limited. The failure of successive governments to develop and invest in strategies that combine supply-side interventions with robust demand-side stimuli left the UK ill-prepared to arrive at an effective employability policy agenda in the face of the 2008 crisis. The long-term unemployed and other vulnerable groups are the victims of this policy failure.

Nor are the long-term unemployed sufficiently supported by a benefits system that provides little by way of disposable income – so that single unemployed people reside in some of the UK's poorest households (Sanderson, 2006) – while meeting housing costs through passported, means-tested benefits (Housing Benefit and Council Tax Benefit). Such a system is inevitably disempowering (Sinfield, 2001), and policy makers have begun to recognise that it means that job seekers can have few of the financial management and budgeting skills they will need when moving into employment (DWP, 2006). Inflexible elements within the benefits system can also throw up additional barriers to work. The financial shock of the sudden withdrawal of housing-related benefits and the potential for delays in regaining eligibility following any return to unemployment can prompt long-term unemployed people to reject any 'risky' opportunities (McQuaid and Lindsay, 2002; Worth, 2003; DWP, 2006). It is also a system that limits the range and geographical focus of unemployed people's job search activities – 'poverty is an isolating experience' for unemployed people (Sinfield, 1981a, p 54), and living in poverty does not make for effective job seeking. There is a need to fundamentally review how unemployment and housing benefits are paid and administered. In order to arrive at more effective policies in this area, we need to move beyond the false dichotomy of debates on balancing rights to 'passive' benefits and responsibilities to participate in 'active' employability programmes (Sinfield, 2007). The reality is that an effective benefits system that lifts people out of poverty while directing them towards support and training is in itself activating and empowering.

Other factors

The McQuaid-Lindsay framework is more broad ranging – for example, we noted the importance of a range of other external factors related to job vacancies (that is, pay and conditions) and employers' credentialism in recruitment (that is, the increasing tendency to recruit over-qualified staff or rely on qualifications as a means of selecting job applicants). In relation to individual factors the framework acknowledges how job seekers' flexibility (in terms of wage demands or ability to travel to work) can set the parameters for the range of opportunities that are available to them.

However, the more important message from this approach – and the key finding from a range of studies – is that a complex range of individual barriers, personal circumstances and external factors *interact* to explain why some people are at greater risk of long-term unemployment, and what the experience of being out of work means to them in terms of social exclusion (Berthoud, 2003, 2007; Green and Owen, 2006; McQuaid, 2006; Carpenter, 2007). It is important that we re-engage with this evidence base in an era of economic crisis. During the UK's long boom, supporters of Work First activation could point to superficial evidence of apparent success in the high job entry rates reported (for a time) by employability programmes and relatively low general unemployment. As noted above, in a high demand economy (even if economic success did not filter down to the most vulnerable people and communities) policy makers were able to reason away long-term unemployment as explained by individual, personal failings and hysterisis effects. The scale and complexity of the crisis that began in 2008 has left these arguments utterly exposed, and the Work First strategies that they informed floundering. The only good news is that understanding and responding to the crisis demands new thinking on employability and unemployment, and/or re-connecting with the experiences and analyses of the past.

Discussion: priorities for policy in an era of crisis

Re-connecting with what unemployment means

Despite relatively high rates of employment in the UK during most of the 1990s and 2000s, many disadvantaged people continued to experience periods of long-term unemployment and the resulting risk of poverty and social exclusion. To adapt the words of Sinfield (1981a) from a time of much higher levels of worklessness, the heaviest and most profound costs of unemployment continued to be borne by many of the poorest and most vulnerable people in society. Indeed, it is not by accident that this chapter opened with the closing words of Sinfield's (1981a) work – in the face of a deepening unemployment crisis he saw the need for activation policies, but also that it was important to consider *all* aspects of employability and the experience of unemployment. Sinfield identified how the unequal distribution of unemployment places the lower-skilled, the low-qualified, those in disadvantaged regions and localities and other vulnerable groups at greater social risk, and how long-term unemployment feeds into poverty and social isolation for the individual and undermines communities. He was also clear that we have a responsibility to try to understand unemployment in context. Reflecting on the earlier insights of C. Wright Mills, he noted the folly of attempts to understand individuals' experiences of unemployment without reference to the social, economic and political contexts that can (especially during recession and its aftermath) limit opportunity. For Mills, when faced with mass job losses, when 'the very structure of opportunities has collapsed', we delude ourselves by seeking solutions based on the idea that individuals' failings can alone explain their unemployment. 'Both the correct statement of the problem and the range of possible solutions require us to consider the economic and political institutions of the society, and not merely the personal situation and character of a scatter of individuals' (Mills, 1959, p 9). The crisis of the early 1980s reminded us that 'Unemployment has to be examined as a characteristic of the society in which we live, not just of those members of it who happen to be out of work at any one time' (Sinfield, 1981b, p 122). This analysis is as relevant in 2010.

There are also political parallels with the unemployment crisis of the early 1980s. At that time the UK's capacity to respond seemed comparatively weak, 'given a government that denies the desirability of bringing about fuller employment ... let alone its responsibility or ability to achieve this' (Sinfield and Showler, 1981, p 5). Almost 30 years on and the modern Conservative Party – or at least David Cameron's rhetoric – now rejects the idea that unemployment is a 'price worth paying' (Dorling, 2009), but Conservative proposals in the field of employability and labour market policy make for grim reading. Centrepieces of the future policy agenda are likely to include: time limits on benefits; compulsory workfare for long-term unemployed people (who will be required to 'work for benefit' on community programmes); and benefit suspensions of three years for those refusing a reasonable job offer (Conservative Party, 2008). There is a commitment to follow the US experiment in privatised workfare despite 'little evidence to suggest the utility of contracting as a strategy for building service capacity or promoting accountability' from US employability programmes (Brodkin, 2005, p 94). Indeed, while the Labour government elected in 1997 oversaw a substantial shift towards contracting out employability provision, it maintained a strong role for the Public Employment Service (Jobcentre Plus) in managing programmes and delivering basic services. There is evidence from other countries that privatising or 'hollowing out' Public Employment Services can affect the quality and continuity of support available to vulnerable groups (Wright, 2008; Lindsay and McQuaid, 2009), yet an expansion of contracting out to all areas of services remains another key theme in the Conservative agenda. Other Conservative positions reflect a strong degree of continuity with policies introduced since 1997, but if anything, the threat of increasingly punitive benefit regulations will inevitably heighten the risk of poverty and social exclusion faced by long-term unemployed people (Crisp et al, 2009). It is also unclear as to what impact promised cuts in public expenditure will have, given that much of the UK's jobs growth during the 1997–2007 period was driven by the expansion of the public sector. Linking supply-side and demand-side elements (services for the long-term unemployed and macro-economic interventions) is key to arriving at a coherent and effective employability policy agenda, so the prioritisation of deficit reduction over continuing macro-economic stimulus is worrying. As Krugman (2009) notes, the usual argument against investing in demand-side stimuli – that by the time the effect filters through, the economy may have recovered anyway – need not trouble us given the depth and scale of the 2008 crisis and aftermath, and its capacity to feed into (long-term) unemployment for some time to come. An effective policy agenda for combating long-term unemployment, and a realistic plan for recovery, needs a continuing commitment to supporting the demand-side of the employability equation.

Re-connecting with the concept of employability

The evidence suggests that long-term unemployed people can face a complex combination of barriers to work, and that many face more (and more severe) barriers than other job seekers. Targeted programmes seeking to address the needs of long-term unemployed people (or those at risk of long-term unemployment) are justified. But they need to be the right kind of programmes. The UK model of Work First activation, which focuses on increasing motivation, generic skills and job search effort, is not equal to the task of addressing the range of barriers faced by the most disadvantaged (see also Dean, 2003). Nor can such programmes (which tend to be rolled out nationally with relatively little regard for local issues) begin to engage with problems such as the concentration of disadvantaged long-term unemployed people in certain regions and neighbourhoods.

Rather, long-term unemployed people need to be able to access high quality human capital development activities addressing, for example, the literacy and numeracy problems that have consistently been shown to limit employability, as well as gaps in occupational and other skills. These individual-focused, supply-side solutions are likely to be more effective where complemented by other targeted interventions that recognise barriers in relation to personal circumstances. Such interventions may involve anything from improving access to transport to signposting people with health problems to appropriate help, or community services that facilitate access to social networks and peer support. It is not that all job seekers, or even all long-term unemployed people, will need access to all of the potential interventions discussed above, but it is important that we are able to provide a menu of options that can be combined to address the range of issues affecting employability.

And crucially, the concept of employability cannot (or at least *should not*) be divorced from the spatial dynamics of local and regional economies (and the broader macro-economic, demand-side issues that will inherently help to define individuals' experiences in the labour market). Regional and local economic development strategies must form a central element of any coherent policy to reduce unemployment and promote the employability of vulnerable job seekers. In an era of crisis, how we understand both employability and long-term unemployment (and our thinking about policy responses) must reflect on the individual and personal barriers faced by job seekers, but also the fundamental social, economic and political structures that are at the root of the problem and its solutions.

Does the concept of employability itself have a role to play? Critics of how employability is used by UK policy makers have fallen into two camps. Some argue that the concept has become so tainted that we must move 'beyond employability' and find new ways of thinking and talking about the problem of unemployment (Peck and Theodore, 2000b). Others have sought to reclaim the language of employability by developing multidimensional models for analysis (McQuaid and Lindsay, 2005). The discussion above has sought to demonstrate that 'employability' – deployed as an holistic concept and framework for analysis – can help us to more fully understand the problems faced by unemployed people, and inform the debate on the mix of policies required to combat labour market disadvantage. This debate is necessary, now more than ever, if we are to arrive at policies that deliver access to employment, and so alleviate the social, economic and psychological damage that often results from the experience of long-term unemployment. As the UK again faces the possibility of a period of prolonged high unemployment, and communities grapple with the social consequences, there is no better time to renew our efforts to understand what unemployment means, map out issues affecting employability and offer advice on what works in supporting long-term unemployed people.

Acknowledgements
I am grateful for the helpful comments of the editors and Adrian Sinfield on an earlier version of this chapter.

References
Arksey, H. and Glendinning, C. (2008) 'Combining work and care: carers' decision-making in the context of competing policy pressures', *Social Policy and Administration*, vol 42, no 1, pp 1-18.

Atkinson, J. and Williams, M. (2003) *Employer perspectives on the recruitment, retention and advancement of low-pay, low-status employees*, London: Government Chief Social Researcher's Office.

Beatty, C. and Fothergill, S. (1997) *Unemployment and the labour market in RDAs*, Salisbury: Rural Development Commission.

Beatty, C. and Fothergill, S. (2003) *The seaside economy*, Sheffield: Sheffield Hallam University.

Beatty, C., Fothergill, S., Houston, D., Powell, R. and Sissons, P. (2009) 'A gendered theory of employment, unemployment, and sickness', *Environment and Planning C: Government and Policy*, vol 27, no 6, pp 958-74.

Begum, N. (2004) 'Characteristics of the short-term and long-term unemployed', *Labour Market Trends*, vol 112, pp 139-44.

Bellamy, K. and Rake, K. (2005) *Money, money, money: Is it still a rich man's world?*, London: Fawcett Society.

Berthoud, R. (2003) *Multiple disadvantage in employment: A quantitative analysis*, York: Joseph Rowntree Foundation.

Berthoud, R. (2007) *Work rich and work poor: Three decades of change*, London: Family Policy Studies Centre.

Blundell, R., Reed, H., van Reenen, J. and Shephard, A. (2003) 'The impact of the New Deal for Young People on the labour market: a four year assessment', in R. Dickens, P. Gregg and J. Wadsworth (eds) *The labour market under New Labour: The state of working Britain*, Basingstoke: Palgrave, pp 17-31.

Brodkin, E. (2005) 'Towards a contractual welfare state? The case of work activation in the United States', in E. Sol and M. Westerveld (eds) *Contractualism in employment services: A new form of welfare state governance*, The Hague: Kluwer Law, pp 73-99.

Bruttel, O. and Sol, E. (2006) 'Work First as a European model? Evidence from Germany and the Netherlands', *Policy & Politics*, vol 34, no 1, pp 69-89.

Cameron, D. (2008) 'A real plan for welfare reform', Speech by Rt Hon David Cameron MP on Conservatives' Green Paper on welfare reform, 8 January 2008 (www.conservatives.com/News/ Speeches/2008/01/ David_Cameron_A_real_plan_for_welfare_reform.aspx).

Carpenter, H. (2007) *Repeat Jobseeker's Allowance spells*, Sheffield: Department for Work and Pensions.

Clasen, J., Gould, A. and Vincent, J. (1997) *Long-term unemployment and the threat of social exclusion*, Bristol: The Policy Press.

Conservative Party (2008) *Work for welfare*, London: Conservative Party.

Crisp, R., Macmillan, R., Robinson, D. and Wells, P. (2009) 'Continuity or change: what a future Conservative government might mean for regional, housing and welfare policies', *People, Place and Policy*, vol 3, no 1, pp 58-74.

Daguerre, A. (2007) *Active labour market policies and welfare reform*, Basingstoke: Palgrave.

Daguerre, A. (2008) 'The second phase of US welfare reform, 2000–2006: blaming the poor again?', *Social Policy and Administration*, vol 42, no 4, pp 362-78.

Danson, M. and Gilmore, K. (2009) 'Evidence on employer attitudes and EQUAL opportunities for the disadvantaged in a flexible and open economy', *Environment and Planning C: Government and Policy*, vol 27, no 6, pp 991-1007.

Dean, H. (2003) 'Reconceptualising welfare to work for people with multiple problems and needs', *Journal of Social Policy*, vol 32, no 3, pp 441-59.

de Koning, J., Layard, R., Nickell, S. and Westergaard-Nielsen, N. (2004) *Policies for full employment*, London: Department for Work and Pensions.

Devins, D. and Hogarth, T. (2005) 'Employing the unemployed: some case study evidence on the role and practice of employers', *Urban Studies*, vol 42, no 2, pp 245-56.

Dex, S. and McCulloch, A. (1997) *Characteristics of the unemployed: Secondary analysis of the Family and Working Lives Survey*, London: Department for Education and Employment.

Dieckhoff, M. and Gallie, D. (2007) 'The renewed Lisbon Strategy and social exclusion policy', *Industrial Relations Journal*, vol 38, no 6, pp 480-502.

Dorling, D. (2009) 'Unemployment and health', *British Medical Journal*, vol 338, pp 1091-2.

DWP (Department for Work and Pensions) (2003) *The UK employment action plan*, London: DWP.

DWP (2006) *A new deal for welfare: Empowering people to work*, London: DWP.

DWP (2007) *In work, better off: Next steps to full employment*, London: DWP.

DWP (2008) *No one written off: Reforming welfare to reward responsibility*, London: DWP.

DWP (2009) *Guide to the Future Jobs Fund*, London: DWP.

European Foundation (2004) *Industrial relations in the United States 2003-4*, Dublin: European Foundation.

Finn, D. (2003) 'The "employment first" welfare state: lessons from the New Deal for Young People', *Social Policy and Administration*, vol 37, no 7, pp 709-24.

Gallie, D., Paugam, S. and Jacobs, S. (2003) 'Unemployment, poverty and social isolation: is there a vicious circle of social exclusion?', *European Societies*, vol 5, no 1, pp 1-32.

GHK (2004) *Understanding performance variations: Synthesis report for Jobcentre Plus*, London: Department for Work and Pensions.

Gore, T. and Hollywood, E. (2009) 'The role of social networks and geographical location in labour market participation in the UK coalfields', *Environment and Planning C: Government and Policy*, vol 27, no 6, pp 1008-21.

Grant, L. (2009) 'Women's disconnection from local labour markets: real lives and policy failure', *Critical Social Policy*, vol 29, no 3, pp 330-50.

Green, A.E. and Hasluck, C. (2009) 'Action to reduce worklessness: what works?', *Local Economy*, vol 24, no 1, pp 73-82.

Green, A.E. and Orton, M. (2009) 'The integration of activation policy at the sub-national level', *International Journal of Sociology and Social Policy*, vol 29, no 11/12, pp 612-23.

Green, A.E. and Owen, D. (2006) *The geography of poor skills and access to work*, York: Joseph Rowntree Foundation.

Halliday, S.A. and Hanson, S. (2004) *Skills for employability: Interim findings*, New Deal for Communities Evaluation Research Report 41, Leeds: Leeds Metropolitan University.

Handler, J. (2006) 'Ending welfare as we know it: welfare reform in the US', in P. Henman and M. Fenger (eds) *Administering welfare reform: International transformations in welfare governance*, Bristol: The Policy Press, pp 117-36.

Hannan, C. (1999) *Beyond networks: Social cohesion and unemployment exit rates*, Colchester: Institute for Social and Economic Research.

Hasluck, C., Elias, P., Green, A.E. and Pitcher, J. (1997) *Identifying people at risk of long-term unemployment*, Sheffield: Employment Service.

Haughton, G., Jones, M., Peck, J., Tickell, A. and While, A. (2000) 'Labour market policy as flexible welfare: prototype employment zones and the new workfarism', *Regional Studies*, vol 34, no 7, pp 669-80.

Hillage, J. and Pollard, E. (1998) *Employability: Developing a framework for policy analysis*, Brighton: Institute for Employment Studies.

HM Treasury (1997) 'Gordon Brown unveils UK Employment Action Plan', Treasury Press Release 122/97, London: HM Treasury.

HM Treasury (2001) *The changing welfare state: Employment opportunity for all*, London: HM Treasury.

HM Treasury (2009) *Securing the recovery: Growth and opportunity*, Pre-Budget report, London: HM Treasury.

Houston, D. (2005) 'Employability, skills mismatch and spatial mismatch in metropolitan labour markets', *Urban Studies*, vol 42, no 2, pp 221-43.

James, R. (2007) 'Job capability match, adviser skills and the five self-efficacy barriers to employment', *Journal of Occupational Psychology, Employment and Disability*, vol 9, no 1, pp 32-40.

Julkunen, I. (2002) 'Social and material deprivation among unemployed youth in Northern Europe', *Social Policy and Administration*, vol 36, no 3, pp 235-53.

Krugman, P. (2009) *The return of depression economics and the crisis of 2008*, London: Penguin.

Layard, R. (2000) 'Welfare-to-work and the New Deal', *World Economics*, vol 1, no 2, pp 29-39.

Layard, R. (2004) *Good jobs and bad jobs*, Centre for Economic Performance Working Paper 19, London: Centre for Economic Performance.

Lévesque, M. and White, D. (2001) 'Capital social, capital humain et sortie de l'aide sociale pour des prestataires de longue durée', *Canadian Journal of Sociology*, vol 26, no 2, pp 167-92.

Lindsay, C. (2007) 'The United Kingdom's "Work First" welfare state and activation regimes in Europe', in A. Serrano Pascual and L. Magnusson (eds) *Reshaping welfare states and activation regimes in Europe*, Brussels: Peter Lang, pp 35-70.

Lindsay, C. (2009) 'Review of A. Daguerre (2007) *Active labour market policies and welfare reform*', *Journal of Social Policy*, vol 38, no 1, pp 180-2.

Lindsay, C. (2010) 'In a lonely place? Social networks, job seeking and the experience of long-term unemployment', *Social Policy and Society*, vol 9, no 1, pp 25-37.

Lindsay, C. and McQuaid, R.W. (2004) 'Avoiding the "McJobs": unemployed job seekers and attitudes to service work', *Work, Employment and Society*, vol 18, no 2, pp 297-319.

Lindsay, C. and McQuaid, R.W. (2009) 'New governance and the case of activation policies: comparing experiences in Denmark and the Netherlands', *Social Policy and Administration*, vol 43, no 5, pp 445-63.

Lindsay, C. and Serrano Pascual, A. (2009) 'New perspectives on employability and labour market policy: reflecting on key issues', *Environment and Planning C: Government and Policy*, vol 27, no 6, pp 951-7.

Lindsay, C., Greig, M. and McQuaid, R.W. (2005) 'Alternative job search strategies in remote rural labour markets: the role of social networks', *Sociologia Ruralis*, vol 45, no 1, pp 53-70.

Lindsay, C., McCracken, M. and McQuaid, R.W. (2003) 'Unemployment duration and employability in remote rural labour markets', *Journal of Rural Studies*, vol 19, no 2, pp 187-200.

Lindsay, C., McQuaid, R.W. and Dutton, M. (2007) 'New approaches to employability in the UK: combining "Human Capital Development" and "Work First" strategies?', *Journal of Social Policy*, vol 36, no 4, pp 539-60.

Lister, R. (2001) 'New Labour: a study in ambiguity from a position of ambivalence', *Critical Social Policy*, vol 21, no 4, pp 425-48.

MacLeavy, J. (2008) 'Neoliberalising subjects: the legacy of New Labour's construction of social exclusion in local governance', *Geoforum*, vol 39, no 5, pp 1657-666.

Macnicol, J. (2008) 'Older men and work in the 21st century: what can the history of retirement tell us?', *Journal of Social Policy*, vol 37, no 4, pp 579-95.

McQuaid, R.W. (2006) 'Job search success and employability in local labor markets', *Annals of Regional Science*, vol 40, no 2, pp 407-21.

McQuaid, R.W. and Lindsay, C. (2002) 'The "employability gap": long-term unemployment and barriers to work in buoyant labour markets', *Environment and Planning C: Government and Policy*, vol 20, no 4, pp 613-29.

McQuaid, R.W. and Lindsay, C. (2005) 'The concept of employability', *Urban Studies*, vol 42, no 2, pp 197-219.

McVicar, D. and Podivinsky, M. (2009) 'How well has the New Deal For Young People worked in the UK regions?', *Scottish Journal of Political Economy*, vol 56, no 2, pp 167-95.

Mead, L. (2001) 'Welfare reform in Wisconsin: the local role', *Administration and Society*, vol 33, no 5, pp 523-54.

Mills, C.W. (1959) *The sociological imagination*, New York, NY: Oxford University Press.

Mitchell, A., Lightman, E. and Herd, D. (2007) 'Work-first and immigrants in Toronto', *Social Policy and Society*, vol 6, no 3, pp 293-307.

Murray, C. (1990) *The emerging British underclass*, London: Institute for Economic Affairs.

Nickell, S. (2001) 'Has UK labour market performance changed?', Speech to the Society of Business Economists, London, 16 May.

Peck, J. and Theodore, N. (2000a) 'Work first: workfare and the regulation of contingent labour markets', *Cambridge Journal of Economics*, vol 24, no 1, pp 119-38.

Peck, J. and Theodore, N. (2000b) 'Beyond employability', *Cambridge Journal of Economics*, vol 24, no 6, pp 729-49.

Ray, K., Hoggart, L., Taylor, R., Vegeris, S. and Campbell-Barr, V. (2009) 'Rewarding responsibility? Long-term unemployed men and the welfare-to-work agenda', *Environment and Planning C: Government and Policy*, vol 27, no 6, pp 975-90.

Sanderson, I. (2006) *Worklessness in deprived neighbourhoods: A review of evidence*, London: Communities and Local Government.

Serrano Pascual, A. and Magnusson, L. (eds) (2007) *Reshaping welfare states and activation regimes in Europe*, Brussels: Peter Lang.

Shuttleworth, I., Tyler, P. and McKinstry, D. (2005) 'Redundancy, readjustment, and employability: what can we learn from the 2000 Harland and Wolff redundancy?', *Environment and Planning A*, vol 37, no 9, pp 1651-68.

Sinfield, A. (1968) *The long-term unemployed*, Paris: OECD.

Sinfield, A. (1981a) *What unemployment means*, Oxford: Martin Robertson.

Sinfield, A. (1981b) 'Unemployment in an unequal society', in B. Showler and A. Sinfield (eds) *The workless state*, Oxford: Martin Robertson, pp 122-66.

Sinfield, A. (2001) 'Benefits and research in the labour market', *European Journal of Social Security*, vol 3, no 3, pp 209-35.

Sinfield, A. (2007) 'Preventing poverty in the European Union', *European Journal of Social Security*, vol 9, no 1, pp 11-28.

Sinfield, A. and Showler, B. (1981) 'Unemployment and the unemployed in 1980', in B. Showler and A. Sinfield (eds) *The workless state*, Oxford: Martin Robertson, pp 1-26.

Smith, A. (2002) *Pathways to work: Helping people into employment: Foreword by Rt Hon Andrew Smith MP, Secretary of State for Work and Pensions*, London: Department for Work and Pensions.

Smith, F., Wainwright, E., Marandet, E. and Buckingham, S. (2008) 'A New Deal for Lone Parents? Training lone parents for work in West London', *Area*, vol 40, no 2, pp 237-44.

Sol, E. and Hoogtanders, Y. (2005) 'Steering by contract in the Netherlands: new approaches to labour market integration', in E. Sol and M. Westerveld (eds) *Contractualism in employment services*, The Hague: Kluwer, pp 139-66.

Such, E. and Walker, R. (2002) 'Falling behind? Research on transmitted deprivation', *Benefits*, vol 10, no 3, pp 185-92.

Sunley, P., Martin, R. and Nativel, C. (2001) 'Mapping the New Deal: local disparities in the performance of welfare-to-work', *Transactions of the Institute of British Geographers*, vol 26, no 4, pp 484-512.

Sunley, P., Martin, R. and Nativel, C. (2006) *Putting workfare in place: Local labour markets and the New Deal*, Oxford: Blackwell.

Taylor, A. (2005) 'What employers look for: the skills debate and the fit with youth perceptions', *Journal of Education and Work*, vol 18, no 2, pp 201-18.

Theodore, N. (2007) 'New Labour at work: long-term unemployment and the geography of opportunity', *Cambridge Journal of Economics*, vol 31, no 6, pp 927-40.

Turok, I. (2007) *Full employment strategies for cities: The case of Glasgow*, Paris: OECD.

van Berkel, R. and Borghi, V. (2008) 'Introduction: the governance of activation', *Social Policy and Society*, vol 7, no 3, pp 331-40.

Waddell, G. and Burton, A. (2006) *Is work good for your health and well being?*, London: Department for Work and Pensions.

Warhurst, C. and Nickson, D. (2007) 'A new labour aristocracy? Aesthetic labour and routine interactive service', *Work, Employment and Society*, vol 21, no 4, pp 785-98.

Webster, D. (2000) 'The geographical concentration of labour market disadvantage', *Oxford Review of Economic Policy*, vol 16, no 1, pp 114-28.

Webster, D. (2005) 'Long-term unemployment, the invention of hysterisis and the misdiagnosis of structural unemployment in the UK', *Cambridge Journal of Economics*, vol 29, no 6, pp 975-95.

Worth, S. (2003) 'Adaptability and self-management: a new ethic of employability for the young unemployed?', *Journal of Social Policy*, vol 32, no 4, pp 607-21.

Wright, S. (2008) *Contracting-out employment services: Lessons from Australia, Denmark, Germany and the Netherlands*, London: Child Poverty Action Group.

SEVEN

Facing the 'dark side' of deregulation? The politics of two-tier labour markets in Germany and Japan after the global financial crisis

Steffen Heinrich[1]

Second thoughts about liberal labour market reform

For much of 2009 Germany and Japan appeared to be among the countries most severely affected by the global economic and financial crisis. Apart from a steep decline in quarterly growth rates, they also experienced dramatic employment adjustment processes unseen perhaps since the 1970s. A closer look reveals, however, that the increased unemployment risk in both countries so far has been shouldered almost exclusively by a distinct class of non-regular employees[2] who together account for over 30% of total salaried employment. By March 2009, for instance, more than a quarter of all temp agency workers in Germany and a similar number in Japan had been made redundant while the figures for regular employment appeared almost unscathed. The current crisis has noticeably elevated public interest in the alleged 'dark side' of deregulation, which includes the risk of a crowding out of regular by non-regular employment, a deterioration of working conditions in general and gaps in the systems of social protection for non-regular employees. German and Japanese media, for example, repeatedly reported on the social hardships faced by some of those who had recently been laid off, such as the realisation that many could not meet the eligibility requirements for unemployment benefits due to termed employment.

They have also questioned the wisdom of German and Japanese governments in the 1990s and early 2000s in gradually liberalising labour law so non-regular employment could expand to its present level. It is not surprising therefore that the 'social costs' of labour market deregulation featured prominently in the general election campaigns in Germany and Japan in late 2009. Yet, whether the present uneasiness with partially regulated labour markets and the strong campaign rhetoric will indeed translate into a re-regulation of labour markets looks anything but certain, not least due to the short time period that has passed since the new government coalitions have taken over.

In order to understand the long-term impact of the crisis it is therefore more sensible to look at the political dynamic of labour market reforms and then to see how this dynamic has changed due to the current crisis. This is what the chapter intends to do. For this purpose it will briefly recapitulate the process of labour law reform in Germany and Japan since the early 1990s and thereby focus on two factors that are likely to play a role relevant in labour market regulation in the current situation: partisan competition (which can be analysed to some degree thanks to almost simultaneous changes in government) and the institutional legacies of traditional German and Japanese employment systems (which appear rather similar when looking at the percentage of non-regular employment in both countries). In the final section it will then evaluate how the current crisis has changed the role and impact of these two factors and how this affects the potential re-regulation of labour markets.

Patterns of two-tierism in German and Japanese labour markets

In neither Germany nor Japan are two-tier labour markets a new phenomenon solely to be associated with labour market reforms of the 1990s and 2000s. Indeed, nearly all industrialised labour markets, whether embedded in coordinated or liberal market economies, distinguish employees in one way or another, for instance between core and periphery, white and blue collar or *ippanshoku* and *sougoushoku*.[3] And when looking at other advanced countries partial deregulation appears to be the norm rather than the exception (see Figure 7.1). Germany and Japan, however, do stand out in several respects. First, both have opted for 'asymmetrical deregulation' (Miura, 2001) or 'semi-liberalisation' of labour law that means that they have gradually deregulated non-regular employment such as temp agency work, fixed-term employment or part-time work (see Tables 7.1 and 7.2). Second, the traditional employment forms (often referred to as *seishain koyou* in Japanese and *Normalarbeitsverhältnis* in German) have shown a surprising resilience despite the jump in non-regular employment (see Figures 7.2 and 7.3) and despite the often alleged 'crumbling' of organised labour and capital.[4] Third, this perseverance of traditional employment is usually credited to the similar dynamics of German and Japanese capitalisms (Thelen and Kume, 1999, 2003; Dore, 2000; Manow, 2001; Streeck, 2001; Vogel, 2003). Simplified, this strand of research argues that the traditional, highly regulated employment systems of Germany and Japan foster the long-term commitment of workers to their employers and offer German and Japanese firms a competitive edge over competitors that operate mainly in liberal market economies. As a consequence, it can be economically sensible for employers to support non-liberal institutions because it grants them economic benefits such as a highly skilled workforce or peaceful labour capital relations. In short, the varieties of capitalism (VOC) literature suggests that current labour market arrangements are still shaped by strong non-liberal institutions as all major parties should have an interest in maintaining the 'comparative institutional advantage' of 'regulated' regular employment. However, it runs into problems when trying to explain the massive expansion of non-regular work since the early 1990s, as this constitutes a significant deviation from the pattern just described. Similar problems afflict simplified models of partisan difference: Neither the German nor the Japanese process of deregulation can confirm assumptions that 'labour-friendly' governments are in general more sceptical towards labour market deregulation or that 'employer-friendly' governments are likely to embrace labour market liberalisation. In reality, Liberal Democratic Party (LDP)-led governments in Japan have maintained a comparatively 'labour-friendly' approach for much of the 1990s (Kume, 1998) and in Germany the centre-left coalition under Schröder enacted several liberal reforms it had strongly opposed when in opposition. Furthermore, almost all OECD (Organisation for Economic Co-operation and Development) countries show similar trajectories, although partisan constellations have varied widely (see Figure 7.1).

But why then have Germany and Japan developed their unique systems of two-tier labour markets? As has been pointed out before, the VOC literature offers a credible explanation for the resilience of the first tier of employment, which has been termed 'regular employment' here. It argues that the success of the German and Japanese economies depends to a large extent on their employment systems and industrial relations as they offer distinct advantages to firms, such as high internal

Figure 7.1: Labour market regulation in selected OECD countries since 1985

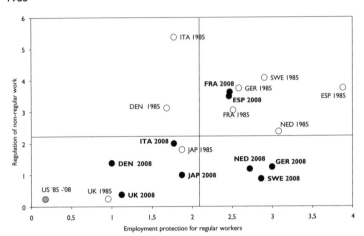

Source: Own compilation based on the OECD's employment protection legislation indicator (EPL) (OECD 2004; Venn 2009). Latest available data in bold. A higher value indicates a higher level of protection/regulation.

labour flexibility and consensual and comparatively peaceful industrial relations (Thelen, 1999, 2001). In the Japanese case lifelong employment almost became a synonym of Japanese capitalism. Although it would be misleading to portray all regular employment as stable 'lifelong employment',[5] certain elements of long-term employment such as the prominence of corporate welfare, long job tenure and the age-related wage structures have been true for the majority of regular workers and even of some non-regular employees. In Germany, regular employment has been characterised by stable, comparatively comprehensive industrial relations that allowed the state to stay out of many regulatory areas because coverage of industrial relations was generally believed to be extensive and comparatively homogeneous. For instance, until recently Germany had no minimum wage legislation (although collective bargaining did set minimum standards for each industry, and it is still limited to selected industries). Although different in many respects, the German and Japanese variants of coordinated labour markets arguably offer similar advantages to employers, such as comparatively peaceful employer–employee relations and high functional flexibility (as German and Japanese employees are generally understood to be keen to acquire firm-specific skills, which could make them unattractive for other employers).[6] However, this requires, the VOC school argues, that employment is long-term, stable and secure so that workers do not fear making long-term commitments.[7] In return employers can build up a loyal, productive and flexible workforce (that is, concerning functional and temporal issues). The argument that 'institutional complementarities' exist, such as between rigid employment protection legislation and firm-specific skill acquisition, appears quite credible when one looks at the relative stability of regular employment and its regulatory environment (Thelen and Kume, 1999; Hall and Soskice, 2001; Thelen, 2001; Hall and Gingerich, 2009). Yet, as has been pointed out before, the VOC school cannot really account for the expansion of non-regular employment, as it suggests that all main actors would have an interest in maintaining and fostering regular employment.

So how can the emergence or rather institutionalisation of the second tier, consisting of various forms of non-regular employment, be explained? Almost all scholars agree that the liberalisation of non-regular work has been a fundamental part of the strategy of governments to increase the external flexibility dimension of labour markets.[8] The push for enhancing labour market flexibility is generally credited to changes in product markets, which have become more competitive and in which demand for manufactured goods and services fluctuates much more than in the past. Enhanced external flexibility enables firms to thrive in such unstable market conditions, for instance by hiring non-regular employees when demand is high without committing themselves to long-term employment or providing costly corporate welfare benefits. Also, deregulation of non-regular employment has been, in Germany in particular, depicted as a policy to fight unemployment as it lowers the threshold for entering the labour market for the long-term unemployed (Schmid, 2003). Sociologists like Kalleberg see a general tendency in western economies towards precarious work patterns that originated in the massive employment adjustment processes after the oil crises of the 1970s (Kalleberg, 2009). As a consequence, firms changed their personnel strategy and increasingly differentiated between core (who would receive corporate welfare and long-term employment) and non-core employees (without or with less welfare entitlements and substantially less employment security). Increasing international market competition, technological advancement and growing mobility of capital, which facilitates 'outsourcing' or 'off-shoring' of jobs, have reinforced this trend, Kalleberg believes. Deregulation could therefore be understood as a more or less inevitable recalibration of labour law to match a changing reality. Some political scientists and scholars of industrial relations, however, see evidence of a general 'crumbling' of social partnership and institutionalised stable employer–labour union relationships in general. This strand of literature argues that the decreasing membership and organisational base of labour unions has made liberal labour market policies politically 'feasible' in the course of the 1980s, 1990s and 2000s because unions have lost much of their ability to resist deregulation (see, for example, Whittaker, 1998; Streeck and Hassel, 2003; Thelen and Kume, 2006). Labour market reforms, according to this view, partly mirror the demise of union strength and indicate a shift in the balance of power between employees and employers, to the advantage of the latter. It implies that unions just barely managed to protect their core constituency.

The insider–outsider theory (Lindbeck and Snower, 2001, 2002) makes a different argument, as it emphasises the influence and power of insiders of a workforce. The mechanism through which the line of conflict between insiders and outsiders emerges is the difference in labour turnover costs that include, for instance, training. Workers with extensive training have a competitive edge over workers without, or with partial, training and can thus achieve better employment conditions. As unions are typically acting on behalf of long-term employees they have an interest in protecting their constituency against employers who would like to cut labour costs, but also against non-core workers who would like to enjoy similar levels of job security and pay.[9] This can make it rational for unions to actively nurture an outsider worker group as they can be sure that this group will be the first to be affected by adjustment processes. However, when it comes to labour market reform, this approach often falls short because labour unions have often been among the fiercest opponents of deregulation of non-regular employment. Yet it highlights the fact that there may be a latent conflict between core and non-core employees (which arguably often, but not necessarily always, coincides with regular and non-regular employment). Indeed, some scholars such as King and Rueda (2008) see this conflict as the biggest 'political challenge' for governments and as a major influence factor for future labour market regulation.

King and Rueda also criticise the standard VOC-based depiction of German and Japanese labour markets as relying mostly on highly skilled and well-protected personnel. Against the background of soaring numbers of non-regular or rather precarious employment they find that 'Our understanding ... still reflects the now disappearing realities [of] the "golden age" of social democratic welfare'. This, they believe, obscures the fact that precarious employment 'will politically test the foundations of the European coordinated market economy' (2008, p 294) because the new class of 'cheap labour'[10] has distinct political interests compared to regularly unionised employed workers. This particularly puts under pressure those who traditionally position themselves as the main advocates of workers' rights and demands, such as social democratic parties and labour union federations. These groups find it increasingly difficult to unify the conflicting preferences of the two labour groups regarding, for example, employment protection or employment maintenance policies. Although King and Rueda's approach does not offer an explanation for the emergence of two-tier labour markets, it does provide an important perspective on the current dynamics of labour market regulation. However, the 'existence of two distinct groups within labour only affects the strategies of partisan governments when there is a conflict between insiders and outsiders' (Rueda, 2005, p 62). So the question here is whether the global economic and financial crisis has indeed intensified such a conflict so that it has become politically salient, say, in the general elections of 2009.

Based on the theoretical considerations just laid out, two hypotheses can be formulated with regard to the two main variables, institutional legacies of traditional employment systems and partisanship.

(1) State regulation is shaped by two conflicting policy goals: the maintenance and support of regular employment (because of the 'comparative institutional advantage' it offers and because of the traditionally well represented interests of those regularly employed) and the wish to maintain or even increase the level of labour market flexibility that has been achieved by partial deregulation. As a consequence, governments will take very different regulatory approaches regarding the two tiers, regardless of the partisan make-up.

(2) For the regulation of non-regular employment, partisanship will increasingly matter. Centre-left parties will increasingly feel threatened by the conflicting demands of workers in the two tiers and thus be comparatively more active in trying to improve social security, wage levels and working conditions for non-regular employees through labour law, because this way they avoid intervening too much in the first tier of regular employment and thus avoid direct confrontations between both worker groups. Centre-right parties on the other hand will above all try to maintain the level of flexibility (deregulation) that has been achieved and be generally less enthusiastic about setting standards through labour law.

Figure 7.2: Regular and non-regular employment in Germany

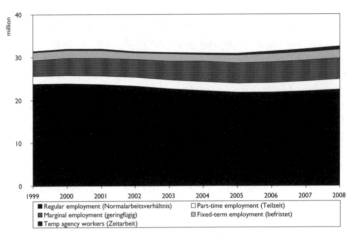

Note: Respondents were asked to characterise their mode of employment and could name several characteristics. The data were adjusted for overlaps using data from 2007 wave, so only part-time workers with non-fixed-term contracts were coded part-timers, only temp agency workers with non-termed contracts as temp agency workers, all others fell under the fixed-term employment category. Marginal employment includes only those who hold no other job.

Source: Own calculations based on panel data from the 'Mikrozensus'.

Figure 7.3: Regular and non-regular employment in Japan

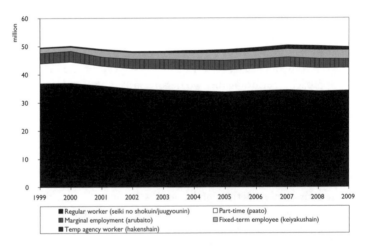

Source: Own calculations based on panel data from Labour Force Survey (Roudou ryoku chousa). Respondents were asked to identify the title of their job (as the employer calls it). The data also included a category for other non-regular employment (around 2% of all employees in 2005), which was not included.

Table 7.1: Patterns of regular and non-regular employment in Germany

	Regular (Normalarbeits-verhältnis)	Part-time (Teilzeit)	Temp agency (Zeitarbeit)	Contract (Befristet)	Marginal (geringfügig)
Regulation	Industry-wide collective bargaining Labour law	Enterprise-based bargaining Labour law	Temp agency industry bargaining Enterprise agreements Labour law	Labour law Industry- and enterprise-based bargaining	Labour law Social security law
Wage standardisation	High within business sectors	High within business sectors	Low compared to regular workers	Varying	Set by social security law (400€ max)
Social and employment protection	High legal hurdles against dismissals Unemployment benefits up to 24 months	High legal hurdles against dismissals Unemployment benefits up to 24 months	Covered but not eligible if consecutive employment <1 year	Covered but not eligible if consecutive employment <1 year	Not covered
Corporate welfare	E.g. corporate pensions	E.g. corporate pensions	Usually without extra corporate benefits	Often not eligible for corporate welfare	None
Profile	Predominantly male (69%)	86% female 60% are between 35 and 55 years	70% male More than 50% are 35 or younger	53% male About 60% are younger than 35	77% female About 50% are between 35 and 55 years of age

Source: Compiled by author. Profile data from Mikrozensus (Statistisches Bundesamt, 2008).

Table 7.2: Patterns of regular and non-regular employment in Japan

	Regular (seishain)	Part-time (paato)	Temp agency (haken)	Contract (keiyaku)	Marginal (arubaito)
Regulation	Firm- and industry-level bargaining Labour law	Firm-level bargaining Labour law	Labour law Firm-level bargaining	Labour law	Labour law
Wage standardisation	Medium to high depending on industry and size of company	Low to medium depending on industry, firm	Varying (equal treatment clause)	Varying	Regional minimum wage legislation
Social and employment protection	High hurdles against dismissals (mainly case law) Unemployment benefits up to 12 months	Entitled to unemployment benefits after 6 months (up to 12 months)	Entitled to unemployment benefits after 6 months (up to 12 months)	Entitled to unemployment benefits after 6 months (up to 12 months)	Entitled to unemployment benefits after 6 months (up to 12 months)
Corporate welfare	Usually firm-specific and non-transferable, can include pension, healthcare, housing	Limited compared to seishain Varying according to firm	Some but usually limited compared to seishain of contracting company	Limited compared to seishain	None
Profile	Predominantly male (70%)	89% female More than 70% are 35 or older	67% female Almost 50% are between 25 and 34 years of age	52% male 50% are between 25-34 and 55-64	51% female Over 80% are younger than 34

Source: Compiled by author. Profile data from the Labour Force Survey 2004 (roudouryoku chousa) (Ministry of Health, 2004).

From de- to re-regulation?

Apart from different partisan preferences, some scholars have suggested that coordinated market economies are characterised by particular decision-making processes that are usually consensus seeking and foster a close relationship between firms, labour unions and the government (see, for example, Regini, 2003). Since there are many 'institutional complementarities', the incentive to jointly discuss measures and legislation should be strong. This should also be true for Japan even though it has famously been described as 'corporatism without labour' (Pempel and Tsunekawa, 1979). Japanese decision-making processes regarding labour legislation have in fact known several corporatist institutions or similar bodies of tripartite consultation and coordination since the 1970s. Most of these survived even the bubble economy and the more 'neoliberal' era of the 1990s (see especially Kume, 1998; Miura, 2002a). In particular, the generally moderate private sector labour unions played an important role in labour policy formulation and even possessed an implicit veto right on labour policy. Until the late 1990s, even LDP-governments would go to great lengths to secure the consent of unions when proposing new legislation. The quasi-veto power of unions resided with the so-called *shingikai*,[11] semi-official institutions in which the main interest groups, academic advisers and ministry officials would discuss new legislative proposals. Proposals had to be agreed on by all participants otherwise they would not be forwarded to the cabinet or parliament.

Due to the relative resilience of corporatist and tripartite coordination in Germany, Japan and other countries some scholars expected labour market reforms would therefore lead to a restoration of corporatist policy making, so that, on the one hand, the continuity of the 'comparative institutional advantage' of traditional employment systems could be ensured, but also, on the other hand, much needed structural reforms could be implemented (Rhodes, 1997). However, when one looks at the reform processes in terms of non-regular employment in Germany and Japan since the early 1990s, the picture looks significantly more complicated. In Japan, the LDP-led governments began ignoring the established *shingikai* after 1998 by setting up new cabinet-level advisory councils (the so-called deregulation commissions) that for the most part consisted of business-friendly academia and ministry officials. The commissions were asked to draw up proposals for the deregulation of markets, among them labour markets, and pass these on directly to the cabinet for approval. Neither the labour unions nor the bodies of coordination between ministry bureaucracy and firms played a decisive role in this period. Only in the autumn of 2007, when the opposition won a majority in the upper house, was this system abandoned due to the opposition's veto power. During the period of non-coordination, however, some major reforms of non-regular employment were implemented such as several revisions of the Temp Agency Act (*roudousha haken hou*) and the Labour Standards Law (*roudou kijun hou*).

The German coordination processes essentially took a similar turn, although tripartite coordination on labour legislation has been much less formal than in Japan. Under the conservative governments of the 1980s the trend seemed to favour an end to policy coordination altogether. Much like the LDP-government in Japan after 1998, the German government tried to implement liberal labour market reforms by appointing a cabinet-level committee. However, all of its proposals eventually failed due to strong opposition from the unions and the social democratic opposition in the second chamber (*Bundesrat*). The late 1990s then did actually see a revival of national-level corporatism, as had been predicted by Rhodes and others, yet the 'alliances for jobs', as they are typically referred to, accomplished little in terms of policy. The coordinative process came to an end in 2002 when the Schröder government set up a commission to make proposals for labour market reform. Although the commission's most important goal was to propose measures to fight structural unemployment in Germany and it produced little in terms of deregulation of non-regular employment (see, for example, Schmid, 2003), its convention signalled a change in the way labour market policies were decided. Indirectly, the commission's work contributed to the reform of the Temp Agency Law (*Arbeitnehmerüberlassungsgesetz*) that effectively meant a comprehensive liberalisation of temp agency work. In sum, the reform process of the 1990s and early 2000s, which could be described here only very briefly, does not confirm the view of a strong relationship between coordinated capitalism and policy making. Instead of mutual coordination, industrial partners and governments appeared to act increasingly independently of each other. Regulation of regular and non-regular employment therefore seems to follow different regulatory dynamics. After the crisis of October 2008 the pattern of two-tierism re-appeared. German and Japanese governments acted quickly to stabilise regular employment (most notably by facilitating work sharing schemes/subsidies for firms to cut working hours instead of reducing their workforce), yet the measures for non-regular employees were limited to more basic issues, such as lowering the eligibility criteria for unemployment benefits, introducing a minimum wage for temp agency workers (in Germany the work sharing scheme was expanded to temp agency workers in the summer of 2009) and expanding training measures (see Table 7.3). Overall, however, Germany and Japan seemed to follow the path of employment stabilisation at all costs which has been visible since the 1970s (Miura, 2002b).[12] That means government policy in the period of the crisis prompted different reactions depending on the tier, with preferential treatment of regular employment.

When one also takes into account developments on the level of industrial relations and the possibility of a conflict between regular and non-regular workers, the picture becomes yet a little more complicated. Judging only from media reports since the crisis, the deterioration of working conditions seems to have progressed quickly due to the expansion of non-regular work. However, before the crisis there had been signs that industrial relations and companies made efforts to balance the relationship between regular and non-regular workers. In Germany, one such example can be seen at BMW. In February 2008 the company had announced it would lay off more than 5,000 temp agency workers. This was an unprecedented announcement that received wide public attention because BMW was still highly profitable at that time and enjoyed a near spotless reputation as a social-minded employer. Although BMW's management emphasised that all temp agency workers would remain employed by their agencies, it declared only a few weeks later that it would voluntarily pay its temp agency workers from now on the same standard wage as its regular employees, with the exception of bonuses. BMW, like some other car manufacturers before it, thus tried to prove to the public how much they cared about temp agency workers, but perhaps also to avoid problems arising from the increasingly controversial relationship between temps and regular workers (*Süddeutsche Zeitung*, 4 March 2008).[13] In Japan, signs of a gradual change became visible in the changing human resources policies of some firms in retailing and finance (Heinrich and Kohlbacher, 2008). The firms effectively abolished the separation between *ippanshoku* and *sougoushoku* careers and also between core and non-core employees. This was to make it easier for non-regular staff to switch to regular employment and to abolish unequal treatment of employees. Clearly both examples have to be assessed with caution, as it is anything but clear whether these instances of change will develop into a major trend that can extend to all firms in the respective industries and employers in other businesses.[14] Nevertheless, they show that developments on the level of industrial relations and firm policy can play an important role for the regulatory situation of non-regular workers, because industrial relations in Germany and Japan may increasingly (co-)determine their actual working conditions.

Finally, how likely is it that re-regulation will become a salient topic for partisan competition? Looking solely at Germany and Japan, the picture looks mixed. While in Japan the Democratic Party of Japan (*Minshu-tou*, DPJ) landed a historic electoral victory in August 2009 with a campaign that emphasised the growing social hardships experienced by non-regular workers, the campaign of the Free Democrats (FDP) and the Christian Democrats (CDU/CSU) in Germany up to the September 2009 election referred to non-regular employment only occasionally and usually in the context of improving the employment prospects of young employees (of whom almost half hold non-regular jobs at least initially). In fact, among the first measures the new coalition partners in Germany agreed on was a partial reform of fixed-term employment.[15] But even in Japan, political measures so far have been constrained to limited state interventions in the form of active and passive labour market measures. Here, however, the exceptional political situation has to be taken into account because 2009 saw only the second genuine change in government in Japan since 1955. Whether this will also lead to a shift in policy is still uncertain, however, due to the heterogeneous make-up of the DPJ.[16] Judging solely from policy proposals, however, a move towards re-regulation looks somewhat more likely in Japan. This is most evident in the fact that the new government is considering outlawing temp agency work in manufacturing. If such legislation was passed, this would indicate a clear departure from the politics of partial deregulation, and it would also show that partisan differences regarding labour market policies do actually matter (see Table 7.3). The change in tone is also evidenced by the fact that the government has invited different social groups to discuss and influence labour legislation. And although the DPJ did not give in to the Social Democratic Party's (*Shamin-tou*, SDP) demand to be awarded the Ministry of Health, Labour and Welfare (MHLW), it did appoint Makoto Yuasa, a well-known activist for public welfare for homeless people,[17] to a new government task force which is to find measures that help to improve employment prospects and security.

In Germany the picture looks more complicated. Because the Social Democratic Party (SPD) has been involved in some major deregulation itself, the obvious opponent of deregulation cannot fill this role convincingly at the moment. This could be taken over by the Left Party, which has been an avid critic of the social democratic reform agenda, but its chances to form a government on the national level are as slim as those of the Japan Communist Party that has been in opposition since the 1950s (*Kyousan-to*, JCP). In recent interview outings and discussions, some SPD leaders have voiced regrets concerning the labour market reform under the second Schröder cabinet, yet the majority of statements point to 'technical insufficiencies' rather than to a general uneasiness with deregulation. Currently, it is mainly the labour union associations that campaign for changes, for example for an 'equal pay' clause which would require firms to pay temp agency workers the same wage as their core workers. The left-of-centre parties, however, have so far shown little enthusiasm for such demands.

In summary, there is little evidence for a major policy shift or a 'reconnection' or 're-synchronisation' of industrial relations and labour market legislation as in the 1970s. At least for the moment, most indicators suggest a continuation of two-tierism in Germany and Japan.

What comes after partial deregulation?

In 2001 Hall and Soskice argued that 'Financial deregulation could be the string that unravels coordinated market economies' so it 'may become more difficult for firms to offer long-term employment' (2001, p 64). Even if the current economic crisis might have more to do with a sudden reduction of exports than with financial deregulation in Germany and Japan itself, the concept of deregulation seems to have lost, at least for the moment, much of its appeal. Yet, would it be reasonable to expect a backlash in the form of re-regulation? Even though one must be cautious, the answer is probably 'no', at least in terms of labour market regulation. While the global economic crisis may be the first major challenge to the newly semi-liberal labour markets, it is unlikely that it alone will initiate a major policy shift. Comparing the measures that have been implemented under the old governments with the measures that have been proposed by the new administrations in Germany and Japan (Table 7.3) shows that the partisan difference is not so big (yet). Of course, much depends on how the economic crisis will unfold from now and how well firms will recover. At the time of writing there were still contradictory signals, with some labour experts still worried that the real test of the current employment systems would not materialise before 2011. If this were true, the political pressure for policy shifts could increase further. On the other hand, rapidly declining unemployment could take out some of the political pressure.

Table 7.3: State and non-state responses to the global economic crisis (October 2009)

	Japan	Germany
Active labour market policies	New training measures announced to take effect in 2010 (old and new government)	Additional training for workers in work-sharing schemes (old government)
Social security and employment maintenance	Expansion of work sharing schemes (*waaku sheringu*) Bill to expand unemployment insurance to non-regular workers was passed in June 2009 (old government)	Massive expansion of work sharing schemes (*Kurzarbeit*), also for temp agencies (old and new governments)
Employment trends	Few dismissals of regular workers Higher dismissal rate of non-regular workers (esp. temp agency workers)	Few dismissals of regular workers Higher dismissal rate of non-regular workers (esp. temp agency workers)
Wages	Dramatic decrease in bonuses Wage hikes are suspended or postponed Higher minimum wages (new government)	Some firms suspend wage hikes, renegotiate collective agreements Income decrease due to work sharing schemes Minimum wage for temp agency workers (old government)
Regulation	Temp agency work in manufacturing to be abolished (proposal by new government still under discussion in early 2010)	Reform of termed-employment (proposal by new government) Freezing of current minimum wage levels, expansion of minimum wage legislation to new industries stopped (new government)

Source: Compilation based on media reports, documents provided by the Federal Agency for Employment in Germany and the Ministry of Health, Labour and Welfare (MHLW) in Japan. See also note 12.

Regarding the question as to what policies are likely in terms of 'political feasibility' and institutional consistency, the evidence points to a continuity of 'two-tierism', except for some minor legal changes to expand the coverage of basic social insurance to non-regular employees. It is noteworthy that the fear of negative trends for regular employment is neither new nor special to the current situation. As Ono observes, it 'is a recurring theme which has evolved over the post-war period in response to fluctuations in the business cycle, not only during the slump years but also during the growth years' (2007, p 3). A similar conclusion can be drawn for Germany, where discussions on the end of the *Normalarbeitsverhältnis* go back to the 1970s (most prominently Mückenberger, 1985). Yet there are two things that are unique to partial deregulation. First, the fact that it is now an easily identifiable group that suffers from unemployment. Second, that regular employment has proven to be so resilient despite the dramatic fall in demand due to the crisis. This can partly be attributed to the massive expansion of work sharing schemes in Germany and Japan, but probably also to the expansion of non-regular work in the 1990s and early 2000s which may have effectively reduced the pressure for dismissals of regular workers after October 2008.

Yet, it should also be kept in mind that the dynamics of non-regular employment are heterogeneous. The different modes of non-regular employment serve different purposes and also differ in their importance for the labour market as a whole. While, for instance, part-time work seems less problematic in Germany because only a comparatively small number of part-timers actually seek full-time employment, this mode of employment is more controversial in Japan, where it is often argued that part-time work is the only work educated women can find after graduation or when returning after child-rearing. The employment forms that most explicitly show signs of precarious and insecure employment are temp agency work and fixed-term employment, and these two forms of employment have thus received most of the recent criticism because many see them as a potential rival to regular employment. More difficult to assess is marginal employment (which in Germany means jobs that pay a maximum of €400 a month [about £358] whereas in Japan *arubaito* are jobs to supplement regular jobs or household work with a minimum wage of ¥717 per hour [in Tokyo; equals about £5]). The number of marginal workers seems dramatic in both Germany and Japan and it is difficult to predict how this kind of employment will develop further, for example, whether it will (or already has) become a permanent mode of employment. So far, many labour market experts see low pay jobs as a solution for unemployment because they make it easier for unemployed or inexperienced workers to enter the labour market. On the other hand, many seem to get stuck in marginal employment. In Japan, workers that rely solely on such work, such as Freeters (a combination of the English word 'free' and the German word for worker, *Arbeiter*) and NEETs (not in education, employment or training) have been in the public spotlight for years. In

Germany, the so-called 'generation internship' (university students who cannot find regular jobs after graduation and instead opt for internships) may be a comparable group. This topic, however, clearly deserves more scholarly attention.

In general comparative terms, it seems as if the lasting functionality of traditional forms of regular employment in Germany and Japan is a blessing and a curse at the same time. It is a blessing because it apparently enables Germany and Japan to limit the overall effect of the current crisis on employment at least this far (see, for example, *The Economist*, 5 November 2009), and to limit non-regular and perhaps even precarious work to an extent. It is a curse because it seems to bar governments from effectively regulating labour markets and adjusting systems of social protection, for instance in the sense of 'flexicurity' which would mean comparable levels of job security and social protection for all workers regardless of their mode of employment (see, for example, Nollert, 2006) for the price of less employment protection overall, which could increase chances for non-regulars to become regular workers. Some of the more pressing social problems, such as low wage levels for unskilled and young workers and limited employment prospects for women (who make up more than 60% of all non-regular employment), may only be addressed with more government interventions, for instance in the form of more ambitious minimum wages or better childcare facilities (Germany and Japan are clearly behind other countries in this aspect). So far, however, German and Japanese governments have left most regulatory answers to the crisis to collective bargaining and have usually intervened only to the benefit of regular employment, by expanding employment maintenance measures, very much as the first hypothesis suggested. It is thus probable that industrial relations will continue to set the pace for non-regular employment as well, even if the decline of organised capital and labour and institutionalised coordinated policy making continues.

Partisanship should not be disregarded as an important influence, however, because there are some differences in the policy positions between the old and the current governments in Germany (see Table 7.3). To a certain degree, the second hypothesis can thus be confirmed as well. However, it could be argued that the latent conflict between insiders and outsiders has not surfaced yet and much of its future significance may hang on how the economic situation will develop from now on. If, however, the economic crisis were to worsen or continue in 2010, the new Japanese government looks more likely to deviate from partial deregulation than the conservative-liberal government in Germany. For the time being, however, scholars interested in the current political dynamics of labour market regulation should focus on changes in industrial relations rather than on legislation.

Notes
[1] Research associate at the Institute of Political Science, University of Heidelberg, Germany and since 2010 research associate at the Institute of East Asian Studies (IN-EAST), University of Duisburg-Essen. A previous version of this chapter was presented at the East Asian Social Policy (EASP) Conference 'Global Economic Crisis and Welfare Restructuring in East and West', 4-5 July 2009, Sheffield.

[2] There are many different definitions in the literature for non-regular employment. Here regular employment stands for salaried, full-time, non-fixed-term employment while non-regular employment stands for all forms of salaried employment that differs from this pattern in one or more aspects.

[3] *Ippanshoku* describes careers in lower management, *sougoushoku* careers in higher-middle and top-level management. Usually the career path is determined at the recruitment stage.

[4] The quality of continuity and change in modern labour markets is a highly relevant question itself, as a comment by Peter Cappelli shows: 'While I have yet to meet a manager who believes that this change has not stood his or her world on its head, I meet plenty of labour economists ... who are not sure what exactly has happened' (quote taken from Kalleberg, 2009, p 6).

[5] On the question of how to define and measure lifetime employment, see Ono (2007).

[6] Labour market flexibility is usually divided into numerical (ease with which the workforce can be reduced), functional (ease with which workers can be assigned to new tasks), temporal (working hours) and wage flexibility. Another possibility is to differentiate between internal and external flexibility. The former describes all elements of labour flexibility that can be achieved inside a firm, and the latter measures outside of a firm, such as outsourcing or hiring of non-regular workers.

[7] It should also be pointed out that the traditional employment systems in Germany and Japan differ regarding the role of corporate and state welfare. Japanese workers are overall much more dependent on corporate welfare even for housing, and until recently had to give up almost all of their entitlements to corporate schemes when leaving their employer. In Germany, state-run social security is in this sense more comprehensive and flexible as it generally does not penalise job

change. However, it differentiates between worker groups, so regular unionised workers on average enjoy higher benefits.

[8] External labour flexibility includes all modes of flexibility that happen outside the immediate realm of the firm. For instance, low employment protection would imply high external flexibility in the sense of high numerical flexibility (Atkinson, 1985).

[9] Labour turnover costs vary depending on the status of a worker. Lindbeck and Snower (2001, 2002) divide workers into three groups: insiders with high labour turnover costs, outsiders with low labour turnover costs, and entrants who may reach insider status in the course of their career but have not done so yet.

[10] Instead of differentiating between regular and non-regular workers, King and Rueda identify a new class of 'cheap labour' that includes many who, in Figures 7.2 and 7.3, would fall under the regular employment category. Workers inside the 'cheap labour' group all lack adequate representation in industrial relations, social protection and adequate pay. King and Rueda also show that this group holds political views markedly different from workers with more favourable working conditions, especially regarding employment protection legislation and welfare policy. Häusermann and Schwander (2009) make a similar argument but they say that work biographies matter more than the current mode of employment.

[11] *Shingikai* can be described as semi-official and semi-formal bodies in the Japanese policy-making system that incorporate members of all groups concerned by the laws discussed. Although most of them are informal, many *shingikai* have been in place for decades (under different names) and even publish records of their proceedings. See Schwartz (1998).

[12] A detailed overview on measures implemented until July 2009 (under the old LDP-led government) can be found at www.mhlw.go.jp/english/policy/affairs/dl/02.pdf. See also the September 2009 issue of *Social Science Japan Newsletter*, University of Tokyo (http://newslet.iss.u-tokyo.ac.jp/ssj41/index.html).

[13] Although the 'equal work equal pay' principle is embedded in German labour law, collective bargaining for temporary agency workers (*Tarifverträge für Zeitarbeit*) allows firms to pay temp agency workers less because the wages in the temp agency industry are usually lower than in other industries.

[14] On the other hand, Charles Weathers, an expert on Japanese industrial relations, argues that this was just an over-reported anomaly. In

fact, non-regular employment would 'continue to replace regular employment' (see http://nbrforums.nbr.org/foraui/list.aspx?LID=5).
[15] The coalition agreement of the new German government foresees legislation to facilitate fixed-term contracts for employees who have been employed by a firm before (*sachgrundlose Befristung*).
[16] In the current cabinet, for instance, over a third of DPJ ministers have a background in the labour movement, but there are almost as many former LDP members in key cabinet positions who generally hold more industry-friendly positions.
[17] Yuasa had been one of the organisers of a 'tent city' in a park close to the central government agencies. Many of its temporary inhabitants were former non-regular workers who had lost company housing together with their job. Although Yuasa resigned in March 2010, he stated that he would continue to cooperate with the government on a case-by-case basis.

References

Atkinson, J. (1985) *Flexibility, uncertainty and manpower management*, Institute of Manpower Studies Report Series, no 89, Brighton: IMSR.

Dore, R. (2000) *Stock market capitalism: welfare capitalism. Japan and Germany versus the Anglo-Saxons*, Oxford: Oxford University Press.

Economist, The (2009) 'Pay for delay', 5 November, p 76.

Hall, P.A. and Gingerich, D.W. (2009) 'Varieties of capitalism and institutional complementarities in the political economy: an empirical analysis', *British Journal of Political Science*, vol 38, no 3, pp 449-82.

Hall, P.A. and Soskice, D. (2001) 'An introduction to varieties of capitalism', in P.A. Hall and D. Soskice (eds) *Varieties of capitalism. The institutional foundations of comparative advantage*, Oxford: Oxford University Press, pp 1-70.

Häusermann, S. and Schwander, H. (2009) *Identifying outsiders across countries: Similarities and differences in the patterns of dualisation*, Working Papers on the Reconciliation of Work and Welfare in Europe, no 09, Edinburgh: RECWOWE Publication

Heinrich, S. and Kohlbacher, F. (2008) 'Sayonara salaryman? Change and continuity in Japan's permanent employment system', *Japan Inc Magazine*, June.

Kalleberg, A.L. (2009) 'Precarious work, insecure workers: employment relations in transition', *American Sociological Review*, vol 74, no 1, pp 1-22.

King, D. and Rueda, D. (2008) 'Cheap labour: the new politics of "bread and roses" in industrial democracies', *Perspectives on Politics*, vol 6, no 2, pp 279-97.

Kume, I. (1998) *Disparaged success: Labour politics in postwar Japan*, Ithaca, NY: Cornell University Press.

Lindbeck, A. and Snower, D.J. (2001) 'Insiders versus outsiders', *Journal of Economic Perspectives*, vol 15, no 1, pp 165-88.

Lindbeck, A. and Snower, D.J. (2002) *The insider–outsider theory: A survey*, IZA Discussion Paper, no 534. Bonn: IZA.

Manow, P. (2001) 'Business coordination, collective wage bargaining and the welfare state: Germany and Japan in historical-comparative perspective', in B. Ebbinghaus and P. Manow (eds) *Comparing welfare capitalism: Social policy and political economy in Europe, Japan and the USA*, London: Routledge, pp 27-51.

Ministry of Health, Labour and Welfare (2004): *Roudou ryoku chousa* [*Labour Force Survey*], Tokyo.

Miura, M. (2001) *Globalization and reforms of labour market institutions: Japan and major OECD countries*, Domestic Politics Project No 4, Heidelberg: Institute of Social Science.

Miura, M. (2002a) 'Atarashii roudou seiji to kyohiken (rengou seiken no seitou seiji to seisaku katei)' ['New labour policy and the right to veto (party politics and policy making in a coalition government)'], *Shakai kagaku kenkyuu zasshi* [*Journal of Social Science*], vol 53, no 2/3, pp 55-78.

Miura, M. (2002b) 'Playing without a net: employment maintenance policy and the underdevelopment of the social safety net in Japan', Paper presented at the Annual Meeting of the American Political Science Association, 29 August–1 September, Boston, MA.

Mückenberger, U. (1985) 'Die Krise des Normalarbeitsverhältnisses. Hat das Arbeitsrecht noch Zukunft?' ['The crisis of regular employment. Is there a future for labour law?'], *Zeitschrift für Sozialreform*, vol 31, pp 415-36, 457-75.

Nollert, M. (2006) 'Soziale Sicherheit und Exklusion im flexiblen Kapitalismus. Eine komparative Analyse und Evaluation von Flexicurity-Politiken' ['Social security and exclusion in flexible capitalisms. A comparative analysis and evaluation of flexicurity policies'], in U. Brinkmann, K. Krenn and S. Schief (eds) *Endspiel des kooperativen Kapitalismus. Institutioneller Wandel unter den Bedingungen des marktzentrierten Paradigmas* [*Cooperative capitalism's endgame: Institutional change under the aegis of the market-centred paradigm*], Wiesbaden: VS Verlag, pp 196-217.

OECD (Organisation for Economic Co-operation and Development) (2004) *OECD employment outlook 2004: Recent labour market developments and prospects*, Paris: OECD Publishing.

Ono, H. (2007) *Lifetime employment in Japan: Concepts and measurements*, SSE/EFI Working Paper Series in Economics and Finance, no 624. Stockholm: Stockholm School of Economics.

Pempel, T.J. and Tsunekawa, K. (1979) 'Corporatism without labour? The Japanese anomaly', in P.C. Schmitter and G. Lehmbruch (eds) *Trends toward corporatist intermediation*, London: Sage Publications, pp 231-70.

Regini, M. (2003) 'Tripartite concertation and varieties of capitalism', *European Journal of Industrial Relations*, vol 89, no 3, pp 251-63.

Rhodes, M. (1997) 'Globalisation, labour markets and welfare states. A future of "competitive corporatism"?', in M. Rhodes and Y. Mény (eds) *The future of European welfare. A new social contract?*, London: Routledge, pp 178-203.

Rueda, D. (2005) 'Insider–outsider politics in industrialized democracies: the challenge to social democratic parties', *American Political Science Review*, vol 99, no 1, pp 61-74.

Schmid, G. (2003) 'Gestaltung des Wandels durch wissenschaftliche Beratung. Das "Bündnis für Arbeit" und die "Hartz-Kommission"' ['Devising change through academic policy advice. The "alliance for jobs" and the "Hartz-commission"'], in S. Ramge and G. Schmid (eds) *Management of Change in der Politik? Reformstrategien am Beispiel der Arbeitsmarkt- und Beschäftigungspolitik. Ein Werkstattbericht* [*Is there a 'management of change' in policy-making? Labour market and employment policies as examples for reform strategies. A review by practitioners*], Berlin: Waxmann, pp 68-94.

Schwartz, F.J. (1998) *Advice and consent: The politics of consultation in Japan*, Cambridge: Cambridge University Press.

Statistisches Bundesamt (2008) *Mikrozensus: Stand und Entwicklung der Erwerbstätigkeit. Band 2: Deutschland* [*Mikrozensus: State and development of employment. Volume 2: Germany*], Wiesbaden.

Streeck, W. (2001) 'Introduction: explorations into the origins of nonliberal capitalism in Germany and Japan', in W. Streeck and K. Yamamura (eds) *The origins of nonliberal capitalism: Germany and Japan in comparison*, Ithaca, NY: Cornell University Press, pp 1-38.

Streeck, W. and Hassel, A. (2003) 'The crumbling pillars of social partnership', *West European Politics*, vol 26, no 4, pp 101-24.

Süddeutsche Zeitung (2008) 'Leiharbeiter sollen Tariflohn bekommen' ['Temp-agency workers to get negotiated wages'], 4 March.

Thelen, K. (1999) 'Why German employers cannot bring themselves to dismantle the German model', in T. Iversen, J. Pontusson and D. Soskice (eds) Unions, employers, and central banks, Cambridge: Cambridge University Press, pp 138-69.

Thelen, K. (2001) 'Varieties of labour politics in the developed democracies', in P.A. Hall and D. Soskice (eds) Varieties of capitalism, Oxford: Oxford University Press, pp 71-104.

Thelen, K. and Kume, I. (1999) 'The effects of globalization on labor revisited: lessons from Germany and Japan', Politics & Society, vol 27, no 4, pp 477-505.

Thelen, K. and Kume, I. (2003) 'The future of nationally embedded capitalism: industrial relations in Germany and Japan', in K. Yamamura and W. Streeck (eds) The end of diversity? Prospects for German and Japanese capitalism, Ithaca, NY: Cornell University Press, pp 183-211.

Thelen, K. and Kume, I. (2006) 'Coordination as a political problem in coordinated market economies', Governance, vol 19, no 1, pp 11-42.

Venn, D. (2009) Legislation, collective bargaining and enforcement: Updating the OECD employment protection indicators, Paris: OECD.

Vogel, S.K. (2003) 'The re-organization of organized capitalism: how the German and Japanese models are shaping their own transformations', in K. Yamamura and W. Streeck (eds) The end of diversity? Prospects for German and Japanese capitalism, Ithaca, NY: Cornell University Press, pp 306-33.

Whittaker, D.H. (1998) 'Labour unions and industrial relations in Japan: crumbling pillar or forging a "third way"', Industrial Relations Journal, vol 29, no 4, pp 280-94.

EIGHT

'Flexibility', xenophobia and exploitation: modern slavery in the UK

Gary Craig

"Slavery ... I didn't know about all these forms that existed. I think it's largely because we aren't expecting it. It is hidden. Generally people would not believe that it is possible under modern conditions. They would say 'No I think you are making it all up', because it's just too incredible." (Archbishop Desmond Tutu, 1999, cited in Craig et al, 2007)

Background

In 2007, commemorative events were held across the UK marking the bicentennial of the abolition of the British transatlantic slave trade, many implying also that slavery had been abolished. Continuing campaigns of the Anti-Slavery Society and others from the mid-19th century onwards indicate, however, that slavery itself had not been abolished. It persists today (Bales, 2004; van der Anker, 2004), but what is less well known is that modern slavery remains a significant facet of the UK economy. Media coverage focuses typically on the treatment of those in slavery in 'less-developed' countries, particularly in Asia and Latin America. Occasional media coverage of horrific events in the UK, such as the drowning of 23 Chinese irregular workers picking shellfish in Morecambe Bay, or the suffocation of migrants in sealed lorries, typically regards these as 'one-offs', not representative of a wider phenomenon. This chapter challenges that perception, arguing that slavery is increasingly common within the UK both directly and indirectly, and that the framework of legislation and policy to address it remains inadequate. It focuses on issues of human trafficking and forced labour, the most common forms of slavery in the contemporary UK, but will also allude to indirect complicity in modern slavery elsewhere. It suggests the need for a much more effective regulatory framework. This is unlikely to happen while the identification of those likely to be in slavery is managed within the context of both a punitive immigration policy and an increasingly deregulated economy. Adel Abadeer (2004) summarises the ways in which modern slavery is obscured within the UK (cited in Craig et al, 2007):

> Modern-day slavery victims are typically very poor, vulnerable and marginalised ... they are unaware of the imperfect nature of contract or of transaction terms, the process of enslavement, and they lack viable secondary sources. The perpetrators, in contrast, exploit the incompleteness of contracts or transactions in terms of the significant information gap between them and the victims ... and the desperate state of the enslaveables that results from their ignorance, vulnerability and the absence of viable alternatives.

Slavery, however defined, is about the removal of liberty from human beings, their treatment as disposable commodities. My colleagues[1] and I define slavery more precisely below. Despite growing evidence to the contrary, there remains a strong view that slavery does not exist in the modern world, having been relegated to the archives of history. Modern slavery is a combination of three elements:

- severe economic exploitation
- the absence of a framework of human rights
- control of one person by another by the threat or reality of coercion or violence.

The issue of violence is not solely a matter of physical violence: a woman trafficked into prostitution can be prevented from freeing herself by psychological threats such as the threat to traffic her daughter also, or to inform her family at home, that, rather than working in a hotel, a bar or a leisure centre – the job she thought she was coming to occupy – she is actually now a prostitute. Any definition of slavery involves boundary difficulties, but this gives us some basis for assessing its scope. Slavery is distinguished primarily from very poor or exploitative working conditions – increasingly familiar in what New Labour has chosen to call its 'flexible labour market'[2] – by the aspect of coercion, 'any situation in which the person has no real and acceptable alternative but to submit to the *abuse* involved' (Weissbrodt and Anti-Slavery International, 2002, para 19, original emphasis). Trafficked adults and children thus fit this definition, whether for sexual purposes or other forms of forced labour.

In seeking to distinguish slavery from severe exploitation, the International Labour Organization (ILO, 2004) has developed six indicators of forced labour. All are present in the UK workforce, typically in combination (Craig et al, 2007; TUC, 2008; Wilkinson et al, 2009):

i Threats or actual physical harm to the worker.
ii Restriction of movement and confinement, to the workplace or to a limited area.
iii Debt bondage: where the worker works to pay off a debt or loan, and is not paid for his/her services. The employer may provide food and accommodation at such inflated prices that the worker cannot escape the debt.
iv Withholding of wages or excessive wage reductions that violate previously made agreements.
v Retention of passports and identity documents, so that the worker cannot leave, or prove his/her identity and status.
vi Threat of denunciation to the authorities, the worker being in an irregular immigration status.

Modern slavery in historical and global contexts

Modern slavery is not an historically isolated phenomenon but a contemporary manifestation of human relations, driven by economic avarice, legitimised by racism. After the global arms and drugs trades, modern slavery is estimated to be the third largest illicit global trade, valued at at least $32 billion per year (Bales, 2007). The bicentenary celebrations promoted a view of Britain as an honourable country, leading the moral struggle against one of the most heinous trades ever. Roughly 16 million Black Africans were forcibly transported across the Atlantic to work as slaves for the rest of their lives. Perhaps 15% of them did not complete the journey, dying en route from disease, sickness or committing suicide. While the contributions of Wilberforce and others are rightly honoured, this perspective on abolition ignored the struggles both of white working people campaigning against slavery – including sailors reporting appalling conditions on slave ships – and of black slaves who fought within both the colonies and Britain against slavery. It overlooked the vast profits made from the exploitation of Africa and the huge wastage of its human resources, legacies resonating today alongside the racism which shapes the socioeconomic outcomes of Black and Asian young people. The abolitionist campaigns need to be understood therefore as broad-based, drawing on all sections of society.

Thanks to Hollywood blockbusters, and to popular academic writing (Walvin, 2007), most people know that slavery was a feature of so-called 'civilised' societies for millennia. Greek and Roman empires were built on slave labour drawn from conquered territories in Asia, Africa and the Gulf. The first black faces seen in Britain were probably Nubian soldiers previously enslaved by Rome. Military conquests and trade were accompanied by capture, exploitation and sale of slaves.

Roughly 11 million slaves were transported by 1900 across the Sahara, the Red Sea and the Indian Ocean (Quirk, 2008). As with the transatlantic slave trade, the driving force was economic, but in a context where slaves crossed boundaries of country and culture in their forced migrations, it was racism – a view from one culture of another's being inherently inferior – that legitimised slave trades. Human trafficking and forced labour now are associated with migration driven generally less by the consequences of war than by the less obvious pressures of poverty and economic dislocation.

British political, economic and religious elites turned slave trading into a state-sponsored industry. Facilitated by its growing maritime, economic and industrial power, Britain responded to the demands of a rapidly growing population for new products – tobacco, chocolate, cotton, minerals – most of all, sugar, 70% of all those surviving the Middle Passage ending up in a sugar colony. Ironically, British world maritime dominance was then used to suppress the trade after 1807. These commodities provide a further link to the present day; many common goods purchased daily from supermarkets, clothing shops and jewellers continue to be produced through the use of slave – often child slave – labour.

Although the slave trades were legally abolished by all European powers by the end of the 19th century, slavery persisted. An important contemporary lesson is that the freeing of slaves as a political act cannot be effective unless they gain, through economic, political and social rehabilitation and their own agency, the political and economic autonomy to become free citizens. This dilemma faces many anti-slavery organisations seeking to emancipate trafficked prostitutes, children working in sweatshops, fishing and stone quarries, forced labourers in brick kilns and agricultural labour: the work of freeing slaves only begins with the act of release (Bales, 2007). Often, 'freed' slaves return to bondage because, for a combination of economic, social and psychological reasons, they are unable to cope with the reality of 'freedom'.

In the 200 years since the 1807 abolition, slavery took many forms, each of which has impacted on present-day demographic and political realities. Africans were transported to the present-day Gulf area; within Central and West Africa, enslavement of African by African or Arab continued, the capture of slaves often accompanied by wars of religious conquest. Thirty per cent of this African population remained enslaved at the beginning of the 20th century. In the 1960s, 200,000 adult slaves remained in the former French colonies, their descendants currently present as familial slaves in the Sahel (*The Times*, 9 March 2007; *The Economist*, 30 October 2008).

By 1900, there were still 2.5 million slaves in British-controlled Northern Nigeria, and slavery was common in both the Muscovy and Ottoman empires. Slaves numbering hundreds of thousands within the Arabian peninsula until the 1960s have now been replaced by migrants from countries such as India, the Philippines and Malaysia, many working effectively as slaves – in construction, as nannies, nurses and cleaners, women's economic contribution often associated with a requirement to perform sexual acts, in conditions so extreme that acts of suicide are not unusual. In 2009, 30 Indian construction workers in Dubai died from heatstroke because their employers refused them shelter and water during one day.[3]

Slavery was formally abolished in India in 1843, but most slaves were transformed overnight into debt bondsmen. In India, the largest single concentration of slaves remains, with tens of millions of adults and children in debt bondage, particularly in agricultural work, a further link between historical and contemporary worlds of slavery. Forced labour remained a familiar part of the colonial landscape throughout much of the early 20th century, most appallingly in the genocidal landscape of the Congo, regarded by Belgium's king as his personal fiefdom (Hochschild, 2006). Although most countries have now formally made slavery illegal, slaves – including many millions of children – remain in many Asian and Latin American countries in more modern industries: brick-making, fish processing, mining, carpet production, charcoal burning, gem-making and the production of fireworks, alongside girls trafficked from neighbouring countries into sexual slavery. The difficulty facing many pursuing abolition is not that slavery is hidden – it is frequently obvious – nor a lack of legislation banning it, but because of complicity between slave masters and the state, particularly police and the judiciary, in maintaining it. Police raids on brothels using trafficked women, or on quarries using child labour, come away empty-handed because agents have been tipped off by corrupt officials.[3]

It is wrong therefore to see modern slavery as isolated from previous manifestations. Although, reflected in international legislation from the 1920s on (Craig et al, 2007), pressure to end slavery has grown; legal instruments and political pressure have failed to abolish it. Slavery simply changes its forms to reflect an industrialised and increasingly globalised world where the migration of labour to new, strange contexts makes it more vulnerable to enslavement.

Ironically, comprehensive data that, during the period when slavery was both legal and diligently recorded,[4] was widely available, is now – in a context of illegality – far less accessible. Estimates of numbers and types of slaves in any country thus come with a health warning as to their approximate, usually understated, nature.[5] The ILO estimates there may be 211 million children aged 5–14 engaged in economic activity, many of them trafficked, most of them working in hazardous situations and at least 8.4 million subjected to the 'worst forms of child labour'. They are concentrated in the Asia–Pacific region, producing goods which go worldwide, most again to the consumer markets of developed countries. Estimates of adults involved in slavery worldwide range from 12 million to 27 million, substantially greater than of those traded across the Atlantic.

Modern slavery worldwide takes many forms, including chattel slavery, forced labour, debt bondage, serfdom, forced marriage, trafficking of adults and children, child soldiers and the severe economic exploitation of children; many of these exist in direct forms within the UK or in other countries linked indirectly to the UK through the supply of goods and services. More recent manifestations here include large-scale farming of cannabis plants by young Vietnamese boys, imprisoned in suburban houses;[6] and the use of children and adults, by criminal gangs, to beg, pickpocket or shoplift.

The most common forms of modern slavery in the UK are of forced labour and human trafficking for sexual purposes (Craig, 2007), examined in more detail below. Forced labour describes the *conditions* under which vulnerable people work; trafficking refers to the *process* by which people are manipulated into vulnerable and exploited situations. Thus trafficked people (for example, who may enter a country *legally* for one form of work but are deceived and/or coerced into an entirely different form) may end up in forced labour, working physically and/or sexually for extremely exploitative employers. Trafficking (CoE, 2004) is distinguished from smuggling in that the latter involves *illegally* transporting people across national borders – the relationship between smuggler and those smuggled may end at that point although many of those smuggled may also end up in forced labour because of their illegal and vulnerable status.

Forced labour in the UK

The ILO (2005a, 2005b; Craig et al, 2007) has led recent attempts to abolish forced labour. It suggests that, despite international trafficking conventions such as the Palermo Protocol (CoE, 2004), there may be 3-4 million adults in Europe without legal papers. While the majority of these 'illegals' or irregular workers may be subject to exploitative working conditions, they would not fit the ILO definition of forced labour. However, within this overall figure, there are half a million people trafficked into the European Union (EU) annually (Floor, 2006), one third for forced labour, the remainder largely for sexual exploitation.

The ILO's indicators mean that forced labourers are operating on the margins of or in illegality. Detailed information about the scope of forced labour in the UK remains extremely difficult to come by, often anecdotal (Dench et al, 2006; Winkelmann-Gleed, 2006; Gupta, 2007), small-scale or journalistic (Pai, 2008), its existence often extrapolated from evidence of extreme exploitation or workers reporting their co-nationals' experience. Evidence suggests that there is a growing problem, requiring stronger intervention by policy makers and those delivering services.

Britain's secret slaves (Anderson, 1993)[7] portrayed domestic slavery (primarily in London). A contemporary report by Anti-Slavery International furnishes greater detail of what is clearly a UK-wide problem, pointing to the systematic global nature of trafficking, resultant on social change, economic and political factors (Skrivankova, 2006, p 20), noting:

> … how widespread and common exploitation in the UK labour market is … exploitative practices such as wage reductions, failure to pay, long working hours, lack of breaks, holidays, health and safety issues, removal of documents, dismissal as a result of complaining about working conditions, and demanding unlawful fees by employment agencies … situations directly or indirectly experienced by … a significant proportion of migrant workers in low-pay sectors … where work can be described by the "three Ds"

(difficult–dangerous–dirty) or where there is a high concentration
of migrant workers....

Trades union-led campaigns to establish the Gangmasters Licensing
Authority (GLA) (Scott et al, 2007) were charged with regulating labour
supply in agriculture/horticulture, food processing/packaging and
shellfish collecting/processing (after the Morecambe Bay tragedy; see
HoC, 2004). Community organisations have also been concerned about
illegality and highly exploitative conditions in certain industrial sectors
(for cleaners, see Artemis, 2006; for domestic workers, see Kalayaan,
2008; for hotels, see TELCO, 2009).

Although forced labour existed in the UK prior to 2004, unexpectedly
large-scale economic migration from the Accession 8 (A8) countries was
a major driver, resulting in hundreds of thousands of workers operating,
often in isolation, with little effective support, some experiencing high
levels of exploitation in the workplace and housing alike (Adamson et
al, 2008). The GLA-led Operation Ruby identified Eastern Europeans
trafficked probably for forced labour but they have been unable to police
most exploited workers' conditions effectively, given limited resources
and remit (Wilkinson et al, 2009). Enhanced levels of in-migration
coincided with 'intensification of work-place regimes in agriculture'
(Rogaly, 2006, p 3), where downward price pressures from retailers are
passed on by labour providers to workers who experience higher levels
of exploitation. Aspects of exploitation are relative, wages considered
exploitative here comparing favourably with wages elsewhere; violence
and coercion are less so.

The greatest driver has been increasing deregulation of the UK
economy making it, the OECD argues, the second least-protected
of all developed countries, after the US, reflected in high proportions
of agency workers in the labour market. Migrant workers, with their
various, confusing immigration statuses and entitlements to work
(including some illegal workers and legal migrants working illegally),
are the largest group most at risk of becoming subjected to slavery-like
working conditions. This has been overlooked in recent media-driven
moral panics about the impact of migrant workers on the UK economy
(which has been shown, in any case, to be either neutral or slightly
benign; see Craig, 2007).

Anderson and Rogaly (2005) summarise overall UK policy approaches
and recent UK legislation with regard to forced labour and people
trafficking. Their analysis of four economic sectors where significant
numbers of migrant workers are found, construction, agriculture/

horticulture, contract cleaning and residential care, asks, rhetorically (p 36):

Are there particular, systematic features in the UK labour market in general, and in these sectors in particular, which create an environment that may actively encourage the exploitation of certain categories of worker? Or are we looking at isolated instances of abuse that can be explained by the profit-maximising behaviour of a small number of unscrupulous employers acting outside the law?

They re-emphasise the flexibility of the UK labour market: 'flexible employment patterns, for instance with regard to working hours; easier hiring and firing of workers; widespread use of short-term contracts; greater flexibility in pay arrangements, linked to performance, for example, and high geographic mobility of the workforce' (Anderson and Rogaly, 2005, p 36). Utilising Anderson and O'Connell Davidson's (2003) work emphasising the demand-led nature of trafficking, they point to constant pressures to cut costs, temporary 'disposable' workers available on demand being laid off when no longer needed. They reported growth in sub-contracting and the creation of long, often opaque, sub-contracting chains as well as outsourcing processes, further obscuring the reality of working conditions from regulatory bodies. In such an environment, labour is treated as a disposable commodity, purchased whenever needed and at very low costs. Other research (Wilkinson et al, 2009) also documents the violence and intimidation meted out to migrant workers, and their substandard working and living conditions, highlighting the inadequacies of current UK statutory protection afforded them.

Enforcement agencies estimate there may be as many as 10,000 gangmasters operating across various industrial sectors, most employing migrant labour; the resources of enforcement agencies – including the core agency, the GLA – are, however, quite inadequate for their task and their powers too narrow. Other main sectors for migrant worker employment unregulated by the GLA include construction, catering, leisure, hotels, cleaning, textiles and social care and healthcare. For example, 5,500 Filipino agency nurses were brought to the UK in 2003 under false pretences (Winkelmann-Gleed, 2006), and are now working excessive hours – often in publicly funded healthcare agencies – paying off large sums (£5,000) as contract fees. Many migrants – apparently working legally – do so under levels of exploitation that meet the ILO definition of 'forced labour'. While there has been growing research on the economic contribution of migrant workers in the UK (see, for example, DBS, 2006; Experian, 2006; Reed and Latorre, 2009), very little has examined issues of exploitation or their need for support, particularly where they work in rural or other isolated situations (NACAB, 2005a, 2005b; Anderson et al, 2006; Fitzgerald, 2007).

One policy problem is that the boundary between severe exploitation and forced labour remains difficult to define precisely. The TUC's Commission on Vulnerable Employment (COVE) (TUC, 2008) identified two million workers in 'vulnerable' employment, most in unorganised sectors, often characterised by subcontracting, agency supply (Markova and McKay, 2008) and complex supply chains (where it was more difficult to monitor or regulate working conditions) (Frances et al, 2005), but they could not explore how many were in forced labour – although seemingly many were. COVE's approach needs to be extended, using local explorations focused specifically on forced labour. The TUC identified fluidity and 'churn' among both workforces and labour suppliers, rapid turnover meaning that accurate policing and data collection was problematic. Estimates of the number of agency workers in the UK range from 0.25 million to 1.25 million, the quarterly Labour Force Survey being unable to identify agency workers. There are other difficult boundary issues: for example are homeworkers, trapped in global supply chains, forced labourers (Oxfam, 2004a)? Another driver has been growing global pressure for economic migration, exploited by criminal gangs in relation to some population groups, such as the trafficking or smuggling of workers from poorer areas of China into the UK. Pai (2008) suggests there may be 300,000 undocumented Chinese workers in the UK, many fitting the ILO definition of forced labour; other estimates suggest even higher numbers (IPPR, 2006).

Many in forced labour may enter the country legally as, for example, A8 Workers Registration Scheme (WRS) workers, slipping into forced labour through a series of pressures – debt bondage, loss of documents, lack of knowledge of rights, disputes with employers – and the general undermining of rights characteristic of a highly 'flexible', unregulated labour market. Others may have arrived as forced labourers, already deeply in debt because of smuggling/travel fees. A third group (for example, students) may have become illegal through failure to observe changing immigration status, increasing their vulnerability to exploitation (Anderson et al, 2006). This group includes many 'refused' asylum seekers, working illegally to mitigate destitution (ICAR, 2006;

Lewis, 2007). Many in forced labour 'choose' it as a survival strategy (Zaranaite and Tirzvte, 2006).

Current evidence suggests then that forced labour within the UK may be a serious and growing issue, arising from the intersection of various circumstances and via different routes, occurring in many industrial sectors with differential gender impacts and difficult to police or quantify. Recommendations for reducing the vulnerability of workers were identified by COVE, directed at a range of agencies, including the government, local government, trades unions, businesses and regulatory bodies. Some, if implemented, might make it possible to regularise the position of those in forced labour, but its report does not address the issue of forced labour directly because of difficulties in gathering data.

Political interest in the concept of forced labour in the UK emerged recently from anecdotal evidence of its growth in industrial sectors where workers are poorly placed to represent their interests. The establishment of a cross-departmental Fair Employment Enforcement Board, the inauguration of a single helpline and government commitment to lead a three-year campaign to increase knowledge among workers of their rights, is belated official acknowledgement of the issue. Additionally, work undertaken by the Home Office/UK Border Agency to establish reporting mechanisms for trafficking victims underpins official recognition of the issue. Action against forced labour under these government programmes, however, presumes coordination of many stakeholders: employers and trades unions, employment inspection agencies, local government, the public services and voluntary organisations. While there is evidence of some willingness to participate, this agenda is confused by the existence of diverse interests and an absence of clarity in crucial areas. The concept of forced labour itself has yet to be interpreted in practical ways relating to the work of many prospective stakeholders, the range of people at risk of being drawn into forced labour and the mechanisms that operate to seal their entrapment currently being understood only in broad sketch terms. Misunderstandings are common, such as the view that its operation is confined to migrants without legal permission to live and work here; it is in fact, as demonstrated, much more widespread. Despite clear evidence of labour trafficking (Skrivankova, 2006), since the 2004 Asylum and Immigration Act there has yet to be a single prosecution brought for trafficking for labour exploitation.

Trafficking for sexual purposes

The US Department of State estimates that at least 800,000 people are trafficked annually across borders worldwide, most of them women and children for sexual purposes, and not including people trafficked *within* countries (UNICEF, 2005). This estimate may be modest as it is believed that more than 500,000 are trafficked into Europe annually. The United Nations (UN) believes that 1.2 million children may be trafficked annually, internally and externally (UNICEF, 2006a).[8]

Evidence of trafficking into and within the UK emerged from the mid-1990s. There is a growing body of accounts of individual victim case histories,[9] but this trade in people is also clandestine, below the radar of policy specialists and politicians. Parliament, however, is becoming sensitised to the problem through debates and the work of the All-Party Parliamentary Group on Trafficking.[10] While the government has begun to prosecute traffickers and criminalise all forms of trafficking – in the 2004 Sexual Offences Act and the 2004 Immigration and Asylum Act – current lack of effective protection for those escaping from trafficking often compounds the abuse that they have already suffered, preventing victims from bringing their plight to the attention of the authorities. As with rape, this leads to under-counting. Many victims are removed as illegal immigrants, with little assessment of risks they may return to and without their traffickers being held to account. The extent of trafficking for sexual exploitation to the UK is unknown but the government suggests 10,000 women and perhaps 3,000-4,000 children have been trafficked here for sexual purposes in the past decade. At any one time about 5,000 child sex workers may be in the UK, most of them trafficked here, 75% of them girls (UNICEF, 2006b).

The larger overall estimates of those trafficked have been challenged, most notably by a reputable newspaper (*The Guardian*, 20 October 2009), which claimed that numbers of those trafficked had been deliberately exaggerated both by evangelistic faith-based groups and by organisations such as the police, in pursuance of their own self-interests. While accurate counting is undoubtedly difficult because of the illegal nature of the activity, this particular account made the somewhat illogical jump from suggesting that numbers had been exaggerated to arguing that trafficking was not a serious problem at all, a statement that flew in the face of the evidence (some of it also published by *The Guardian* in later days) both from women who had been trafficked, organisations involved in helping them (eg ECPAT UK, 2009) and their ongoing records and the accounts of other journalists including, ironically, Pai (2008), who had been funded by the same newspaper to explore the area of trafficking, identifying it as a serious and widespread issue (see note 5). The growth of the problem is suggested by the fact that although the National Criminal Intelligence Service (NCIS, 2002) once also argued that there was no evidence of large-scale trafficking into the UK, this view is now generally accepted as indefensible.

Sexual trafficking is an aspect of human trafficking with its own dominant characteristics. Analysis of global migration trends suggests that almost half of all migrants are women. However, although many women and men migrate for reasons to do with poverty (the push factor) and economic betterment (the pull factor), gender relations – in particular power disparities between men and women – are an important context (Piper, 2005). Human trafficking is dominated by the trafficking of women and children by men. Several non-governmental organisations (NGOs)[11] have emerged recently to address specific aspects of trafficking and long-established children's organisations such as UNICEF, NSPCC and Barnardo's are focusing on child trafficking as cases come to their attention (Pearce et al, 2009). The growing volume of policy, practice and research reports point to continuing difficulties in getting reliable quantitative data (UNICEF, 2003), although there is little dispute about its qualitative dimensions. Growing concern among NGOs has largely driven the introduction of legislation, the development of a Home Office-led UK Action Plan on Trafficking and the establishment of the police-led UK Human Trafficking Centre (UKHTC). Research on sexual trafficking is better developed than on other forms of trafficking but remains largely limited to mapping the problem, reviewing legal frameworks and developing policy responses. Again, boundary issues are problematic, as children and younger people may be trafficked both for labour and sexual purposes and there is also considerable difficulty in determining the age of many young people. Many trafficked young people may be brought in by an alleged relative for educational purposes or placed with private foster carers without official supervision. Trafficked children may have been physically abducted but many are trafficked with the compliance of family members who believe they are being offered a chance to better themselves, not knowing their children may be destined for sexual exploitation. The case of Victoria Climbié is an extreme example – in her case it was for domestic labour. Families are often also coerced through physical threats, debt bondage or pressure from threats of voodoo/juju cults.[12]

Early research (Levy, 1991) suggested that the 'movement of children across international borders for abusive purposes' might incorporate at least four different kinds of phenomena: forced marriages; trafficking of children for sexual exploitation; economic exploitation of children (including the UK as a staging post between Africa and Europe); and trafficking of children for inter-country adoption (involving corruption and exploitation) (Leifsen, 2008). Concern about child sex trafficking in the UK originally focused on the experience of unaccompanied girls (one as young as 12) and young women, mostly from West Africa, arriving at Gatwick airport and, being minors, placed in care in a 'safe' house. Many of these girls and others arriving elsewhere rapidly disappeared, being later identified as sex workers in Italy. Attempts to quantify the extent of this phenomenon failed because of a failure to track them. It was known that more than 60 passed through one West Sussex hostel in less than three years.[13] More recent cases have been reported of young people being detained in, but again disappearing from, children's homes near Heathrow airport. Criminals trafficking young people into the UK appear to respond to policing initiatives by adapting their approaches and using other routes (Dottridge, 2006).

Investigations by children's charities have identified sexual trafficking both *through* the UK to other destinations, and *to* the UK, with young people 'hidden' among the inflow of refugees seeking asylum, ending up as sex workers (including boy prostitutes in refugee dispersal areas). Trafficked children have now been identified as coming from a widening range of sources including many South East Asian countries; a growing number from West, North and Central Africa; from East and Central Europe (especially Balkan and Baltic countries); and, most recently, from the Caribbean. ECPAT UK also suggests that a significant number of young adults may have been trafficked, particularly from South Asia, for the purposes of forced marriage (Bokhari, 2009).

The NSPCC (2006) recorded a 'dramatic' rise recently in referrals of trafficked children to its sexual exploitation service, suggesting that trafficking of children, through deception, manipulation and coercion, may be easier than trafficking in women, because of children's increased levels of dependency on adults. A further ECPAT UK study (2007) noted that dozens of children had gone missing, probably into sexual trafficking, in three regions of the UK.

Trafficking of women is a more extensive and better-recorded phenomenon although hard data remains difficult to come by; no attempt has yet been made to determine whether global figures allow for those who are re-trafficked. An early study identified 71 women trafficked for prostitution in 1998 (Kelly and Reagan, 2000) but suggested that the real figure might have been 20 times higher, the latter figure (1,420) later cited by the Solicitor-General. In 2006, the Home Office produced an unofficial estimate of 400 women trafficked into prostitution, again widely regarded as a serious under-estimate. A study of the sex industry (Poppy Project, 2004) in London found that 85% of women working off streets, mostly from Eastern Europe, had been trafficked into prostitution in the UK: 10 years earlier the figure was nearer 10% (see also Somerset, 2002). A number of recent police raids have led to court cases, for example in Sheffield and Hull, in which several people trafficking women for sexual activity have been imprisoned. Both victim and trafficker were generally from Eastern/South East Europe but traffickers have also been identified from China. A major campaign by the police in 2006[14] suggested that where less than 10% of all brothels or other sex establishments were visited, 'several thousand more victims remain to be found'. In the police Reflex campaign, for offences associated with trafficking, a total of 1,456 arrests were made in 2004/05 and the more recent Pentameter 2 exercise, accompanied by a public awareness campaign (Blue Blindfold), similarly identified thousands of potential adult victims of trafficking.

Many women will have been trafficked as a result of responding to advertisements offering specific kinds of better-paid employment in the UK or even offers of marriage, to help improve their quality of life. Often women are trapped not only by physical threats but also by debt bondage as they struggle to repay the costs of bringing them to the UK; other control techniques involve physical and emotional violence (including rape, torture and beatings), the use of drink and drugs and economic coercion of women and their families.[15] Trafficked women arrive in the UK by every conceivable mode of transport, including on foot. Some may have suffered rape during ethnic conflict and, having been ostracised from their communities, may arrive ostensibly as refugees (which is how they may wish to be perceived).

Most commentators agree that the origins of trafficking lie in conditions in the sending countries, often characterised by poverty, a lack of basic education, by poor attention to human rights and, frequently, by a recent record of conflict, ethnic cleansing and war, leading to considerable demographic dislocation and migration. The impact of globalisation of labour markets is also substantial; essentially, trafficking for sexual purposes reverses the dynamic from one where those owning capital (sex tourists) move to labour (those offering sexual services, for example, in South East Asia) to the converse, where labour is moved to meet the demands of capital on the latter's own territory. Moldova is a typical example; one seventh of the population is estimated to have emigrated in the past few years to seek work. In three years, 1,131 Moldovan victims of child trafficking have been identified.[16] As Masika (2004) notes, the fundamental requirement to combat trafficking is thus to address the impoverishment of many countries and to ensure strategies are developed that reduce the vulnerability of communities at risk. At present, responses are characteristically driven by a sense of political crisis (for example, over immigration) in receiving countries.

UK policy concern has been translated into legal instruments since 2002. Laws have been passed covering issues of trafficking (previously not existing as a distinct crime). Since 2004, all forms of trafficking have been made illegal and traffickers may receive sentences of up to 14 years' imprisonment.[17] Initially, trafficking was defined by government in terms only of prostitution but now incorporates forced labour and domestic servitude; the assets and cash of people traffickers can be seized.

The European Convention for the Protection of Human Rights and Fundamental Freedoms is the overarching policy and political framework covering the treatment of refugees, the right to be free from torture, inhumane or degrading treatment and the prohibition of slavery and forced labour. Here, slavery is interpreted to imply a ban on trafficking. The Council of Europe, as well as requiring binding standards of human rights among member states, has introduced a treaty and protocol specifically addressing trafficking. It proposes measures to prevent and combat trafficking, provide better victim protection, and has established a monitoring body to review progress in implementation.[18] However, although most countries have adopted laws to combat trafficking, policy and practice responses vary quite widely between countries. The general view of the UK position from those working in the field is that legal frameworks are largely adequate in principle – although the UK has only just ratified the Council of Europe Convention on Action Against Trafficking in Human Beings – but that policy and practice responses are inadequate. For example, the TUC (2006) points out that trafficking victims in general appear to have no enforceable employment rights, possibly contributing to the deaths of the Morecambe Bay cockle-pickers.

One major police and policy response was to establish the UKHTC (in Sheffield), in late 2006.[19] It is still too early to assess its effectiveness but it is hoped that it will address the lack of effective communication between police, immigration and both statutory and voluntary social services agencies. Commentators remain critical of the government, which appears far more concerned with tracking and capture of traffickers, with immigration (for example, the fear that illegal economic migrants may abuse the provisions of the Convention) and law enforcement, than with victims' needs and rights.[20] More widely, the government approach appears not to link the trafficking dynamic to the underdevelopment of many, particularly African, countries.

Home Office criteria for identifying trafficked women and allowing them to remain within the UK are thus criticised as being too narrowly drawn, not recognising the need for building trust between authorities and victims of trafficking. These criteria are that women should have been brought to the UK, forcibly exploited, working in prostitution and willing rapidly to cooperate with the authorities;[21] such conditionality can be counterproductive in terms of building relationships of trust. Women identified during police raids are often regarded as illegal immigrants first, and trafficked victims second, often leading to their deportation back to their country of origin where they may face hostility from the host community and re-trafficking or punishment from the trafficking gangs. The UN High Commission for Refugees argues that people who experience sexual violence (including sexual trafficking) should be given refugee status under the UN 1951 Convention on the Status of Refugees. To date, 'only a few trafficked persons ... have been granted refugee status or humanitarian protection in the UK on the basis of their trafficking experience' (Young and Quick, 2006), usually then only on appeal.

What is to be done?

It is clear that the growth of modern slavery within the UK, while driven by racism and economic greed, has effectively been aided by successive governments' stance towards labour market deregulation. While (unlike virtually every other West European country) the UK government's decision not to place obstacles in the path of East and Central European migrant workers wishing to work in the UK following the 2004 EU enlargement was shaped by the desire to have a 'flexible' response, its consequences, in an increasingly unregulated labour market, one where trades union influence is at a low ebb, has been that possibly tens of thousands of workers have slid into forced labour. The only attempt to regulate the most exploitative industrial sectors, the GLA, is poorly resourced, operating within very narrow limits. Given this narrow purview, any gangmaster exploiting workers feeling the hand of the GLA on their shoulder can simply shift to another, unregulated, sector or, as many do, play games, closing down companies and then opening new ones under slightly different auspices (Wilkinson et al,

2009).The growth of xenophobic responses to migrant workers means their vulnerability is obscured (Craig, 2007).

A fourfold response is needed: the government should urgently extend the GLA's remit and its resources; trades unions should target those sectors where exploitative gangmasters are known to operate; exploited workers who have slipped into slavery need to be offered an amnesty from deportation – perhaps their only hope of protection; and the public at large, including those working within advice centres, housing providers and so on, need to scrutinise those with whom they come into contact to ensure that they are not in situations of severe exploitation.

In relation to human sex trafficking, while the government has ratified the Council of Europe Protocol and established the UKHTC, its approach to trafficking remains driven by an emphasis on criminality and on immigration control, despite the fact that many victims enter the UK legally. Organisations working with trafficking victims argue that border officials should be better trained to spot potential victims; monitoring of them post-arrival would help to ensure their protection. For adults who are 'rescued' as a result of police raids, their chances of remaining within the UK and gaining decent work depend critically on their willingness to cooperate with the police in tracking down their traffickers. This may sound unproblematic but they and their families may be at risk of injury or even death if they do so. If they refuse to do so, they may be deported and returned to their countries of origin to face humiliation and the possibility of being re-trafficked. A much clearer focus on the needs of victims is required. For young people and children, there needs to be better investigation and protection on arrival: there are well-recorded processes whereby young people arrive in this country, are taken into care and then 'escape', being trafficked either internally in the UK or to other European destinations.[22]

There is also a role for the wider public. Incidents are reported where residents in neighbourhoods have complained about overcrowding and noise among migrant worker populations. A little neighbourly investigation might reveal the economic hardship which many such workers face, forcing them into such situations.These investigations can be reported to local authority public health and housing departments, advice centres or fire and rescue services, with a view to exploring the levels of exploitation that such workers face (Adamson et al, 2008). Similarly, as Pai shows, many brothels using trafficked women or cannabis factories operate in otherwise unremarkable urban and suburban streets. As the theme of the Blue Blindfold campaign suggests, much can be done to help victims by everyday observation of the unusual.

On a wider canvas, we noted that many of the goods and services available on an everyday basis in the shops in an average UK high street are produced under slavery-like conditions – including the use of child labour – in other countries. Initiatives are being developed in the UK, of which the Fairtrade movement is probably the most well known, to ensure that those who produce such goods and services obtain just rewards for their labour. In specific sectors such as cocoa and chocolate, ethical trading initiatives – alliances of voluntary organisations, trades unions and businesses – are slowly drawing in companies to sign up to ethical employment and purchasing policies.[23] Achievements are modest to date but their impact is slowly growing and the public education work they do has an important role in reaching a much wider public. Many large companies – Tesco, Marks and Spencer, Gap, Primark, Sainsbury's among them (Oxfam, 2004c; Action Aid, 2005; Corporate Watch, 2005; Monbiot, 2005) – have been named and shamed in the media as a result of activists' investigations. These companies often hide behind both agents who manage workforces – here and abroad – and behind complex supply chains where it is virtually impossible to discover who is responsible for the conditions of workers. End user companies then deny responsibility for unethical behaviours elsewhere.[24] It is the responsibility of all to ask awkward questions about how companies such as Primark can possibly sell t-shirts at £3 and trousers at £8, or the conditions under which red roses grown in Kenya or cocoa beans grown in the Côte d'Ivoire are produced and, when dissatisfied with the answers, to take our business elsewhere.

However, again, government too has a responsibility. Its approach has been to argue for voluntary codes of practice and it does not yet police companies in any meaningful way, another aspect of its 'flexible' approach. Action Aid and others argue that a voluntary approach is insufficient, needing to be underpinned by minimum legal standards. These would incorporate requirements that the government should extend company law to place legal duties on companies to take account not just of their company's interests but also of its wider stakeholders – notably employees, suppliers, local communities and on the environment – in decision making. Political campaigning with government on a range of issues is also important. The critical factor driving people to migrate is poverty: development aid programmes should build in understandings of and links to issues around slavery and its causes, and sanctions against those perpetuating it. It is now relatively straightforward – Bales (2007) has done this – to identify the general characteristics of countries likely to be involved in exporting migrants into slavery, and indeed both Bales (2007) and Arocha (2008) have provided a taxonomy of these issues; while further research is probably needed, there is enough general guidance for aid donors to consider attaching conditions about anti-slavery campaigns to aid programmes and to inform local policy and action.

We noted that the campaign to abolish the slave trade in 1807 was a broad-based one, uniting a range of people from differing backgrounds, classes and interests. This can be a model for action now, seeking to create broad-based campaigns, informed by moral outrage, exploiting all the forms of political action open to us, to end this appalling trade. Like the transatlantic slave trade, we are all compromised by modern slavery because we all benefit from it; we all therefore have a moral duty to stop it. Bales argues that modern slavery could be halted within a generation by effective, targeted political and economic actions: everyone has a role to play in achieving this.

Notes

[1] This chapter owes much to the work that has been developed collectively at the Wilberforce Institute for the study of Slavery and Emancipation (WISE) in Hull over the past few years. In particular I would like to acknowledge collaborations with Mick Wilkinson, Joel Quirk, Kevin Bales and Aline Gaus at WISE and with Aidan McQuade and Klara Skrivankova (Anti-Slavery International), Jonathan Blagbrough (freelance researcher), Don Flynn (Migrants' Rights Network), Farrah Bokhari (ECPAT UK) and Oxfam UK.

[2] The two New Labour Prime Ministers, Tony Blair and Gordon Brown, have frequently celebrated the fact that the UK has a flexible labour market, indeed one which is now regarded as probably the most flexible in Western Europe. However, flexibility appears to be a code for high levels of exploitation including low wages, long hours, insecure contracts, poor working conditions and little trades union organisation or protection.

[3] See the report of a study tour undertaken for the Mahatma Gandhi Memorial Committee in early 2009 for details of modern slavery in India and of Indian migrant workers operating in slave-like conditions in other countries. Copies of the report are available from me at g.craig@hull.ac.uk

[4] For example, WISE holds detailed records, including names of slaves transported and originating ports, of thousands of transatlantic slave journeys.

[5] I had a conversation with a senior police official searching for trafficked women in local brothels. The local chief constable suggested

that there might be one such brothel locally.The police investigation found more than 50 involving several hundred prostitutes, many of them trafficked.

6   And not just in the suburbs. In June 2009, a cannabis 'factory' managed by a number of East Asians and located in a small rural village in North Yorkshire was raided by police.

7   For a more recent account of the plight of migrant domestic workers in the UK with proposals for remedies, see Anderson (2004).

8   The ILO (www.ilo.org) suggests that there may be 1.4 million trafficked migrants worldwide forced into commercial sexual exploitation.

9   See, for example, Wainwright (2006); Stratton (2005).

10   See, for example, Parliamentary Debate, 24 May 2007; HoC (2009).

11   For example, ECPAT UK (www.ecpat.org.uk); Eaves Housing (www.eaves.org.uk).

12   See *The Guardian*, 3 May 2005.

13   This 'Newbridge' phenomenon is described at greater length in UNICEF (2003) and in Somerset (2002).

14   Pentameter 2 (see www.pentameter.police.uk).

15   The physical and mental health effects on victims of sexual trafficking are recorded at www.lshtm.ac.uk/hpu/docs/stolensmiles.pdf. The first prosecution under the 2003 Sexual Offences Act was of two Albanian traffickers who lured Lithuanian women to the UK, took their passports and forced them to act as prostitutes to pay off their air fares.The traffickers were given 18 and 19 years' imprisonment.

16   'Ending child trafficking' (see www.unicef.org.uk/unicefuk/policies/policy_detail.asp?policy=30).

17   See, for example, the 2002 Proceeds of Crime Act; the 2003 Sexual Offences Act; and the 2004 Asylum and Immigration Act.

18   *Ad hoc Committee on Action against trafficking in Human Beings*, Council of Europe Convention (revised draft), 5 July 2004.

19   www.ukhtc.org/

20   See, for example, Baroness Scotland, Home Office Minister of State, cited in *Hansard* House of Lords written answers, 2 November 2006: 'the government are examining how the Council of Europe's Convention's approach could best be harmonised with effective immigration controls', a comment which came back to haunt her as she was later found to be employing an irregular worker.

21   Although the period of 'reflection' has been extended, there is still an implicit pressure on victims to cooperate with the police regardless of fears for their own or their families' safety.

[22] Interestingly, Italy and Nigeria (as receiving and sending countries respectively) launched a joint research study some years ago into trafficking of young women. Although UKHTC is building links with police forces in other countries, including potential sending countries, the UK government could learn much from an exercise of this kind.

[23] www.ethicaltrade.org

[24] Gap, for example, found that the sale of clothing such as cotton dresses, was supported by up to a dozen different production processes – harvesting, refining weaving, cutting, dyeing, sewing, ornamenting, etc – each managed by different suppliers, many of them using child labour. Gap's response has been to bring all those processes 'in-house' where it can supervise them effectively although it also recognises that the impact of this in terms of price rises may reduce its market share against more unscrupulous companies. On the other hand, an enhanced reputation also led to increased sales in some areas.

References

Action Aid (2005) *Rotten fruit: Tesco profits as women workers pay a high price*, London: Action Aid.

Adamson, S., Craig, G. and Wilkinson, M. (2008) *Migrant workers in the Humber*, Hull: Humber Improvement Programme.

Anderson, B. (1993) *Britain's secret slaves: An investigation into the plight of overseas domestic workers*, London: Anti-Slavery International.

Anderson, B. (2004) 'Migrant domestic workers and slavery', in C. van den Anker (ed), *The political economy of new slavery*, Basingstoke: Palgrave, pp 107-17.

Anderson, B. and O'Connell Davidson, J. (2003) *Is trafficking in human beings demand driven?*, Geneva: International Organisation for Migration.

Anderson, B. and Rogaly, B. (2005) *Forced labour migration to the UK*, London: Trades Union Congress.

Anderson, B., Ruhs, M., Rogaly, B. and Spencer, S. (2006) *Central and East European migrants in low-wage employment in the UK*, York: Joseph Rowntree Foundation.

Arocha, L. (2008) 'Modern slavery', PhD thesis (unpublished), Roehampton: University of Roehampton.

Artemis (2006) 'Underground Londoners' [DVD] (http://creativecommons.org/policy).

Bales, K. (2004) *Disposable people: New slavery in the global economy*, Berkeley, CA: University of California Press.

Bales, K. (2007) *Ending slavery*, Berkeley, CA: University of California Press.

Bokhari, F. (2009) *Stolen futures*, London and Hull: ECPAT UK and WISE.

CoE (Council of Europe) (2004) *Ad hoc committee on action against trafficking in human beings*, Strasbourg: CoE.

Corporate Watch (2005) *Off the peg: Tesco and the garment industry in Asia*, London: Corporate Watch.

Craig, G. (2007) 'They come over here.... And boost our economy', *Regional Review*, University of Leeds, Summer, 33-35.

Craig, G., Gaus, A., Wilkinson, M., Skrivankova, K. and McQuade, A. (2007) *Contemporary slavery in the UK: Overview and key issues*, York: Joseph Rowntree Foundation.

DBS (Dundee Business School) (2006) *Tayside migrant labour population study*, Dundee: DBS.

Dench, S., Hurstfield, J., Hill, D. and Akroyd, K. (2006) *Employers' use of migrant labour*, Home Office Online Report 03/06, London: The Stationery Office.

Dottridge, M. (2006) *Action to prevent child trafficking in South Eastern Europe*, Geneva: UNICEF/Terre des Hommes.

ECPAT UK (End Child Prostitution, Child Pornography and the Trafficking of Children for Sexual Purposes) (2007) *Missing out*, London: ECPAT UK.

ECPAT UK (2009) *Bordering on concern: Child trafficking in Wales*, London: ECPAT UK.

Experian (2006) *Migrant workers in West Yorkshire, North Yorkshire and the Humber*, Bradford: Learning and Skills Council Yorkshire and Humber.

Fitzgerald, I. (2007) *The informational needs of Polish migrant workers*, Leeds: Yorkshire and Humber Trades Union Congress.

Floor, M. (2006) 'UNHCR's role in combating human trafficking in Europe', *Forced Migration Review*, no 25.

Frances, J., Barrientos, S. and Rogaly, B. (2005) *Temporary workers in UK agriculture and horticulture*, London: Department for Environment, Food and Rural Affairs.

Gupta, R. (2007) *Enslaved*, London: Portobello.

HoC (House of Commons) (2004) *Gangmasters (follow-up): Eighth report of session 2003-4*, HC 455, Environment, Food and Rural Affairs Committee, London: HoC.

HoC (2009) *The trade in human beings*, Home Affairs Committee, HC23-1, London: The Stationery Office.

Hochschild, A. (2006) *King Leopold's ghost*, Basingstoke: Pan.

ICAR (Information Centre about Asylum and Refugees) (2006) *Destitution amongst refugees and asylum seekers*, London: ICAR.

ILO (International Labour Organization) (2004) 'Human trafficking and forced labour exploitation: guidelines for legislators and law enforcement', in B. Anderson and B. Rogaly (2005) *Forced labour and migration to the UK*, London: TUC/COMPAS, p 16.

ILO (2005a) *A global alliance against forced labour*, Geneva: ILO.

ILO (2005b) *Human trafficking and forced labour exploitation: Guidelines*, Geneva: ILO.

IPPR (Institute for Public Policy Research) (2006) *Irregular migration in the UK*, London: IPPR.

Kalayaan (2008) *The new bonded labour?*, London: Kalayaan and Oxfam.

Kelly, L. and Reagan, L. (2000) *Stopping traffic*, Police Research Series Paper No 125, London: Home Office.

Leifsen, E. (2008) 'Child trafficking and formalisation', *Children and Society*, vol 22, no 3, pp 212-22.

Levy, A. (1991) 'Cross-border movement for abusive purposes: the adequacy of UK safeguards', *Childright*, issue 159, pp 608-10.

Lewis, H. (2007) *Destitution in Leeds*, York: Joseph Rowntree Charitable Trust.

Markova, E. and McKay, S. (2008) *Agency and migrant workers*, London: Trades Union Congress.

Masika, R. (ed) (2004) *Gender, trafficking and slavery*, Oxford: Oxfam.

Monbiot, G. (2005) 'The price of cheap beef: disease, deforestation, slavery and murder', *The Guardian*, 18 October.

NACAB (National Association of Citizens' Advice Bureaux) (2005a) *Supporting migrant workers in rural areas: A guide to Citizens Advice Bureaux initiatives*, London: NACAB.

NACAB (2005b) *Home from home? Experiences of migrant workers in rural parts of the UK, and the impact on local service providers*, London: NACAB.

NCIS (National Criminal Intelligence Service) (2002) *UK threat assessment of serious and organised crime* (www.ncis.co.uk/ukba/threat4.asp).

NSPCC (National Society for the Prevention of Cruelty to Children) (2006) *Tackling human trafficking – Consultation on proposals for a UK action plan*, London: NSPCC.

Oxfam (2004a) *Made at home*, Oxford: Oxfam.

Oxfam (2004b) *Trading away our rights: Women working in global supply chains*, Oxford: Oxfam.

Oxfam (2004c) *Stitched up*, Oxford: Oxfam.

Pai, H.-H. (2008) *Chinese whispers*, London: Penguin Books.

Pearce, J., Hynes, P. and Bovarnick, S. (2009) *Breaking the wall of silence*, London: NSPCC.

Piper, N. (2005) 'Gender and migration', Paper prepared for the Policy Analysis and Research Programme of the Global Commission on International Migration (www.gcim.org).

Poppy Project (2004) *Sex in the city: Mapping commercial sex across London*, London: Poppy Project.

Quirk, J. (2008) *Unfinished business*, Paris: UNESCO.

Reed, H. and Latorre, M. (2009) *The economic impacts of migration on the UK labour market*, London: Institute for Public Policy Research.

Rogaly, B. (2006) *Intensification of work-place regimes in British agriculture*, University of Sussex Migration Working Paper No 36, Brighton: Institute of Development Studies.

Scott, S., Geddes, A., Nielson, K. and Brindley, P. (2007) *Gangmasters Licensing Authority annual review*, Nottingham: Gangmasters Licensing Authority.

Skrivankova, K. (2006) *Trafficking for forced labour: UK country report*, London: Anti-Slavery International.

Somerset, C. (2002) 'The trafficking of children into the UK for sexual purposes', *Childright*, no 186, pp 19-20.

Stratton, M. (2005) 'The people traffickers', *The Yorkshire Post*, 9 May.

TELCO (2009) *Rooms for change*, London: London Citizens.

TUC (Trades Union Congress) (2006) *Tackling trafficking through workers' rights*, London: TUC.

TUC (2008) *Hard work, hidden lives*, London: Commission on Vulnerable Employment.

UNICEF (2003) *End child exploitation, stop the traffic!*, London: UNICEF UK.

UNICEF (2005) *The true extent of child trafficking*, London: UNICEF.

UNICEF (2006a) *Child trafficking*, London: UNICEF UK.

UNICEF (2006b) *Commercial sexual exploitation*, London: UNICEF UK.

van den Anker, C. (ed) (2004) *The political economy of new slavery*, Basingstoke: Palgrave.

Wainwright, M. (2006) 'Pregnant girl left in street after being held captive in brothel', *The Guardian*, 11 July.

Walvin, J. (2007) *A short history of slavery*, Harmondsworth: Penguin.

Weissbrodt, D. and Anti-Slavery International (2002) *Abolishing slavery and its contemporary forms*, HR/PUB/02/4 (www.antislavery.org/english/resources/reports/download_antislavery_publications/slavery_reports.aspx).

Wilkinson, M., Craig, G. and Gaus, A. (2009) *Turning the tide*, Oxford: Oxfam.

Winkelmann-Gleed, A. (2006) *Migrant nurses, motivation, integration, contribution*, Oxford: Radcliffe Medical Press.

Young, W. and Quick, D. (2006) 'Combating trafficking in the UK', *Forced Migration Review*, no 25.

Zaranaite, D. and Tirzite, A. (2006) *The dynamics of migrant labour in South Lincolnshire*, Nottingham: EMDA.

NINE

Mi Familia Progresa: change and continuity in Guatemala's social policy

Elena Gaia[1]

Introduction

Catching up on recent trends in social assistance in Latin America, in April 2008 Guatemala introduced *Mi Familia Progresa* (MIFAPRO) (My Family is Moving Forward), a conditional cash transfer (CCT) programme. Pioneered in Latin America by Brazil and Mexico during the 1990s, CCTs have acquired prominence in social policy debates over the past 10 years and have spread across all Latin America and many other countries around the world.[2]

Used in developmental or humanitarian contexts, CCTs are a form of social assistance that links the provision of cash to the behaviour of the target population, who are required to perform certain verifiable actions such as securing minimum investments in children's education and health. Generally these programmes seek to sustain or increase demand for and consumption of goods and services purchased in the market – for example, food – and/or provided by the state – for example, health and education (Farrington and Slater, 2006). In this sense, they normally combine two sets of objectives: the cash transfer component aims at short-term poverty[3] reduction, either in the form of prevention or alleviation, while the conditionality relates to long-term improvements in human development. Conditionality is supposed to incentivise this investment but also places 'emphasis on the participants' active management of their risk through "co-responsibility" [...] where beneficiaries contribute their labour for the implementation of projects'

(Molyneux, 2006, p 434). Although the incidence of such programmes in total social spending is very small compared to other sectors of social policy,[4] there is a growing consensus among scholars that they represent a new generation of social policy (Rawlings, 2004; Molyneux, 2008). In particular, it is argued that programmes of this type have brought about significant innovations in social assistance policies, for instance by promoting transparency and efficiency over past legacies of paternalism and clientelism (de la Brière and Rawlings, 2006; Barrientos and Santibañez, 2009). Other scholars have been more sceptical as to 'the potential of these programmes to substantially re-orientate welfare systems and promote equitable public policies' (Lloyd-Sherlock, 2008, p 621).

The adoption of this type of instrument for the first time in the history of Guatemala's welfare provision, coupled with the increasing amount of resources mobilised for it, triggers questions as to whether this country, for a long time considered a laggard in social policy in Latin America, is now undergoing a process of change and reform in this realm. The aim of this research is to foster a better understanding of the progress and challenges of social development and social policy in an under-researched developing country such as Guatemala, and to contribute to ongoing debates about the implications of CCT programmes in Central and Latin America. The chapter builds on two main bodies of literature: on the one hand, research on the political economy of social policy reform, both in advanced and developing countries; on the other hand, the literature regarding social assistance and poverty reduction in developing countries and Latin America in particular. Interviews with key informants[5] in Guatemala complement the review of official documents and secondary data.

The chapter carries out an analysis of the Guatemalan programme, focusing on its design, set up and execution so far. The analysis is conducted against the backdrop of the general social policy context in the country since the end of the civil war in 1996, in order to determine the extent to which this initiative represents a change in Guatemala's social policy. The analysis of policy change will consider the following specific dimensions: the context into which the new programme has been inserted, the policy instrument, the content of the policy and its consequences, as well as the politics surrounding the initiative. Given the short life of the programme, any assessment of the results and the impact of *Mi Familia Progresa* is beyond the scope of this chapter.[6]

The study concludes that *Mi Familia Progresa* represents continuity more than change in Guatemala's social policy. Although MIFAPRO could become an important step further in the advancement of welfare entitlements in the country, its residual nature hampers its transformative potential. In terms of the broader implications for social policy in Central and Latin America, the findings of this chapter confirm the general consensus on the need to insert current CCT programmes into broader and more inclusive social and economic policies.

The structure of the chapter is as follows. The first section gives an overview of social indicators and social policy trends and identifies the main characteristics of Guatemala's social policy since 1996. The next section is dedicated to a detailed analysis of the content of *Mi Familia Progresa*, with some insights into its potential consequences. In the third section I bring together the main findings of the analysis conducted in the previous section to show that MIFAPRO represents continuity more than change in Guatemala's social policy. In the conclusion, I summarise the main findings of the chapter and speculate on their broader implications for social policy in the region.

Social policy and development in Guatemala after 1996

Despite being classified as a middle-income country by The World Bank, Guatemala has one of the highest poverty rates and most unequal income distributions in Latin America. Half of the population (6.6 million people) live below the national poverty line,[7] and 15% – 2 million – in extreme poverty[8] (INE, 2006). Since 2000, poverty declined by 9 percentage points, while extreme poverty has remained the same. Poverty and deprivation are concentrated in the rural areas and highly correlated with ethnicity as 56% of people in poverty and 68% of people in extreme poverty belong to the indigenous population. With respect to inequality, estimates show that the top quintile has a consumption share of 51%, while that of the lowest quintile is 6%, indicating the persistence of substantial disparities (The World Bank, 2009b). Due to the low starting levels for many social indicators, in particular extreme poverty, malnutrition, primary school completion and persistence rates, Guatemala has a long way to go before its social indicators match those of other comparable countries in the region (The World Bank, 2009b).

Contemporary social policy-making in Guatemala is conditioned by broader unresolved socio-economic and political issues. Thirty-six years of civil war, military rule and violent repression of dissent have left the country without strong civil society and political actors pushing for the expansion and institutionalisation of social policy. Elites, supported by enclave economies based on exports of primary goods, have been dominating the state apparatus and have used the fiscal capacity of the state for the extraction of rents, without providing the counterpart collective goods neither in infrastructure nor in regulation or social services (Filgueira, 2005). During the structural adjustment reforms of the 1980s and 1990s, as social policy became increasingly associated with poverty alleviation rather than social inclusion, historically and newly excluded sectors were left without institutionalised forms of protection or, at best, very weak forms of protection. Eventually, the advent of democracy brought about a basic consensus on rights to well-being and institutional responsibilities for delivering them enshrined in the Peace Accords of 1996. This has been compounded by the establishment of the Millennium Development Goals, imposing strong commitments upon the state. As a result, public social spending as a percentage of GDP has increased dramatically since 1996, although still remaining among the lowest in Latin America; however, social spending as a share of total public expenditure is above the regional average (The World Bank, 2009b). Tax efforts in Guatemala remain low, at around 12% of GDP in 2007, below the regional average for Latin America for the same year calculated at around 15% (ECLAC, 2009). Although the peace negotiations and resulting accords generated new opportunities for the engagement and participation of civil society in public sector reform, most of this participation has been merely cosmetic (Freedom House, 2006). Thus, decision-making has remained highly centralised and rather exclusionary, with the executive overshadowing Congress. Moreover, issues of state legitimacy and the persistent challenges to deepening democracy and rule of law also affect public social policy making in Guatemala. The country falls short of a consolidated and professional civil service, thus impeding the consolidation of state policies over time. Corruption and lack of transparency have also been major issues, with both the Guatemalan Institute of Social Security (IGSS) and the Superintendence of Tax Administration (SAT) embroiled in corruption allegations (Freedom House, 2006).

Ultimately, the lack of well-functioning labour and financial markets and the high degree of labour informality indicate that Guatemala has not been able to achieve the commodification of labour 'while social protection and the formation of human capital are minimally decommodified' (Martinez Franzoni, 2008a, p 87). If participation in the labour market is not a way out of poverty for the majority of the population, with the features outlined, the capacity of the state to compensate for the inadequacy and inequitable outcomes of imperfect markets in such an unequal society is limited (Gough, 2008). In such a context, families continue to play a central role as 'social policy remains residual in terms of the services provided (very basic), their coverage (very limited), and the amount and source of resources programs receive (largely contingent on international cooperation or loans, unpaid work, and co-payments by recipients)' (Martinez Franzoni, 2008a, p 91).

As to the policy instruments that have been enacted since 1996, public social expenditure has concentrated on education, with half of the investment targeted to primary education and around 10% on each of the other three levels. While primary education is mostly public and managed by the central government, secondary education is private. Spending on education and health displays the highest degrees of progressivity and incidence on the poorest quintiles of the population. Social protection expenditures, including social security, social assistance and social funds, amounted in 2003 to 3.8% of GDP (The World Bank, 2005), below the regional averages in Central and Latin America. Social security represented two thirds of the social protection budget and the social funds used almost one fifth of the budget (The World Bank, 2009b). By 2006 only 3.4% of workers affiliated to the IGSS were extremely poor and 22.6% were poor (The World Bank, 2009b). A limited number of formal workers and public officers are enrolled, while the vast majority of the population, represented by the informal sector workers, agriculture and secondary labour force, is excluded. Health insurance through the IGSS has an overall low coverage, leaving 94.5% of the poor and 97.2% of the extreme poor uncovered (The World Bank, 2009b).

Social assistance accounted for 16% of total social protection expenditure in 2003, with expenditure being channelled mainly to a host of different small programmes (21 in total in 2003) in education (school meals, scholarships, subsidies to school and transport, materials) and, to a lesser extent, early child care and subsidies for fertilisers, electricity and housing (The World Bank, 2009b). The fragmentation and dispersion of efforts in social assistance across multiple small and uncoordinated initiatives is coupled with institutional fragmentation leading to the dispersion and duplication of responsibility across multiple government entities, para-statal bodies and social funds. Seventeen per cent of the population is covered by at least one of these programmes and coverage for each of the lowest three quintiles and for the extreme poor and all poor people is 20% (The World Bank, 2009b). Absolute incidence varies substantially among the social programmes with some being pro-poor, such as school supplies and school meals, but others highly regressive (school transport subsidy, scholarships, health programmes). As such, the technical and administrative capacity required for a successful targeting cannot be taken for granted. Criteria for targeting social assistance have differed widely across programmes, with some using geographic criteria (although rarely based on poverty maps) and others using broad categorical eligibility, for example, girls in poor rural areas, victims of human rights violations, orphans, poor elderly, landless peasants, breast-feeding mothers, refugees, etc). Furthermore, these initiatives are seldom monitored and evaluated due to the lack of adequate mechanisms to do so (The World Bank, 2009b).

To sum up, the previous insights from the available literature on Guatemala make it possible to identify a number of broad characteristics of Guatemala's social policy. The broader context of social policy in Guatemala has been characterised by: (a) focus on poverty reduction – mainly in the dimension of access to education, health and nutrition – as the main goal of social policy; (b) low mobilisation of domestic resources and low expenditure; (c) elitist and exclusionary decision-making practices, concentrated in the central government; (d) low state legitimacy resulting in lack of transparency, high risks of corruption and clientelism, and discontinuity between governments; and (e) residual state intervention and underdeveloped markets leading to a central role of families and women in securing welfare. In terms of the choice of policies to address the issues identified, the emphasis has been on the provision of basic social services, with social insurance and social assistance playing a minimal role both in terms of coverage, resources committed and incidence. As to the specific features of previous social assistance programmes, these have been characterised by: (a) low coverage and regressive incidence; (b) dispersion of efforts across multiple small and uncoordinated initiatives and institutional fragmentation; (c) limited targeting capacity and lack of monitoring and evaluation mechanisms. Bearing these features in mind, I now turn to examine in detail how *Mi Familia Progresa* fits into the scenario just sketched.

Mi Familia Progresa: the programme, its settings and its consequence

Coverage, targeting and conditionalities

In order to increase the human capital of younger generations and break with the intergenerational cycle of poverty, MIFAPRO provides two types of monetary transfer,[9] both targeted to women in households living below the extreme poverty line. A monthly health and nutrition transfer of around US$ 18 (£11.57) is paid to mothers of children under the age of six, to pregnant women and to breast-feeding mothers, on the condition that they attend health centres to receive a basic package of nutritional and preventive maternal-child healthcare services. An education transfer of US$18 is paid to families with at least one child between the ages of 6 and 15 attending primary school or preschool. The two types of transfer are not mutually exclusive and they can be cumulated, while the amount provided is not adjusted to the number of children, size of the family or other special conditions.

The cash transfer of US$18 represents 10% of the average monthly consumption of an extremely poor household, estimated in 2006 to be US$193 (approximately £124) (INE, 2006), while the combined cash transfers for health, nutrition and education, US$36 (£23), represent around 20%. At the end of 2008, the total amount of cash transfers handed out topped US 13 million (approximately £8,349,500) and benefited 280,939 families (Gobierno de Guatemala, 2009). This represents 0.2% of total government spending and 0.03% of gross domestic product (GDP) in 2008. In November 2009, the programme reached more than 450,000 households, thus almost attaining the goal of 500,000 set for 2009, which would benefit a total of three million Guatemalans, almost half the total population estimated to be living in poverty.

Targeting in MIFAPRO is based on a combination of regional criteria and means-testing. Forty-six municipalities were prioritised in the first phase of the programme on the basis of poverty maps previously elaborated from the 2002 Census and from the two rounds of the Guatemalan living standards measurement survey conducted in 2000 and 2006. The use of poverty assessment tools previously elaborated in the country is also a welcome change as it tries to build public social interventions on the best evidence available, thus reducing the scope for discretion and corruption. Furthermore, by building upon the previous efforts of data collection, MIFAPRO is displaying some degree of continuity in social policy between governments. Compared to the methods used for targeting previous cash transfers, MIFAPRO has undoubtedly made a huge step forward by incorporating the most advanced methodological devices[10] applied in other similar initiatives and developed with the help of international donors such as The World Bank. By the end of 2008, 89 municipalities were incorporated and in the third phase of the programme, begun in March 2009, another 47 municipalities were integrated.

The introduction of the conditionalities in MIFAPRO is a novelty within the spectrum of previous social assistance programmes in Guatemala. The main issue that future evaluations of the programme will need to address is whether this type of intervention, focused on boosting demand, is appropriate to achieve improvements in education and health indicators and whether it is supported by a sufficient level of services' supply, so as to avoid generating additional compliance costs for beneficiaries. It is worth mentioning that the use of conditionalities in MIFAPRO draws on the standard CCT model adopted across Latin America and popularised by the main lending international institutions in the region – namely The World Bank and the Inter-American Development Bank.[11] Indeed, this type of social assistance fits well into the recent approaches to social protection elaborated by The World Bank which combine an emphasis on individual responsibility and on households, communities and markets as the primary providers of social protection with a residual view of the role of public intervention in social welfare; accordingly, states should step in only as a last resort, with minimal support targeted to the neediest groups, who are in turn required to actively participate in sharing the responsibilities and costs of social development (Molyneux, 2007).

Some considerations can be made, at this stage of the implementation of MIFAPRO, as to the potential of these design features to produce an impact on beneficiaries' well-being and general education, health and nutrition indicators. With regards to the goal of smoothing consumption and reducing malnutrition, it is debatable whether a cash transfer of US$18 is able to make a substantial difference within a household's budget when the estimated cost of the minimum level of food consumption to secure survival was calculated in 2006 to be US$400 (£257) per person per year. Similarly, the average monthly value of the basic food basket, based on a model household of 5.38 members,[12] was calculated to be around US$197 (£127) in 2007 and US$ 233 (£150) in 2008 (INE, 2009). This translates into an average[13] per capita monthly value of around US$36 that is evidently well above the amount assigned, especially since the transfer is not provided per child but as a lump sum per household and not indexed to inflation. In this sense, as was found for other similar programmes elsewhere (Barrientos and Santibáñez, 2009), the poverty impact of the programme may be stronger on the poverty gap than on the poverty headcount. Moreover, since poorer families often have more members, the fixed amount of the transfer means a lower per capita transfer to these households (The World Bank, 2009b). The recent introduction of a third cash transfer specifically targeted at improving nutrition is a useful addition towards securing the attainment of the programme's objectives. If the contribution of the cash transfer to alleviate malnutrition and hunger in the short term remains to be proven, even more difficult to disentangle are the potential impacts of the programme in terms of fighting chronic malnutrition and reducing poverty in the medium and long term. Indeed, MIFAPRO is far from tackling more fundamental and unresolved structural issues, such as land tenure, access to markets and rural infrastructure that could have stronger and more durable impacts on food security as well as on poverty. In this sense, the programme cannot substitute for broader structural interventions to improve agricultural production for the local market through investments in resources and technology with the aim of making communities self-sustaining and food-secure in the long term. While MIFAPRO may help in poverty alleviation, sustained poverty reduction will only be achieved by creating stable and decent employment opportunities and by addressing other social reforms such as land, pensions, labour market and taxation, aimed at achieving a universal minimum level of protection based on rights.

As far as education is concerned, lack of money is definitively an important reason for not attending school, especially at the beginning of primary and of middle school (INE, 2002). Thus, MIFAPRO is well suited to tackle demand-side constraints in access to education. Conversely, supply-side factors have a very low relative weight in explaining drop-out from primary school and lack of enrolment in secondary education; this is probably due to efforts to expand the coverage of public education and achieve almost universal primary education since 1996. Still, besides lack of money, the attitudes of parents either directly through parental authority or indirectly through their effect on the perceptions and feelings of the child accounts in total for 38.1% of the motives for non-attendance (INE, 2002). This points to a much broader process of awareness raising in education that needs to be addressed either by this programme or through complementary interventions, if MIFAPRO is to attain its objectives in terms of educational outcomes.[14]

As for health, in 2006 when asked about the reasons for not seeking medical attention in the event of health problems, 41.2% of people living in extreme poverty mentioned lack of money (INE 2006). However, supply-side barriers to access health were especially important for the extreme poor, the indigenous and rural households (The World Bank, 2009b). Besides, Guatemalan private expenditure on health is estimated at 62.3% (WHO, 2008) of total health expenditure and it consists almost exclusively of out-of-pocket payments (91.4%), thus placing a very heavy burden on households' finances. Health insurance (mainly public) has an extremely low overall coverage (12.9% of the population), leaving

94.5% of the poor and 97.2% of the extreme poor uncovered. For all these reasons, the cash transfer from MIFAPRO can help households to smooth health expenditures and is likely to have a positive impact on access to health services, provided that it is coupled with improvements in supply and quality of services in the rural areas. The fact that the programme has prioritised almost exclusively rural areas is indeed an indication that there is an attempt towards reversing structural regional and rural/urban imbalances.

Official reports of MIFAPRO's execution in 2008 recognise that monitoring of compliance with the conditionalities was generally not enforced and lax at best. This was due to the speed at which the programme started its operations, without having previously put in place the adequate institutional apparatus. The widespread lack of information regarding the programme both among beneficiaries and staff employed in education and health services, which in turn was the result of insufficient interinstitutional coordination among the public entities involved in the initiative, contributed to a great extent to making the first phase of *Mi Familia Progresa* a de facto unconditional cash transfer programme. In 2009, interinstitutional coordination has been improved and a more ambitious plan to monitor and to secure the compliance with conditionalities has been designed. It remains to be seen whether the additional costs of this complex structure will produce the expected results in terms of improving the effectiveness of the programme.

As far as the targeting method chosen is concerned, by focusing on extremely poor households with children or pregnant women, the programme is not only excluding those households in extreme poverty without these characteristics but also ignoring the remaining four million people who continue to live below the poverty line. Thus, although overall coverage is wider than in previous social assistance programmes, *Mi Familia Progresa* perpetuates the exclusionary and residual nature of previous state efforts in social protection. The narrow targeting adopted could ultimately delegitimise the whole initiative in the eyes of those who feel arbitrarily excluded. This can jeopardise its future consolidation and extension, while generating social fracture and resentment among the population and towards the government. It is true that, considering the limited financial resources available, putting in place a targeted cash transfer programme seems better than simply sticking to the status quo outlined in the first section. As was observed in other similar experiences, scaling up and expanding the coverage and eligibility criteria of an existing programme is easier than setting up a totally new initiative. This is especially relevant at a time of global financial and economic crisis, where governments are increasingly using existing social policies to mitigate the social consequences of the crisis. However, a clear vision in the government about the role and the transformative potential of this type of initiative is missing, thus maintaining *Mi Familia Progresa*, for the moment, within the ranks of previous minimalist initiatives.

Institutional configuration

Mi Familia Progresa was initiated under the auspices of the Social Cohesion Council, a new interinstitutional body created by President Alvaro Colom and coordinated by the First Lady, Sandra de Colom, to bring together efforts in social development at the national level. This is a clear example of what Molyneux has defined as 'the rise of parallel institutions to assist in the delivery of social welfare' (2008, p 784). *Mi Familia Progresa* has been strongly identified with central government, the President and, even more, the First Lady. However, neither the First Lady nor the Social Cohesion Council she chairs was granted a formal status within the political and legal constitution of Guatemala. Hence, they could not be held accountable to the national parliament nor audited by public auditing bodies. Therefore, the choice to execute the new cash transfer programme (financed out of public funds) through the Social Cohesion Council cast shadows on the transparency and accountability of *Mi Familia Progresa* and provoked accusations about a potentially hidden agenda of the presidential couple. As a consequence, in 2009 MIFAPRO was transferred to the Ministry of Education, to be administered through a public trust fund. Even though this new configuration improves the transparency of the programme since these types of social funds are audited, commercial law rather than state procurement rules is the applicable regulatory framework for these types of financial instruments, leaving more room for discretionary management. Still, the integration of the programme into the public education system helps to consolidate and legitimise it, contributes to mitigate its inherent residual nature and represents a move away from the dispersion of efforts that has characterised social policy in Guatemala so far. However, the creation by the Colom administration of a number of other social programmes, smaller in scale than MIFAPRO but somehow complementing it, to address food security, education and youth criminality in urban areas (Gobierno de Guatemala, 2009), suggests that fragmentation of social interventions is not being consistently reversed by this government.

Governance and management

Mi Familia Progresa was centralised from the start, with minimal involvement of municipalities and communities. In this sense, MIFAPRO retains a typical feature of public social policy making in Guatemala. Still, national experts on the issues of transparency and governance consider that the choice of a centralised management for this programme was appropriate, as local authorities in the country do not often enjoy a creditable reputation. The programme is proceeding to a partial decentralisation in 2009. Two main aspects regarding the programme's governance and management raise interesting issues: delivery mechanisms and access to information.

The delivery of cash transfers in MIFAPRO is carried out through a complex mechanism of payment events (*eventos de pago*). The First Lady and the President often attend these rallies, transforming them into occasions to increase the visibility of the presidential couple within the rural constituencies that strongly contributed to President Colom's victory in the 2007 elections. This modality differs markedly from the methods developed and used in similar initiatives in Latin America, where beneficiaries receive the transfers through magnetic cards linked to individual bank accounts. The gathering of beneficiaries from the same geographical area during these events is likely to have both negative and positive impacts. On the one hand, the organisation of these rallies puts a burden not only on the programme's but also the beneficiaries' budgets and time, as they have to cover the costs of transport to the location of the event, walk long distances where transport is not available and abandon their work and/or care activities. A further point is that, given the precarious security conditions looming in the country, having women travel back home from these events carrying a consistent amount of cash is likely to make them more vulnerable to attacks and robbery. On the other hand, collective attendance of beneficiaries can be an effective way of ensuring transparency both in the selection of beneficiaries and in the delivery of transfers as participants are witnessing the process. Additionally, these public payment events provide a space for direct interaction between beneficiaries, possibly favouring forms of organisation and collective action. In this sense, the programme could also have potential transformative effects on social cohesion and empowerment among the beneficiaries.

The most contested issue surrounding MIFAPRO both in general public debates and in the national parliament has been access to personal data identifying the beneficiaries of the programme. Accusations of partisanship in the prioritisation of beneficiaries were triggered by the lack of clarity and transparency about the general selection criteria. A huge controversy surrounds the disclosure of personal identification numbers, since MIFAPRO's initial agreement with beneficiaries was that all the information retrieved from them would be kept confidential. Given the country's history, citizens are sensitive about diffusing personal identification information, as this was used in the past by state and military apparatuses to persecute and 'disappear' thousands of innocent people. Thus, legitimate transparency claims are clashing with the right to protect the identities and personal information of the beneficiaries of public social programmes. This shows that the establishment of more formal social rights to security and well-being has not been coupled with the enhancement of procedural rights, rule of law, accountability and transparency. Having the first without the second may ultimately jeopardise the attainment of the common goal of improving people's well-being and security.

Efforts have been made since April 2008 to improve the management of the programme and correct some of the initial shortcomings in access to information regarding the programme, in the design of a mechanism to deal with complaints, in the methods to check compliance with conditionalities and in the provision of a monitoring and evaluation system. These efforts have been triggered by a spectrum of actors in constant expansion. Members of Parliament have promoted hearings and legal actions to improve the disclosure of information, while civil society organisations have been monitoring the initiative closely and providing technical advice. The programme's staff have also autonomously initiated various upgrading of procedures following initial feedback, independent journalistic investigations and protests by beneficiaries. Additionally, the local academic community has participated in the debate and begun generating new research studies as well as changes in curricula to prepare future cohorts of social programmes' administrators.

Financing

In its first year of execution, *Mi Familia Progresa* was financed by domestic resources through budgetary transfers from other ministries and public institutions. As Table 9.1 shows, most of the funds came from the budgets for public education and health, with complementary funding from another three institutions.

Table 9.1: Sources of funding of MIFAPRO in 2008

Source	Amount (US$)
Ministry of Education	11,432,787
Institute for Municipal Support	43,750
Ministry of Public Health and Social Assistance	6,250,000
Presidency's Secretariat of Social Welfare	4,375,000
First Lady's Social Committee	1,000,000
Total	23,101,537

Source: Author's elaboration based on reports by MIFAPRO

This seems to confirm what was found elsewhere in terms of the political and financial feasibility of cash transfer programmes. Thus, the case for cash transfers might appear easier to make where these programmes are partial substitutes for existing social policies and simply require the reallocation of resources from one budget line to another (Slater, 2008).

Nevertheless, the use of budgetary transfers raises a number of questions. First, transferring significant amounts of resources that were originally assigned in the budget process to other types of spending is not a particularly transparent way of spending public money. This is especially true in the case of Guatemala, since the government has the faculty of authorising and executing these transfers to MIFAPRO without having to go through the normal legislative process in the national parliament. Second, it must be carefully assessed within which budgetary lines funds are reallocated. In the case of MIFAPRO, given the constraints in terms of supply of these basic services in the country, the reallocation of funds to MIFAPRO in order to increase the use of basic social services by the more excluded sectors of the population reduces the overall budget for improving the supply-side of these basic services: this may ultimately jeopardise the whole rationale of the conditionalities linked to the cash transfers. In addition, by transferring resources from budget lines already assigned to social spending, the overall level of financial resources available for social policy does not increase. In this sense, a better option would be to reallocate funds from other budgetary lines such as military spending.

Overall, the provision of domestic funding for MIFAPRO represents a positive move towards improving the social contract between the Guatemalan state and its citizens, as it symbolically sanctions the right of the state to use public money collected through general taxation to be redistributed in cash to the most disadvantaged and excluded sectors of the population. Yet, the overall redistributive impact of

MIFAPRO will have to be assessed by factoring in not only the extent to which the expenditures made are reaching the poorest quintiles of the population, but also the degree of progressivity of the tax system that finances all public spending, including MIFAPRO. Eventually, domestic resources for *Mi Familia Progresa* will be topped up in the years to come by international funds provided through a loan from the Inter-American Development Bank. This is likely to trigger further impacts on accountability, state–society relations and national ownership of the programme, as the state will have to respond to donors alongside its own citizens.

Mi Familia Progresa: change or continuity?

In the first section I identified the main features of social policy making in Guatemala since 1996, while in the second section I discussed a number of issues raised by the design and implementation of the new CCTs programme in Guatemala. Merging all these discussions together, I address here whether MIFAPRO represents a change or continuity in Guatemala's short history of public welfare.

The choice of the policy instrument and the settings of MIFAPRO display both change and continuity with respect to previous and existing social policies in Guatemala. To begin with, the choice of the CCT tool is new to the country's tradition of social transfers and demonstrates a good intention and attempt to take stock and learn from other experiences in the Central and Latin American region. While the attainment of MIFAPRO's educational and health objectives seems within reach, it is not yet clear whether this type of intervention and the level of the benefits provided will be enough to lift people out of poverty. In this sense, the introduction of improved techniques may not be reflected in changes in the outcomes of this programme compared with previous initiatives or with alternative policies that could be pursued (for instance, by increasing the amount of resources channelled to supply-side interventions in social services). Putting in place a targeted cash transfer programme shows at least an attempt to change the status quo outlined in the first section. As was observed in other similar experiences, and especially in times of crisis, scaling up and expanding the coverage and eligibility criteria of an existing programme is easier than setting up a totally new initiative. Still, a full appreciation of a potential shift towards more progressive social spending will have to be done by weighing the impact of the programme against the effects of the rest of social expenditure. In this sense, the transfer of funds to the programme from the education and health budgets diverts funds from the social expenditure that displays the highest degree of progressivity and could jeopardise the pre-conditions for the conditionalities.

In terms of targeting and coverage, it is the first time that a programme has been deliberately targeted to the poorest sectors of the population, especially those in rural areas; indeed, the rapidity with which resources were made available, the number of families reached so far and the volume of transfers scaled up in just several months during 2008 show that attempts to mitigate the elitist and regressive nature of previous social policy are being made. The programme represents a measure of formalisation of the system, as previously excluded sectors are included for the first time in a public social protection scheme. However, the extension and inclusion pursued by MIFAPRO so far still leaves half of the people in poverty unattended and therefore does not allow the programme to move the social policy agenda away from previous residual approaches.

The initial placement of MIFAPRO under the institutionally ambiguous Social Cohesion Council (other established institutions could have been more adequately placed to coordinate the execution of the programme) signals the persistence of institutional fragmentation and precariousness. The integration of the programme into the Ministry of Education in 2009 has improved interinstitutional coordination across the different sectors of social policy involved, although the establishment of a trust to administer it does not represent a clear institutionalisation of MIFAPRO. On similar grounds, the institution of other smaller programmes to tackle poverty mainly in urban areas indicates that the dispersion of efforts into multiple small initiatives persists.

Implementation capacity is a domain where progress has been made but considerable challenges remain. On the one hand, MIFAPRO makes use of advanced targeting tools and methodologies neglected by previous initiatives. This reflects a change in the type of actors involved in influencing the choice of policy instruments, with external actors such as The World Bank and the Inter-American Development Bank playing an increasingly important role, together with strengthened cooperation with other countries in the region. On the other hand, the introduction of conditionalities may constitute a change only in the technique but not in the outcomes of the policy. It is not clear so far whether the additional costs of monitoring compliance will be matched by improved outcomes. Furthermore, in its first year, speeding up the transfer process was prioritised over the consolidation of an adequate and competent organisational and bureaucratic structure to carry out the monitoring of compliance with conditionalities and to evaluate the progress made. This indicates that reaping political benefits was more important than securing a better delivery of welfare.

In terms of the broader social policy paradigm, *Mi Familia Progresa* continues to display many of the typical features of past public policy making in Guatemala. Social expenditure and mobilisation of domestic resources in general, and for MIFAPRO specifically, remains low. The total share of government social expenditure has not been increased as the expansion of social policy is being pursued through budget transfers and/or international loans with different implications for transparency, accountability and national ownership of social programmes.

In terms of the welfare mix, with its narrow focus on extreme poverty, and in spite of the considerable absolute numbers of people reached, *Mi Familia Progresa* perpetuates the residual nature of public social intervention in Guatemala for three main reasons. First, although MIFAPRO is an adequate instrument to tackle some identified constraints to improving welfare, it remains a limited and isolated initiative and has not been complemented by other efforts to respond to numerous other identified social needs in health, education and nutrition. Second, the promotion of sustainable livelihoods and decent employment as tools for the long-term eradication of poverty is not integrated into the social protection strategy embodied by *Mi Familia Progresa*, further diminishing its transformative potential. These first two considerations are both related to the fact that an overall strategy for the sustainable eradication of poverty is still missing. Hence, 'there is a renewed interest in social programmes, but less in a comprehensive social policy to constrain inequalities and enhance wellbeing' (Gough, 2008, p 1).

Third, families continue to play a central role in the provision of welfare not only through market, community and informal mechanisms but also now within state policies. Thus, families, but in reality mothers, are responsible for complying with the conditionalities imposed by MIFAPRO and for approaching the programme at given times and places to be able to receive the transfer. Targeting the cash transfers onto women may indeed assist them in their responsibilities as carers and empower them to some extent through encouraging a more leading role in managing household resources; however, the fact that women are included in the programme as 'mothers' and 'carers' may turn out to reinforce traditional gender roles, while complying with the tasks and requirements of the programme adds to the total workload of poor women with the risk of overburdening them (Molyneux, 2007). Thus,

MIFAPRO seems to endorse what have been pointed out as different logics for children and their mothers in this type of programme: 'the former are invested in as citizens, their capabilities and life chances are expanded through education and health; the mothers, meanwhile, are treated as having responsibilities rather than needs and rights' (Molyneux, 2007, p 30). It is still to be demonstrated in the case of MIFAPRO whether this type of beneficiaries' involvement will have positive effects on social cohesion and women's empowerment.

This last point brings about a further consideration about the persistence of an exclusionary decision-making process in Guatemalan social policy. MIFAPRO started as a top-down, centralised initiative, strongly identified with the presidential couple and with an involvement of beneficiaries only at the bottom end of the process. It is true that at the national level MIFAPRO has become a very debated, visible and contested issue. This seems to be in line with the new directions and developments in Latin America's social policy indicated by Barrientos et al (2008). However, it is mostly the political establishment and urban upper middle classes that participate in these debates. Although the participation of different civil society actors has increased during the implementation phase and has helped improve some aspects of the design and management of the programme, beneficiaries' contribution to decision making has been unsatisfactory. This indicates that the heated contestation surrounding *Mi Familia Progresa* does not necessarily reflect the rise of a new type of social mobilisation around social assistance programmes, as argued by Barrientos et al (2008). On the contrary, the enormous space given in public debates to this initiative hides, and may even jeopardise, the real social mobilisation of the excluded sectors of the population over the fundamental and unresolved issues of the country: land reform, access to markets and opportunities for economic development, and respect for human rights.

Ultimately, lack of transparency and accountability continues to plague state intervention in social policy, as procedural rights, such as access to information about the selection criteria, are not extended at the same time as social rights. The massive use of budget transfers by the government without the approval of Congress and the recent creation of the trust fund under the Ministry of Education reveal failures in achieving a fully transparent financial management. As a consequence, and despite the transparent design of the delivery mechanism, risks of clientelism and corruption remain high. At the same time, the programme also shows an effort to build on work done during previous governments in terms of mapping the extent and depth of poverty and other social issues; in this sense, it is a timid attempt to break with the usual discontinuities in social policy between governments.

Based on these findings, I conclude that *Mi Familia Progresa* does not represent a substantial change in the structure and direction of Guatemala's social policy. Positive changes in policy instruments and settings do not outweigh continuities that act to reinforce the current paradigm and are not able to produce permanent and radical solutions to the problems of extreme poverty and inequality that the country faces. MIFAPRO could potentially be a step further in the process of endogenous and incremental acquisition of more equal rights and freedoms begun in 1996 by the Peace Accords and triggered by the failure of 36 years of civil war to achieve a radical transformation and re-foundation of the social contract among citizens and between these and the state. However, the transformative potential of such an initiative has not been understood and pursued so far, as narrow targeting, additional responsibilities imposed on families and women, limited state capacity, political opportunism and constrained resources have relegated the programme to a residual and exclusive safety net. Thus, the positive effects of a programme such as *Mi Familia Progresa* cannot make up for broader failures in state action to build a more universal, inclusive and rights-based society. The case of *Mi Familia Progresa* confirms that, no matter how well implemented, CCT programmes alone cannot be expected to deliver more inclusive citizenship, overcome alienation and initiate a positive dynamic of social reproduction capable of challenging the path dependency of extreme inequality (Copestake, 2007). For the moment, social rights to security and well-being remain fragile in Guatemala: while some gradual improvement in average welfare is clearly visible, the overall economic, political and social system remains remarkably resilient and intact in its unequal structural conditions.

Conclusion

In this chapter I have shown that the introduction of a new cash transfer programme, *Mi Familia Progresa*, in Guatemala represents continuity more than change in the country's efforts to improve and expand welfare provision. MIFAPRO has the potential to become an important step forward in the advancement of welfare entitlements, but its residual nature and the lack of state action on other dimensions of economic and social development hamper the contribution of this initiative to a structural transformation of society. Thus, social rights in the country remain fragile and the overall economic, political and social system is resilient in a number of aspects and intact in its unequal structural conditions.

In terms of future directions, despite constant attacks by the press and the national parliament, no one has seriously challenged the institution of MIFAPRO as such; rather, criticisms have concentrated on the ways the initiative has been put into practice so far. This would seem to indicate that there is consensus among political parties represented in the national parliament and across public opinion about investing collective resources in the poorest sectors of the population. There may be windows of opportunity to transform this initiative into a more institutionalised and long-term commitment. It is less clear whether similar prospects exist with regards to the broader structural interventions needed to bring about a socially inclusive structural change.

The findings of this chapter contribute to our understanding of the challenges of social development and social policy in a relatively under-researched developing country such as Guatemala. The disputes surrounding MIFAPRO and the other initiatives that the current government is promoting indicate the difficulty of pursuing change in a context characterised by long-term inequalities, weak state legitimacy and exclusionary patterns of economic development and decision making. They also add further insights to ongoing debates about the implications of CCT programmes in Central and Latin America. In particular, the evidence presented here supports the argument that *Mi Familia Progresa*, as other similar programmes executed in the region, is contributing to shift the social policy agenda to a 'new social policy system' (Filgueira, 2005, p 38), promoted by market-oriented social reformers and characterised by targeted social policies and by moves from supply-based social policies to demand-based social policies or from financing supply to financing demand (Barrientos, 2004; Filgueira, 2005). However, the specific characteristics of this new agenda are likely to be different in countries with more consolidated public welfare provision and longer traditions of democracy and rule of law than in countries like Guatemala and some of its Central American neighbours, with lower or non-existent levels of state welfare provision. In this sense, future research on CCTs will need to incorporate to a much greater extent the welfare regime approaches currently being applied to the study of Latin American social policy.[15] This will help us to understand how the same types of social assistance programmes may fit in countries with different political regimes, levels of development and trajectories of social policy.

Notes

[1] Research Analyst at the United Nations Research Institute for Social Development (UNRISD). Please address any correspondence to efmgaia@gmail.com. An earlier version of this chapter was presented at the Social Policy Association conference in 2009, 'Policy Futures: Learning from the Past?', Edinburgh, 29 June–1 July 2009. Suggestions from Silke Staab and Pon Souvannaseng on the earlier draft and comments from the editors of the *Social Policy Review* greatly improved the chapter. Any remaining errors are all mine.

[2] Some of the most cited and studied programmes include the *Programa Nacional de Educacion, Salud y Alimentación* (PROGRESA, later renamed *Oportunidades*) in Mexico, *Programa de Asignación Familiar II* (PRAF II) in Honduras, *Red de Protección Social* (RPS) in Nicaragua, *Bolsa Familia* in Brazil, Program for Advancement through Health and Education (PATH) in Jamaica, *Familias en Acción* in Colombia and *Red Solidaria* in El Salvador. See also The World Bank (2009a) for a global overview of existing CCT programmes.

[3] Poverty is a contested concept. I agree that poverty is a relative and multidimensional phenomenon, comprising multiple deprivations in material, symbolic and relational aspects (Townsend, 1979; Lister, 2004). However, in this research the term 'poverty' is used occasionally as a synonym with 'income poverty' and therefore measured in terms of individual or household income. This limitation of scope is necessary because of lack of data on multidimensional poverty in Guatemala.

[4] In this chapter social policy is defined as state intervention that directly affects social welfare, social institutions and social relations, involving overarching concerns with redistribution, production, reproduction and protection (UNRISD, 2005). The focus of this chapter is solely on the intervention of public institutions in social protection, as state intervention shapes the conditions for the involvement of other actors and is shaped by these in turn. For discussions on the role of private actors in providing welfare in Guatemala, see The World Bank (2003, 2009b).

[5] In-depth interviews with national policy analysts and members of civil society organisations that follow the policy process closely were conducted in Guatemala in January 2009. MIFAPRO's staff, despite many attempts, refused to be interviewed. Email correspondence with staff from the Mexican programme *Progresa/Oportunidades* and from The World Bank provided additional information.

[6]   In January 2009 it was established that the programme would be evaluated externally by the *Instituto Nacional de Salud Pública*, a Mexican institution involved in the evaluation of *Oportunidades* in Mexico, in collaboration with the National Statistical Institute of Guatemala (INE). This will be financed by a grant from the Inter-American Development Bank.

[7]   The national poverty line under which a person is considered to be in poverty is based on the estimated cost of the minimum level of food consumption necessary for survival plus the minimum estimated costs for additional basic services, housing, transport and other non-food items. The poverty line was calculated in 2006 to be US$821 (6,574 quetzels or approximately £528) per capita per year.

[8]   The poverty line under which a person is considered to be in extreme poverty is based on the estimated cost of the minimum level of food consumption necessary for survival and was calculated in 2006 to be US$400 (3,206 quetzels or approximately £257) per capita per year.

[9]   In May 2009, MIFAPRO started to provide a third additional nutrition transfer of US$13 (£8.36) targeted to a pilot of families with children under the age of six, aimed at combating chronic child malnutrition. The transfer is conditional on mothers administering a number of food supplements and attending nutrition-related training.

[10] To determine whether a household is extremely poor and whether it is eligible to be incorporated into the programme, a proxy means test (PMT) model is used, elaborated with technical assistance from The World Bank.

[11] In particular, these agencies have been actively engaged in supporting and conducting feasibility studies and evaluations of CCT programmes, they have fostered debates around the effectiveness of these initiatives and provided technical advice to governments and, most importantly, financial resources to run pilot programmes and scale up existing ones.

[12] This value was calculated from the Family Income and Expenditures Survey 1979–81 and is currently used by the National Statistical Institute of Guatemala as the reference average to devise the cost of the basket of basic goods. Data collected during the 2002 Census show that the mean number of people in a household has been slightly reduced to 5.09.

[13] Not adjusted to the different energy and nutritional requirements for adults and children.

[14] A positive move in this direction has been the establishment in August 2008 of a complementary programme under the Ministry

of Education called *Mi Familia Aprende* (My Family Learns), with the aim of training the parents and carers who are beneficiaries of MIFAPRO. The training modules, held for a couple of hours every three weeks, include topics related to values, health, nutrition and education. Since it targets adults with the right to vote and not children directly, this initiative has, nonetheless, been criticised as being used as a clientelistic tool to create and reinforce constituencies in support of the ruling party for the general elections to be held in 2011 (*El Periódico*, 2009).

[15] See, for instance, Mesa-Lago (1978); Huber (1996); Barrientos (2004); Gough et al (2004); Filgueira (2005); Martínez Franzoni (2008b).

References

Barrientos, A. (2004) 'Latin America: towards a liberal-informal welfare regime', in I. Gough and G. Wood (eds) *Insecurity and welfare regimes in Asia, Africa and Latin America: Social policy in development contexts*, Cambridge: Cambridge University Press, pp 68-121.

Barrientos, A., Gideon, J. and Molyneaux, M. (2008) 'New developments in Latin America's social policy', *Development and Change*, vol 39, no 5, pp 759-74.

Barrientos, A. and Santibañez, C. (2009) 'New forms of social assistance and the evolution of social protection in Latin America', *Journal of Latin American Studies*, vol 41, no 1, pp 1-26.

Copestake, J. (2007) *Multiple dimensions of social assistance: The case of Peru's Glass of Milk Programme*, WED Working Paper 21, ESRC Research Group on Wellbeing in Developing Countries, Bath: University of Bath.

de la Brière, B. and Rawlings, L. (2006) *Examining conditional cash transfer programs: A role for increased social inclusion?*, Social Protection Discussion Paper No 0603, Washington, DC: World Bank.

ECLAC (Economic Commission for Latin America and the Caribbean)/ CEPAL (2009) *Estadísticas de América Latina y El Caribe* (http://websie. eclac.cl/sisgen/ConsultaIntegrada.asp?idAplicacion=6&idTema=140 &idioma=e).

El *Périodico* (2009) 'Mi Familia Aprende, un programa destinado a la formación de adultos', 19 February (www.elperiodico.com.gt).

Farrington, J. and Slater, R. (2006) 'Cash transfers: panacea for poverty reduction or money down the drain?', *Development Policy Review*, vol 24, no 5, pp 499-512.

Filgueira, F. (2005) *Welfare and democracy in Latin America: The development, crisis and aftermath of universal, dual and exclusionary social states*, Mimeo, Programme on Social Policy and Development, Geneva: UNRISD.

Freedom House (2006) *Countries at the crossroads. Country report –
Guatemala* (http://freedomhouse.org/modules/publications/ccr/
modPrintVersion.cfm?edition=7&ccrpage=31&ccrcountry=115).

Gobierno de Guatemala (2009) *Primer año de Gobierno. Informe*,
Guatemala: Gobierno de Guatemala.

Gough, I. (2008) *Social policy for sustainable wellbeing*, Briefing Paper 4/08,
ESRC Research Group on Wellbeing in Developing Countries, Bath:
University of Bath.

Gough, I. with G. Wood, A. Barrientos, P. Bevan, P. Davis and G. Room
(eds) (2004) *Insecurity and welfare regimes in Asia, Africa and Latin America:
Social policy in development contexts*, Cambridge: Cambridge University
Press.

Huber, E. (1996) 'Options for social policy in Latin America: neoliberal
versus social democratic models', in G. Esping-Andersen (ed) *Welfare
states in transition: National adaptations in global economies*, London: Sage
Publications, pp 141-91.

INE (Instituto Nacional de Estadística) (2002) *XI censo nacional de
población y VI de habitación*, Guatemala: INE.

INE (2006) *Encuesta nacional de condiciones de vida (ENCOVI)*, Guatemala:
INE.

INE (2009) *Canasta básica de alimentos* (www.ine.gob.gt/index.php/
estadisticasdeprecios/58-estadisticasdeprecios/137-cba).

Lister, R. (2004) *Poverty*, Cambridge and Malden, MA: Polity Press.

Lloyd-Sherlock, P. (2008) 'Doing a bit more for the poor? Social
assistance in Latin America', *Journal of Social Policy*, vol 37, no 4, pp
621-39.

Martínez Franzoni, J. (2008a) 'Welfare regimes in Latin America:
capturing constellations of markets, families, and policies', *Latin
American Politics and Society*, vol 50, no 2, pp 67-100.

Martínez Franzoni, J. (2008b) 'Three welfare regimes, three critical
paths to strengthen redistribution', Paper presented at the XIII
Congreso Internacional del CLAD sobre la Reforma del Estado y de
la Administración Pública, Buenos Aires, Argentina, 4-7 November.

Mesa-Lago, C. (1978) *Social security in Latin America: Pressure groups,
stratification, and inequality*, Pittsburgh, PA: University of Pittsburgh Press.

Molyneux, M. (2006) 'Mothers at the service of the new poverty agenda',
Social Policy and Administration, vol 40, no 4, pp 425-49.

Molyneux, M. (2007) *Change and continuity in social protection in Latin
America. Mothers at the service of the state?*, Programme on Gender and
Development, Paper No 1, Geneva: UNRISD.

Molyneux, M. (2008) 'The "neoliberal turn" and the new social policy in Latin America: how neoliberal, how new?', *Development and Change*, vol 39, no 5, pp 775-97.

Rawlings, L. (2004) *A new approach to social assistance: Latin America's experience with conditional cash transfer programs*, Social Protection Discussion Paper No 0416, Washington, DC: World Bank.

Slater, R. (2008) *Cash transfers, social protection and poverty reduction*, Background paper commissioned for the UNRISD Flagship Report on Poverty Reduction and Policy Regimes, unpublished report available at www.unrisd.org/unrisd/website/document.nsf/%28htt pPublications%29/207C8A9E75D293EAC12574FE003A4780?Op enDocument

Townsend, P. (1979) *Poverty in the United Kingdom*, Harmondsworth: Penguin.

UNRISD (United Nations Research Institute for Social Development) (2005) *Transformative social policy: Lessons from UNRISD research*, UNRISD Research and Policy Brief no 5, Geneva: UNRISD.

World Bank, The (2003) *Poverty in Guatemala. A World Bank country study*, Washington, DC: The World Bank.

World Bank, The (2005) *Guatemala public expenditure review. A World Bank study*, Washington, DC: The World Bank.

World Bank, The (2009a) *Conditional cash transfers. Reducing present and future poverty*, Washington, DC: The World Bank.

World Bank, The (2009b) *Guatemala poverty assessment. Good performance at low levels*, World Bank Report, Washington, DC: The World Bank.

WHO (World Health Organization) (2008) *World health statistics. Core health indicators – Guatemala* (http://apps.who.int/whosis/database/ core/core_select_process.cfm?country=gtm&indicators=nha).

Part Three
Service user involvement

Majella Kilkey

Service users and social policy: developing different discussions, challenging dominant discourses

Peter Beresford

Introduction

In 2008, in its third edition and for the first time, *The student's companion to social policy*, published by Wiley-Blackwell and with a testimonial from the Social Policy Association describing it as 'an essential text for all social policy students', examined the 'role of users in determining welfare policy' (Alcock et al, 2008, p xix). This contribution was itself written from a 'service user perspective' by a member of a service user organisation and movement (Beresford, 2008). This reference to 'users', that is to say, people on the receiving end of welfare policy and practice, not only marks a departure for this particular social policy text, but it also contrasts with a broader tendency in academic social policy writing, which has historically tended to be dominated and largely constructed by social policy academics and other professional 'experts'. This has been to the exclusion of people identifying as coming from the perspective of direct experience as 'end users'.

The aim of this chapter is to look more closely at the recent contribution of service users and their organisations to the reconceptualisation of social policy. It explores the fresh insights and approaches that they have offered; the complex, often highly ambiguous ways in which these have been addressed and incorporated in public policy; and how this may helpfully be challenged.

An overlooked issue

Typically current and recent social policy textbooks to be found on library and bookshop shelves, even those offered as standard texts or key introductions, tend to have little or nothing to say about, or to report from, people as welfare state service users (for example, Pierson, 2001; Dean, 2006; Lavalette and Pratt, 2006; Pierson and Castles, 2006, Pierson, 2006; Alford, 2009). They seem to have particularly little to say about the organisations and movements developed by such service users. Thus, for instance, a social policy text whose focus is specifically 'social welfare movements' acknowledges in its introduction that it 'barely discusses' the modern service user movements, like the disabled people's and psychiatric system survivors' movements (Annetts et al, 2009, p 12). Yet these can be seen as the movements most closely associated with social policy, indeed in some cases, being traceable to and generated by it and in the case of the disabled people's movement, with a history stretching back more than a generation to the 1960s and 1970s (Campbell and Oliver, 1996).

Policy prioritising of user and public involvement

Such omissions are difficult to understand as merely accidental. More to the point, they also stand in some contrast to developments in actual social policy. Emerging in the late 1970s as part of the New Right political agenda of Margaret Thatcher and her governments, an increasing emphasis in social and indeed public policy more generally, has been placed on the active involvement and engagement of 'public', 'patients' and 'service users'. This trend was reinforced under New Labour governments where there has been increasing political and policy rhetoric about the 'active citizen' and the 'public consumer', with increasing requirements for public, patient and user involvement and engagement across public policy. There are now widespread requirements for such involvement in legislation, policy guidance and government statements. It extends across a wide range of public policies as well as to evaluation, research and standard setting. It has become part of the rhetoric and currency of modern politics and policy making. It is associated with public petitions on the Prime Minister's website, local referendums and deliberative structures like citizens' juries, as well as user involvement forums and officers, a 'czar' for involvement and local NHS PALS (Patient Advice and Liaison Services) established by government to support patient and public involvement in local health services.

We thus start with a tension in any discussion of 'service users' and 'user involvement' in academic social policy. Such discussion is relatively under-developed. Academics like Marian Barnes who have focused on such issues, particularly in the context of health and social care, are unusual (Barnes et al, 2007). A key expression of this tension is that while in public policy, across the major political parties, there has been a general sign-up to the virtues and value of public involvement, academic social policy discourse has had only a limited engagement with such concerns and does not have a strong canon of work critiquing it. Much more attention has been paid in academic social policy to the supply-side of social policy than to the role of its recipients or 'consumers', to what might be called the viewpoints of 'the demand-side'.

We can only guess why this is. It seems likely that the inherent paternalism of traditional Fabianism, which has been the dominant strand in UK academic social policy discourse, with its presumption of the 'expert' construction of social policy, has a bearing on this. It is something about which we can gain some additional insights by exploring important early case studies of UK 'user involvement' and user movements.

Disabled people's movement: a case study of competing ideologies and discussions

There have been different strands in the development of service users' efforts to get involved. And different user movements have approached involvement in different ways. For example, the mental health service users/survivors movement has tended to be more closely linked with the service system than the disabled people's movement. It has also been suggested that these movements have based their efforts to be involved on different understandings and expectations (Barnes et al, 1999).

Historically, the UK disabled people's movement has tended to focus on developing its own ideas, theories, organisations and models of service, rather than seeking to inform and prioritising the reform of dominant structures (Campbell and Oliver, 1996). Just how big a departure and how much of a challenge this could be to traditional social policy approaches and understandings can be seen from discussions held early in the history of the disabled people's movement between a traditional organisation *for* disabled people and a founding organisation *of* disabled people, where control lay formally and explicitly with disabled people. An agreed account of these discussions was published (UPIAS/Disability Alliance, 1976) and the present comments are based on this. The disability organisation was the Disability Alliance, and the disabled people's organisation was UPIAS, the Union of the Physically Impaired Against Segregation. Significantly Disability Alliance was mainly represented by its co-founder, Peter Townsend, a key figure in modern academic social policy and social policy reform, while UPIAS spokespeople include founders of the UK disabled people's movement such as Vic Finkelstein and Paul Hunt.

The agreed aim of the meeting between the two organisations, subject to their 'prior agreement' to a set of 'fundamental principles of disability' identified by UPIAS, was to explore how disabled people 'could become more active in the disability field' and consider a 'long-term programme of action' to make that possible (UPIAS/Disability Alliance, 1976, p 3). These 'fundamental principles' were that:

> ... disability is a situation, caused by social conditions, which requires for its elimination:
>
> (a) that no one aspect such as incomes, mobility or institutions is treated in isolation;
> (b) that disabled people should, with the advice and help of others, assume control over their own lives;
> (c) that professionals, experts and others who seek to help must be committed to promoting such control by disabled people. (UPIAS/Disability Alliance, 1976, p 3)

Although both organisations said they had signed up to these principles, UPIAS was not convinced that the Disability Alliance and Peter Townsend actually had, instead seeing them as:

- pursuing the income issue in isolation – 'it is only one aspect of [disabled people's] oppression';
- maintaining an approach with 'a small number of [non-disabled] experts' having the central role and most disabled people left 'largely passive';
- seeking to educate the public through 'expert' information, with a 'narrow concentration on parliamentary pressure' rather than working for the 'mass participation of disabled people' which UPIAS saw as crucial;
- not making serious efforts to involve disabled people.
  (UPIAS/Disability Alliance, 1976, p 4).

UPIAS interpreted Peter Townsend's and the Disability Alliance's focus on a comprehensive state income for disabled people as perpetuating their social and economic dependence. It regarded the Alliance's reliance on a medically based model of assessing disability – what people 'couldn't do' – rather than a social model – providing the support they needed to live independently – as keeping control with social administrators and taking it from disabled people. UPIAS was critical of what it saw as 'the willingness of the incomes "experts" to use disabled people to give authority to their own social interests' (UPIAS/Disability Alliance, 1976, p 16). Peter Townsend, on the other hand, genuinely seemed unable to understand why UPIAS held so determinedly to its own processes and values, wondering why it was 'making such heavy weather of them' (UPIAS/Disability Alliance, 1976, p 8), and saying that the failure to ensure large-scale involvement of disabled people in the Disability Alliance was no more than 'a problem of time and organisation' (UPIAS/Disability Alliance, 1976, p 6).

Adam Lent, in his examination of British social movements, concluded:

> The meeting was supposedly designed to see whether UPIAS could join the Alliance and whether Alliance members would be allowed to affiliate to UPIAS. In effect, however, it simply emphasized the irreconcilability of the old moderate approach and the new, self-organised radicalism. (Lent, 2002, pp 107-8)

This dialogue also highlighted the distance between traditional Fabian approaches to social policy and new participatory ones, where groups on the receiving end of social policy challenged the right of others to speak for them, developed their own collectivities, ideas and theories, rejecting traditional 'expertise' and emphasising the expertise that came from direct or lived experience. Not only were the process, aims and the understandings of the two far apart from each other, but this distance was also exacerbated by the apparent inability of either party to understand the other.

User involvement: a contested concept

If academic social policy started from a position of restricted understanding of service user movements and user involvement, this has not been helped by the limited attention it has subsequently given them. The under-development of academic social policy discussion of user involvement means it is not well placed to illuminate a chronology of at least 25 years' political, policy and practice concern with public involvement, with all the complexities and subtleties that entails. Basic questions still need to be addressed and that will be part of the aim here. Crucially, since academic social policy discussions have so far had only a limited engagement with service users and their perspectives and institutions, it will focus particularly on the roles and perspectives of service users in relation to user involvement.

The increasing interest in public, patient and user involvement in public policy does not mean, however, that issues are uncontested. Instead what emerges within the frameworks and terminology of user involvement are complex and fierce but also often unrecognised tensions and conflicts. Underpinning these are the competing value systems of the major sources of interest in such involvement. These are: (a) state managerialist/consumerism and (b) service user or citizen interest in democratisation and empowerment. Both the methods and the purposes of these two ideologies tend to be different.

The managerialist/consumerist approach starts from the market ideology of the new political Right combined with the 'new public management' (NPM) ideas from the 1980s (Simmons et al, 2009). It is concerned with gaining public, patient and service user information and experience to inform services and provision. It has predominated in both state and service system discussions and developments in user involvement. It is primarily concerned with individual involvement and individualising involvement and follows from ideological commitments to the market, purchase of services and the marketisation of welfare, emphasising *consumer choice*. The democratic or empowerment approach developed by service users and their organisations is concerned with increasing the say and control that people have over their lives and the policies and services that intervene in them. This approach to user involvement, which has been based particularly on collective action, has been developed by service users and their organisations and highlights power and the redistribution of power in society and services, emphasising *citizen control* (Beresford, 2001).

There can be little question that increasing state interest in user involvement has gained a degree of public support and enthusiasm. It has been officially associated with a rhetoric of devolution, decentralisation, 'shifting control from Whitehall', activating citizens and challenging paternalism. In the fields of health and social care, where user involvement has been particularly developed, it has gained a significant response from service users over the years, both individually and collectively, with relatively large-scale participation in high-profile consultations, people joining participatory structures such as local involvement networks (LINks), the successor to PALS, and responding to invitations to 'get involved'. It has acted as an opportunity, an impetus and sometimes a funding source for service users seeking to input their views and experiences and for these to influence and improve policy and provision.

Concerns about incorporation

At the same time, service users who have got involved have expressed growing concerns about what they feel they actually achieve through such involvement. This is often compounded by a lack of feedback and a sense that decisions were already made before their views were sought. Increasingly there is talk among service users of being 'over-consulted' and 'all-consulted-out'. Service users frequently interpret their experience of formal user involvement as 'tokenistic' and a 'tick-box exercise' (Campbell, 1996, 2009). Such views are regularly encountered among members of service user organisations, which are under constant pressure to respond to a wide range of consultations and participatory initiatives. Some explanation of this is likely to be found in the often conflicting reasons why people get involved and the rationale of most involvement exercises. When asked why they get involved, people as service users are most likely to say it is in order to achieve change in line with securing their rights and needs (Branfield et al, 2006).

As we have seen, however, the prevailing purpose of involvement initiatives is to gain people's views as part of a consumerist/managerialist agenda. The expectation of existing decision makers tends to be that it is then their own judgements and interpretations of what needs to be done that will be acted on. Service users serve effectively as little more than a data source, as they would do in conventional market research, which offers the closest parallel. It is the lack of fit here between democratic/empowerment and consumerist/managerialist approaches to involvement, which is likely to explain the frequent frustration and disappointment expressed by people who get involved about what it actually achieves. Indeed, since dominant approaches to involvement have tended to be tied to a market and managerialist-based ideology, service users who are not supportive of this may not see adding to its evidence base as consistent with their interests. Such involvement may actually have complex and contradictory consequences for service users, their organisations and movements.

Should we be getting involved?

This raises some large issues about user involvement for service users, their organisations, and indeed for academic social policy too. Should service users be getting involved in such schemes? If not, what should they be doing? This has been a long-standing conundrum for service users and their organisations. Structures for involvement offer them opportunities to seek to exert influence, but equally may constantly be pulling in a different direction to them, with conflicting aims and goals. They can take much energy and resources. So should service users get involved in the hope of challenging these, or do they merely reinforce and legitimise them by getting involved? On the other hand, sometimes getting involved in this way can pay off in terms of having an effect, building links, gaining credibility and securing some support. Some service users and service user organisations may not be fully aware of these tensions, but others certainly are. It is very difficult to predict which schemes and initiatives may be helpful or unproductive. These are key questions for individuals and organisations that are likely to have very limited time and resources.

It may be helpful for service users to ask themselves some basic questions about any involvement opportunity:

- Is there a realistic chance of making a difference in this case?
- Is this involvement in line with our core aims and goals?
- Is it consistent with a social rather than an individual medicalised interpretation of service users' needs?
- Can we achieve the same or more in a different way?
- Does it enable us to work together as we wish to in line with our values and philosophy?

Developing counter discourses

In this way, it may become clearer if through such involvement service users, their organisations and movements are able to advance their own discourses or are merely being sucked into the dominant discourses of the state and service system. Over the years, the service user movements have developed their own cultures, histories, bodies of knowledge, ways of organising and collective working, ideas, theories and skills. As Oliver and Barnes have observed, a major achievement of the UK disabled people's movement has been to develop and sustain its own counter-discourse to traditional medicalised individual interpretations and responses to disability:

> From relatively small beginnings and with remarkably limited resources, disabled people and their organisations have successfully challenged professional wisdom and intransigence. In so doing, they have generated a range of policy initiatives enabling ever-increasing numbers of disabled people to live independently within the local community. (Oliver and Barnes, 1998, p 92)

The survivors movement, by contrast, which has operated more closely within the service system, has been much less successful in developing a counter to the medical model of mental illness and the drug-based treatments that continue to predominate in the mental health field. Much energy has been expended in participatory processes, seeking to reform existing services, but activists seriously question how much has been achieved (Campbell, 2009). Survivors and their organisations have nonetheless developed ideas and approaches which challenge traditional understandings of 'mental illness', generating new ideas and thinking about self-harm, eating distress and hearing voices (Beresford and Campbell, 2004; Romme et al, 2009). As with other user movements, they have also prioritised the right of service users to speak for themselves, to be treated as equals and to be respected for who they are.

Co-option and appropriation

However, state and service system interest in user involvement does not only mean that service users may run the risk of becoming incorporated unintentionally and unwillingly into dominant consumerist/managerialist agendas by feeding into them. There have also been clear signs that the state and service system are also appropriating and subverting service user ideas and initiatives to support such consumerist/managerialist agendas. Thus service users not only run the risk of being co-opted into dominant discourses; their independent initiatives and developments are also being appropriated. As yet much more attention seems to have been paid to the first of these issues than to the second. In addition, while service users may have some control over the first – by choosing whether or not to engage with dominant structures for participation – they do not have the same control over the second. It is difficult to see what they can do to prevent their ideas and initiatives being colonised by local and central state and service systems that are far more powerful than them.

Undermining of service users' innovations

Two important examples of this development can be found in state support for policies of:

- personalisation and self-directed support, and
- co-production.

Personalisation and self-directed support

In 2007, at a national conference bringing together policy makers and service users, David Behan, the Department of Health's Director General of Social Care, set out the government's plans for the future of adult social care. He said:

> The current system of social care needs to be transformed, to a new set of arrangements. This is what we are setting out in our vision. It is a transformation in the way that services are commissioned, developed and delivered. This needs to be based on services being 'personalised' around individual needs, so they are tailored to people's particular circumstances and requirements. (quoted in Beresford and Hasler, 2009, p 45)

This vision had been officially announced in the same year in a 'concordat' called *Putting people first* (HM Government, 2007; Glasby and Littlechild, 2009, p 82), which was signed by six government departments and a series of national health, social care and local government organisations. 'Transformation' was also the word used in this document, which talked of a 'shared vision and commitment to the transformation of adult social care' (HM Government, 2007, p 2). The key proposals of *Putting people first* included:

- Personal budgets for everyone eligible for publicly funded adult social care support other than in circumstances where people require emergency access to provision.
- Direct payments utilised by increasing numbers of people.

- A universal information, advice and advocacy service for people needing services and their carers irrespective of their eligibility for public funding.
- Person-centred planning and self-directed support to become mainstream and define individually tailored support packages.

(HM Government, 2007, pp 3-4)

The government also allocated more than half a billion pounds, an unprecedented sum in the usually impoverished field of adult social care, to fund its three-year programme for the transformation of social care. It had earlier commissioned an independent university-based evaluation of the social care individual budget pilots, known as the IBSEN evaluation (Glendinning et al, 2008). However, it did not even wait until these findings were available before committing itself to this radical policy shift and large-scale investment.

Personalisation and self-directed support were presented very much as a 'user-led' policy, putting service users at the centre and offering them greater 'choice and control' (Glasby and Littlechild, 2009, p 83). Interestingly for a document concerned with user-centred support, although *Putting people first* was signed up to by a wide range of social care organisations, this did not include any service user organisations. Moreover, although this has not always been recognised on the ground, pressure for personalisation and individual budgets did not primarily come from service users. Instead it had come mainly from voluntary organisations like In Control and Mencap and increasingly allies in statutory organisations, like the Care Services Improvement Partnership (Waters and Duffy, 2007; Hatton et al, 2008).

I gained a different picture of service user views on this subject over time from being involved in a national service user organisation and network in close touch with local service users and their organisations, and listening to what service users said at meetings, events and conferences, nationally and locally. Service users, including mental health service users, disabled people, people with learning difficulties, older people and others, reported:

- Their lack of effective involvement in this change.
- Their fears about losing existing services through them being closed and uncertainty about what the alternatives actually put in place would be.
- Worries that the move to personalisation was a new way in which government was trying to make cuts.

- Big questions about how two parallel systems – existing services and the new arrangements for support linked with individual budgets could possibly be sustained to ensure real choice, at a time of limited budgets.

It is important to remember the rapidity with which government and policy makers adopted the policies of individual budgets and personalisation. Rapid reform has not historically been a characteristic of social care. Yet here was a policy with a very limited evidence base and little clarity about its actual meaning or implications, which was adopted and where national implementation was expected to be achieved, all within a space of five or six years. It would entail an expansion of a policy approach from one tested on a few hundred people, to what was intended to be the standard offer for many hundreds of thousands of social care service users.

What seemed to catch the attention of policy makers and politicians and what advocates of individual budgets and personalisation highlighted was that it could offer 'better for less'. Service users would be able to benefit from customised packages of support for less than it cost to provide traditional service-led standardised provision (Leadbeater et al, 2008). Financial calculations for individual service users were based on calculations about the allocation of existing funding, divided according to the needs externally calculated for any individual, then often top-sliced for administrative costs. This has come to be called 'RAS', the term coined by In Control, the 'resource allocation system' (Duffy, 2005). Given that existing funding for social care is still seen as inadequate and unsatisfactory, given existing needs and means-testing arrangements, given that the findings of the IBSEN evaluation challenged assumptions that individual budgets could be provided on a significantly cheaper basis than other service approaches, we have to suspect any such RAS-based system of assessment and allocation will inevitably be tied to an arbitrary rationing role.

However, proposals to extend individual or personal budgets are not restricted to social care. The plan is also to trial them in the NHS. Lord Darzi's 2008 report on NHS reform reflected this. While calling for the extension of personal budgets to the health service, key to his recommendations was the extension of the role of the market in the NHS framed in terms of repeated arguments for greater consumer 'choice' (Darzi, 2008). His proposals also raise the question of how the introduction of personal budgets pioneered in residual means-tested social care services can be squared with the universalist 'free at the point of delivery' founding principles of the NHS (Beresford, 2009).

This raises broader issues about the ideological underpinnings of personalisation and individual budgets as currently being developed and implemented in English social care. Questions are increasingly being raised about this policy development (Gibson et al, 2009; Prideaux et al, 2009). There has been growing concern that as it is being developed and implemented, it is actually increasingly serving and advancing a neoliberal ideology. It is associated with cuts in services, attacks on welfare professionals, with professional social workers replaced by unskilled workers, the individualisation and commodification of need, transferring responsibility from the state to the individual, ignoring issues of inequality and deprivation and marketising welfare (Ferguson, 2007; Scourfield, 2008; Roulstone and Morgan, 2009).

This is in sharp contrast to the developments from which it originated. Individual budgets, although this has sometimes been denied or ignored, have their origins very clearly in the direct payments pioneered by the UK disabled people's movement (Brindle, 2008a). Direct payments were introduced into social care following campaigning by disabled activists by the 1996 Community Care (Direct Payments) Act. They grew out of two of the major philosophical and theoretical developments initiated by the disabled people's movement. These are the social model of disability, which draws a distinction between individual (perceived) impairment and disability, the negative societal reaction and the philosophy of independent living. The latter, which follows from the social model, challenges traditional assumptions of disabled people's need for support as defining them as dependent. It sees independence as meaning autonomous decision making rather than the physical capacity to carry out all activities of daily living unaided (Campbell and Oliver, 1996; Morris, 2004). The provision of appropriate support and equal access to mainstream life and services are seen as requirements for independence. Thus instead of seeing service users as having deficits or pathologies, the philosophy of independent living includes in its definition of independence ensuring people the support to live their lives on as equal terms as possible.

Direct payments were therefore developed as part of the disabled people's movement's liberatory and emancipatory objectives. Direct payments were not conceived of as some kind of consumerist exchange relationship, but rather to ensure the support necessary for independence and increased equality. Thus:

- the level at which funding would be set needed to be consistent with the goals and values of independent living;
- the package of support paid for by these payments would be under the disabled person's control;
- they would have infrastructural support to operate their direct payments, to match their particular needs and circumstances, offered ideally by a local user-controlled organisation or 'centre for independent living';
- disabled people would also have independent advocacy, advice and information to help them make their own assessment of what support they needed to live independently (Campbell and Oliver, 1996).

It is important to note that none of these elements have been routinely matched in the development of individual budgets. The expectation has frequently been that these would be run by people's families, funding ceilings have been restricted by available funds, no infrastructure of support was identified as necessary and user-controlled organisations were not central to the thinking or operation of individual budget pilot schemes.

While government concern with individual budgets, as we have seen, has been to expand them massively, with some local authorities enthusiastic early starters, the story of direct payments has been very different. Their expansion was slow, patchy, uneven across different regions, restricted to certain user groups and they were developed in ways which service users frequently saw as over-bureaucratic and over-controlled, limiting the independence and autonomy of their users and undermining their liberatory values (Pearson, 2000; CSCI, 2004; Riddell et al, 2005; Davey et al, 2007). Nonetheless, in principle, service users who accessed them generally valued them (Maglajlic et al, 2000; Stainton and Boyce, 2004). On the other hand, while service users accessing individual budgets in special pilots have tended to be enthusiastic, service users more generally have tended to be cautious and concerned about the wholesale shift to personalisation and self-directed support (Glynn et al, 2008).

We can see the transformation of the idea of direct payments initiated by the disabled people's movement, into the personalisation, self-directed support and individual budgets espoused by the state, as fundamental in its effect. The nature, aims and philosophy of the development are changed. We can see a development reconstructed from the liberatory and emancipatory ideal of disabled people, to become part of a neoliberal project of governments committed to increased privatisation and the containment or reduction of public welfare spending. The empowering and democratising philosophy of direct payments has been replaced by the consumerism of individual budgets. Ironically some service users who have been able to access individual budgets have praised them for their flexibility over direct payments that they previously received. Yet the difference has been related to the bureaucratisation and 'over-policing' of direct payments by some local authorities, rather than the originating principles established by the disabled people's movement.

Co-production

The term 'co-production' is a very recent arrival to public and social policy. It has been defined as:

> An innovative approach to service development and practice that brings together service users and practitioners in a collaborative relationship, drawing on service users' strengths and abilities in the problem solving process. (Hunter and Ritchie, 2007, back cover)

There is now a growing literature on the subject, as well as an increasing number of events, studies and consultants focusing on it (for example, Alford, 2009; Needham and Carr, 2009). There is an emphasis in such discussion on partnership, involvement and empowerment. Discussions chime closely with long-term preoccupations of service users and their movements. These include, for example, the importance of equality in relationships and roles, the need to move away from passive roles for service users in service provision and development and an emphasis on the skills and contributions of people as service users and members of the public. It reflects service users' efforts to develop 'user-led' and more 'user-centred' services, which can be traced to the 1970s and 1980s.

What is interesting is that, although indebted to their discussions and proposals, the terminology does not seem to come from service users. Co-production, like personalisation, is another piece of jargon that has been developed within the service system. It is not a term that has been initiated or owned by service users. Moreover, so far at least, service users have not been central in the development of discussion under this heading, even though it emphasises the importance of their involvement, partnership and capacity. So, for instance, a current edited collection which aims to add to the research-based evidence on this subject offers nine chapters, only one of which is authored by someone who writes from a 'service user' perspective (Hunter and Ritchie, 2007). Some texts pay minimal attention to service user organisations or movements, but are written much more from a managerialist/consumerist perspective (Alford, 2009).

Broader undermining of service user-related ideas and developments

Unless service users are full and equal partners in the intellectual as well as practical development of this initiative, it is difficult to see how it will avoid ultimately disempowering rather than empowering them, adding to their responsibilities, rather than democratising policy and provision. One of the sub-texts of such co-production seems to be the part that service users can play in running and managing services and supporting each other. True co-production means shifting resources to service users and their organisations, not just shifting responsibility and effort.

So far, it can be argued inadequate attention has been paid to the components that will need to be put in place to make this possible. The first of these is capacity building for individual service users, to ensure that they are adequately equipped for new, more active roles in policy and provision. From experience we know that this means the provision of more independent advocacy, advice, accessible information and support. If a wide range of service users is to be involved, then effective policies and practices for access and support will also need to be put in place (Beresford and Croft, 1993). These are still generally at an early stage in their development. Second, service users will need the support of their own local user-controlled organisations and centres for independent living. The evidence is that such organisations are insecure and under-funded. They are overstretched and lack capacity (Branfield et al, 2006), an issue we will return to later. They lack the resources to provide the essential infrastructural base to make ideas of 'co-production' meaningful, especially in a time of public spending cuts.

It is also important to recognise that service users, their organisations and movements have not always seen 'collaborative working' with the state and services system, for that is what co-production essentially means, as the most helpful route to secure their rights and needs. Some of the best developments have come from service user organisations themselves taking the lead (Campbell and Oliver, 1996). That, as we have seen, is how direct payments originated. This must still happen. It should not be restricted by a pre-occupation with 'co-production'. Instead there should continue to be resources and opportunities to experiment with and develop user-controlled initiatives, schemes and services.

A broader issue

Other ideas and developments have also emerged in social policy which build on concepts, values and aspirations of service users, but which have been advanced by others and have become deeply ambiguous. Three such ideas are 'recovery', 'social capital' and 'social inclusion'. All three of these reflect the desire of service users and their movements to be recognised as active, contributing citizens. All have gained some support from service users. But all have also mainly been developed by state and service providers, rather than service users and their organisations, and can be seen to be at least contentious in their role and purpose.

Recovery

The idea of recovery has recently gained major interest in UK mental health policy and practice. There is talk of a 'recovery movement' (Pilgrim, 2008). Many service users value the idea of recovery because it does not write them off as irreparably damaged or defective, but instead offers hope and the possibility of positive outcomes for their lives (Turner-Crowson and Wallcraft, 2002). However, other survivors are highly critical of the concept's essentially medicalised basis and the associated emphasis on 're-ablement' and moving people to employment. While the philosophy of independent living developed by disabled people emphasises people's potentially continuing need for support to live their lives to the full, recovery instead implies that such support may become unnecessary and be withdrawn as people 'recover'. For this reason, some survivors see recovery as at least consistent with, and in some cases supportive of, the neoliberal agenda of cuts, integration into the labour market and increasing reliance on people's self-help and 'looking after themselves'.

Social capital

The concept of social capital, which has gained international importance and been associated with international development, acknowledges and recognises service users' own strengths and resources. It takes account of and seeks to foster the networks and relationships that people may have. It challenges institutionalising assumptions that see solutions only through the provision of formal services, which have historically often restricted people to and resulted in an over-reliance on such formalised and professionalised settings and professional relationships (Brindle, 2008b).

But it is also seen and can be experienced as gender-biased, placing an over-reliance on women's traditional role in the private and community spheres. It may also serve as a means of co-opting and harnessing service users' networks and relationships to purposes defined by the state and services system, in order to compensate for and maintain a system of inadequate formal services (Morris, 1993; Stolle and Lewis, 2002).

Social inclusion

One of the key concerns of service user movements from their beginning has been to challenge the exclusion of service users and the many different barriers that they face. This has been most explicitly argued by the UK disabled people's movement. As two of its founding members, Ken and Maggie Davis, wrote, disability was redefined through the social model, 'in terms of social exclusion and thus as a particular form of social oppression' (Oliver and Barnes, 1998, p xii). Based on a 'barriers' approach to challenging such disability, the campaigning of the disabled people's movement can be seen as a struggle to secure inclusion in mainstream life and services, after a history of social exclusion in western societies like Britain (Campbell and Oliver, 1996).

There has been an equivalent interest in such inclusion and participation on the part of all service user movements. The concept of social inclusion was championed by New Labour from its election to power in 1997 and became a key touchstone for the development and evaluation of social policy. However, as its critics have evidenced, this was an idea of social inclusion based primarily on moral regulation and people's incorporation into the labour market through being pressured into paid employment (Levitas, 2005). Whereas for service users and their organisations employment has been seen as a right to which service users should have equal access and entitlement, under dominant definitions of social inclusion it has been framed as an obligation which they seem often to be suspected of trying to duck.

An interesting case study of the clash between service users' and state ideologies over such social inclusion is offered by 'modernisation' policy in relation to day services for mental health service users. Current policy has been towards 'disinvestment' from such day centre provision on the grounds it is 'segregating' and poor quality, the same negative criticisms that service users traditionally made about such 'special' services. Instead there has been an increasing emphasis on employment-based schemes. Service users and supportive practitioners, however, have argued that the actual effect of such policy is frequently to withdraw services from people, which may be valued and which are certainly better than nothing, without providing appropriate alternatives or challenging the discriminatory nature of the labour market, which is key to their social exclusion (Beresford and Bryant, 2008).

Conclusion

This discussion suggests that service users and their movements may be challenged in two key ways under mainstream politics and social policy. They can be at risk of being incorporated in proposals and developments that are antithetical to their self-defined interests through engagement in participatory schemes operating under the broader managerialist/consumerist user involvement project. But equally, their own independent and liberatory ideas and developments are liable to be subverted and presented back to them in regressive ways by policy makers, the state, market, the third sector and the service system.

It is no longer enough for service users to operate in separatist ways – as to some extent the UK disabled people's movement did in its initial stages – to avoid the risk of incorporation and subordination. It is no longer sufficient for us as service users to work in collective rather than individualised ways, or to avoid responding to dominant agendas, if we wish to advance our own. What has characterised social policy in an age of user and public engagement – and current social care reforms epitomise this – is increasing ambiguity, uncertainty and contradiction. What this means is that as service users, and in their service user movements, people will need to be as clear as they can be about their own values and principles and be constantly monitoring politics, policies and practice – and their own involvement in them – in relation to them.

This process of service users' liberatory ideals constantly being subverted in the policy and political process may be seen as calling into question the very value of such efforts. This may be especially true if we see, as many service users do, the processes of developing ideas and policy formation as ones which take place between competing interests of local and central state, the market, workers and service users, where there are great inequalities of power. But we need to be aware of – while not overstating – the progressive changes (in legislation, policy, culture and people's lives) that there have been which have their origins in service users' collective action and movements. Nonetheless this issue of the regressive restructuring of service user developments needs to be given more serious and careful consideration in academic social policy as well as among service users and their organisations.

For service users and their organisations, it raises a number of questions about what they can and should be doing to resist such negative consequences of their action. The UK disabled people's movement long held a distrustful view of traditional political structures and processes, prioritising the development of its own collective action and organisations as part of a broader programme for securing disabled people's human and civil rights. Since then, with the emergence of more opportunities and encouragement, disabled people have become more closely and directly involved in government bodies, forums and parliamentary processes. However, their organisations and those of other service users remain insecure and under-funded, despite the setting up of the government's Office for Disability Issues, cross-departmental sign-up to principles of independent living and a commitment initially emanating from the Prime Minister's Strategy Unit to support and establish a national network of user-controlled or 'user-led' organisations (ULOs) (PMSU, 2005).

As relationships between service users and their organisations and government have become more complex, with aims and roles more unclear, it becomes even more important for service users to be critiquing and evaluating what they do, their independent efforts and those advanced in association with the government, to build the evidence base of what outcomes are achieved and what goals secured by each of them.

It may now be appropriate for service users to reaffirm their focus on:

* developing their own independent organisations and finding ways of making them more financially independent and viable;
* strengthening their networks with each other – both geographically and across user groups – and building on their shared experience to strengthen their solidarity;
* developing more proactive strategies in their own approaches to user involvement which encourage more diverse involvement;
* forming positive alliances with practitioner and carer organisations which are supportive of their values and philosophy (like, for example, Carer Watch and the Social Work Action Network); and
* negotiating from such enhanced platforms more effectively and on more equal terms with existing powerholders and policy makers.

The crucial achievement of service user movements as of other liberatory and new social movements has been the raising of people's consciousness. This has transformed the understanding of themselves of many thousands of disabled people, people with learning difficulties, mental health service users/survivors, older people and others, in the UK and globally. It has helped to transform their expectations, abilities, self-confidence and capacity to exert pressure for change. It enables them to formulate their own definitions of their experience and the world and their own critiques of what is needed. This is the most effective basis for working for change. It makes it possible for growing numbers of people as service users to make sense of what is actually happening to them and in society more generally and to steer change in line with their rights, desires and ambitions. It also provides the force for change to counter the dominance of state and market.

There are also implications here for academic social policy. It needs to be focusing far more on the complex issues raised by participation and the emergence of service users as individual and collective actors in social policy. These are indisputably now central to public policy. Hopefully it may take on these tasks in partnership with service users and their organisations, developing alliances with them as historically it has with traditional charitable and top-down initiators of reform.

In their 1998 discussion of disabled people and social policy, Mike Oliver and Colin Barnes argued that disabled people:

> have no choice but to attempt to build a better world.... We all need a world where impairment is valued and celebrated and all disabling barriers are eradicated. Such a world would be inclusionary for all. It is up to everyone, but especially those involved in the development and implementation of social policy – both planners and practitioners – to nurture it and help make it a reality. (Oliver and Barnes, 1998, p 102)

They also argue that 'a successful outcome might only be achieved by the further development of a bottom-up approach to policymaking' (Oliver and Barnes, 1998, p 92).

The present discussion started out by considering different discourses that have developed in social policy. It has shown how liberatory discourses can be overpowered and subverted. But it has also argued for the development of creative alliances and partnerships between discourses, like those of academic social policy and service user movements that have previously sometimes been either opposed or distant from each other. This is likely to have valuable effects in challenging reactionary dominant discourses that have previously overshadowed and undermined both.

References

Alcock, P., May, M. and Rowlingson, K. (eds) (2008) *The student's companion to social policy* (3rd edn), Oxford: Wiley-Blackwell.

Alford, J. (2009) *Engaging public sector clients: From service delivery to co-production*, Basingstoke: Palgrave Macmillan.

Annetts, J., Law, A., McNeish, W. and Mooney, G. (2009) *Understanding social welfare movements*, Bristol: The Policy Press in association with the Social Policy Association.

Barnes, M., Sullivan, H. and Newman, J. (2007) *Power, participation and political renewal: Case studies in public participation*, Bristol: The Policy Press.

Barnes, M., Harrison, S., Mort, M. and Shardlow, P. (1999) *Unequal partners: User groups and community care*, Bristol: The Policy Press.

Beresford, P. (2001) 'Service users, social policy and the future of welfare', *Critical Social Policy*, vol 21, no 4, pp 494-512.

Beresford, P. (2008) 'Welfare users and social policy', in P. Alcock, M. May, and K. Rowlingson (eds) (2008) *The student's companion to social policy* (3rd edn), Oxford: Wiley-Blackwell

Beresford, P. (2009) 'Personal health budgets for the UK NHS: a revolution for the patient?', Guest Editorial, *Patient*, vol 2, no 2, pp 1-4.

Beresford, P. and Bryant, W. (2008) 'Saving the day centre', *Society Guardian*, 11 June, p 6.

Beresford, P. and Campbell, P. (2004) 'Participation and protest: mental health service users/survivors', in M.J. Todd and G. Taylor (eds) *Democracy and participation: Popular protest and new social movements*, London: Merlin Press, pp 326-42.

Beresford, P. and Croft, S. (1993) *Citizen involvement: A practical guide to change*, Basingstoke: Macmillan.

Beresford, P. and Hasler, F. (2009) *Transforming social care: Changing the future together*, Uxbridge: Brunel University Press.

Branfield, F. and Beresford, P. with Andrews, E.J., Chambers, P., Staddon, P., Wise, G. and Williams-Findlay, B. (2006) *Making user involvement work: Supporting service user networking and knowledge*, York: York Publishing Services for the Joseph Rowntree Foundation.

Brindle, D. (2008) 'Tireless champion of autonomy: profile of disability campaigner, John Evans', *Society Guardian*, 22 October, p 7.

Brindle, D. (2008b) *Care and support: A community responsibility?*, Viewpoint, York: Joseph Rowntree Foundation.

Campbell, J. and Oliver, M. (1996) *Disability politics: Understanding our past, changing our future*, London: Routledge.

Campbell, P. (1996) 'The history of the user movement in the United Kingdom', in T. Heller, J. Reynolds, R. Gomm, R. Muston and S. Pattison (eds) *Mental health matters*, Basingstoke: Macmillan in association with the Open University, pp 218-25.

Campbell, P. (2009) 'The service user/survivor movement', in J. Reynolds, R. Muston, T. Heller, J. Leach, M. McCormick, J. Wallcraft and M. Walsh (eds) *Mental health still matters*, Basingstoke: Palgrave/Macmillan, pp 46-52.

CSCI (Commission for Social Care Inspection) (2004) *Direct payments: What are the barriers?*, London: CSCI.

Darzi, A. (2008) *High quality care for all: NHS next stage review final report* (Darzi Report), London: The Stationery Office.

Davey, V., Fernandez, J.-L., Knapp, M., Vick, N., Jolly, D., Swift, P., Tobin, R., Kendall, J., Ferrie, J., Pearson, C., Mercer, G. and Priestley, M. (2007) *Direct payments: A national survey of direct payments policy and practice*, London: Personal Social Services Research Unit, London School of Economics and Political Science.

Dean, H. (2006) *Social policy*, Short Introductions Series, Cambridge: Polity Press.

Duffy, S. (2005) 'Individual budgets: transforming the allocation of resources for care', *Journal of Integrated Care*, vol 13, no 1, pp 8-16.

Ferguson, I. (2007) 'Increasing user choice or privatizing risk?: the antinomies of personalization', *British Journal of Social Work*, vol 37, no 3, pp 387-403.

Gibson, B.E., Brooks, D., DeMatteo, D. and King, A. (2009) 'Consumer-directed personal assistance and "care": perspectives of workers and ventilator users', *Disability & Society*, vol 24, no 3, pp 317-30.

Glasby, J. and Littlechild, R. (2009) *Direct payments and personal budgets: Putting personalisation into practice* (2nd edn), Bristol: The Policy Press.

Glendinning, C., Challis, D., Fernández. J.-L., Jacobs, S., Jones, K., Knapp, M., Manthorpe, J., Moran, N., Netten, A., Stevens, M. and Wilberforce, M. (2008) *National evaluation of the individual budget pilot projects: Final report*, York: Social Policy Research Unit, University of York.

Glynn, M., Beresford, P., Bewley, C., Branfield, F., Butt, J., Croft, S., Dattan Pitt, K., Fleming, J., Flynn, R., Patmore, C., Postle, K. and Turner, M. (2008) *Person-centred support: What service users and practitioners say*, York: York Publishing Services for the Joseph Rowntree Foundation.

Hatton, C., Waters, J., Duffy, S. et al (2008) *A report on In Control's second phase: Evaluation and learning 2005–7*, London: In Control Publications.

HM Government (2007) *Putting people first: A shared vision and commitment to the transformation of adult social care*, London: HM Government.

Hunter, S. and Ritchie, P. (2007) *Co-production and personalisation in social care*, London: Jessica Kingsley Publishers.

Lavalette, M. and Pratt, A. (eds) (2006) *Social policy: Theories, concepts and issues*, London: Sage Publications.

Leadbeater, C., Bartlett, J. and Gallagher, N. (2008) *Making it personal*, London: Demos.

Lent, A. (2002) *British social movements since 1945: Sex, colour, peace and power*, Basingstoke: Palgrave Macmillan.

Levitas, R. (2005) *The inclusive society? Social exclusion and New Labour* (2nd revised edn), Basingstoke: Palgrave Macmillan.

Maglajlic, R., Brandon, D. and Given, D. (2000) 'Making direct payments a choice: a report on the research findings', *Disability & Society*, vol 15, no 1, pp 99-113.

Morris, J. (1993) *Independent lives? Community care and disabled people*, Basingstoke: Macmillan.

Morris, J. (2004) 'Community care: a disempowering framework', *Disability & Society*, vol 19, no 5, pp 427-42.

Needham, C. and Carr, S. (2009) *Co-production: An emerging evidence base for social care transformation*, SCIE Research Briefing 31, London: Social Care Institute for Excellence.

Oliver, M. and Barnes, C. (1998) *Disabled people and social policy: From exclusion to inclusion*, London: Longmans.

Pearson, C. (2000) 'Money talks?: Competing discourses in the implementation of direct payments', *Critical Social Policy*, vol 20, no 4, pp 459-77.

Pierson, C. (2006) *Beyond the welfare state: The new political economy of welfare* (3rd edn), Cambridge: Polity Press.

Pierson, C. and Castles, F.G. (eds) (2006) *The welfare state reader* (2nd edn), Cambridge: Polity Press.

Pierson, P. (ed) (2001) *The new politics of the welfare state*, Oxford: Oxford University Press.

Pilgrim, D. (2008) '"Recovery" and current mental health policy', *Chronic Illness*, vol 4, no 4, pp 295-304.

PMSU (Prime Minister's Strategy Unit) (2005) *Improving the life chances of disabled people*, London: Cabinet Office.

Prideaux, S., Roulstone, A., Harris, J. and Barnes, C. (2009) 'Disabled people and self-directed support schemes: reconceptualising work and welfare in the 21st century', *Disability & Society*, vol 24, no 5, pp 557-69.

Riddell, S., Pearson, C., Jolly, D., Barnes, C., Priestley, M. and Mercer, G. (2005) 'The development of direct payments in the UK: implications for social justice', *Social Policy & Society*, vol 4, no 1, pp 75-85.

Romme, M., Escher, S., Dillon, J., Corstens, D. and Morris, M. (2009) *Living with voices: 50 stories of recovery*, Ross-on-Wye: PCCS Books.

Roulstone, A. and Morgan, H. (2009) 'Neo-liberal individualism or self-directed support: are we all speaking the same language on modernizing adult social care?', *Social Policy & Society*, vol 8, no 4, pp 333-45.

Scourfield, P. (2008) 'Going for brokerage: a task of "independent support" or social work?', Advance access publishing, 21 October, *British Journal of Social Work*, doi:10.1093/bjsw/bcn141.

Simmons, R., Powell, M. and Greener, I. (eds) (2009) *The consumer in public services: Choice, values and difference*, Bristol: The Policy Press.

Stainton, T. and Boyce, S. (2004) '"I have got my life back": users' experience of direct payments', *Disability & Society*, vol 19, no 5, pp 443-54.

Stolle, D. and Lewis, J. (2002) 'Social capital: an emerging concept', in B. Hobson, J. Lewis and B. Siim (eds) *Contested concepts in gender and social politics*, Cheltenham: Edward Elgar Publishing, pp 195-230.

Turner-Crowson, J. and Wallcraft, J. (2002) 'The recovery vision for mental health services and research: a British perspective', *Psychiatric Rehabilitation Journal*, vol 25, no 3, pp 245-54.

UPIAS (Union of the Physically Impaired Against Segregation)/Disability Alliance (1976) *Fundamental principles of disability: Being a summary of the discussion held on 22nd November, 1975 and containing commentaries from each organization*, London: UPIAS and the Disability Alliance.

Waters, J. and Duffy, S. (2007) *Individual budgets: Report on individual budget integration*, London: In Control Publications.

ELEVEN

Participation and social justice

Marian Barnes with Colin Gell and Pat Thomas

Introduction

Advocacy of participation by 'the public' and of service users in decision making about public policy and services has multiple origins. In the late 1980s it was claimed by sections of the Left as a radical idea that would renew the public sector in order to resist attacks from Prime Minister Margaret Thatcher and others who sought to replace public services with private markets (Deakin and Wright, 1990). In contrast, for the neoliberals of the political Right, consumerist strategies were a way of limiting the power of professionals and rolling back the state. Creating active consumers was part of the strategy of market making. For New Labour in government, initiatives to involve the public and service users have reflected aspirations to improve services, create more assertive consumers, enable more accountability and to generate greater legitimacy for public service decision making (Barnes et al, 2004). For users of welfare services and for deprived and disadvantaged communities the right to have a say about services and policies is a matter of civil rights and social justice (for example, Beresford et al, 1999). From whatever perspective, changes in public service governance and service delivery that have taken place over the last 20–30 years represent a substantially different way of imagining the relationship between the state and its citizens from that which characterised the first 20–30 years of the welfare state.

One group of people who have both demanded and been invited to have their say is those who use mental health services. Colin Gell argues the importance of this:

a Because any business or service that does not enable this will not meet what it set out to do and could potentially lose its business. The development of Foundation Trusts could see competition increase and inappropriate trusts could be shunned by commissioners.
b The most successful businesses regularly ask their customers about what they want. M&S and Tesco are always asking their customers.

Most importantly it is morally right that organisations that use our money should be accountable to us, particularly those providing health and social care. Instinctively most service users know what is right for them and what is not.

By the end of the first decade of the 21st century participation has become official policy: from the 'real people' exercising 'real power' in relation to local government (CLG, 2008); to the 'ordinary people only' sought by the National Health Service (NHS) to take part in the, now defunct, patient and public involvement forums (Martin, 2008); through the communities to be engaged in processes of crime reduction (Prior et al, 2006); to the experts by experience whose knowledge is sought in the delivery of health and social care services. This is not only a phenomenon of the UK policy scene; across the globe citizens are being activated, empowered, encouraged or coerced into taking part in public policy making and service delivery (Cornwall and Coelho, 2007). Participatory governance, co-production, choice and control are part of the language of welfare and public policy more generally.

However, in spite of broad acceptance of user and citizen participation in the governance, design and delivery of public services, there are a number of issues that continue to offer conceptual, practical and political challenges in terms of the way in which opportunities for participation are designed. The impact of such activity is also uncertain. In view of the diverse aspirations of government and public officials, of users and of citizens, what has been achieved by it and does more participation mean more socially just decision making and outcomes? A social policy perspective on user involvement and public participation requires us to address the extent to which such initiatives can be considered to be contributing to the creation of a more just society and it is this issue that is the focus of this chapter.

The chapter is based on a plenary presentation at the 2009 Social Policy Association conference in Edinburgh. It brings together perspectives from activists in the mental health service user movement and the carers' movement and a researcher who has studied such developments and been an ally of participants within them. Colin Gell, a founder member of the Nottingham Advocacy Group (NAG) and Pat Thomas, chair of Birmingham Carers Association, each have more than 20 years' experience of activism. They illustrate from their direct experience the argument that I (Marian Barnes) am making here based on my own and others' research and analysis. While the particular examples of carer and mental health service user involvement are used to illustrate the argument, the chapter aims to offer an analysis that is broadly relevant to citizen and user involvement in different contexts.

Voice, knowledge and representation

One of the key principles guiding participatory approaches to governance and service delivery is that those whose lives are affected by public services and policies have a right to a say about them. But the possibility for absolutely everybody affected to be directly involved in decision making is constrained by practicalities. Thus, one enduring issue and point of contention within user and public participation is how and on what basis some, rather than all, of those affected get to take part. Assumptions about the appropriate representation of service users and citizens shape the way in which 'legitimate' participants are determined and the basis on which different identities, experiences, interests or perspectives can be represented within policy and service decision making (see, for example, Barnes et al, 2003).

Another set of issues concerns the value accorded to different types of knowledge within service and policy decision making: what types of knowledge should be recognised and valued? Should one type of knowledge be prioritised over others? And is it possible for new understandings to be generated through dialogue between 'professional' and 'experiential' knowledge?

These questions about representation and knowledge are linked. The concept of 'voice' implies a role for users and citizens in contributing to policy making. But on what basis? Should their contribution be legitimated by forms of election and accountability, that is, by an extension of the principle of representation familiar within democratic politics, or by reference to the personal knowledge and/or expertise they have to contribute? There is evidence of both tension and confusion over whether participation should be based on principles of 'local representation', which emphasises the role of participants as representatives of a constituency and thus enhancing the legitimacy of decision making, or 'local knowledge', which assumes that better decisions will be made as a result of drawing on lay or experiential knowledge. Barnes et al (2008) explored these issues in a study of citizen-centred governance in a number of policy contexts (for example, Sure Start, foundation hospitals, local strategic partnerships, school governors, young people's participation in neighbourhood renewal), which revealed that each principle was more or less evident as a basis on which people were invited or encouraged to take part in different cases, but that there was rarely an explicit decision to adopt one or other as the basis on which participative practices should be developed. In some instances this led to confusion, frustration and sometimes conflict between citizens and officials who had different ideas about who should be regarded as legitimate participants. The principles of local knowledge and local representation are relevant to diverse contexts in which citizens and service users are included in dialogue about policies and services, whether these are locality-based initiatives aiming to engage a range of people living in the local area, or service-based initiatives seeking to involve those who need to use those services on a regular basis. In the next section we consider 'local representation' and 'local knowledge' in more detail.

Local representation

Concern about the 'representativeness' of citizen/user participants is frequently used to question and sometimes challenge the legitimacy of these processes (for example, Barnes, 2002).

Colin offers a view from his experience of representing mental health service users in many different contexts:

"We need to address 'representativeness' and 'professional users'. You will never get true user representation, just as you will never get true medical or social work representation. So let's go with 'good as it can be'. Try and ensure that whoever is a representative has access to and consults with a wider group of

> people. And why should service users not be professional? Why shouldn't people make a life/living through giving their knowledge and experience to bettering services? Most professional users I know are still part of a local, regional or national network and do their best to encourage wider involvement. Let's celebrate the success of service user involvement – don't knock it!"

The discourse of 'local representation' is concerned with the democratisation of public policy making in a plural and diverse society – what has been called 'deepening democracy' (Fung and Wright, 2003). It is based on the argument that democratic capacity is enhanced by providing new opportunities for a variety of relevant stakeholders to be a formal part of the decision-making process in relation to specific areas of policy or service delivery, rather than relying on the very limited form of democracy enabled by choosing generic decision makers via the electoral process – local councillors and Members of Parliament (MPs). Typically, this form of representation is achieved by allocating reserved seats on the management board of a governance body to relevant sections of the community – the boards of many New Deal for Communities initiatives operated in this way and foundation trusts also operate a system of allocated board places for patient and public member representatives.

The case for local representation rests on a number of principles (Skelcher, 2003). One is that public policy programmes directed at discrete localities or publics should include the affected groups in the governance of that initiative. Including representatives of those who will be affected enhances the democratic quality of decision making, but democracy itself also benefits. This is because the involvement by citizens in local governance is also considered to have an educative effect, promoting good citizenship and a healthy democratic life in society – values that are considered important in their own right.

This approach has a number of institutional and design implications. First, there need to be mechanisms that enable individuals to be elected or nominated by particular constituencies, and second, there needs to be a system that enables the chosen representatives to be accountable to those constituencies. The legitimacy of their input derives from this accountability relationship. That is, it reflects an expansion of the principles of representative democracy. It assumes there is an identifiable – and organised – constituency to be represented and it also assumes that there are mechanisms and opportunities for representatives to consult and give account to those organised constituencies. This can be the case when, for example, service users and carers have created their own organisations from which participants in service decision making can be chosen. As Colin argues: "When seeking 'representation', work with established user organisations that have a wideish membership".

Perversely, there have been instances where it is precisely such formal mandated positions that have led to accusations of 'non-representativeness'. A study considered the experiences of a high profile disabled people's coalition which had a formal representative structure that meant that the disabled people who took up roles on policy bodies adopted a position that had been decided on by their council (Barnes et al, 1999). These individuals were there formally to represent the disabled people's coalition, were expected to do so on the basis of a previously debated position and to report back to members that they had done so. But officials from the local authority decided that the positions being argued by representatives did not 'represent' what they presumed to be the position of disabled people in the area who were not members of the coalition. Hence they also invited people from other disability organisations (which did not have these accountability structures) to take part. Their involvement was invited rather than the result of selection and mandate and arguably much less capable of being demonstrably 'representative' in terms of formal democratic principles.

As Colin has suggested, there need to be pragmatic responses to the issue of representation – people should not be excluded from taking part in decision making because the formal conditions for ensuring election and accountability do not exist. The response of the local authority in this case appeared to be driven by the fact that they were not happy with the positions being taken by coalition representatives, rather than that they wanted to enlarge opportunities for participation. But there are other, more principled arguments for suggesting that a system based on mandated representation may not always be appropriate. This can constrain the development of deliberative policy making. Because participants are there to represent a particular interest or identity, whether that be a neighbourhood, an ethnic group, an age group or a group of people using a particular service, rather than to contribute on the basis of their local or experiential knowledge, a formal requirement to act as a mandated representative can mean that it is hard to engage in an exchange of ideas that might generate different ways of thinking about things – the approach that is promoted by advocates of deliberative democracy (for example, Dryzek, 2002).

There are other aspects to the problematic nature of representation in practice. Often people may be invited to represent others simply because they are a 'service user'. Participation is sought on the basis of single characteristics which are considered to define the individual and enable them to speak on behalf of others with similar characteristics: as a carer, a mental health service user, an old person, as someone living in a particular neighbourhood. Yet each of these identities constitute only one dimension of the lives of the people involved and while, for example, an older person who uses social care services may be 'typical' of others with similar needs for support, they may be reluctant to 'speak on behalf of' others with whom they have no contact and whose life experiences may be very different.

One of the dynamics that Barnes et al (2006) reflected on in a study of participation across a range of different policy areas was the significance of the processes of identity construction that take place – sometimes across lines of difference, through the process of participation. Examples included: women from different generations who felt that their way of looking at other women had changed through involvement in a women's advice centre, and older people who developed a collective sense of tolerance and respect through working with men and women of different ethnicities and class positions through their involvement in an older people's forum. Rather than *starting off* with a collective sense of a shared identity, this is something that is often generated through involvement – a process that has previously been identified in studies of social movements (Melucci, 1996). Carers can come to understand their shared identity with other carers through taking part in carers' groups (Barnes, 2006, chapter 7). Users of mental health services recognise that similar experiences of mental health problems and of service use can contribute to a shared understanding and the ability to propose alternative responses as a result of taking part in advocacy and user groups (Barnes and Bowl, 2001). Forums that enable debate and exploration of positions may be more creative – both of ideas and identities – than those where people are expected to come to represent pre-determined positions. This is enabled through collective action in groups such as NAG and the Birmingham Carers Association, but is harder to achieve in the spaces to which public officials 'invite' individuals to 'represent' others. This introduces the significance of the second principle on which participation is and can be based.

Local knowledge

The idea of 'local knowledge' comes from the critique of the role of state-sponsored experts in the policy-making process, whether they be 'professionals' or 'bureaucrats'. It promotes and validates knowledge held by actors who have previously been excluded from or had only a marginal role in such processes – poor citizens, service users and groups organised around various identities and interests. The term 'local knowledge' has been adopted by policy analysts to refer to 'the very mundane, but still expert knowledge, understanding of and practical reasoning about local conditions derived from lived experience' (Yanow, 2003, p 236). The term 'local' in this context refers less to a defined geographical space than to a 'location' within a community of meaning, which could derive from the shared experience of discrimination among Black Americans living in the southern states of the US in the 1960s, or the shared knowledge of environmental changes following the Chernobyl nuclear disaster among shepherds in the Cumbrian hills. Equally it could refer to the analyses and strategies that people living with mental health problems have developed to deal with the discrimination they face. Participatory practices in public governance focus attention on the type of knowledge that is necessary for and recognised as legitimate in reaching policy decisions, on who has access to such knowledge and how it can be utilised in democratic debate (for example, Fischer, 2000).

One argument for practices such as citizens' juries and other deliberative forums is that they not only enable lay citizens to *access* knowledge that has previously been accessible only within professional knowledge communities, or bureaucratic systems, but also that they open up such expert knowledge to lay scrutiny – for example in the process of witness questioning that takes place in citizens' juries (see, for example, Barnes, 1999; Davies et al, 2006) – and that they enable policy to be deliberated by reference to different types of knowledge. The experts are exposed to questioning on the basis of the lay, experiential or local knowledge of users and citizens. This may suggest that recognised 'expertise' is partial, inadequate or just plain wrong. Less formal processes are evident in other participatory forums (such as neighbourhood conferences) that are based in principles of local knowledge.

Local knowledge can be contrasted with the technical and universalising claims of scientific knowledge in two key ways. First, local knowledge is particular, embedded in understandings of how things work in specific contexts and based in practical reasoning. Second, it encompasses meanings, values, emotions and beliefs as well as cognition.

Purely technical solutions to policy problems and those that are based on the assumption that people make decisions based solely on rational choices often fail because they do not recognise the significance of non-cognitive factors in affecting social behaviour (Yanow, 2003).

Pat summarised what it is that lay carers learn and the expertise they develop through the experience of care giving. She has cared for her disabled son since his birth. Trevor is now in his 40s and lives on his own with support. Pat's list of what she has learned to do highlights the overlap with what paid care workers might consider 'professional' expertise. In her case, and that of other carers, Pat's expertise has developed from the particular circumstances in which she and Trevor have negotiated his needs for support:

- Organisation and things to do
- Sort out day care transport
- Doctors and hospital appointments
- Special footwear
- Liaise with social workers, physiotherapist and psychologist
- Get appropriate adaptations and wheelchairs
- Organise respite
- Deal with sexual problems
- Shopping, household and personal
- Pension entitlements
- Adapt clothing
- Washing, ironing
- Organise suitable holidays
- Medication
- Deal with behaviour problems
- Give emotional support

Pat also captures the significance of the emotional dimension of the experience of carers. Under the heading 'What a carer may be feeling' she highlights important aspects of what caring can mean for care givers:

- Anger
- Guilt
- Isolation
- Loneliness

- Poverty
- Exhaustion
- Low self-worth
- Cheated in employment and relationships because of caring role
- Life not worth living
- A sense of loss
- Depression
- Let down by professionals
- Fear of my own death – what wil happen to my son?

Pat's personal analysis constitutes a powerful indication of the experiential knowledge that carers can contribute to decision making. Individually and collectively the understanding that carers develop about what caring means is not only a valuable resource to decision makers, but also offers insight into the ways in which 'socially just' responses need to take on board the emotional dimensions of this experience as well as the practical support needs necessary to sustain caring relationships. Such knowledge and experiences may be accessed and reflected through research that explores carers' lives (for example, Barnes, 2006), but this is not the same as carers themselves communicating directly what caring means to those with responsibilities for making policy and designing services. I have argued elsewhere the importance of encompassing the 'intelligence of the emotions' (Nussbaum, 2001) in the context of public and user participation (Barnes, 2004, 2008). Ruling emotions 'out of order' in the context of deliberation not only risks excluding particular ways of expressing experience, but also of excluding important aspects of the experience itself.

Colin offers a specific illustration of how the meaning and the emotional dimension of experience needs to be taken into consideration in planning services for people with mental health problems. He goes on to describe how this knowledge contributed by service users led to a significant change in service design.

"For a number of years there has been disquiet about the appropriateness of acute in-patient wards. The idea of 'postcode' wards is redundant. Supposing a woman is experiencing a life crisis that is considered best treated in an in-patient setting. Would she really be happy with being admitted to our 'postcode' wards?

- She would be going from a situation where there is freedom and choice about a way of life to living in a unit with 20+ other people.
- At least half those people are not there by choice; the law decrees that they are there so they are going to be pretty angry. Any chance of therapy for voluntary people is remote.
- At least half will be men, what would she feel about sharing living space with other men? Many women going into care have been the victims of some abuse. Why put them into a very dangerous situation? Women should have the choice of female-only wards.
- The idea of people wanting to be with people from their village/town/district is a myth. With the continuing stigma around mental ill health in most communities people do not want their 'difficulty' known about in the place where they live, 'The street loony'.
- Why put 20+ people with a whole range of problems/needs together simply because of their postcode? In my little road we have a person with a blood disorder, a chap with heart problems and an older lady at risk of a stroke, but we don't put them in the same place simply because of postcode. So why do we do this in mental health when people are experiencing one of the most difficult times of their life? A nonsense. How can we expect ward staff, many recently qualified, to deal properly with all those needs? What happens is the most 'disturbed'/active people attract all their time and a lot of voluntary people feel left out.
- If we need wards then why not arrange them around 'needs', with the capacity to specialise and for people to move across areas depending on their need increasing or decreasing? Staff development would not suffer if they too could move around.
- The 'postcode' system seems to exist purely for administrative requirements and doctors being able to see all their patients in one area. Perhaps the last statement is the nub of the matter.

So given all that, the people in Nottingham started to raise the issue at the Citywide Council, Acute Ward Forums and other events. Four or five years ago the trust was looking to replace two worn-out wards with a new build. Service users questioned the sense in just moving the same style of service from old to new accommodation. They suggested a fresh look at providing in-patient care. It was suggested that the space be used to provide female-only accommodation, a male-only ward, a separate high support unit and an activities centre that could be used by everyone. The new unit was built in the style described. The Psychiatric Intensive Care Unit, at the request of service users, was renamed a Mental Health Intensive Care Unit. Alongside this new unit Nottingham has looked at the other acute wards. An assessment ward has been established – 40% of people admitted to the ward are discharged in seven days, others going to treatment wards. Nottingham is moving towards 'needs' wards, giving greater flexibility when there is a need for people to be admitted.

All this because of the imagination of service users and that idea being implemented. Not earth-shattering but extremely important in that a more appropriate service is now evolving. Other trusts are now starting to look at ridding us of the outdated, inappropriate 'postcode' system."

The case for citizen participation based in the principle of local knowledge is that good decision making requires access to lay and experiential knowledge as well as to technical, professional and scientific knowledge. Thus public services can benefit from enabling citizens and service users to contribute to service planning and development. But it has also been argued that recognition of this form of knowledge is necessary for 'cognitive justice' to be achieved (Visvanathan, 2005). Thus the benefit that is experienced also accrues to those whose knowledge is valued and recognised, particularly when the holders of this type of knowledge have previously been ignored or regarded as incompetent to contribute to decision making.

Visvanathan was writing about the situation in India where western 'experts' came up against indigenous knowledge systems that suggested these expert proposals for, for example, agricultural development, were flawed because they did not recognise that 'nature was not just an object of an experiment or a resource but part of a way of life' (Visvanathan, 2005, p 89). But the significance of cognitive justice also applies within the policy systems of western states. This argument suggests that recognition of the local or experiential knowledge of service users and citizens is in itself a dimension of social justice. Many of the recent and contemporary struggles around public and social policy issues can be understood as struggles between expert and local knowledge. These include environmental struggles, struggles around AIDS and genetic technologies (see, for example, Fischer, 2000; Leach et al, 2005). The claims made by disabled people, mental health service users and others who live with long-term medical conditions or who care for people who do so are also based in experiential knowledge which challenges professionalised explanations and characterisations of their problems and thus proposes sometimes radically different solutions to those problems (for example, Campbell and Oliver, 1996; Barnes and Bowl, 2001).

Those who promote the principle of local knowledge as a basis for participation identify deliberative policy making as essential to the implementation of this principle. What this means in practice are deliberative forums, citizens' juries and community conferences that bring together individuals from a range of relevant publics to discuss and debate their needs and possible policy options. These are often face-to-face forums, but can also be undertaken remotely using web technology. Rather than participants representing previously determined positions, they bring different knowledge and insight to a process of dialogue that has the potential to generate new understandings. The creation of deliberative forums does not mean that power relationships are neutralised and that all voices are equally influential (Young, 2000), but at their best they can 'produce challenges to the status quo and some element of transformation – if not in terms of quantifiable outcomes, then at least in terms of attitudes and orientations of public officials' (Barnes et al, 2007, p 202).

So what might we conclude about the comparative merits of local representation and local knowledge as a basis on which citizen and user involvement might be sought in processes of governance and service delivery? On the one hand, it may be inappropriate to assume that broadening participatory practices can and should be achieved by requiring conformity to principles based in representative systems of democracy. Practices that are based in principles of local knowledge can arguably enable those who are not organised into clear constituencies to bring greater diversity of experience and perspective to public decision making. On the other hand, it can be argued that 'rights to representation' are necessary to ensure real commitment – the rather weak 'duty to involve' enshrined in law is perhaps inadequate as a means of ensuring broad-based representation, and if justice is to be served then those previously excluded should have a right to have their voices heard and this might be better achieved via enhanced representation rights (although see Barnes and Coelho, 2009).

Achieving social justice?

Decisions about the principles that determine who is able to take part in public policy making constitute one dimension of the relationship between participation and social justice. Normative or structural factors that exclude individuals or groups of individuals from having a say can be considered unjust in the context of an apparent commitment to participative decision making. But it is also important to consider the consequences of participation – does more broadly based decision making lead to more socially just outcomes? The example that Colin described indicates that involving service users can make a difference to specific aspects of the way in which services are designed and delivered. But case studies of participation across a range of sectors highlight the barriers to institutional change and the far from 'empowering' practice that is evident in some cases (Barnes et al, 2007). Service users and carers have experienced frustration at the slow pace of change and some have been angry about endless 'consultation' without any commitment to action. One school of thought suggests that, far from public participation providing opportunities for service users and citizens to become 'empowered' through offering major challenges to policy makers and those who deliver services, the participatory turn is all about creating responsible citizens who won't rock the boat (for example, Newman, 2005).

So can we see participation and involvement as routes to securing social justice? Experience of injustice is certainly one motivator for participation and, while this is by no means the only purpose proposed by government, participation in a range of contexts has been seen as a route to reducing social exclusion, deprivation and inequalities by official proponents of such practices. However, macro-level statistics do not indicate much evidence of success in this respect – for example, during the period in which public participation has been official policy for the NHS, health overall has improved, but health *inequalities* have slightly increased (for example, Dorling, 2008).

But in order to understand the potential relationship between user involvement, public participation and social justice we need to be clear what we mean by 'social justice'. Our argument here is that this needs to be understood by reference to both recognition and redistribution. Social justice is a matter not only of the way in which material goods and resources, and opportunities such as access to education and healthcare are distributed, but also of the respect and value that are received by different groups within the population.

Axel Honneth argues that 'what those affected regard as "unjust" are institutional rules or measures they see as necessarily violating what they consider to be well-founded claims to social recognition' (Fraser and Honneth, 2003, p 133). The claims of service user groups and of other citizens who have sought to have their experiences acknowledged and their knowledge respected are often responses to the failure on the part of institutions of the welfare state to offer them recognition and respect. In some instances the recognition that is sought is fundamentally that of recognising the existence of social groups with specific needs. Thus, there could have been no policies, strategies or services designed to support carers without recognition that the role of 'carer' is a distinct and significant one – a recognition that has been fought for by the carers' movement since its early days in the 1960s (Barnes, 1997). Beyond this, recognition also involves respect for self-determination on the part of groups previously considered incompetent to define their own needs and propose their own solutions. Thus mental health service users would not have been invited to play a part in service development without recognition that those who live with mental illness should not be defined by their diagnoses. A key contribution of the pioneering NAG and of others that followed on at local and national level has been to achieve recognition of the humanity of those who live with mental illness and of their capacity to transcend its disabling effects.

At an individual level there are many personal testimonies to the positive impact on service users and carers of recognition of the value of what they can contribute. The following quotes of what participation has meant to individual mental health service users come from a history of NAG (Barnes, 2007):

"In some ways it turned out to be a positive step for me. It changed my life around from something that was killing me, virtually, to something that I finally got some kind of reward in."

"It's given me a life and without it I wouldn't have dreamed of doing half the things I do now. It's given me confidence, assurance…. I get up now and speak at a conference quite happily. A few years ago I would have no more done that than fly!"

"If I didn't do this I would be adrift. I would have nothing to do. I enjoy doing it. I enjoy doing it because I am working with people who are ill and I am still a service user myself. But I am a long way down the road from where they are. And you know it's nice to be able to work in that field and think you are contributing to someone's recovery in a way. Although it's a very small way, I mean it takes a long time to get anything done, but I enjoy doing it."

"[It's been] huge for my own personal self-esteem. I've started very small and suddenly realised that I was capable of a bit more and a bit more and a bit more, and now that I'm working full-time it's just lovely, it really is."

"Well it's refreshing to know in this troubled world, that there are
people committed to speaking up for those who can't themselves.
And that is not because of any intellectual or organic incapacity.
It's because in plain English, they are having an unjust service....
I am able to make a difference, I can inform other people who
will listen to me."

Pat offers a similar reflection of the impact of the recognition she has
received for her contribution as a carer and what this has meant for her.

When my disabled son was born my own self-worth suffered. As a mother
I felt it must be my fault I had a disabled child. I also felt that my other son
suffered having a disabled brother. My husband felt left out at times and
my able-bodied son felt pushed out which caused me to have problems
psychologically. I found a role in life by becoming a pioneer for carers to
get respect from social services and the local authority. It has been a long
and difficult journey that is not over yet. I have seen many changes over
the years and I would like to think I have made a difference for carers.
Each experience we have makes us the person we are now. I have met
some wonderful and interesting people. I feel because of people like me,
carers now have the respect they deserve and some acknowledgement of
the wonderful work they do. Carers can become very strong of character.
We have to be as carers in fighting for those we love, but through the
work I have done with Birmingham Carers Association I have met with
politicians, councillors and directors of social services. I firmly believe they
respect the knowledge I have from my role as a carer, and I have enjoyed
the challenge of being a carer too.

However, it is unlikely that the significance of that recognition can be
sustained without material evidence of service change and changes in
the lives of those who live with mental illness or disability, and those
whose lives are bound up with them as family members and carers. An
important dimension of recognition is evidence that action has been
taken in response to the input made to a process – being invited to
give voice to experiences that are continually ignored does not offer
recognition.

The introduction to this chapter noted that user involvement and
public participation were once radical ideas that have now gained
official acceptance. Studies of social movements demonstrate what can

happen when radical ideas that challenge the status quo get adopted by the mainstream and start to become taken for granted in official policy (see, for example, Lovenduski and Randall, 1993, in relation to what happened to the British feminist movement). They may be selectively adopted, co-opted, adapted and perhaps corrupted. NAG's experience of being claimed as a 'partner' by local services but then losing out when services were re-organised and advocacy services re-tendered is in many ways not surprising (Barnes, 2007). But hard as it is for those who see the groups and organisations they have created run out of steam or become overlooked, perhaps we should not judge success by what happens to any individual user group. Rather we should think about the underlying changes that have taken place, how they have been achieved and what they mean for current service users and citizens. For example, the insertion of a social inclusion and social justice theme in the newly created National Mental Health Development Unit offers some evidence of the change in the frames within which issues of mental health are being addressed (www.its-services.org.uk/nmhdu/en/our-work/promoting-social-inclusion-and-social-justice/). Recognition that policies regarding mental health should focus on issues of social justice as well as on service delivery and clinical treatments can be considered a major achievement of the user/survivor movement as a whole. And while carers may still be campaigning for a level of financial support that truly reflects the significance of the role they play in caring for disabled, frail or ill family and friends, the carers' movement can point to significant levels of support that have become available since Mary Webster first named the 'problem' of unpaid care in the early 1960s (Barnes, 2010: in press).

Nancy Fraser's (1997) analysis of the relationship between recognition and redistribution is helpful in enabling us to reflect on the significance of what has been achieved. Her argument is that both recognition and redistribution are necessary to social justice and she relates each to different types of policy response: those that offer affirmation, and those that seek transformation. Using 'race' and gender as her exemplars, she argues that a combination of transformative redistribution and recognition is most effective in terms of strategies for achieving social justice. While policies that emphasise 'affirmation' have a tendency to reinforce racial and gender differentiation, transformative strategies oppose what she describes as the 'congealing' of differences, and hierarchical relationships based in gendered and racialised identities. By addressing the deep structures that produce racialised and gendered attitudes and structures, transformative recognition strategies destabilise existing differentiations between groups. And in relation to redistribution, this is less likely to result in resentments caused by perceived 'special treatment' for particular groups.

We can apply this to the situation of people with mental health problems and of carers, the two groups that have been the focus for examples explored in this chapter. One of the key achievements of the mental health service user or survivor movement has been the way it has challenged both assumptions about the nature of mental illness, and social policies that have separated out those who live with mental health problems – to mark them out as different and in many cases 'suspect' citizens, or in some instances to deny them the status and practice of citizenship. The impact of such policies and practices have not only impacted negatively on those who have received psychiatric diagnoses but have also had damaging effects on social relations more broadly, summed up perhaps in the words of a woman involved in NAG talking in the early 1990s. Talking about a mental health awareness campaign the group was planning, she described a response to a request for involvement that demonstrated the 'othering' of those who live with mental illness:

> ... a vicar's wife once said "what if I invite these people into my home? How would they be?" And I said "well, they'll be like you, they'll have two eyes, and a nose and a mouth and two ears". You know, they think they're going to see something weird and they don't know that perhaps they'll have a nervous breakdown and start with a mental illness. (quoted in Barnes and Shardlow, 1996, p 126)

The early years of the user and carer movements were marked in some instances by competitive tensions between those seeking recognition for each group. In particular some parts of the disability movement rejected the concept of care and resisted the idea that carers' voices should be heard (Wood, 1991). More recently there has been increasing recognition that oppositional stances between user and carer groups are not helpful, and that the interests of each in securing good quality services and support are complementary. There is also a recognition that, for example, disabled people can be parents, people with learning difficulties care for elderly parents, elderly spouses and partners care for each other, that is, that it is possible to be both a carer and a user, at the same time or at different stages of life. The government's carers strategy recognises that becoming a carer is a common experience (HM Government, 2008), and one expression of that recognition is £255 million new investment in carer support. None of us can be sure we won't need to use mental health services, or that we won't be a care giver or a care receiver or even simultaneously occupy both positions.

In the early days of the user and carer movements it was important to emphasise the distinctiveness of different identities. Claims for recognition were based on such distinctiveness and the right to representation on this basis. We are now at a point where it is easier to 'come out' and claim an identity in this way, precisely because of the success of both user and carer movements in securing recognition and respect. Perhaps we are also at a point where dialogue between those who bring different knowledge and experience from different standpoints, but a shared interest in and commitment to social justice for those, for example, who live with mental health problems and for those who care for and support them, is more capable of challenging the deep-seated attitudes and assumptions that disadvantage both.

Conclusion

The right to a voice is a necessary but not sufficient condition for achieving social justice. There are plenty of examples of poor practice in user involvement and public participation and it would be naive to assume that this alone will resolve the multiple injustices that derive from structural as well as recognitional disadvantages and inequalities. However, the social policy terrain is transformed from a time when those subject to the decision making of professionals and policy makers could do little more than accept what was offered or go without. What Pat has described as a process of 'chipping away' to make a difference has created an entirely new context within which public policy deliberations take place, a context in which the question is not whether, but *how* service users and citizens can play a part in ensuring just decision making. In order to ensure that this is indeed the case, official acceptance needs to be accompanied by a continuing understanding of the radical significance of such participation and by a constant questioning of its transformative potential.

References

Barnes, M. (1997) *Care, communities and citizens*, Harlow: Addison Wesley Longman.

Barnes, M. (1999) *Building a deliberative democracy: An evaluation of two citizens' juries*, London: Institute for Public Policy Research.

Barnes, M. (2002) 'Bringing difference into deliberation. Disabled people, survivors and local governance', *Policy & Politics*, vol 30, no 3, pp 355-68.

Barnes, M. (2004) 'Affect, anecdote and diverse debates. User challenges to scientific rationality', in A. Gray and S. Harrison (eds) *Governing medicine: Theory and practice*, McGraw Hill/Open University Press, pp 122-32.

Barnes, M. (2006) *Caring and social justice*, Basingstoke: Palgrave.

Barnes, M. (2007) *A final brick in the wall? A history of the Nottingham Advocacy Group* (www.brighton.ac.uk/sass/contact/details.php?uid=mb12).

Barnes, M. (2008) 'Passionate participation: emotional experiences and expressions in deliverable forms', *Critical Social Policy*, vol 28, no 4, pp 461-81.

Barnes, M. (2010: in press) 'Caring responsibilities: the making of citizen carers?', in J.E. Newman and E. Tonkens (eds) *Active citizenship in Europe*, Amsterdam: University of Amsterdam Press.

Barnes, M. and Bowl, R. (2001) *Taking over the asylum: Empowerment and mental health*, Basingstoke: Palgrave.

Barnes, M. and Coelho, V.S. (2009) 'Social participation in health in Brazil and England', *Health Expectations*, vol 12, pp 226-36.

Barnes, M. and Shardlow, P. (1996) 'Identity crisis: mental health user groups and the "problem of identity"', in C. Barnes and G. Mercer (eds) *Exploring the divide: Illness and disability*, Leeds: The Disability Press.

Barnes, M., McCabe, A. and Ross, L. (2004) 'Public participation in governance: the institutional context', in *Researching civil renewal: A set of scoping papers prepared for the Home Office Civil Renewal Unit*, Civil Renewal Research Centre, University of Birmingham.

Barnes, M., Newman, J. and Sullivan, H. (2006) 'Discursive arenas: deliberation and the constitution of identity in public participation at a local level', *Social Movement Studies*, vol 5, no 3, pp 193-207.

Barnes, M., Newman, J. and Sullivan, H. (2007) *Power, participation and political renewal: Case studies in public participation*, Bristol: The Policy Press.

Barnes, M., Harrison, S., Mort, M. and Shardlow, P. (1999) *Unequal partners: User groups and community care*, Bristol: The Policy Press.

Barnes, M., Newman, J., Knops, A. and Sullivan, H. (2003) 'Constituting the public for public participation', *Public Administration*, vol 81, no 2, pp 379-99.

Barnes, M., Skelcher, C., Dalziel, R. and Beirens, H. (2008) *Designing citizen centred governance*, York: Joseph Rowntree Foundation (www.jrf. org.uk/publications/desiginig-citizen-centred-governance).

Beresford, P., Green. D., Lister, R. and Woodard, K. (1999) *Poverty first hand: Poor people speak for themselves*, London: Child Poverty Action Group.

Campbell, J. and Oliver, M. (1996) *Disability politics: Understanding our past, changing our future*, London: Routledge.

Communities and Local Government (2008) *Communities in control: Real people, real power*, Cm 7427, London: HM Government.

Cornwall, A. and Coelho, V.S. (eds) (2007) *Spaces for change*, London: Zed Books.

Davies, C., Wetherell, M. and Barnett, E. (2006) *Citizens at the centre: Deliberative participation in healthcare decisions*, Bristol: The Policy Press.

Deakin, N. and Wright, A. (eds) (1990) *Consuming public services*, London: Routledge.

Dorling, D. (2008) 'Inequality downturn', *National Health Executive Journal*, vol 2, no 3, pp 16-17.

Dryzek, J. (2002) *Deliberative democracy and beyond: Liberals, critics, contestations*, Oxford: Oxford University Press.

Fischer, F. (2000) *Citizens, experts and the environment: The politics of local knowledge*, Durham, NC and London: Duke University Press.

Fraser, N. (1997) *Justice interruptus: Critical reflections on the post-Socialist condition*, London: Routledge.

Fraser, N. and Honneth, A. (2003) *Redistribution or recognition? A political–philosophical exchange*, London: Verso.

Fung, A. and Wright, O. (eds) (2003) *Deepening democracy: Institutional innovation in empowered participatory governance*, London: Verso.

HM Government (2008) *Carers at the heart of 21st-century families and communities: A caring system on your side, a life of your own*, London: Department of Health.

Leach, M., Scoones, I. and Wynne, B. (eds) (2005) *Science and citizens: Globalization and the challenge of engagement*, London: Zed Books.

Lovenduski, J. and Randall, V. (1993) *Contemporary feminist politics*, Oxford: Oxford University Press.

Martin, G. (2008) '"Ordinary people only": knowledge, representativeness, and the publics of public participation in healthcare', *Sociology of Health and Illness*, vol 30, no 1, pp 35-54.

Melucci, A. (1996) *Challenging codes: Collective action in the information age*, Cambridge: Cambridge University Press.

Newman, J. (2005) 'Participative governance and the remaking of the public sphere', in J. Newman (ed) *Remaking governance: Peoples, politics and the public sphere*, Bristol: The Policy Press.

Nussbaum, M.C. (2001) *Upheavals of thought: The intelligence of the emotions*, Cambridge: Cambridge University Press.

Prior, D., Farrow, K., Spalek, B. and Barnes, M. (2006) 'Anti-social behaviour and civil renewal?', in T. Brennan, P. John and G. Stoker (eds) *Re-energizing citizenship: Strategies for civil renewal*, Basingstoke: Palgrave-Macmillan, pp 91-111.

Skelcher, C. (2003) 'Governing local communities: parish-pump politics or strategic partnerships?', *Local Government Studies*, vol 23, no 4, pp 1-16.

Visvanathan, S. (2005) 'Knowledge, justice and democracy', in M. Leach, I. Scoones and B. Wynne (eds) *Science and citizens: Globalization and the challenge of engagement*, London: Zed Books, pp 83-94.

Wood, R. (1991) 'Care of disabled people', in G. Dalley (ed) *Disability and social policy*, London: Policy Studies Institute.

Yanow, D. (2003) 'Accessing local knowledge', in M.A. Hajer and H. Wagenaar (eds) *Deliberative policy analysis: Understanding governance in the network society*, Cambridge: Cambridge University Press, pp 228-46.

Young, I.M. (2000) *Inclusion and democracy*, Oxford: Oxford University Press.

TWELVE

Involving disabled children and young people in research and consultations: issues, challenges and opportunities

David Abbott

Sometimes I watch the world around me going completely mad. Can we enjoy each other for ourselves, including taking time to help each other out without being measured, even if it takes time and energy? I want access to ideas, to learning, to different ways of life – to engage in thinking with other people. To have all that we need to communicate, even if it's non-verbally. All this is a lot to ask, but it is possible and essential for an ongoing and productive life. (MacKeith, 2003)

Introduction

Maresa MacKeith is a young disabled woman who communicates non-verbally using assisted technology. She makes a powerful case for the value and purpose of communication. Disabled children and young people have a long history of exclusion in important aspects of their life – from education, friendships, from active citizenry, from participation. In their interactions with the many professionals, statutory services, and increasingly, researchers who engage with them, there have in the past been too few attempts to find out what the views of disabled children and young people are. Morris (1998a, 1998b) chronicled what seemed to be a common approach when, in her research about disabled children in the looked-after system, she reviewed case files where professionals were obliged to fill in what the views of the disabled child were. In too many cases what was recorded were comments such as 'child unable to communicate', 'child does not talk', or even more commonly, the section was left blank.

There is now a much stronger ethical, policy and legal framework in place that starts from the premise that everyone can communicate. There has been a great deal of social policy research that has explicitly prioritised the voice and views of disabled children and young people. Doing it, and doing it well, is not without challenges, and this chapter reviews 'where we are at' in terms of meaningfully engaging with disabled children and young people in research and in the range of consultations about public services that are supposed to support them. This chapter reviews the existing research and literature concerning the involvement of disabled children and young people in consultation and research activity. It discusses the case for doing it, the detail of how people do it, the ethical issues involved and an overview of some of the methodological and other challenges involved in doing it in a non-tokenistic way.

Current context regarding consulting with/research about disabled children and young people

It is still relatively recently that researchers and services have thought that including disabled children directly in research was a worthwhile or feasible activity, with researchers such as Ward (1997), Beresford (1997) and Morris (1998a, 1998b) being early proponents of this inclusive approach. There is now a substantial body of research that includes direct consultation with disabled children (for example, Shakespeare et al, 1999; Stalker and Connors, 2003; Townsley et al, 2004; Franklin and Sloper, 2007; Lewis et al, 2007). It is increasingly recognised that disabled children can, however severe the barriers they face, usefully be included in the research process, either as participants, as researchers or as advisers to research projects. Morris (2002, 2003) has written widely on the involvement of children with communication impairments both in services and in research. The importance of directly determining the views of young disabled people has been illustrated by two pieces of research: that of Franck and Callery (2004), who suggest that children's views can differ significantly from their carers', and Mitchell and Sloper (2002), who found that children and their parents prioritise different things as being important within their lives.

One of the most recent, largest audits of disabled children's views of life and of services was the Audit Commission work (Audit Commission, 2003a, 2003b) that showed that families were in contact with a large number of public services on an almost daily basis. Levels of awareness about entitlements were low and the report acknowledged that services agreed that 'if families did not accept what was on offer, they risked being left without any support at all'. The 133 young people in the study (aged 7–19) said, of their interaction with services, that professionals often did not speak to them at all. While parents in the study prioritised education, health, housing and social care, children and young people talked about play, leisure, friendships and school.

Developments in this area mean that we now, more often than not, ask *how* we should include and work in partnership with disabled children and young people, as opposed to *whether* we should. There is no shortage of government policy and guidance driving this forward – the 1989 and 2004 Children Acts; the National Service Framework for children, young people and maternity services (2004); Article 12 of the United Nations (UN) Convention on the Rights of the Child; and Article 7 of the UN Convention on the Rights of Persons with Disabilities (2006).

Cavet and Sloper (2004) and Watson et al (2007) review the range of issues that disabled children and young people have expressed themselves about in research and consultation exercises. These include school life, play and leisure, residential services, transition and information. Less research has been done on the impact or outcomes of seeking the views of disabled children – whether in traditional research, or in decision making and involvement in individual decisions, or as part of service consultations. Franklin and Sloper (2006) interviewed 21 disabled children and young people (the majority of whom had learning difficulties) about their views on the participation they had been involved in. The children and young people said that they had few opportunities to express their views about the services they received, or the professionals who worked with them. For some young people, there was limited understanding of the purpose of the participation they had been involved in. Despite this, they reported enjoying taking part, especially if it was creative or fun. The socialising aspects of group activity were regarded as particularly positive and children and young people said that they would like more opportunities to get involved.

The evidence on what difference it makes to be exposed to the views of disabled children and young people is rarely drawn together, either as an overview of substantive findings or in terms of the methods used to elicit those views. We also do not have a developed overview of how frontline staff and practitioners involve young disabled people, as opposed to researchers, or particular groups like Triangle,[1] who have developed considerable expertise. There has also been a tendency, when focusing on how disabled children and young people get and experience services, to focus on social care and education and less on health. The data that do exist are, according to Franklin and Sloper (2005), 'disparate', and they highlight a lack of evidence on how children's input and involvement leads (or does not lead) to change. Sloper and Lightfoot (2003) conducted a national survey of all health authorities and National Health Service (NHS) trusts in England and uncovered just 27 initiatives involving consultation with physically disabled or chronically ill children in England. Only half of these said that they fed back to the children on the results of the consultation.

There are practice and organisational developments in the area of participation and disabled children and young people, and a number of resources to help researchers and practitioners (The Children's Society, 1997, 2001; Marchant et al, 1999; Triangle and NSPCC, 2001; Morris, 2002; Marchant and Jones, 2003). Making Ourselves Heard is funded by the True Colours Trust and is a project that aims to ensure the active participation of disabled children and young people in all decisions directly affecting them; in the development of their local communities; in the strategic planning of services; and in all aspects of the work of the Council for Disabled Children. The group has produced 'Top tips for participation: what young disabled people want':

- Respect us
- Be open and honest with us
- Prove you're listening to us
- Make sure we get something out of it
- Give us time
- Involve us from the start
- Listen to us
- Make it fun
- Involve *all* of us
- Support us to make our own decisions

(www.ncb.org.uk/cdc/moh_toptips_poster.pdf)

What do we know about *how* to do it?

Franklin and Sloper (2009) argue that the evidence base around good practice in disabled children's participation in decision making about their lives is under-developed. Most work about how to find out more about the lives of disabled children and young people does, however, have some consistent messages (Morris, 1998c; Abbott, 2004; Franklin and Sloper, 2006, 2009; Knight et al, 2006). These include having an assumption that *everyone* can communicate. The literature suggests that we should be prepared to adopt a range of methodological approaches, bearing in mind that one size will not fit all, given differences in age, cognitive ability and experience related to impairment. The key recommendation is to be flexible where possible. Another theme identified in this work is to consider the trade-offs between methodological 'gold standards' and including as many and as wide a group as possible. It is possible to get so stuck on trying to be perfect that it prevents anything getting done. It is important to recognise the amount of time, money and skill that is required, but equally important not to mystify the skill required, or limit it to a very small number of people as this will not encourage more people to try and improve at doing it. The literature also highlights the need to be clear about the point of the research or consultation exercise and, where possible, check that there is shared understanding between the participants and the researchers. Disabled children and young people are often subject to 'gatekeepers' who have a say in what they can and cannot do. This is true for all children, but previous research with disabled children and young people points to the particular barriers that may be put in the way, for example, other people saying that a disabled child/ young person will not be able to take part or have anything useful to say because of the nature or level of their impairment. Finally, as a point of good practice and principle, we should think carefully about how to let disabled children and young people know what the research has found out in ways which are interesting and accessible to them.

It is not clear how far good practice suggestions like the ones above are adopted in everyday consultation exercises or research. What is probable is that without explicit commitment to including 'hard-to-include' disabled children and young people, they are likely to be left out. We have also not known that much about the efficiency of different methods that *do* attempt to be flexible and tailored more closely to individual need. Porter et al (2008) included an evaluative aspect in their work that used six different methods to obtain disabled students' views on their school. Some of the most important messages were that being or feeling disabled changes over time and can be dependent on changes in health and particular experiences of having needs well met, or poorly met. Responses to questions about disability, impairment and life experiences will vary accordingly. Negative-sounding terminology and wording in research tools can lead to under-reporting and lower response rates. The authors recommended a social model of disability approach to questions, for example, collecting information about what children and young people can do and what is going right, as well as carefully framing questions about barriers and problems, such as, 'how are you prevented from…?'. Porter et al's study also found that asking (direct) questions is not always the best way to elicit information. It may be better exploring one-off concrete examples or vignettes. The authors suggested that while it was relatively easy to get superficial information on likes and dislikes, it was harder to get a deeper level of reflection. They reported, for example, that while students said that smiley/sad faces that rated their experience were the most liked, it was written comments that provided the most insights into specific barrier/support issues. One research tool involved using an online questionnaire to rate experience in schools. Staff said that the most 'fruitful' question in the questionnaire was the 'wild card question' – 'if you had a magic wand what would you change about the school?'.

Franklin and Sloper (2008) and Kirby et al (2003) describe the continuum of participation and warn against making assumptions that there is a hierarchy of preferred method or outcome. So, for example, for children and young people with the highest levels of cognitive impairment, being asked to choose between two options can constitute significant consultation and feedback and should be viewed as being as valid and as useful as other levels of participation.

Asking disabled children and young people about the services they receive

As noted above, there is an established body of work which details research findings about various aspects of the lives of disabled children and young people. Much of this includes, but does not focus exclusively on, children's views about services or the professionals that support them. In response to what is known about the problems faced by disabled children and young people (and their families) around achieving 'ordinary family life', and goals which are on a par with non-disabled children and young people, there has been a great deal of policy and guidance from the government which aims to improve service delivery. It is only more recently that work has been developed to assess or conceptualise desired outcome measures (which are service-focused) for disabled children and young people and their families.

Apart from small-scale evaluations, most research with disabled children has included reflections on services as a part (and often a minor part) of the research. There has been some reluctance in the past to ask disabled children and young people exclusively about statutory services and instead to do semi-structured interviews which focus on the whole of their lives. There are a number of reasons behind this. Researchers have been wary of seeing disabled children and young people as the sum of their interactions with services and professionals and have been keen to collect data about broader aspects of their lives/identity. In addition, given that disabled children and young people and their families often experience services as uncoordinated, inflexible and not meeting their needs, research tools/methods which dwell on service-related topics could be quite a negative experience and one which focuses on deficits. Interviews focusing on services in isolation could be boring and difficult to engage children and young people about and it can also be hard for disabled children and young people to always differentiate between professionals and services, or to know what services they receive, as they are not likely to be organising them or be the interface with them. If awareness about rights and entitlements is quite low then responses may be based on unacceptably low expectation levels. Finally, focusing on what services do/offer could miss important gaps in need. For example, research with disabled children and young people has often tended to highlight unmet need around play, leisure and social opportunities. These topics, often at the top of the list of priorities for disabled children and young people, would probably not have arisen if research had focused wholly on the experiences of services and service delivery/interaction with professionals. A good example of this was the work of Connors and Stalker (2003) that took a broad and methodologically innovative approach to data collection. Their study 'bucked the trend' by describing the largely positive view of themselves and the world that disabled children and young people had.

This is not to say that the experience of service delivery and views on related outcomes cannot be elicited from disabled children and young people. Beresford et al (2007) interviewed 95 families (29 disabled children directly, including children with complex needs and communication impairments) in three local authorities about what outcomes disabled children wanted to achieve from service provision, within the context of the *Every Child Matters* outcomes framework (be healthy, stay safe, enjoy and achieve, make a positive contribution, achieve economic well-being). In common with other studies, the researchers used questions that adopted a wider focus than services and tried to frame the idea of 'outcomes' into something meaningful and accessible for disabled children and young people. The project was named The 'What Matters?' Research Project and the information sheet for children explained the project like this:

We are talking and listening to children and young people about what matters to them. We would like to visit you and find out what you want to do. What makes you happy? What makes you sad? What's exciting, what's boring? What stops you doing what you like to do? What you tell us is important. The people who help disabled children and their families want to improve the support and help they give. (Beresford et al, 2007)

The interview then adopted drawing, writing and symbol techniques to collect information about a map of the child's life, positive and negative aspects of life, exploring what would make it better, new experiences and opportunities and aspirations. The study concluded that the *Every Child Matters* outcomes *were* relevant to disabled children with some important caveats: communication was an important omission from the outcomes and a priority for disabled children and young people; there were differences in meaning around outcomes for disabled children as compared with non-disabled children; and there was a hierarchy of outcomes, that is, a need to achieve some outcomes before others could be achieved. Some were regarded as fundamental outcomes (being healthy, being able to communicate and staying safe), while others were thought to be 'higher level outcomes'.

Two of the three local authorities in the study subsequently piloted tools to help them record and assess outcomes for families: one focused on 'parental well-being'; the other sought to create and record a discussion between parent, child and worker around areas of importance for child and parental well-being. In this part of the study, the researchers found a number of issues arising about perceptions of what outcomes were, and whether or not they were helpful: there were considerable differences in how staff understood what an outcome was; about half of the parents appeared not to understand the outcomes approach; of those staff that did understand outcomes, they liked the shift from 'what is available' to a more creative, solution-focused way of working with families, but some staff felt this raised unrealistic expectations; and similarly, some parents who were positive said it helped them think outside the 'service box'.

This study is helpful because it suggests that you can extrapolate data about descriptions and views of life in general, and use that data to suggest to what degree outcomes set by government and/or services are being met. A similar approach was adopted in Wales in a large-scale consultation exercise designed to inform the children and young people's National Service Framework (Turner, 2003) which found that the main messages from disabled children and young people relating to services were: that attitudes and behaviour of staff had the greatest impact on disabled children and young people's experiences of accessing services; that there were major gaps in the provision of information about the roles and responsibilities of services and individual staff; that accessing services remained problematic as did the lack of choice about services, especially leisure services; and that there was a lack of consistency around disabled children and young people's participation in important decisions about their lives.

Ethical issues

It is important to remember that all the usual ethical issues that apply to research with non-disabled children also apply to disabled children, with some possible additions.

Accessibility

Information about research or consultation exercises must be meaningful and accessible to those who are the focus of the work. This may mean information sheets, consent forms and interview tools being appropriate to the cognitive ability and communication needs of the child/young person.

Confidentiality/disclosure

Previous research with disabled children has suggested that some research participants want assurances of total confidentiality and suggest that anything else would compromise the trust that the person may have in the process/research. We know that this is simply not permissible. Participants can be given assurances about how their data will be anonymised and treated in accordance with Data Protection Act principles, but they also need to know that if they disclose on the survey/in interview that they, or some other child, is at risk, then action will be taken.

Sensitive questions and impact of research on children

Interviews with disabled children and young people run the risk of eliciting a lot of 'deficit-type' information – barriers that the person faces, things that they cannot do or have difficulties with, and so on.

There should be space in or at the end of interviews to encourage the child/young person to discuss things that come up for them either with the interviewer or with people they trust – their friends – but also other adults like parents or teachers. There should be included some additional points of contact, for example, ChildLine, information about independent advocacy, and so on. The development of wording around sensitive questions – perhaps around health, impairment, pain, relationships, friendships and bullying – is just one area where getting advice from disabled children and young people users is really helpful.

Making a difference

Whether or not research makes a difference to people's lives by bringing about change is subject to a whole host of, sometimes unpredictable, factors. The ethical issues here are to be clear with children about what research can and cannot do, that is, that taking part will not necessarily/ automatically lead to change in their own lives but that there is a commitment to do something with the data collected.

Feeding back results

As well as simply being good practice, it is also ethically right to let people who take part in research know what the conclusions are, and in ways that they can understand. It may be that individual feedback is not practicable but that findings are distributed via websites, other established information sources or regional/local events/seminars.

Involving children in the design and implementation of research

A step beyond involving disabled children and young people as participants is to involve them at a much earlier stage when thinking about what things actually need to be researched, how and by whom. The government expects all central government departments to show how they are involving children and young people in the design, provision and evaluation of services (CYPU, 2001). The Department of Health accepts that there is an expectation that children and young people will be routinely involved in service development locally and nationally (DH, 2002). There are some fairly established templates for involving disabled children in large-scale exercises – a good example is the *Quality Protects* reference groups of disabled children and young people (JRF, 2001). It is seen as good practice to work with existing groups (bearing in mind that it is important they represent as well as possible the range of ages, ethnic backgrounds and support needs in the population of disabled children and young people) when doing work like this rather than setting up and then disbanding groups to work on standalone projects. This develops skill and experience among disabled children and young people in the practice of participation and consultation. It is not clear how far research commissioners, funders and large government departments 'practise what they preach', that is, involve disabled children and young people in the commissioning, funding and decision-making processes even though this seems to be a prerequisite for those that apply for or are awarded funding.

The challenge of meaningful involvement: things that are hard to talk about

It would be a mistake to suggest that involving disabled children and young people in research and consultations is easy. It is challenging, especially including those who communicate non-verbally or who have significant learning disabilities. Sometimes I am concerned that research which does this, including my own, airbrushes out/over some of the challenges. It may be that as a result people think it is easier than it is, are reluctant to talk about their mistakes, slow to acknowledge their own disabilist prejudices and lead commissioners and research funders to under-estimate the costs (in time and money) of including all disabled children and young people. My own personal and professional experiences (which I note I am reluctant to disclose) include failing to admit my own anxieties about meeting disabled children and young people who did not use words to communicate and who were reliant on medical technology which I found scary. This led to me shortening some interviews because I felt anxious, frightened and incompetent. But this was a difficult admission and I persuaded myself and others that I had done a good job when I had not.

On other occasions I have asserted my more powerful position and not owned up to the tokenism of *some* of my approaches to involving disabled children and young people. For example, subtly trying to get disabled young people who had been co-researchers to accept gift vouchers as payment instead of a fee because of the associated difficulties for me in dealing with the university finance office regulations and the young person's disability benefit situation. In another instance, asking young disabled people on a project advisory group how best we might disseminate research findings, I was certain they would say, 'make a DVD' (which they did) when I knew we did not have the money to do more than produce an easy-read summary. Instead of being up front about this I thought I had to let them say what they wanted and then work to dissuade them that their idea was viable.

Finally, my own discriminatory and unhelpful prejudices about disability and disabled people which I think operate at a relatively subconscious level have also affected my approaches. Looking back over a number of research studies, I wonder if I have at times uncritically accepted the views of disabled children and young people almost as if they were sacrosanct. Underlying this was a patronising belief system that it was so incredible that they could express themselves (the 'overcoming the odds' stereotype) that everything they said must be 'completely true' and that sometimes competing/conflicting views from, for example, parents, siblings, professionals, could not be as true. Another stereotype relates to having an unhelpful assumption about young disabled people that they would be 'good'. A group of young disabled people who were acting as advisers to one of my studies were put up for a night in a hotel so that they could attend our work meeting. They ran up huge telephone, room service and mini bar bills that I was left to deal with. I realised I had not expected them to behave the way any group of non-disabled young people might behave. Finally, I recall asking a young disabled person to help me co-write an easy-read version of research findings. He refused and said he thought it 'dumbed down' the work and was patronising. I was shocked and irritated and realised that I thought I was doing him a favour by asking/involving him and that he would be grateful and compliant.

I would like to think these were all 'early career' mistakes and I find it hard to write them here, but in being honest about the challenges and the things that go well, as well as badly, it may be that there are more authentic opportunities to learn from people who are skilled at working effectively and mindfully with disabled children and young people.

Conclusion

This chapter has charted the progress in approach and methods that have taken place over the last decade or so in involving disabled children and young people in research and consultations. It is entirely right that those who are the subjects of research – or even partners in research – are as fully involved as possible.

The new orthodoxy of consultation and involvement needs some reflection, however. Are we honest about what we are doing and how? Do we know what difference it makes to outcomes for disabled children and young people? Recent research about transition to adulthood for young disabled men (Abbott and Carpenter, 2010) found several men unhappy about being consulted and asked for their views by professionals about their futures. They had not been given information about what was possible so they did not know how to answer and felt professionals got exasperated with them as a result. Others were tired of saying what they would like to do only to be told that it was not possible. Do we know if disabled children and young people want to take part in more research and consultation about the services that are supposed to support them? Or do they actually just want those services to improve and get on with it? Lewis (2010) makes an important contribution in an article which refers to 'the promotion of "child voice" as "a moral crusade"'. Lewis asks how we deal with what children do *not* say as well as what they do and questions how well we really document and understand *non*-participation.

Nonetheless, there is a resounding message from disabled children and young people that they want to be included in important decisions about their own life and will no longer tolerate research that attempts to find out about the reality of their lives without asking them. There are now well-developed methodologies, guides and templates for doing this well and for including disabled children who were always previously excluded. But perhaps it is time to reflect on how effective these strategies for inclusion have been and if there is still room for improvement. Honest reflection about the strengths and weaknesses in this work, as well as an examination of our motivations and our value base, will perhaps lead to a more authentic inclusion of, and partnership working with, disabled children and young people.

Note

[1] Triangle is an independent organisation which works with children and families and which has developed particular expertise in communicating with children without verbal communication (www. triangle.org.uk).

References

Abbott, D. (2004) 'Involving disabled children in research', in S. Becker and A. Bryman (eds) *Understanding research for social policy and practice: Themes, methods and approaches*, Bristol: The Policy Press, pp 171-4.

Abbott, D. and Carpenter, J. (2010) *Becoming an adult: Transition for young men with Duchenne Muscular Dystrophy (DMD)*, London: Muscular Dystrophy Campaign.

Audit Commission (2003a) *Services for disabled children: A review of services for disabled children and their families*, London: Audit Commission.

Audit Commission (2003b) *Let me be me: A handbook for managers and staff working with disabled children and their families*, London: Audit Commission.

Beresford, B. (1997) *Personal accounts: Involving disabled children in research*, SPRU Papers, London: The Stationery Office.

Beresford, B., Parvaneh, R. and Sloper, P. (2007) *Priorities and perceptions of disabled children and young people and their parents regarding outcomes from support services*, York: Social Policy Research Unit, University of York.

Cavet, J. and Sloper, P. (2004) 'Participation of disabled children in individual decisions about their lives and in public decisions about service development', *Children & Society*, vol 18, pp 278-90.

Children's Society, The (1997) *I'll go first: The planning and review toolkit for use with children with disabilities*, London: The Children's Society.

Children's Society, The (2001) 'Ask us', CD-ROM summarising key messages from a multimedia project to involve disabled children in policy development on *Quality Protects*, London: The Children's Society.

Connors, C. and Stalker, K. (2003) *The views and experiences of disabled children and their siblings: A positive outlook*, London: Jessica Kingsley Publishers.

CYPU (Children and Young People's Unit) (2001) *Learning to listen: Core principles for the involvement of children and young people*, London: Department for Education and Skills.

DH (Department of Health) (2002) *Listening, hearing and responding: Department of Health action plan – Core principles for the involvement of children and young people*, London: DH.

Franck, L. and Callery, P. (2004) 'Re-thinking of family-centred care across the continuum of children's healthcare', *Child: Care, Health and Development*, vol 30, pp 265-77.

Franklin, A. and Sloper, P. (2005) 'Listening and responding? Children's participation in healthcare within England', *The International Journal of Children's Rights*, vol 13, no 1-2, pp 11-29.

Franklin, A. and Sloper, P. (2006) 'Supporting the participation of disabled children and young people in decision making', *Research Works*, York: Social Policy Research Unit, University of York.

Franklin, A. and Sloper, P. (2007) *Participation of disabled children and young people in decision-making relating to social care*, York: Social Policy Research Unit, University of York.

Franklin, A. and Sloper, P. (2009) 'Supporting the participation of disabled children and young people in decision making', *Children & Society*, vol 23, no 1, pp 3-15.

JRF (Joseph Rowntree Foundation) (2001) *Consulting with disabled children and young people*, York: JRF.

Kirby, P., Lanyon, C., Cronin, K. and Sinclair, R. (2003) *Building a culture of participation: Involving children and young people in policy, service planning, delivery and evaluation. Research report*, London: Department for Education and Skills.

Knight, A., Clark, A., Petrie, P. and Statham, J. (2006) *The views of children and young people with learning disabilities about the support they receive from social services: A review of consultations and methods*, London: Thomas Coram Research Unit, University of London.

Lewis, A. (2010) 'Silence in the context of "child voice"', *Children & Society*, vol 24, no 1, pp 14-23.

Lewis, A., Parsons, S. and Robertson, C. (2007) *My school, my family, my life: A study detailing the experiences of disabled children, young people and their families in 2006*, London: Disability Rights Commission.

MacKeith, M. (2003) 'Personal assistants and how they affect my life', Personal correspondence.

Marchant, R. and Jones, M. (2003) *Getting it right: Involving disabled children in assessment, planning and review processes*, Brighton: Triangle.

Marchant, R., Jones, M., Julyan, A. and Giles, A. (1999) *Listening on all channels: Consulting with disabled children and young people*, Brighton: Triangle.

Mitchell, W. and Sloper, P. (2002) 'Quality services for disabled children', *Research Works*, York: Social Policy Research Unit, University of York.

Morris, J. (1998a) *Still missing? Volume 1: The experiences of children and young people living away from their families*, London: The Who Cares? Trust.

Morris, J. (1998b) *Still missing? Volume 2: Disabled children and the Children Act*, London: The Who Cares? Trust.

Morris, J. (1998c) *Don't leave us out: Involving disabled children and young people with communication impairments*, York: Joseph Rowntree Foundation.

Morris, J. (2002) *A lot to say: A guide for social workers, personal advisors, and others working with young people with communication impairments*, London: Scope.

Morris, J. (2003) 'Including all children: finding out about the experiences of children with communication and/or cognitive impairments', *Children & Society*, vol 17, no 5, pp 337-48.

Porter, J., Daniels, H., Georgeson, J., Feiler, A. and Hacker, J. (2008) *Disability data collection for children's services: Draft report*, London: Department for Children, Schools and Families.

Shakespeare, T., Barnes, C., Priestly, M., Cunninghambirley, S., Davis, J. and Watson, N. (1999) *Life as a disabled child: A qualitative study of young people's experiences and perspectives*, Leeds: Disability Research Unit, University of Leeds.

Sloper, P. and Lightfoot, J. (2003) 'Involving disabled children and chronically ill children and young people in health service development', *Child: Care, Health & Development*, vol 29, no 1, pp 15-20.

Stalker, K. and Connors, C. (2003) 'Communicating with disabled children', *Adoption & Fostering Journal*, vol 27, no 1, pp 26-35.

Townsley, R., Abbott, D. and Watson, D. (2004) *Making a difference? Exploring the impact of multi-agency working on disabled children with complex healthcare needs, their families and the professionals who support them*, Bristol: The Policy Press.

Triangle and NSPCC (2001) 'Two-way street', Communicating with disabled children and young people video pack, Leicester: NSPCC.

Turner, C. (2003) *Are you listening? What disabled children and young people in Wales think about the services they use*, Cardiff: Barnardo's, NCH and Children First.

Ward, L. (1997) *Seen and heard: Involving disabled children and young people in research and development projects*, York: Joseph Rowntree Foundation.

Watson, D., Abbott, D. and Townsley, R. (2007) 'Listen to me, too! Lessons from involving children with complex healthcare needs in research about multi-agency services', *Child: Care, Health & Development*, vol 33, no 1, pp 90-5.

THIRTEEN

Responding to unhappy childhoods in the UK: enhancing young people's 'well-being' through participatory action research

Charlie Cooper

Background

There is a wealth of evidence pointing to a decline in young people's emotional 'well-being' in the UK – particularly among the most disadvantaged – in the last 20 years (Collishaw et al, 2004). The 2007 United Nations Children's Fund's (UNICEF) assessment of children's and young people's well-being in 21 'advanced' nations placed the UK bottom (UNICEF, 2007). A similar study of young people's well-being in 2009 for the Child Poverty Action Group (CPAG) placed Britain 24th out of 29 European states (CPAG, 2009). Other studies suggest a decline in young people's well-being in relation to educational experience (Primary Review, 2007), employment opportunities (Shaheen, 2009), mental health problems (Revill and Lawless, 2007), access to public space (Mayall, 2001), trust and belonging (NEF, 2009), age discrimination (Davies, 2009) and the pressurised socio-cultural context caused by a consumerist society (Layard and Dunn, 2009). At the same time, a commitment to promoting well-being is embedded in the stated aims of all government departments (UK government website, 2006), a commitment that is shared by the Conservative opposition (Walker, 2007). Despite this apparent consensus, however, 'well-being' remains a contested concept that can be understood and represented in different ways. Because of this, the need for well-being research is recognised within the social policy field (nef, 2004). To date, much of the existing literature has been focused on evaluating the impact of health and social care services on well-being (Bauld et al, 2006). Arguably, well-being is only partially affected by such provision and is something pursued and experienced within a broader socio-cultural context (Wilkinson, 2005; Camfield and Crivello, 2009). More specifically, our sense of well-being and the strategies we deploy to attain it will be socially and culturally determined. Consequently, understanding well-being requires consideration of our aspirations, the societal preconditions perceived necessary to achieve these and the socio-cultural factors shaping our perceptions (McGregor, 2006).

With these concerns in mind, the central aim of this chapter is to contribute to current debates within well-being studies (nef, 2004; van Praag and Ferrer-i-Carbonell, 2004; Layard, 2005; Dolan et al, 2006; McGregor, 2006; Hothi et al, 2008; The Young Foundation, 2008) by mapping out a novel and radical social policy research agenda for exploring the welfare aspirations of disadvantaged young people (13- to 19-year-olds), and the strategies that might be deployed to achieve these. The approach outlined seeks to address a perceived need in the sociology and social policy literature for new fieldwork strategies better able to respond to the challenges facing disadvantaged young people in contemporary society. The methodology proposed is one grounded in the tenets of critical pedagogy and feminist traditions which espouse the notion that, by facilitating the authentic involvement of the research participants throughout the research process, they can be empowered with the capacity to engage effectively in collective action directed at bringing about positive social change. Accordingly, the research agenda proposed aims not only to bring to light important lessons for social policy makers and practitioners concerned with supporting young people to fulfil their wants and needs, it also aims to contribute to the development of new exploratory paradigms that value the potential of research to bring about real improvements in the way disadvantaged young people experience and attain social well-being. At the same time, the research agenda proposed can be expected to contribute to the development of well-being theory by acknowledging the broader socio-cultural context within which young people's expectations and experiences are constructed.

'Well-being' and the state

Philosophical interest in 'well-being' and the societal conditions needed to attain it go back a long way. Aristotle (384–322 BC) believed well-being derived from fulfilling ambitions and experiencing pleasures as free responsible citizens (Dean, 2006). In the 18th century Jeremy Bentham argued that humans were essentially 'rational' pleasure seekers and that political philosophy should therefore concern itself with how best to maximise pleasure and minimise pain. As quantifying 'pleasure' and 'pain' is an impractical task, what came to matter was whether or not people could fulfil their desires and the main constraint on this was seen to be income. After the Second World War, the proxy used to measure the well-being of a nation came to be gross domestic product (GDP) and the task of politics became focused on choosing whichever social order would best maximise this (Burchardt, 2006). Bentham shared Adam Smith's (1776 [1986]) assertion that a *laissez faire* political economy was best equipped to encourage the pursuit of economic self-interest and, thereby, to optimise economic growth and well-being. However, the human suffering experienced by many under a *laissez faire* political economy inspired later theorists to focus on its limitations; in particular, its tendency to generate 'anomie' (Durkheim, 1933), 'alienation' (Marx, 1976), the erosion of 'community' (Tönnies, 1887 [1955]), the depersonalisation of social relations (Simmel, 1907 [1978]) and the corruption of the human soul (Nietzsche, 1901 [1968]). Despite this, British governments throughout the 19th century continued to pursue *laissez faire* policies, exacerbating widespread poverty and social unrest in the process (Burden et al, 2000). The persistence of these domestic problems in Britain, combined with military and economic concerns abroad, persuaded the state to incrementally abandon the *laissez faire* political economy from the beginning of the 20th century and to accept greater responsibility for managing economic and social well-being.

The gradual abandonment of the *laissez faire* political economy reached a peak after the Second World War under policies shaped by Keynesian welfare 'social democratic' principles. While there are conflicting interpretations concerning whose interests the welfare state best served – particularly in relation to 'race' and 'gender' (Williams, 1989) – post-war social policies did lead to appreciable improvements in the material well-being of the working classes (Byrne, 2006). In the 1970s, however, the Keynesian welfare 'consensus' came under increasing strain due *inter alia* to contracting global markets. Since this time, governments have embraced neoliberalism and policies emphasising financial deregulation, labour market flexibility, regressive tax regimes and cuts in welfare entitlement. Evidence suggests that these reforms have had profoundly harmful consequences for social relations (Wilkinson, 2005; Dentith et al, 2009; Wilkinson and Pickett, 2009), a corollary of which is the growing body of data alluded to above suggesting that the well-being of children and young people in particular has declined since the 1980s. We now live in a 'post-industrial society' characterised by the shift from a manufacturing to a service sector economy (Bell, 1973), and social changes that have included: a 'crisis of masculinity' for young working-class males caused by the erosion of employment opportunities and, because of this, their prospects of marriage – constituting for many young men the loss of a clearly defined role (Campbell, 1993); an increase in the number of women entering the labour market that has contributed to the 'dual bind' of women's exploitation in both the workplace and the home (Hamnett et al, 1989); and the intensification of Anglocentric perspectives on 'race' and ideology that continues to shape policies designed to control (black) immigration to the UK and to assimilate those (black) migrants already settled here (Cooper, 2008). These economic and social changes will have had and are having profound consequences for the way young people experience well-being.

Well-being theory and research

As mentioned above, since the Second World War the main proxy used to measure the well-being of a nation came to be GDP. However, the GDP model offers only a restricted understanding of well-being based on a narrow set of economic indicators. While the UN Development Programme's Human Development Index adds health and education indicators, this is again limited and ignores other well-being characteristics (Chan et al, 2008). More recently, broader understandings of well-being have emerged based on psychosocial and subjective accounts of how people evaluate their lives holistically (Dolan et al, 2006; Stenner et al, 2008). These come closer to John Rawls' (1971) understanding of the importance of 'self-respect' for well-being and the need for social institutions to support people to access the resources necessary for them to attain this as a right of citizenship. The new economics foundation (nef) has attempted to identify what these resources might include, suggesting *inter alia* the need for a quality work environment; time to spend with friends and family; an education system that promotes curiosity and creativity; a health system that promotes holistic well-being; and opportunities for meaningful democratic engagement in decision-making processes (nef, 2004). These resource requirements are consistent with Doyal and Gough's (1991) theory of human need. However, while subjective accounts of well-being and the societal conditions needed for it to flourish offer additional insight, what they lack is acknowledgement of 'false consciousness' and the way in which expectations are shaped by cultural hegemony (Chan et al, 2008). As the Well-being in Developing Countries (WeD) Economic and Social Research Council (ESRC) research team at the University of Bath argue, what is perceived as a need or want, and whether this has been satisfied, is a culturally specific social construction (McGregor, 2006). People's autobiographies will largely reflect internalised values forged by powerful cultural influences. In recognition of these concerns, it is argued that a more innovative interpretivist approach to researching well-being is needed and that this can be found in the epistemological principles of critical pedagogy and feminist action research (Freire, 1996; Dentith et al, 2009). Such a mode of enquiry is particularly suited to explorations with socially marginalised communities because it has the capacity to empower the research subject by fully involving them throughout the research process and making it possible for them to see their world from a less partial and fatalistic standpoint (Dentith et al, 2009), and to recognise the role of human agency and its potential for changing one's situation for the better. More specifically, the key aim of such an enquiry is to make a genuine difference to the well-being of the participants through applying an approach that facilitates their transformative awareness and ability to escape the power that cultural imperatives hold over all of us and, in doing so, bring about positive social change.

Researching young people

Throughout modernity, research with young people in Britain has traditionally focused on youth as *the* problem – particularly a *male* problem. Moreover, historically the 'voice' of young people has been marginalised in social research and they have largely been treated as passive recipients of 'expert knowledge' (France, 2007). While this focus is changing to some extent in late modernity – with greater attention now given to difference, diversity and the problems faced *by* young people and the creative strategies they deploy to deal with these (see, for example, Ridge, 2003) – mainstream research influencing government policy continues to be dominated by neopositivist interpretations that continue to focus on youth as *the* problem (France, 2007) and somehow in deficit (Cooper, 2009). A key influence here, for example, is the work of the local well-being projects (LWPs) under the guidance of Richard Layard at the London School of Economics and Political Science. Layard advocates the practice of cognitive behaviour therapy (CBT) to enhance the 'emotional resilience' of young people to deal 'more constructively' with difficult social circumstances (The Young Foundation, 2008). Under the New Labour government, youth policy (DfES, 2005, 2006) has increasingly focused on such targeted interventions in an attempt to 'incentivise' young people 'at risk of social exclusion' to become more accountable for their own social development by overcoming their 'cultural deficits' – that is, their flawed attitudes to work, schooling and training, and their 'risky' 'anti-social' behaviour – and become more responsible. What these approaches lack, however, is acknowledgement of the broader socio-cultural context within which young people strive to attain well-being in post-industrial Britain, a context that has become increasingly unsupportive under neoliberalism (Elias, 2000; Wilkinson, 2005; Cooper, 2008; Rodger, 2008; Wilkinson and Pickett, 2009).

Alternative models of well-being research with young people

In response to recent developments in the sociology of childhood championing young people's competence as social actors (James et al, 1998), there has been growing recognition of the need to listen to young people and to acknowledge their agency. Established views about the abilities of young people to participate creatively in research that concerns them – including the desirability of entrusting them with the tools to reassess the world in which they find themselves and empowering them to transform unjust social relations through research – have been redefined (Dentith et al, 2009). In parallel with this change, children's and young people's rights to participate in decision making concerning their lives have been enshrined in legislation; in particular, the 1998 Human Rights Act and Article 12 of the UN Convention on the Rights of the Child. These developments are beginning to reposition young people towards the centre of the research process through the adoption of models built on participatory action research (PAR) (Nieuwenhuys, 2004); or, more specifically, youth PAR (Dentith et al, 2009).

Youth PAR seeks to permit young people to explore, reflect and act on their social world and, in doing so, strengthen their capacity for self-determination. PAR involves a dialogical approach where the researcher and research population co-investigate dialectically the object of the study, a process Paulo Freire (1996) described as 'conscientisation'.

The 'subjects' of the research are fully involved in the research process and its outcomes, ensuring that they share the status, the sense of self-efficacy and the self-esteem traditionally only claimed by the researcher (Dentith et al, 2009). Research themes are discussed not in a vacuum but in the context of power relations and their structural manifestations. As Giroux (2000) argues, such a methodology is particularly appropriate to research with disadvantaged young people increasingly exposed to the commercial pressures of consumerist society, because it presents genuine opportunities for fostering what C. Wright Mills (1959) called a 'sociological imagination' and the means to perceive more clearly what is happening to us and to discover alternative routes for self-development. It allows the fatalism ('false consciousness') often apparent in the statements of the oppressed to be exposed and countered (Mayo, 2004).

Young people facing difficult situations will already be more actively engaged in negotiating their place in the world and in devising efficacious coping strategies than is commonly acknowledged (James et al, 1998; Ridge, 2003). By recognising this and respecting the integrity of young people to think critically and act capably – in contrast to the 'deficit model' of youth – PAR builds on their lived reality and provides them with the conditions to strengthen their knowledge, their skills and their confidence, and empowers them to participate directly and collectively in action for positive social change. In this way, PAR represents a form of qualitative research that aims to produce knowledge and action of direct use to the research population (Nieuwenhuys, 2004). Implementing PAR requires the researcher to adopt a less directive role than in more conventional social studies and instead play the part of 'intellectual mediator', facilitating an open dialogue in which various values and positions can be mapped out, evaluated and challenged. Because the approach seeks to maximise the expression of views and interpretations from a range of perspectives informed by different contexts, it does not have a distinct set of methodologies as with conventional research. Instead, PAR adopts tools of research and dissemination conducive to the type of wide-ranging dialogue it seeks to facilitate, deploying new and creative techniques such as storytelling, poetry, game playing, drawing pictures, photography and video (Nieuwenhuys, 2004) to complement group discussions and interviews.

While there has been increasing support for participatory and emancipatory paradigms in social research in recent times, this has largely been in the interest of academic careers rather than in the interest of the respondents themselves (Lloyd et al, 1996; Dwyer, 2008). Intended beneficiaries may have been 'consulted' by the researcher on aspects of the research but this has rarely led to genuine power sharing (Nieuwenhuys, 2004). Through PAR, the respondents themselves will be encouraged to be involved in shaping the research agenda, defining and refining the research problem, devising the research strategy, engaging in various forms of data collection, and analysing and disseminating the findings. This approach contrasts with conventional research wedded to predetermined agendas and methodologies (Nieuwenhuys, 2004), allowing possibilities for generating findings not yet imagined and yet concerned with what could be (and should be) in a socially just world (Dentith et al, 2009).

PAR requires precise planning and preparation by the principal researcher through preliminary enquiries with representatives from the research population that aim to identify the key themes that are likely to be of central concern to them and in need of investigation. At the end of the research process, arrangements will be put in place to discuss with representatives from the research population what (if anything) they want to do with the research findings, including deliberating on what are the possibilities for translating these into tangible outcomes. A fundamental aim of PAR is to ensure that the research structure genuinely acknowledges the lived realities of the respondents' life experiences and that the research process leads to genuine material improvements in their well-being.

A toolbox for implementing PAR, described in one of my previous pieces of work (Cooper, 2008), can be found in Niels Åkerstrøm Andersen's (2003) assessment of the utility of the discourse analyses of Michel Foucault, Reinhart Koselleck, Ernesto Laclau and Niklas Luhmann. His textbook synthesises the theoretical contributions of these writers and offers a practical approach to deconstructing normative understandings and subjecting these to critical scrutiny, thereby offering possibilities for facilitating more meaningful insights into the nature of social relationships and, for the purpose of well-being research with young people, for generating a more progressive vision of social welfare.

Drawing on Foucault's (2005) *The archaeology of knowledge*, Andersen outlines a framework for critically analysing moral interpretations of 'social reality', raising such questions as who or what determines what is 'good' and acceptable (and, as a consequence, what is 'bad' and unacceptable)? What knowledge sources (or 'discourses', ie ideas and ways of representing 'social reality' through communication) have been excluded from such determinations? How are the subjects of dominant discourses represented and what are the effects of these representations

– inclusion and welfare support, or exclusion and criminalisation? And finally, who gains most from these discursive practices?

Andersen then illustrates how Koselleck's work (in Brunner et al, 1990) on the history of concepts offers a terrain on which counter-positions to dominant discourses can be forged. By emphasising the contestability of ideas, Koselleck focuses attention onto their ambiguity (that is, concepts can never be a true representation of reality, otherwise they would not be concepts) and thereby underlines the potential for counter-discourses around which alternative concepts can be formulated. There are always possibilities, therefore, for resisting dominant discourses and the concepts they are based on through the presentation of counter-discourses and concepts. This notion is supported by Laclau and Mouffe in *Hegemony and socialist strategy* (2001), which examines hegemony in action; that is, the way that power is acted out and reinforced throughout society via social institutions, thereby sustaining the interests of the status quo. Here, Laclau and Mouffe offer suggestions for organised resistance, arguing that because hegemony is something contingent which has to be constantly strived for (a 'battle of fixating'), hegemonic consent can never be fully secured. As a consequence, there is always potential for counter-hegemonic projects against dominating discourses. This is also close to Foucault's (1979) notion that 'there are no relations of power without resistance' and the potential for 'reverse discourse'. Possibilities always exist, therefore, for counter-hegemonic projects to develop wherever dominating discourses seek to impose discipline and control.

Finally, Luhmann's (1995) thesis on social systems offers a framework for scrutinising the motives of social institutions and bringing them to account. He describes these social institutions (scientific, political, social, economic, judicial, the media, etc) as the 'function systems' of modern society and argues that we need to examine how they observe and explain 'social reality'. Luhmann explains how 'observations' involve the selection of distinctions; that is, we cannot observe social phenomena without first having selected a means of distinguishing the way we see and name. These ways of distinguishing will always accord with particular predetermined judgements and therefore what is seen and named will always possess characteristics that are not indicated because other ways of distinguishing were not chosen. In brief, all observations will have blind spots. The task, therefore, is to illuminate these blind spots through what Luhmann calls 'second-order observations' that reveal the way social institutions only observe and represent what their choice of distinction permits them to see.

In short, Andersen's framework offers an appropriate toolbox for academics and community and youth workers to both research and work with young people in ways that facilitate:

- the unravelling and scrutinising of dominant discourses, to appraise the 'commonsense' notions of 'truth' they stake claim to, and to appraise whose interests are being served by these claims;
- the generation of counter-discourses that expose contradictions within dominant discourses and allow alternative 'truths' that may serve the interests of a broader constituency to be engendered;
- the identification of possibilities for counter-hegemonic projects and the potential sites of conflict for engaging in these; and
- the development of strategies for exposing the limited assumptions underpinning the activities of social institutions and calling these to account.

Bamber and Murphy (1999) outline a similar approach from their experience of critical youth work practice. They describe a 'holistic project' for youth work – one that strives to help young people to become (in Freire's term) 'fully human' – which takes as its starting point 'the interests and inclinations of groups of young people' (Bamber and Murphy, 1999, p 231) themselves (although this agenda will be subject to negotiation in order to counter populist authoritarian claims based, for example, on racist preconceptions). Central to this project is recognition of the issue of 'power' and 'the capacity of a select few to influence the manner in which the many make sense of the world' (Bamber and Murphy, 1999, p 231); that is, addressing how 'people's awareness is socially constructed' (Bamber and Murphy, 1999, p 231) through what Gramsci (1971) termed 'hegemony'. More specifically, critical youth work practice seeks to help people both to understand their situation (for example, their disadvantage) and to challenge it through a three-stage process:

- Stage one: developing a group's critical awareness of an issue or problem through open dialogue and counter-arguments (supported by evidence and logical argument).
- Stage two: developing a sense of the group's shared commitment to deal with the issue (is there a consensus in favour of doing something?).
- Stage three (where a consensus in support of action exists): planning for and mobilising action to deal with the issue or problem

– reflecting on and learning from the outcome of this action (clarifying what can be done realistically).

This and Andersen's approach are similar to one proposed for transformative practice by Ledwith and Springett (2010) which involves four interlinked stages in the process:

- questioning the status quo and dominant ideology
- identifying the key sites of intervention in the process of disempowerment
- creating new ways of seeing and making sense of the world (epistemology)
- creating new ways of being and acting in the world (ontology).

(Ledwith and Springett, 2010, p 23)

In relation to participatory practice with young people, Ledwith and Springett refer to the work of Mo Griffiths, who:

... talks about the "little stories" that link voice to narrative making that vital connection between the deeply personal and the profoundly political "by taking the particular perspective of an individual seriously; that is, the individual as situated in particular circumstances in all their complexity [and linking this] to grander concerns like education, social justice and power" (Griffiths, 2003, p 81) (Ledwith and Springett, 2010, p 25)

Ledwith and Springett suggest connecting the 'little stories' of young people within a collective narrative situated within social trends supported by statistical evidence. The evidence they draw on includes the UNICEF report on children's and young people's well-being (UNICEF, 2007, discussed above) and Tomlinson and Walker's (2009) assessment of child poverty in the UK (showing not only that one in three children grow up in poverty but that these figures are skewed disproportionately in relation to class, 'race', gender and 'disability'). This analysis leads Ledwith and Springett to cite Damian Killeen, a consultant on social justice and sustainable development, who adopts a 'rights-based' approach to PAR in asking 'is poverty in the UK a denial of people's human rights?' given that 'poverty and discrimination contravene the Universal Declaration on Human Rights' (Ledwith and Springett, 2010, p 25). A similar rights-based approach was recently adopted by a research partnership between Save the Children (Northern Ireland), The Prince's Trust (Northern Ireland) and Queen's University, Belfast, into the well-being of some of the most marginalised young people in Northern Ireland (McAlister et al, 2009). The research highlighted how young people in Northern Ireland experience a lack of respect and age discrimination in all areas of society but particularly in the sphere of participation in key decisions affecting their lives, a flagrant breach of the UN Convention on the Rights of the Child. As a consequence, they were left feeling 'undermined, unimportant, excluded and resentful' (McAlister et al, 2009, p 156) in their communities. Consequently, building safer, inclusive communities requires greater mutual respect and genuine opportunities for young people to be listened to so that the structural, cultural and sectarian contexts shaping their life chances and well-being can be better understood. This understanding contrasts with contemporary mainstream social policies largely aimed at addressing 'youth problems' by prioritising 'changing individuals' behaviours rather than challenging and adapting the institutional processes that contextualise the lives of children and young people' (McAlister et al, 2009, p 15).

Working with young people and communities in the ways described in this section opens up real possibilities for exploring the social context shaping experiences and lived realities, and generating a broader perspective on well-being that takes account of structural issues such as: relationships in the workplace; social protection and healthcare; housing and the local environment; education and training; personal safety and security; and opportunities to influence decision-making processes. Working in these ways, possibilities emerge for forging networks and constituencies of support for alternative social policy arrangements in a range of settings to deal more effectively with these issues: issues likely to have substantive implications for social well-being. In the penultimate section that follows, we suggest a major area of public concern about the 'problem of youth' in contemporary Britain where youth PAR might lead to a radically different perspective on the nature of the problem and what might be done about it – the apparent rise of a criminal sub-culture within sections of Britain's youth. The discussion includes reference to a research technique I have used in my own teaching with social sciences undergraduates and community and youth work students that attempted to facilitate critical engagement with the topic.

Radical potential of PAR: imagining what could and should be in a socially just world

A major area of concern in British society in recent times has been the effects of cultural change on working-class young people – in particular, the apparent rise of narcissism, amorality and 'anti-social' criminal behaviour among them. In February 2007, following the fatal shooting of three teenagers in London, the then Prime Minister Tony Blair spoke of the rise of a 'specific criminal culture' among some young people (BBC News, 2007, p 1). The notion of the emergence of a criminal culture in British society has been underpinned in mainstream criminology. For example, in *Criminal identities and consumer culture*, Hall et al (2008) argue that disadvantaged young people commit crime because it offers them the most optimum prospect of attaining the material trappings of success in contemporary society. This all takes place in a context where 'cool individualism' and the desire to consume these symbols of success at any cost have displaced traditional loyalties and trust. From the 1960s, it is argued, 'more and more individuals were enrolled into consumer culture, becoming ever more active in its reproduction and less interested in the politics of social democracy' (Hall et al, 2008, p 201). According to Hall et al, the key motor driving this development has been the remorseless (and invariably unethical) marketing practices of private corporations and the creation of new generations of young narcissistic egotists committed to fantasies of distinction. For these young people, theirs is 'a life motivated by the ... perception of a constant struggle with hostile others in a dog-eat-dog world, a "war of all against all" in a Hobbesian state of nature' (Hall et al, 2008, p 192). Effectively, over the past 50 years there has been a discernible and corrosive psychosocial paradigm shift where the conspicuous consumption of individuals has replaced traditional working-class solidarity as the means of attaining ontological well-being. Much of this appears to restate Merton's (1938) understanding of how social disorder is the consequence of the promotion of infinite material aspirations in an unequal society – only, for Hall et al, things have got infinitely worse. There has been a radical cultural shift caused by many young working-class people abandoning 'politics, class loyalties and egalitarian ethics' (Hall et al, 2008, p 216). Increasingly, hedonism, amorality, competitive individualism and crime 'is manifested throughout the social order' (Hall et al, 2008, p 210). According to these political and academic perspectives, crime and deviance in contemporary times can be explained by the occurrence of a psychosocial conceptual shift where social distinction and well-being now relies on fulfilling individualised consumer fantasies rather than collectively fighting for social improvement. As we have argued in the previous section, the major effect of these perspectives has been to privilege policies recommended by Layard and measures aimed at incentivising young people to take greater responsibility for overcoming their 'cultural deficit' – in the interest of their and everyone's well-being. Meanwhile, the broader socio-cultural context within which young people strive to attain well-being remains beyond scrutiny. PAR offers an opportunity to address this lacuna.

In *Criminalising social policy*, John Rodger (2008) offers a different focus of understanding for exploring the 'problem of youth' by concentrating more on the decline in government support for welfarism and the emergence of what he observes as 'de-civilising tendencies' in British society. He draws largely on Norbert Elias' (1978, 1982, 2000) notion of a 'de-civilising process' which, with qualifications,[1] is helpful in understanding the changing character of social relationships in recent times. With industrialisation, the advancement of state welfare and the growth of political democracy, networks of interdependence between different social interests grew stronger and people developed a greater sensitivity about the effects of their behaviour on others, described as 'the civilising process'. However, with deindustrialisation, welfare retrenchment and the centralisation of political power, this process has gone into reverse. Changes caused by transformations in labour market relations – that is, the loss of sustainable employment and the erosion of collective bargaining power – led to a breakdown in interdependence and, with this, a decline in empathy for others. This decline in empathy for others led to popular electoral support for political projects favouring less solidaristic social policies, such as the sale of council housing, benefit cut-backs and competition between schools. This has weakened the efficacy of the state to manage social tensions (now redefined as 'anti-social' behaviour) through social welfare measures. As a corollary, governments turn instead to authoritarian criminal justice sanctions – social policy is effectively criminalised and increasingly 'viewed in terms of its direct consequences for incivility and crime' (Rodger, 2008, p xii).

As with Hall et al, Rodger recognises a cultural shift in British society and the rise of materialist consumerism at all levels of the social stratum. However, for Rodger, in order to understand the nature of this shift, it is more fruitful to focus on the change that occurred at the level of 'official and popular thinking' (Rodger, 2008, p xii) – particularly under New Labour – about incivility and deviance, and 'how best to manage problem populations who are socially excluded from consumer society' (Rodger, 2008, p xvi) rather than at the level where young working-class people seemingly reject 'traditional' working-class values. Throughout the last decade, the increasing politicisation of crime and deviance has led to policies 'geared less to addressing the underlying social needs of troubled citizens than to their subjugation to the demands of a society unwilling to tolerate disorder (stylistically and behaviourally) in key areas of social and economic life' (Rodger, 2008, p 57). Alongside the weakening of economic and social interdependency over the past 30 years has been declining political participation for the marginalised (no longer deemed worthy of representation). Effectively, the economic, social and political context within which social interrelatedness is played out has become 'de-civilised', and mutual trust between people and empathy for 'the other' has evaporated. In such a context, differences between social categories, particularly based on 'race' and culture, become overstated – black youth, travellers, refugee children and asylum seekers have been particularly let down by social policy choices in recent times (Bawden, 2008) – and violence, aggression and incivility towards the other intensifies. This scenario is evident throughout 'de-civilised' Britain, just as much in the harmful behaviour of the powerful ('legitimised' violence and aggression, domestically and abroad) as in the harmful events experienced on the 'mean streets' of run-down inner-city neighbourhoods ('illegitimate' incivility and criminalised behaviour). It is the social context responsible for determining these harms that has become increasingly 'anti-social' and amoral. Moreover, it is those wedded to the neoliberal assignment, and the managerialist techniques responsible for its operationalisation, who should be the primary focus of inquiry.

PAR has the potential to expose these realities and to assess the social and cultural context within which young people seek well-being. By unravelling and scrutinising contemporary mainstream accounts of the 'problem of youth' – explanations largely founded on neopositivist and realist perspectives focused on populist authoritarian notions of 'dysfunctional' youth (feral and out of control due to inadequate parenting and broken neighbourhoods) – PAR holds prospects for re-focusing the nature of the debate onto the structural context for living in Britain. A technique I have used with students to facilitate such critical engagement with this topic is to show them two media clips from YouTube which portray contrasting perspectives on the 'problem of youth': one, a poem 'No respect' by Laura Walsh (available at www.youtube.com/watch?v=B8tLd0XWYm4 at the time of writing); the other, a talk on youth and restorative justice by Phil Gatensby (available at www.youtube.com/watch?v=9xFG2t5JIFU at the time of writing).

Laura Walsh's poem is a powerful, highly emotive presentation backed by techno music and fast-moving images portraying vandalism, verbal abuse, thieving, guns and knives, drug (ab)use, and devils and hell fire. Walsh is from Liverpool and she states that her poem 'illustrates some of the facts of current gang culture and have [sic] highlighted the futility of such behaviour and suggests an alternative path from a lifestyle of drugs and violence'. The essential message is that youth crime and deviance is caused by a lack of self-control and free choice, and cannot be linked to educational disadvantage and social deprivation. Young people needed to be more responsible for their own actions. In contrast, Phil Gatensby, a restorative justice activist in Canada, focuses extremely calmly on the responsibility of adults to do more to address the underlying societal problems young people face and not merely react to the symptoms (that is, drug use and crime). In the course of critically reflecting on these two media clips, students invariably see beyond mainstream discourses on youth crime and engage with broader understandings that give greater recognition to the social and its interrelationship with dominant power structures.

An illuminating example of such recognition is Danny Dorling's analysis of knife crime. While much of the research evidence suggests that many teenagers carry knives in order to protect themselves against attacks – 'a "logical" response by children who fear for their safety on the street' (Curtis, 2008, p 8) – the state's response to this 'logic' has become increasingly punitive. For example, the use of Section 60 of the 1994 Criminal Justice and Public Order Act, which permits the police to stop and search even when there are no grounds for suspicion, rose by 386% between 2005 and 2007 – disproportionately targeting young black men – with 'those found with a knife ... now being dealt with by the courts rather than being cautioned' (Travis, 2008, p 4). In November 2009, Jack Straw announced plans to give 'knife killers' a 25-year minimum sentence (*The Guardian*, 2009).

Dorling's analysis of this issue offers a more nuanced understanding that draws attention to context:

Behind the man with the knife is the man who sold him the knife, the man who did not give him a job, the man who decided that his school did not need funding, the man who closed down the branch plant where he could have worked, the man who decided to reduce benefit levels so that a black [sic] economy grew, all the way back to the woman who only noticed "those inner cities" some six years after the summer of 1981, and the people who voted to keep her in office. The harm done to one generation has repercussions long after that harm is first acted out. Those who perpetuated the social violence that was done to the lives of young men starting some 20 years ago are the prime suspects for most of the murders in Britain. (Dorling, 2008, p 41)

By tracing back the chain of responsibility for a social problem in this way, PAR allows the aetiology of that problem to be disentangled and, subsequently, for counter-discourses to be generated that expose contradictions within dominant accounts and permit alternative understandings to arise.

Another example of such recognition is in relation to the contemporary concern about young people's use of illegal drugs under the 1971 Misuse of Drugs Act. Young people prosecuted for taking illegal drugs – effectively, prosecuted 'for little more than youthful experimentation' (Lloyd, 2009, p 24) – have been left stigmatised with all that entails for well-being. Moreover, the criminalisation of certain drugs means that users are reluctant to approach social institutions for help and support in relation to health and welfare, with profound consequences for their well-being and that of others. As Lloyd points out, 'The biggest growth of HIV/Aids outside Africa is in injecting drug users' (Lloyd, 2009, p 24). Where drugs have been decriminalised – such as Switzerland – there is evidence of 'less crime, death and disease and fewer new users' (Lloyd, 2009, p 24). By engaging people in informed open dialogue, PAR offers genuine opportunities for generating greater critical awareness of such issues and, subsequently, possibilities for developing a shared commitment to deal with these through building counter-hegemonic projects that expose the flawed assumptions underpinning the activities of social institutions – in the case of this latter point and for the purpose of this chapter, the development of strategies that expose the limited assumptions underpinning the activities of the criminal youth justice system and their understanding of the 'problem of youth', and calling these to account.

As Dorling et al (2008) imply, the criminal justice system works to a limited understanding of the 'problem of youth', shaped by mainstream criminological thinking that encourages a restricted view of human suffering that neglects (more serious) social harms, harms largely caused by the activities of the powerful:

The omission of these harms is largely a result of ... [mainstream] criminology's proximity to the criminal law and its 'common

> sense hierarchy of morality', which prioritises acts of intent over indifference.... Naturally, this limits the scope of the sub-discipline's gaze to 'intentional harm', rather than the broader notion of 'preventable harm'.... (Pemberton, 2008, p 75)

The tendency in mainstream criminology is to maintain a focus on 'individual level harms' resulting from the low-level crimes and incivilities of the powerless, rather than the distress experienced as a consequence of the political and economic choices (and the accompanying indifference) of the powerful (such as those choices that lead to school exclusion, unemployment, poverty and homelessness). Consequently, possibilities for imagining more productive ways of responding to human suffering are foreclosed. Here, we share Simon Pemberton's view that a more fruitful way of understanding threats to social well-being is through the development of a social harm perspective which focuses on the nature and relative impact of harms people bear. The basis for such a perspective, argues Pemberton, can be found in the discipline of Social Policy:

> Primarily, the discipline's focus on improving human well-being through social action is an obvious attraction to the social harm perspective. The humanistic concerns that are integral to the discipline are more closely allied to those of the social harm perspective. Thus, social policy debates around well-being are potentially of great utility to the perspective, because they provide an understanding of human "needs" and the conditions necessary for their fulfilment. (Pemberton, 2008, p 78)

A social harm perspective rooted in social policy discourse could facilitate a more fertile contemporary debate focused on 'a wider range of harms, including structural harm' (Pemberton, 2008, p 79). Adopting such an approach through PAR has the potential to refocus attention onto the more significant harms wrought by 30 years of neoliberalism in Britain (described by Dorling above) or Britain's drug laws (described by Lloyd above). It also offers hope of arriving at a collective agreement that something should be done – where there is a consensus in support of social action to deal with the issue or problem – and reflection on what can realistically be done.

PAR is, therefore, unapologetically political and aims to challenge oppressive practices and structures, and realise change. Its potential is highly potent. It offers the opportunity to see the corrosive effects of neoliberal capitalism on societies through a wider lens. Here we find value in Sullivan's (2002) claims on the enduring relevance of Marxism for understanding contemporary times. In particular, he refers to the work of the Frankfurt School and its focus on the cultural consequences of capitalism and the way in which desires are increasingly shaped by the culture industry – what Marcuse (1964) described as the production of 'false needs'. Moreover, as Sullivan argues, our ability to realise this has become increasingly obscured 'by the persistent propagation of a myth, namely that liberty is synonymous with the vacuous choice between various brands and gadgets' (Sullivan, 2002, p 49). Sullivan reminds us of how Marx distinguished between *having* and *being*, and the corrosive impact of materialistic desires:

> 'Private property has made us stupid and partial, that an object is only ours when we have it, when it exists for us as capital or when it is directly eaten, drunk, worn, inhabited, etc, in short utilized in some way' [Marx, 1966]. Instead, we realize our true human potential not through the possession of material objects, but through productive, creative activity, through the expression of our unique individuality by which we achieve recognition and spiritual satisfaction. (Sullivan, 2002, pp 56-7)

Exposing this reality would, Marx believed, generate the anger and outrage necessary for the oppressed to forge a plan of action for social change. Aside from its tendency to perpetuate social injustice, the dehumanising effects of capitalism *also* contain the seeds of social transformation. It is essential for us to retain this fundamental tenet of Marxism; that is, 'the potential for self-empowerment among the masses, based on the conviction that they can bring about change' (Sullivan, 2002, p 75).

Marx believed that the key to social transformation was education or, more specifically, an education process that facilitated a critical self-awareness of the structural determinants of oppression and social injustice, and allowed the formation of a cohesive political strategy for social change. Moreover, Marx saw possibilities for generating, through education, *creators* rather than *consumers* that would, thereby, challenge the force of consumer society. Social change therefore rests on the belief that humans can develop themselves sufficiently to create their own authentic worlds counter to the commodified extensions of their identity. We therefore need to build political support for social research paradigms and welfare practices geared to fostering human emancipation, love and compassion, rather than merely serving the interests of the status quo – things that could and should be in a socially just world.

Conclusion

Evidence demonstrates a decline in the well-being of young people in the UK. Although there have been government policy statements in response to this, well-being itself remains a contested and contestable concept. Meanwhile, mainstream well-being research has largely retained a limited focus, particularly on health and social care. In more recent times there has been growing recognition of the need to facilitate the participation of young people in social research. A key aim of this chapter has been to contribute to this recent development by outlining a radical research agenda for investigating the well-being experiences and needs of young people and for assessing how best to respond to these. The approach we have described is one committed to achieving positive social change. It is an approach which recognises that building support for such a commitment requires the kind of effective engagement we have described and the establishment of what Margaret Simey, a feminist community activist of the 1920s, described as a 'sense of outrage' (Dalrymple and Burke, 2006, p 282) at the unjust, brutalising social context in which many disadvantaged young people are expected to survive. Only by generating such outrage are we likely to galvanise people into social action. As we have argued, engendering this anger is likely to come about through locating individual problems and suffering within their broader social context. It will then be translated into social action through recognising people's agency and believing in their collective ability to bring about structural change and, with this, happier childhoods.

Note

1 This suggestion is qualified by acknowledging that any attempt to define what is 'civil' and, consequently, what is 'uncivil' is problematic. Such normative values are highly contentious and much depends on who is doing the defining.

References

Andersen, N.Å. (2003) *Discursive analytical strategies: Understanding Foucault, Koselleck, Laclau, Luhmann*, Bristol: The Policy Press.

Bamber, J. and Murphy, H. (1999) 'Youth work: the possibilities for critical practice', *Journal of Youth Studies*, vol 2, no 2, pp 227-42.

Bauld, L., Clarke, K. and Maltby, T. (eds) (2006) *Social Policy Review 18: Analysis and debate in social policy, 2006*, Bristol: The Policy Press for the Social Policy Association.

Bawden, A. (2008) 'A fight for what is right', *Education Guardian*, 5 February, p 5.

BBC News (2007) 'Fathers "must fight gang culture"', 16 February, p 1 (http://news.bbc.co.uk/1/hi/uk_politics/6367273.stm).

Bell, D. (1973) *The coming of post-industrial society: A venture in social forecasting*, Harmondsworth: Penguin.

Brunner, O., Conze, W. and Kosselleck, R. (eds) (1990) *Geschichtliche Grundbegriffe, Historisches Lexikon zur politisch-sozialen Sprache in Deutschland*, Stuttgart: Klett-Cotta.

Burchardt, T. (2006) 'Happiness and social policy: barking up the right tree in the wrong neck of the woods', in L. Bauld, K. Clarke and T. Maltby (eds) *Social Policy Review 18: Analysis and debate in social policy, 2006*, Bristol: The Policy Press for the Social Policy Association, pp 145-64.

Burden, T., Cooper, C. and Petrie, S. (2000) *'Modernising' social policy: Unravelling New Labour's welfare reforms*, Aldershot: Ashgate.

Byrne, D. (2006) *Social exclusion* (2nd edn), Maidenhead: Open University Press.

Camfield, L. and Crivello, G. (2009) 'Editorial', *Social Indicators Research*, vol 90, no 1, pp 1-3.

Campbell, B. (1993) *Goliath: Britain's dangerous places*, London: Methuen.

Chan, C.K., Ngok, K.L. and Phillips, D. (2008) *Social policy in China: Development and well-being*, Bristol: The Policy Press.

Collishaw, S., Maughan, B., Goodman, R. and Pickles, A. (2004) 'Time trends in adolescent mental health', *Journal of Child Psychology and Psychiatry*, vol 45, no 8, pp 1350-62.

Cooper, C. (2008) *Community, conflict and the state: Rethinking notions of 'safety', 'cohesion' and 'wellbeing'*, Basingstoke: Palgrave.

Cooper, C. (2009) 'Rethinking the "problem of youth": refocusing on the social and its interrelationship with dominant power structures', *Youth & Policy*, 103, summer, pp 81-92.

CPAG (Child Poverty Action Group) (2009) *Child wellbeing and child poverty: Where the UK stands in the European table*, London: CPAG.

Curtis, P. (2008) 'Fear factor leading teenagers to carry weapons, says report', *The Guardian*, 14 February, p 8.

Dalrymple, J. and Burke, B. (2006) *Anti-oppressive practice: Social care and the law*, Maidenhead: Open University Press.

Davies, C. (2009) 'British children "face discrimination daily"', *The Observer*, 29 March, p 14.

Dean, H. (2006) *Social policy*, Cambridge: Polity Press.

Dentith, A.M., Measor, L. and O'Malley, M.P. (2009) 'Stirring dangerous waters: dilemmas for critical participatory research with young people', *Sociology*, vol 43, no 1, pp 158-68.

DfES (Department for Education and Skills) (2005) *Youth matters*, London: Secretary of State for Education and Skills.

DfES (2006) *Youth matters: Next steps*, London: Secretary of State for Education and Skills.

Dolan, P., Peasgood, T., Dixon, A., Knight, M., Phillips, D., Tsuchiya, A. and White, M. (2006) *Research on the relationship between well-being and sustainable development*, Final report for Defra, 22 August (www.stopstansteadexpansion.com/documents/SSE18_Appendix_11.pdf

Dorling, D. (2008) 'Prime suspect: murder in Britain', in D. Dorling, D. Gordon, P. Hillyard, C. Pantazis, S. Pemberton and S. Tombs, *Criminal obsessions: Why harm matters more than crime* (2nd edn), London: Centre for Crime and Justice Studies, King's College London, pp 25-41.

Dorling, D., Gordon, D., Hillyard, P., Pantazis, C., Pemberton, S. and Tombs, S. (2008) *Criminal obsessions: Why harm matters more than crime* (2nd edn), London: Centre for Crime and Justice Studies, King's College London.

Doyal, L. and Gough, I. (1991) *A theory of human need*, Basingstoke: Macmillan.

Durkheim, E. (1933) *The division of labour in society*, New York, NY: Macmillan.

Dwyer, P. (2008) 'The roles of welfare service users and academics in research, policy and practice', *PolicyWorld: Newsletter of the Social Policy Association*, Autumn, p 10.

Elias, N. (1978) *The civilising process: Volume 1. The history of manners*, Oxford: Blackwell.

Elias, N. (1982) *State formation and civilisation*, Oxford: Blackwell.

Elias, N. (2000) *The civilising process: Sociogenetic and psychogenetic investigations*, Oxford: Blackwell.

Foucault, M. (1979) *The history of sexuality, Vol 1, An introduction*, London: Allen Lane.

Foucault, M. (2005) *The archaeology of knowledge*, London: Routledge.

France, A. (2007) *Understanding youth in late modernity*, Maidenhead: Open University Press.

Freire, P. (1996) *Pedagogy of the oppressed*, London: Penguin Books.

Giroux, H.A. (2000) *Stealing innocence: Youth, corporate power, and the politics of culture*, New York, NY: St Martin's Press.

Gramsci, A. (1971) *Selections from the 'Prison notebooks'* (translated and edited by Q. Hoare and G. Nowell Smith), New York, NY: International Publishers.

Guardian, The (2009) 'Knife killers will get 25-year minimum sentence, says Jack Straw', 11 November (www.guardian.co.uk/uk/2009/nov/10/knife-murder-sentences-raised).

Hall, S., Winlow, S. and Ancrum, C. (2008) *Criminal identities and consumer culture: Crime, exclusion and the new culture of narcissism*, Cullompton: Willen Publishing.

Hamnett, C., McDowell, L. and Sarre, P. (eds) (1989) *The changing social structure*, London: Sage Publications.

Hothi, M. with Bacon, N., Brophy, M. and Mulgan, G. (2008) *Neighbourliness + empowerment = wellbeing: Is there a formula for happy communities?*, London: The Young Foundation.

James, A., Jenks, C. and Prout, A. (1998) *Theorizing childhood*, Cambridge: Polity Press.

Laclau, E. and Mouffe, C. (2001) *Hegemony and socialist strategy: Towards a radical democratic politics* (2nd edn), London: Verso.

Layard, R. (2005) *Happiness: Lessons from a new science*, London: Penguin.

Layard, R. and Dunn, J. (2009) *A good childhood: Searching for values in a competitive age*, London: Penguin.

Ledwith, M. and Springett, J. (2010) *Participatory practice: Community-based action for transformative change*, Bristol: The Policy Press.

Lloyd, M., Preston-Shoot, M., Temple, B. with Wuu, R. (1996) 'Whose project is it anyway? Sharing and shaping the research and development agenda', *Disability & Society*, vol 11, no 3, pp 301-15.

Lloyd, T. (2009) 'The drugs debate: legalise or not', *The Observer*, 20 September, pp 24-5.

Luhmann, N. (1995) *Social systems* (translated by J. Bednarz and D. Baecker), Palo Alto, CA: Stanford University Press.

Marcuse, H. (1964) *One-dimensional man*, Boston, MA: Beacon Press.

Marx, K. (1976) *Capital: Volume 1: A critique of political economy*, Harmondsworth: Penguin.

Mayall, B. (2001) 'Understanding childhood: a London study', in L. Alanen and B. Mayall (eds) *Conceptualizing child–adult relations*, London: Routledge, pp 114-28.

Mayo, P. (2004) *Liberating praxis: Paulo Freire's legacy for radical education and politics*, Rotterdam: Sense Publishers.

McAlister, S., Scraton, P. and Haydon, D. (2009) *Childhood in transition: Experiencing marginalisation and conflict in Northern Ireland*, Belfast: Queen's University, Prince's Trust and Save the Children.

McGregor, J.A. (2006) *Researching wellbeing: From concepts to methodology*, WeD Working Paper 20, Bath: University of Bath.

Merton, R.K. (1938) 'Social structure and anomie', *American Sociological Review*, vol 3 no 5, pp 672-82.

nef (new economics foundation) (2004) *A well-being manifesto for a flourishing society*, London: nef.

nef (2009) *National Accounts of Well-being in Europe* (www.nationalaccountsofwellbeing.org/).

Nietzsche, F. (1901 [1968]) *The will to power*, London: Weidenfeld & Nicolson.

Nieuwenhuys, O. (2004) 'Participatory action research in the majority world', in S. Fraser, V. Lewis, S. Ding, M. Kellett and C. Robinson (eds) *Doing research with children and young people*, London: Sage Publications, pp 206-21.

Pemberton, S. (2008) 'Where next? The future of the social harm perspective', in D. Dorling, D. Gordon, P. Hillyard, C. Pantazis, S. Pemberton and S. Tombs, *Criminal obsessions: Why harm matters more than crime* (2nd edn), London: Centre for Crime and Justice Studies, King's College London.

Primary Review (2007) *Community soundings: The Primary Review regional witness sessions*, Cambridge: University of Cambridge.

Rawls, J. (1971) *A theory of justice*, Cambridge, MA: Harvard University Press.

Revill, J. and Lawless, J. (2007) 'Suicide fears for under-14s', *The Observer*, 16 December, p 2.

Ridge, T. (2003) *Childhood poverty and social exclusion: From a child's perspective*, Bristol: The Policy Press.

Rodger, J.J. (2008) *Criminalising social policy: Anti-social behaviour and welfare in a de-civilised society*, Cullompton: Willan.

Shaheen, F. (2009) *Sticking plaster or stepping-stone? Tackling urban youth unemployment*, London: Centre for Cities.

Simmel, G. (1907 [1978]) *Philosophy of money*, London: Routledge & Kegan Paul.

Smith, A. (1776 [1986]) *The wealth of nations, Books I–III*, London: Penguin.

Stenner, P., Barnes, M. and Taylor, D. (2008) 'Editorial introduction – psychosocial welfare: contributions to an emerging field', *Critical Social Policy*, vol 28, no 4, pp 411-14.

Sullivan, S. (2002) *Marx for a postcommunist era: On poverty, corruption, and banality*, London and New York, NY: Routledge.

Tomlinson, M. and Walker, R. (2009) *Coping with complexity: Child and adult poverty*, London: Child Poverty Action Group.

Tönnies, F. (1887 [1955]) *Community and association*, London: Routledge & Kegan Paul.

Travis, A. (2008) 'Met defends stop-and-search tactics as it claims limited success in reducing knife crime', *The Guardian*, 18 November, p 4.

UK Government website (2006) 'Sustainable development – wellbeing: government departments and other organisations' (www.sustainable-development.gov.uk/what/priority/wellbeing/ogds.htm#audit).

UNICEF (United Nations Children's Fund) (2007) *Child poverty in perspective: An overview of child well-being in rich countries*, Florence: UNICEF.

van Praag, B. and Ferrer-i-Carbonell, A.D.A. (2004) *Happiness quantified: A satisfaction calculus approach*, Oxford: Oxford University Press.

Walker, D. (2007) 'The greatest gift that we possess', *Society Guardian*, 5 October (www.guardian.co.uk/society/2007/oct/05/comment.publicservices).

Wilkinson, R.G. (2005) *The impact of inequality: How to make sick societies healthier*, Abingdon: Routledge.

Wilkinson, R.G. and Pickett, K. (2009) *The spirit level: Why more equal societies almost always do better*, London: Penguin.

Williams, F. (1989) *Social policy: A critical introduction*, Cambridge: Polity Press.

Wright Mills, C. (1959) *The sociological imagination*, New York, NY: Oxford University Press.

Young Foundation, The (2008) 'Wellbeing home' (www.youngfoundation.org.uk).

FOURTEEN

Service users as peer research interviewers: why bother?

Rachel Harding, Grahame Whitfield and Neil Stillwell

Introduction

Drawing on two studies completed within the social housing sector, this chapter asks if there are advantages to peer interviewing, whereby those currently or recently receiving services interview their peers as part of a research project. Contribution is made to the broader methodological debate of how service users should be involved in research about their lives. Along with contributions from a peer interviewer, we examine the benefits to peer interviewers themselves, and whether there are any positive differences for the people being interviewed. This chapter argues that there are clear methodological advantages to peer interviewing as it can lend vital insights from rapport with those often regarded as 'hardest to reach'. The chapter also discusses peer interviewing in terms of strategic risk and limitations, as well as practical and ethical considerations. Ways of developing peer research in general are also suggested.

What is peer interviewing?

Historically, 'professional researchers' determined what data were to be collected, how they were to be collected, how they were analysed and what the findings meant (Hanley, 2005; Beresford, 2007). This structural exclusion of the perspective of people being researched (in this case service users) and the notion of them as only having a voice as 'subjects' has increasingly become a problematic issue, particularly in applied social policy research and in research about how health and social services interventions are delivered (Smith, 2004; Thornicroft and Tansella, 2005).

However, service user involvement – and peer research specifically – is an increasingly debated area in social research (McLaughlin, 2005). The focus of this chapter is on peer interviewing, but support for it and user involvement more generally falls into three broad camps (Becker et al, 2006). Some champion it as the only meaningful way to do applied social policy research. Others have serious reservations about its effectiveness. Still more feel they ought to engage with this approach but do not know exactly how. Peer research thus has the potential to engage or alienate researchers as well as policy makers and service providers.

Peer research has been termed 'participatory action research' in methodological literature (Becker and Bryman, 2004). Peer *interviewing* concentrates on one approach to fieldwork, particularly qualitative fieldwork. It is one aspect of peer research and should be viewed in context of the wider debates on peer research but distinct from 'user-led' research. The distinction lies in that 'user-led' research is managed by service users and sometimes without professional input, whereas peer research is often managed by professional researchers but includes roles for service users as part of a project's design. Peer research therefore involves people who are currently (or have recently been) receiving services as interviewers of others receiving similar services. It is the gathering of data from interviews alongside people who share experiences with those who are themselves being interviewed. It is a process of joint interviewing between a researcher and someone who has direct experience of the issue being explored.

Beresford (2002) identifies two approaches to research with 'user' involvement that are inherently conflicting. The *consumerist* approach seeks to manage the delivery of services, while the *democratic* approach offers empowerment to those receiving services. One retains power for the 'professional', while the other seeks to share it with service users. In many ways, peer interviewing can be considered a methodological approach that aims to facilitate the data gathering of research. However, while not disregarding the empowering process that peer interviewers find beneficial, the focus is on enabling the person being interviewed to do so on common ground. There is also an underlying assumption that this also produces better quality ('more grounded') data.

In this chapter, the term 'peer interviewer' is preferred to 'service user', 'user' or 'client' interviewer. This is in recognition of the fact that those interviewing alongside professional researchers might no longer be in receipt of services. It is the commonality of experience and its benefits and limitations that is explored here, whether or not that experience of receiving services is concurrent with the role undertaken as an interviewer. Taylor (2005) rightly raises concerns of inadvertently stigmatising peer researchers. It would be a hindrance to identify peer interviewers as part of the social 'problem' studied *only* in order that they qualify as people to be involved at all. Furthermore, McLaughlin (2005) writes that it is difficult to draw boundaries between 'users' and 'professionals' given that some 'users' might become professionals, and some professionals might themselves become or already be (or have been) 'users'. In addition, in this chapter, the term 'researchers' denotes professionally trained members of the project team with responsibility for the project's success and all peer interviewer involvement.

An overview of the studies and how the peer interviewing worked

This chapter draws on two studies conducted in the field of homelessness research. The first was funded by Nottingham City Council to explore day centre services for homeless and vulnerably housed people, namely those who held their own tenancy or owned their own home but were nevertheless at risk of becoming homeless through complex needs from substance use to debts and arrears (Smith and Harding, 2005). The second investigated tenancy support for formerly homeless substance users (Harding et al, 2007; Bowpitt and Harding, 2009) and was funded by a service provider. Peer interviewing was a core feature of the design of both studies, with formerly homeless people being joint interviewers alongside the researchers. Thus those who had been homeless and were using services at one day centre were recruited to joint interviews at other day centres (Smith and Harding, 2005). In this way, and having been a user of the tenancy support service for street homeless people with substance use problems, a contributor to this chapter was recruited to joint interview in the study (Harding et al, 2007; Bowpitt and Harding, 2009).

This was a deliberate attempt to undertake the research with homeless people as equal partners in the conduct of the research, so that people with experience of the subject of the study undertook a vital role in its design and specifically the fieldwork. Research *with* those who are usually seen as recipients of social welfare is an aim of other studies. For example, Dwyer and Hardhill (2008) recruited older people as peer interviewers of a study about older people; Sutton et al (2007) designed research fieldwork with the distinct groups of young people being studied to include and share ownership of the methods.

Considerable preparation was made in advance of the actual interviews to ensure both peer interviewers and project researchers were clear as to their respective roles during the interview. It was also necessary to ensure the peer interviewers were equipped with the interviewing skills required, since these cannot be assumed by virtue of their being 'service users' themselves (Smith et al, 2002; McLaughlin, 2005). It was not expected that peer interviewers would have the same set of skills as the project researchers, and neither was it anticipated that the project researchers would have the same immediate insights as the peer interviewers. It was found, however, that the 'professional' and 'service user' perspectives could complement each other for a more comprehensive interviewing strategy. It was not assumed that the peer interviewers would or should cope with sole responsibility for the interviews, given that the pressure to do so could well be unfair (see Clark et al, 2005), potentially exploitative and difficult given their limited research skills. As such, while responsibility for managing the interview situation remained with the project researchers, the emphasis in the interview was that the homeless people being interviewed should be able to respond directly to the peer researcher as much as possible.

To support the peer interviewers in doing this, a meeting was held to agree the interview schedule, and amendments to the draft topic guide were made accordingly regarding the wording, objectives and sequence of the questions. Openness to the peer interviewer's views at this early planning stage was crucial in striving towards seeking knowledge from both the '(outside) professional' and the '(inside) service user' world (Warren, 2000). The peer interviewers then familiarised themselves with the agreed semi-structured qualitative schedule, practising on each other and suggesting final amendments as necessary. Clark et al (2005) comment that the opportunity to learn (or re-learn) research and interviewing skills can be exciting, rewarding and enormously empowering for peer researchers and can offer a significant contribution to a project's success.

During the ensuing interviews, the peer interviewers introduced the interviewee to the aim of the research, explaining what would be involved and seeking their informed consent. They also undertook the specific role of leading on the interview questions. In this way, the homeless person being interviewed was able to respond directly to another who had also experienced homelessness. Their significant contribution lay in allowing those with personal experience of the issue being studied to take the lead in the interview situation (Smith et al, 2002). Any prompting, re-wording or re-phrasing was undertaken by the project researchers as appropriate. Thus the project researchers only became involved when they felt departure from the prepared interview schedule was necessary to elicit sufficient data in answering the research questions, when peer researchers had raised pertinent new issues that it was felt needed to be explored in more detail or when peer interviewers got into difficulties. Effectively, the project researchers were assuming the role of immediate 'support person' (Smith, 2004), enabling the peer interviewers to carry out their task effectively and satisfactorily.

During the interviews, the peer interviewers were careful not to assume a commonality of experience with the people being interviewed (Smith et al, 2002). There was an emphasis on listening as a key component to the qualitative interviewing process (Mason, 2002). Professionalism was thus upheld, with each interview seeking to uncover the articulated experiences of others (Arksey and Knight, 1999), and not subject them to having to appreciate the views of an interviewer. The peer interviewers also contributed to the research project as a whole, for example approving the report for accessibility and offering valuable criticism, a task identified in other participatory studies (Smith, 2004; McLaughlin, 2005; Northway and Wheeler, 2005).

Benefits to peer interviewers: a personal reflection

This section explores the personal benefit of peer interviewing from the perspective of a peer interviewer. While Neil was initially recruited as a service user, he is no longer in formal receipt of the services he jointly researched. However, he continues to be called on as a peer interviewer. The text in this section is the result of several discussions to set down not only the benefits but also the possible risks to a service user becoming a peer interviewer. Neil asked for this section to be co-written in the first person rather than by means of the use of selective quotes to convey his experience more effectively. Therefore, while not directly authored by himself, he has approved it for this publication as an accurate representation of his experiences and views.

Self-esteem and 'giving back'

As someone involved as a peer interviewer, I have benefited from the experience in a number of different ways. Taking part in research interviewing is often a tremendous boost to my individual confidence and self-esteem. But it was also a chance to return through interviewing something of what I had earlier received when a service user.

Taking part in the interviewing was an opportunity to turn what I would call the negative experience of homelessness into something positive and useful. It's not that interviewing equates to that of a support worker's task, but there is clearly a satisfaction in having a turn to enable another homeless person to express their views about their experiences and aspirations. Whereas being homeless had been a profound experience of exclusion, peer interviewing allowed me to be included on relatively equal footing within a team of professionals.

However, there is the issue of addressing the vulnerability of peer interviewers, given that there can be a personal history of not succeeding, and then giving up, lacking the resources to try again. My nature has always been, if I cannot succeed the first time, I stop. As long as I do not feel out of my depth with the interview, I can give it my best.

For this reason, preparation is crucial for me. It is very important that this is done professionally and thoroughly so that peer interviewers have a minimum amount of worry about carrying out an interview. Equipping peer interviewers with clear guidelines so that they know what to do and how to do it, and checking that they feel able to do such a task is essential. It's about making everyone safe and removing as much as possible the risk of things going wrong. Imbuing people with a feeling that it is something they will find manageable and achievable is much more likely to produce a good peer interview.

Participating and responsibility

The participatory role in itself is not to be underestimated for those undertaking peer interviews. My own personal story includes receiving sufficient personal encouragement from support staff to gain a sense of positive self-esteem and confidence. Having benefited from such support, the process of contributing to the research team is a continuation of this personal encouragement. In particular, it was having research professionals *trusting* me with leading on a peer interview that was a very meaningful benefit to undertaking the task. It gave me a feeling of pride and affirmation, an enormous sense of well-being that experts or 'research professionals' had trust in my ability to do the job. And after interviewing, de-briefing not only gives the chance to divest of any stress from hearing current homeless people's accounts, but also because it is affirming and being appreciated for having done the job well.

However, although I had been homeless, my experience is personal and particular to me. In no way is it helpful to assume a commonality, because it is not going to do anything or achieve anything to say 'I know how you feel' or 'I know what you're going through'. It can, in fact, be quite patronising to make these assumptions, and it's more likely to risk offending the person being interviewed. This in itself could irrevocably damage the integrity of the interview. Everybody's experience or struggle with homelessness is completely unique; even if they are going through the same sort of things as I went through, it will be unique for them in the way they react to the situation.

It's also crucial that I am able to listen to what other homeless people had to say and not assume I would 'know' by virtue of having been homeless once myself. Whatever the apparent commonality of experiences, interviewing requires basic skills of listening and respect for another's view. It is important to listen because everybody's going to face things differently, to see them differently. Peer interviewers must be able to listen when undertaking interviewing to contribute to the success of the fieldwork.

Empathy versus stigma

Of course there are potential dangers of former homeless people judging others who are currently homeless. It is not uncommon for such stigma to occur even if someone has experienced something like homelessness for themselves. They can display discriminatory behaviour against another in a similar situation. Being empathic and non-judgemental are two desirable qualities in a peer interviewer. When faced with a homeless person, it would be damaging to the interview, and indeed the project as a whole, if the peer interviewer were to reveal scorn or dislike towards the social status of a homeless person being interviewed. My own feelings are along the lines that because I have been there, and I have been homeless, I have seen what goes on and how nasty being homeless really is. It's important to have the tools to avoid negative behaviour towards those who remain homeless.

As said above, personal confidence and self-value have come from the support I received. As a peer interviewer, I have been able to face what I have been through and utilise the experience positively. After all, it is an integrity that would benefit any member, professional or service user, of any research team.

Perceived benefits to those interviewed by their peers

Probably the least understood area of peer research, and one that lacks substantial empirical study to date, is whether those interviewed by their peers do in fact benefit in any way. Unpicking (as far as possible) what was done in the two studies discussed in this chapter does shed some light on the question.

All those interviewed for the research studies by a peer interviewer alongside a researcher gave their informed consent for this. All were also offered the choice of being interviewed by a researcher only. Interestingly, all chose to be interviewed with a peer interviewer. Having a peer interviewer appeared to facilitate the interview in two ways.

First, there was an immediate and relaxed manner on the part of the person being interviewed. It would appear that there was indeed a methodological advantage to peer interviewing, as opposed to being interviewed by researchers alone. Smith et al (2002) have similarly noticed this on the part of the peer interviewers. While it might be unjustified to suggest that without the peer interviewer the interview would have been difficult, there was a perceived benefit in assuming a commonality of language. Less experienced interviewers of homeless people might require secondary questions eliciting explanations of specific language. The 'street language' or terminology, namely jargon peculiar to sleeping rough, drug and alcohol use and so on, can inhibit the natural flow of an interview if it is interrupted with a need for clarification with 'non-homeless' phraseology or language.

Having a peer interviewer did not necessitate such 'translations', and the interview was able to proceed with the interviewed person's own choice of words understood and recognised. Clarification was sought where an account was complex. For example, inasmuch as peer interviewing requires the interpretation of the social world within the vocabulary of those who have lived what is being researched, doing so with just such people lends integrity to a study. In this way, the terms of reference of those being researched were retained (Harding and Hamilton, 2009). This interpretation was led by the researchers, with contributions from the peer interviewers. As Smith et al (2002) writes, it should not always be assumed that peer interviewers themselves fully understand all that is told them by those they are interviewing.

Second, there was a notable levelling of power relations in the interview situation. Again, it is unhelpful to suggest that an interview by a professional and experienced researcher would not be a good one. However, that a homeless person was addressing a peer interviewer who had themselves been homeless facilitated rapport. Essential to any qualitative interview, rapport facilitates a dialogue necessary for the gathering of rich data, even if the situation remains contrived (Duncombe and Jessop, 2002). Observing this dynamic of two people with the core experience of homelessness in common, the researchers were able to see an interview unfold that did not have the added ingredient of vulnerable people relating to professionals, academics or those 'outside' the direct experience of the social issue being investigated (Warren, 2000).

Methodological benefits

In many ways, peer interviewing can be located within standpoint epistemology. Feminist standpoint epistemology, for example, is a particular understanding of the world to be researched, especially a woman's world, and engaging in this requires particular skill as well as specific experience. Harding (1987, p 185) writes of '... the intellectual and political struggles necessary to see nature and social life from the point of view of that disdained activity which produces women's social experiences...'. There is, it is argued, a distinctive experience of human relationships that is peculiar to women (Stanley and Wise, 1983). Thus, according to this argument, female researchers with this approach will uncover different data and in different ways from male researchers.

This kind of argument, while generally argued to have originated in feminist approaches, has been adopted and developed in respect of research on and involving people from different ethnic groups, religions, sexualities and in terms of disability and long-standing illness (Beresford, 2002). It is essentially a political 'participatory rhetoric' (Beresford and Croft, 2004, p 61). In respect of disability, particularly mental health and learning disability (Beresford, 2005; UFM, 2005), the often cited, 'Nothing about us without us' has been a powerful slogan used in campaign literature, research and by policy makers (DH, 2001).

A standpoint epistemology would therefore contend that homeless people are best placed to provide meaningful and informed insight into the experience of homelessness and to relate to other homeless people. This supports the use of peer interviewing as part of exploring the social world with the advantage of a particular point of view, namely that of people who themselves have specific experience of an issue or phenomenon. To see them as key to the research in question is to acknowledge their unique contribution to its answer. However, peer interviewing does not refer to standpoint epistemology alone. We would argue that this is fundamentally about doing qualitative research with people in vulnerable or disadvantaged circumstances *properly*. It involves those belonging to the social issue studied in a positively democratic way. As Beresford (2005, p 12) says of 'user involvement': 'It is a systematic process of discussion and negotiation – which is what the best practice always has been'.

Doing this *with* homeless people themselves is the next step to understanding their social world as best as possible, a progress from data sources to joint data gatherers. It can be argued that if researchers want to gather data from homeless people, there is already an assumption that they have a specific contribution that must be included in a project's design. Carr (2007) points out that resisting this opportunity for participation would have effectively denied any such research discourse. Qualitative research undertaken with peer interviewers challenges academics, policy researchers, policy makers and service providers to appreciate in more depth what it is that other people have lived.

These challenges can be direct in terms of preferred methods but also result in a greater appreciation of research, its process and outputs (Smith et al, 2002). As mentioned above, peer research also suggests that those with a particular experience have a crucial role in its investigation. Peer interviewing is therefore about doing research (literally) alongside those who also belong with the people being studied.

For example, one interviewee listened to the short introduction of the peer interviewer stating they had been homeless themselves, and then commented, "Good – you've been through it too". There followed a short exchange comparing experiences and services used between interviewee and peer interviewer. This appeared to 'seal' the common ground and established a rapport that would not necessarily have been possible with a researcher alone.

Furthermore, another interview paused when an interviewee did not understand the prepared question being asked from the schedule. The researcher intervened and paraphrased, but only when the peer interviewer then put the paraphrased question into more familiar 'street' language did the interviewee understand. It is possible that the trained skills of a researcher would have failed where the added familiarity of street jargon from the peer interviewer succeeded in the homeless person being able to answer the interview question.

Validity and other issues

It would be right to suggest that the impact of peer research and interviewing is still to be tested, and its value proved (Becker et al, 2006;

Taylor and Le Riche, 2006). It is important not to make too sweeping an assumption about how the benefits argued for here may be generalised; they remain perceived and not necessarily examined for themselves, and there is an inherent danger in assuming peer interviewing is good in respect of the people being interviewed in all circumstances (Smith et al, 2002). There is also a need to critique the benefits to 'professionals' which itself is not to be assumed (McLaughlin, 2005). It would certainly appear at the time of writing that formal evaluation of peer interviewing is still to be undertaken.

How to do this is, of course, another matter. Indeed, proving anything within qualitative research is fraught with difficulty, not least that qualitative researchers usually prefer terms such as 'building theory' or 'suggesting evidence', rather than 'causation' or 'proof' (Henn et al, 2006). Yet it would be possible to ask at the end of an interview why a person chose, and gave their consent to, being peer interviewed, and whether they would do so again.

Alternatively, a project could be organised into two groups, one with peer interviewers and one with professional researchers alone. Seeing whether data was richer from the peer interview group would help with a peer interview evaluation. Regarding homelessness in particular, exploring whether 'hard-to-reach' groups found it easier to participate because of having peer interviewers would add substantial argument to the advantage of peer research.

Examining peer research in this way would contribute to the literature 'from the receiving end'. It would give a balance to the increasing number of publications written from the point of view of the academic supporters of peer researchers (Lowes and Hulatt, 2005). It would also enable the debate to move beyond the notion that peer research is about wanting to appear to do the right thing without necessarily undertaking anything of consequence (Steel, 2005).

Identifying and managing risks

Certainly, peer interviewing brings its own complicated risks of having people with experience of a social problem (current or recent) interviewing those who are themselves defined and identified, if only for research purposes, by the same social phenomenon. For example, and following on from the above discussion of empathy and stigma, psychology literature includes theories about how stigma can be used to preserve the interests of self, whatever those interests and threats are perceived to be (Neuberg et al, 2003). Stigma can therefore be used to bolster an individual's positive perception of themselves at the expense of an open and favourable attitude to others. Encountering homelessness in others can result in stigma and other negative or hostile attitudes, even when someone has been homeless themselves.

If there are indeed methodological benefits to researching *with* as well as researching *on* people, and these are largely reliant on theories of knowledge sources (Warren, 2000; McLaughlin, 2005), then the validity of a project is strengthened rather than weakened by including peer interviewing. Most of the concerns about peer interviewing, and peer research in general – trusting people to behave ethically and professionally – are usually present within any research team. These are justified concerns, yet not insurmountable ones: the management of a research team with peer interviewers might be more taxing, but essentially it remains similar to managing a team of professionals alone (Smith et al, 2002).

The way that the peer interviewers contributed to the project teams described here is quite specific. In many ways it is hierarchical and sits with the 'collaborative' user involvement type identified by Hanley et al (2004, quoted in McLaughlin, 2005), and critiqued by Rose (2003). The 'pairing' of the 'professional' with a 'service user' interviewer model lends itself to the project researchers having a more controlling and superior role than the peer interviewers.

While this did not assign menial tasks (Smith et al, 2002) to the 'service users' in the projects described earlier, given the methodological significance of the interview dynamic observed, neither was it to exercise any functional dichotomy within the team overall, depending on 'professional' or 'service user' status. The point of assigning these different roles was to demonstrate clear accountability to funders and to offer the necessary supportive structure to the peer interviewers themselves (McLaughlin, 2005). It facilitated a supervisory framework that benefited the peer interviewers, most of whom were new to research, and this was a priority.

Unless proper consideration is given to *how* peer interviewers are to be meaningfully involved as well as to *what* their role could be, the responsibility of including 'service users' will remain questionable and risk undermining the power sharing sought within such an inclusive project (Cornwall and Jewkes, 1995; Smith, 2004). Nevertheless, user-led research projects seeking more autonomous roles for 'service users' with greater levels of control and involvement would still benefit from considering the various issues raised and discussed in this chapter.

Developing peer research

Ultimately, peer interviewing is only one aspect of peer research. Involvement in other significant aspects such as proposals, design and planning, data analysis, report and publication writing (Birch and Miller, 2002) is not only called for but also sought by funders (McLaughlin, 2005). It is also not necessary to limit peer research to qualitative design, even though many peer research projects appear to have such a preference (Lewis and Lindsey, 2000), but make quantitative and mixed methods possible, within the abilities of the peer researchers themselves (Smith et al, 2002). To re-iterate, peer researchers would complement and not conflict with 'professionals', given that it is often impossible to suggest any demarcation along the lines of either skills or experience.

Given that funding bodies are moving towards considering research outcomes as much as the standard outputs (Burns and MacKeith, 2006), it can be argued that 'service users' should have a contribution as decision makers, grant approvers and application assessors as with other professionals. At this point in time it remains something of a vision; many formal bodies remain sceptical of funding 'user-controlled' research (Tew, 2008), and professionals might question the direction of change sought through participation (Stickley, 2006). Yet, as Smith et al (2002, p 199) write, it is about 'the encouragement of insight and creativity in the research act'.

Limitations and responsibilities of including peer interviewers

Peer interviewing remains limited in a number of ways. Regarding homeless people, the selection of suitable interviewers demands applying a criteria of reliability, individual personal confidence and sufficient stamina. It could be disastrous for a research project if a homeless person's substance use, drinking levels or housing situation left them unfit or too mentally and physically exhausted to be included. Significant delays in fieldwork can jeopardise the likely success of a project.

Furthermore, there are ethical considerations of inadvertently exploiting vulnerable people for the sake of including them as peer interviewers, which would not only be morally questionable but also tantamount to sheer tokenism (Hodge, 2005). As Smith (2004, p 337) writes, 'Good intentions are not enough'. It is therefore usually people who have survived homelessness successfully enough who get selected as peer interviewers. Often, they are no longer homeless themselves or with any accompanying issues, but sober, intelligent, physically and mentally well, housed individuals with enough confidence to undertake such a challenge. It is also necessary to add that being suggested or nominated by a well-meaning support worker is not sufficient to assume the individual is sufficiently motivated to deliver the peer researcher role to the standard required.

Briefing and de-briefing is critical to protecting the well-being of a peer interviewer. They must be aware that they can hear difficult stories, particularly accounts that might evoke personal or even painful memories of being homeless themselves. Although each person's homelessness is unique, hearing accounts of common themes (for example insecurity, fear, shame, stigma and sheer physical and mental hardship) can remind someone of the panic of being homeless. Coping with these and other feelings as a peer interviewer can be difficult. Ensuring effective briefing both before and after an interview must be part of the responsibility of a researcher in involving peer interviewers.

It is also important to pace the interviews appropriately. The demands of qualitative interviewing can be significant for a peer interviewer (Clark et al, 2005). This can be the case with all qualitative interviewers, and sometimes the demands may cause difficulties or require adjustments to the fieldwork. Avoiding unnecessary risks associated with tiredness of some of the peer interviewers will help maximise the benefits for all involved in the research. Simply reducing the number of interviews carried out in a day will contribute significantly towards the most effective collection of qualitative data.

To carry out peer interviewing it is necessary to secure resources of both time and funding (Smith et al, 2002; McLaughlin, 2005). Fieldwork might well take longer with peer interviewers than without, and this should be accounted for in planning the research timetable. Having a group of peer interviewers rather than just one individual would help share the commitment and responsibility of joining 'professional' researchers in the fieldwork. This would also allow for peer support within the peer interviewers group; additional support would be gained from meeting and discussing with the other interviewers. Sufficient funding would pay for financial acknowledgement of the peer interviewers' time and work on the research project. While it remains discretionary as to how much each peer interviewer is to be paid, it is advisable to keep a record as to the number of interviews completed, or the number of training, question design and analysis sessions attended. This way a 'one-off' payment can be made on completion of the person's time with the project. Provided the sum amount does not exceed individual capital of £6,000, payment in the form of gift or store vouchers for example, will be considered 'irregular (one-off) charitable or voluntary payments' (CPAG, 2007, p 921) rather than regular income and therefore not jeopardise benefit claims. In both projects mentioned, peer interviewers were also given an open reference to assist with employment and/or voluntary work applications on satisfactory completion of their interviewing role.

Further ethical issues

Ethical dilemmas associated with peer interviewing include that of confidentiality. Of the two studies on which this chapter draws, the day centres review included one such organisation that refused to have peer interviewers because of concerns of confidentiality. The research team accepted the decision made by the centre but were aware that this was likely being made with at least some degree of prejudice. There is, of course, no guarantee that a peer interviewer would treat the personal accounts and details of those they interview as confidential (Smith et al, 2002), any more than such a guarantee can be assumed with 'professional' researchers. While it would be the researchers' decision that the project was suitable for peer interviewing, a risk potentially remains.

It is accepted that the world of homelessness is not only tightly knit, but it also carries its own danger and potential to intimidate and harm those vulnerable within it (Johnsen et al, 2005). Careful selection, preparation, training and briefing will go some way to minimise this risk. However, it is possible to make those being invited for interview aware of the risks without undermining the peer interviewers at the point of consent. This would perhaps be a statement of greater integrity than offering any *guarantee* of confidentiality (see Bryman, 2004). While not wanting to shift ethical responsibility from the researcher to the researched, peer interviewing should be agreed by all parties. Ultimately, it is the researchers managing the project who would be accountable for any issues arising from including peer interviewers.

Intellectual property and ownership of the project, its outputs and any outcomes is also a potentially contentious area. Smith et al (2002) write of how the young people involved as 'co-researchers' wanted to own the dissemination process as much as the academic team, given that it was detailed accounts of their lives and experiences that were to be presented and disseminated. It is essential to negotiate ownership of these from the outset, signing agreements if necessary.

Even so, it is not always possible to anticipate issues that can arise from any research project, and not everything can be agreed by all parties in advance. In the two Nottingham projects, peer interviewers were brought in after securing funding. Peer interviewers in one project were anonymously acknowledged in the research report. With the other, the peer interviewer's name was included as author of the report as he had assisted with its final draft, but not included on an academic chapter to which he had not contributed.

Conclusion

The benefits of peer interviewing are therefore that it complements academic professionalism with knowledge from those who have first-hand experiences as service users. The methodological advantages of peer interviewing in gaining data from people who might otherwise be 'hard to reach' are vital for social research. Peer interviewing can be managed as with any other research team issue through lines of accountability by project leaders, thus satisfying funding requirements for risk minimisation. While it remains 'untested', peer interviewing also appears to benefit those being interviewed, particularly regarding rapport. For these reasons, even taking into account the potential risks and uncertainties, peer interviewing is worthy of serious consideration when designing social research.

References

Arksey, H. and Knight, P. (1999) *Interviewing for social sciences: An introductory resource with examples*, London: Sage Publications.

Becker, S. and Bryman, A. (eds) (2004) *Understanding research for social policy and practice*, Bristol: The Policy Press.

Becker, S., Bryman, A. and Sempik, J. (2006) *Defining 'quality' in social policy research. Views, perceptions and a framework for discussion*, Lavenham: Social Policy Association.

Beresford, P. (2002) 'User involvement in research and evaluation: liberation or regulation?', *Social Policy and Society*, vol 1, no 2, pp 95-105.

Beresford, P. (2005) 'Theory and research practice of user involvement in research: making the connection with public policy and practice', in L. Lowes and I. Hulatt (eds) *Involving service users in health and social care research*, Oxford: Routledge, pp 6-17.

Beresford, P. (2007) 'User involvement, research and health inequalities: developing new directions', *Health and Social Care in the Community*, vol 15, no 4, pp 306-12.

Beresford, P. and Croft, S. (2004) 'Service users and practitioners reunited: the key component for social work reform', *British Journal of Social Work*, vol 34, pp 53-68.

Birch, J. and Miller T. (2002) 'Encouraging participation: ethics and responsibilities', in M. Mauthner, M. Birch, J. Jessop and T. Miller (eds) *Ethics in qualitative research*, London: Sage Publications, pp 91-106.

Bowpitt, G. and Harding, R. (2009) 'Not going it alone: social integration and tenancy sustainability for formerly homeless substance users', *Social Policy and Society*, vol 8, pp 1-11.

Bryman, A. (2004) *Social research methods* (2nd edn), Oxford: Oxford University Press.

Burns, S. and MacKeith, J. (2006) *Explaining the difference your project makes: A BIG guide to using an outcomes approach*, Oxford: Big Lottery Fund.

Carr, S. (2007) 'Participation, power, conflict and change: theorizing dynamics of service user participation in the social care system of England and Wales', *Critical Social Policy*, vol 27, pp 266-76.

Clark, M., Lester, H. and Glasby, J. (2005) 'From recruitment to dissemination: the experience of working together from service user and professional perspectives', in L. Lowes and I. Hulatt (eds) *Involving service users in health and social care research*, Oxford: Routledge, pp 76-84.

Cornwall, A. and Jewkes, R. (1995) 'What is participatory research?', *Social Science and Medicine*, vol 41, no 12, pp 1667-76.

CPAG (Child Poverty Action Group) (2007) *Welfare benefits and tax credits handbook* (9th edn), London: CPAG.

DH (Department of Health) (2001) *Valuing people*, London: The Stationery Office.

Duncombe, J. and Jessop, J. (2002) '"Doing rapport" and the ethics of "faking friendship"', in M. Mauthner, M. Birch, J. Jessop and T. Miller (eds) *Ethics in qualitative research*, London: Sage Publications, pp 107-22.

Dwyer, P. and Hardhill, I. (2008) *Older people and village services: Research report to Age Concern in the Midlands and Eastern regions of England*, Nottingham: Nottingham Trent University.

Hanley, B. (2005) *Research as empowerment?*, York: Joseph Rowntree Foundation.

Hanley, B., Bradburn, J., Barnes, M., Evans, C., Goodare, H., Kelson, M., Kent, A., Oliver, S., Thomas, S. and Wallcraft, J. (2004) *Involving the public in NHS, public health and social care: Briefing notes for researchers*, Eastleigh: Involve.

Harding, R. and Hamilton, P. (2009) 'Working girls: abuse or choice in street level sex work?', *British Journal of Social Work*, vol 39, no 6, pp 1118-37.

Harding, R., Lafond, N. and Stillwell, N. (2007) *Tenancy support for substance users: A study of the Handel Street tenancy support team*, Nottingham: Framework Housing Association.

Harding, S. (1987) 'Is there a feminist methodology?', in S. Harding (ed) *Feminism and methodology*, Milton Keynes: Open University Press, pp 1-14.

Henn, M., Weinstein, M. and Foard, N. (2006) *A short introduction to social research*, London: Sage Publications.

Hodge, S. (2005) 'Participation, discourse and power: a case study in service user involvement', *Critical Social Policy*, vol, 25, pp 164-79.

Johnsen, S., Cloke, P. and May, J. (2005) 'Day centres for homeless people: spaces of care or fear?', *Social and Cultural Geography*, vol 6, no 6, pp 787-811.

Lewis, A. and Lindsey, G. (2000) *Researching children's perspectives*, Buckingham: Open University Press.

Lowes, L. and Hulatt, I. (2005) *Involving service users in health and social care research*, Oxford: Routledge.

Mason, J. (2002) *Qualitative researching*, London: Sage Publications.

McLaughlin, H. (2005) 'Young service users as co-researchers', *Qualitative Social Work*, vol 4, no 2, pp 211-28.

Neuberg, S., Smith, D. and Asher, T. (2003) 'Why people stigmatise: toward a biocultural framework', in T. Heatherton, R. Kleck, M. Hebl and J. Hull (eds) *The social psychology of stigma*, New York, NY: The Guildford Press, pp 31-61.

Northway, R. and Wheeler, P. (2005) 'Working together to undertake research', in L. Lowes and I. Hulatt (eds) *Involving service users in health and social care research*, Oxford: Routledge, pp 199-208.

Rose, D. (2003) 'Collaborative research between users and professionals: peaks and pitfalls', *Psychiatric Bulletin*, vol 27, pp 404-6.

Smith, D. and Harding, R. (2005) *Review of day centres providing services for homeless people in Nottingham city*, Nottingham: Framework Housing Association.

Smith, R. (2004) 'A matter of trust: service users and researchers', *Qualitative Social Work*, vol 3, pp 335-46.

Smith, R., Monaghan, M. and Broad, B. (2002) 'Involving young people as co-researchers: facing up to the methodological issues', *Qualitative Social Work*, vol 1, pp 191-207.

Stanley, L. and Wise, S. (1983) *Breaking out: Feminist consciousness and feminist research*, London: Routledge and Kegan Paul.

Steel, R. (2005) 'Actively involving marginalized and vulnerable people in research', in L. Lowes and I. Hulatt (eds) *Involving service users in health and social care research*, Oxford: Routledge, pp 18-29.

Stickley, T. (2006) 'Should service user involvement be consigned to history? A critical realist perspective', *Journal of Psychiatric and Mental Health Nursing*, vol 13, pp 570-7.

Sutton, L., Smith, N., Dearden, C. and Middleton, S. (2007) *A child's-eye view of social difference*, York: Joseph Rowntree Foundation.

Taylor, D. (2005) 'Governing through evidence: participation and power in policy evaluation', *Journal of Social Policy*, vol 34, no 4, pp 601-18.

Taylor, I. and Le Riche, P. (2006) 'What do we know about partnership with service users and carers in social work education and how robust is the evidence base?', *Health and Social Care in the Community*, vol 14, no 5, pp 418-25.

Tew, J. (2008) 'Researching in partnership: reflecting on a collaborative study with mental health service users into the impact of compulsion', *Qualitative Social Work*, vol 7, pp 271-87.

Thornicroft, G. and Tansella, M. (2005) 'Growing recognition of the importance of service user involvement in mental health service planning and evaluation', *Epidemiologia e Psichiatria Sociale*, vol 14, no 1, pp 1-3.

UFM (user focus monitoring group) (2005) 'A hard fight: the involvement of mental health service users in research', in L. Lowes and I. Hulatt (eds) *Involving service users in health and social care research*, Oxford: Routledge, pp 41-7.

Warren, S. (2000) 'Let's do it properly: inviting children to be researchers', in A. Lewis and G. Lindsey (eds) *Researching children's perspectives*, Buckingham: Open University Press, pp 122-34.

Index

Pensions Acts (2007; 2008) 71
Pensions Commission (2002) 71-2,
74, 78, 80
Pentameter 2 exercise 187
Personal Accounts (formerly NPSS)
71, 74, 82, 85, 87, 88
personalisation 236-41
PFI (Private Finance Initiative) 52,
54, 55
Poppy Project 187
Porter, J. 279, 280
positive welfare 32-4, 36
poverty 6, 33, 34, 73, 111, 125, 135,
176, 191, 199-223, 301
PPI (public and patient involvement)
60, 61, 79
The Prince's Trust (NI) 302
Private Finance Initiative *see* PFI
privatisation 24-6, 27-8, 52, 53, 138
'problem of youth' 295, 305, 307-8
prostitution *see* sex trafficking
public consultation 59-63
Public Employment Service 138
public and patient involvement (PPI)
60, 61
public–private partnerships (PPPs)
52
Putting people first (HM Government)
236-7

Q

Qualifications and Curriculum
Authority (QCA) 18
Quality Protects (Joseph Rowntree
Foundation) 284-5
Queen's University (Belfast) 302

R

Rawls, J. 294
Reflex campaign 187
research and consultations 8, 227-51,
253-90, 291-315, 317-35
'resource allocation system' (RAS)
238
Respect Agenda 34, 41
Rio Group 97, 98
Rodger, J. 304-5
Rogaly, B. 180-1
Rueda, D. 154-5
Rutter, Sir M. 44

S

Save the Children (NI) 301-2
*Schools: Building on success: Raising
standards, promoting diversity,
achieving results* (DfEE) 22
Schools Standards and Framework
Act 1998 21-2
Scottish Parliament 54
self-directed support 236-41
Seligman, M. 43
semi-normative budget lines 4, 97,
98-9, 110, 111
service reconfiguration 59-63
service user involvement 7-10
concept of 'voice' 255-6, 287
consumerist vs democratic 318
democratic/empowerment
approach 232, 233
disabled children 8, 275-90
local knowledge 255, 260-5
local representation 255, 256-9
managerialist/consumerist
approach 232, 233, 235
participation 253-74
peer research interviewing 317-35
recognition and redistribution
269-70
social change 292
research and consultation and
227-51
young people's well-being 8, 291-
315
sex offenders 35
sex trafficking 6, 174, 179
Sexual Offences Act 2004 184
Simey, Margaret 310
Sinfield, A. 121, 122, 137
slavery 173-90
Sloper, P. 277, 278, 280
Snower, D.J. 154
social capital 132-3, 243-4
Social Cohesion Council
(Guatemala) 209, 214
social democracy 72, 75, 76, 77,
79-80, 81, 82, 88, 293
Social Democratic Party (*Shamin-tou*,
SDP) (Japan) 162
Social Democratic Party (SPD)
(Germany) 162
Social Exclusion Unit (SEU) 36
social inclusion 244-5

Work and Pensions, Department of
(DWP) 71
World Bank 6, 201, 203, 205, 206,
214

Y

young people 291-2, 295-302
Young Person's Guarantee 134